WITHIN WALLS

Within Walls

*Private Life in the German
Democratic Republic*

PAUL BETTS

OXFORD
UNIVERSITY PRESS

OXFORD
UNIVERSITY PRESS

Great Clarendon Street, Oxford OX2 6DP

Oxford University Press is a department of the University of Oxford.
It furthers the University's objective of excellence in research, scholarship,
and education by publishing worldwide in

Oxford New York

Auckland Cape Town Dar es Salaam Hong Kong Karachi
Kuala Lumpur Madrid Melbourne Mexico City Nairobi
New Delhi Shanghai Taipei Toronto

With offices in

Argentina Austria Brazil Chile Czech Republic France Greece
Guatemala Hungary Italy Japan Poland Portugal Singapore
South Korea Switzerland Thailand Turkey Ukraine Vietnam

Oxford is a registered trade mark of Oxford University Press
in the UK and in certain other countries

Published in the United States
by Oxford University Press Inc., New York

© Paul Betts 2010

British Library Cataloguing in Publication Data

Data available

Library of Congress Cataloging in Publication Data

Data available

Typeset by SPI Publisher Services, Pondicherry, India
Printed in Great Britain
on acid-free paper by
MPG Books Group, Bodmin and King's Lynn

ISBN 978–0–19–920884–5

1 3 5 7 9 10 8 6 4 2

Contents

Acknowledgements

It is a great pleasure to convey my gratitude to those people and institutions that have made it possible for me to research and write this book. First of all, I would like to thank the National Endowment for the Humanities for generously awarding me a Research Fellowship in 2006–7, which enabled me to spend the year in Berlin gathering most of the archival material for this book. I am also grateful to the Graham Foundation for a summer research grant in 2005 to conduct most of the research for Chapter 4. I greatly profited from my two-month fellowship in 2007 as a Visiting Scholar at the Zentrum für Zeithistorische Forschung in Potsdam, and special thanks to Martin Sabrow and Christoph Classen for their interest and support. The University of Sussex gave me two timely single-term research leaves (2007 and 2009) to help me finish the manuscript, which made all the difference. The staffs at the Bundesarchiv in Berlin/Lichterfelde and Dahlwitz-Hoppegarten, the Deutsches Tagebuch-Archiv in Emmindingen, the Bundesbeauftragte für die Unterlagen des Staatssicherheitsdienstes der ehemaligen DDR (BstU), the Havemann-Gesellschaft-Archiv, the Kempowski-Biografien-Archiv in Berlin's Akademie der Künste, the Berlinische Galerie, the Landeskirchenarchiv, and Landesarchiv in Berlin were very helpful with my many questions and requests. I would like to single out Dr Klaus Dettmer and Bianca Welzing at the Berlin Landesarchiv for their extraordinary assistance in locating obscure sources *hors-piste*, as well as to Jürgen Stenzel at the Landeskirchenarchiv for furnishing me with hard-to-get sources and further contacts.

I would like to thank the people whom I interviewed for this project; I greatly appreciated their time and candour in discussing the past, often in very personal ways, and, as promised, have rendered them anonymous. Thanks as well go to those people who took the time to fill out detailed questionnaires on private life in the GDR, which were invaluable. Angela Brock deserves special mention in this regard. As part of a British Academy Fellowship, she masterfully conducted (and transcribed) some two dozen interviews for this project, and helped me with other sources, including friends of her family. Esther von Richthofen also was gracious enough to interview several people for this project, including members of her own family.

Two chapters were published in earlier forms. Chapter 4 first appeared as 'Building Socialism at Home: The Case of East German Interiors', in Katherine Pence and Paul Betts (eds.), *Socialist Modern: East German Everyday Culture and Politics* (Ann Arbor: University of Michigan Press, 2008), 96–132, while Chapter 5 was published as 'Property, Peace and Honor: Neighborhood Justice in Communist Berlin', *Past & Present*, 201 (Nov. 2008), 215–54. I wish to thank both publishers for permission to republish material from them in these chapters.

A number of friends and colleagues read drafts of individual chapters at various stages, and I am indebted to them for their constructive criticism. They include Robert Moeller, Alon Confino, Dagmar Herzog, Corey Ross, Jens Gieseke, Stefan-Ludwig Hoffmann, Rod Kedward, Inga Markowits, Greg Castillo, Nick Stargardt, John Lowerson, Jennifer Evans, Kathy Pence, David Crowley, and my sister Sharon Stella Betts. Saul Dubow read most of the chapters, and I benefited from his sharp editorial eye and characteristic range. Gerhard Wolf and Kevin Reynolds kindly helped me with the illustrations down the stretch. Christopher Wheeler has been a model editor for his encouragement, interest, and professionalism, and Matthew Cotton and Claire Thompson ably shepherded the manuscript to the finish line with impressive dispatch. Jane Robson copy-edited the book with great care, and the manuscript is better as a result of her meticulous work.

I thank my family 'across the pond' for their continued presence and support, especially my parents, Petra and Charles, my brother-in-law, David Leven, and my sister Sharon. My partner Sylvie heard every aspect of this book in embryonic form, greeting it all with a healthy mix of interest and occasional scepticism that helped drive the project. She has been there at every step, in ways that matter most. This book is dedicated to her, and our two daughters, Lucie and Anna, my own private sphere.

List of Illustrations

Every reasonable effort has been made to contact all copyright holders; any omissions will be rectified in subsequent printings if notice is given to the publishers.

Introduction

Privacy in an Enclosed State

In July 2006 a privately funded museum dedicated to commemorating everyday life in the former German Democratic Republic was opened on the banks of the Spree River in central Berlin, the so-called DDR-Museum. This popular 'hands-on experience of history' expressly aimed to go beyond the misdeeds of the Stasi and Berlin Wall border guards so as to display the 'life of the people in the dictatorship'. In it visitors are treated to the sights, sounds, and smells of the defunct regime, including the starchy fragrances of select GDR foodstuffs, rattling phone-tapping machines, grainy television programmes flickering in a dark East German living room as well as a simulated drive in a noisy Trabant around one of the former capital's residential estates.[1] No less interesting is the way that the museum represents private life in the former socialist state. In a display area dedicated to recounting the country's infamous 'Sword and Shield' Ministry of State Security, or Stasi for short, visitors can read the description: 'Like an octopus, the Stasi had the country in its grip: its tentacles reached all corners of life. Society was infested with spies. Mail was opened and bank accounts monitored; there was no private sphere, no secure rights.' And yet, just a few steps further in another room designated the 'Garden Gnome Idyll', or *Gartenzwergidylle*, the museumgoer is presented with the following statement on the wall above the displayed trinkets: 'The summer house was more than just a green retreat. It symbolized the desire for harmony beyond the world of politics. The Party viewed this withdrawal into privacy (*Rückzug ins Private*) with mixed feelings. Still, the retreat to country idylls was better than fleeing to the West.' This may be so, but what is striking is the strange contradiction itself—that is, how could a museum claim in one room that there was 'no private sphere' and then in the next declare that the Party saw 'this retreat into privacy with mixed feelings'? The private sphere, paradoxically, was somehow there and not there at the same time.

This book initially emerged from conversations that I had with East Germans in the mid-1990s about this very paradox. People spoke very movingly about their lost world, both critically and sympathetically, and many insisted that their biographies do not accord with the stock supply of crude epithets used to describe East Germany's failed communist state, be it SED-Tyranny, Red Dictatorship, or Stasi-State, to name only a few of the most common. That perhaps was predictable enough. What surprised me was how often what they themselves called the private sphere came up in their recollections and reassessments. Of course what they meant by private life differed enormously—ranging from black market activities to personal hobbies, domestic upkeep to summer house gardening, cherished solitude to conviviality with family and friends. If nothing else, such first-narratives of private pursuits in the GDR seemed to fly in the face of the media-driven fascination with the dark machinations and supposedly limitless reach of East Germany's latter-day Leviathan. Over the course of the 1990s dozens of best-selling histories, television programmes, and exhibitions popularized these stereotypes by repeatedly trawling the GDR's lurid underworld of unfreedom, surveillance, and mass-produced misery. Anna Funder's much-publicized 2003 travelogue, *Stasiland*, is only one recent instalment in this abiding interest in the 'wild, wild East', offering a picture of GDR life dominated by Stasi henchmen, ideological cranks, shameless opportunists, and crushed idealists. In its own way, Florian von Donnersmarck's 2006 Oscar-winning film, *The Lives of Others*, reinforced these Stasicentric views of the GDR. Historians, for their part, have often peddled similar imagery in portraying the GDR as twentieth-century Germany's 'second dictatorship', framing East German history in terms of its more famous forerunner's patent abuse of state power, civil law, and designated 'enemies of the state'.

No doubt there is a good amount of truth in many of these accounts of the doomed experiment in creating a New Jerusalem in East Germany. Even the most diehard GDR sympathizers would be at pains to deny the regime's low regard for civil rights and genuine democratic culture. But is it accurate to conclude that GDR society was inescapably held in the grip of a walled-in 'totalitarian state?' Did the GDR state really succeed in completely doing away with civil society and even private life, making good with characteristic Prussian diligence Lenin's infamous comment that 'under communism nothing is private'? A remarkably large proportion of the literature produced in the 1990s was inclined to answer in the affirmative to these questions in one way or another. Nowhere is this more striking than in the ever-expanding literature on 'red totalitarianism', whose GDR variant has invariably focused on the nefarious activities of the legendary Stasi and its elaborate surveillance empire. Such characterizations informed a whole cottage industry of studies in the 1990s dedicated to recounting the state's brutal and obsessive tyranny over its citizens. Other works, to be sure, have taken issue with this so-called totalitarian school. Those who have detailed the stories of individual resisters, church leaders, and/or civil rights movements, for example, have pointed up the limits of state power by stressing the heroic—if belated—reassertion of civil society. Underlying all of these studies, though, is the assumption that social politics centred exclusively on the control of—and resistance to—the Socialist Unity Party-dominated public sphere.

By contrast, the private sphere is left virtually unremarked, presumably because it is seen as either insignificant or non-existent. This is unfortunate, not least because one can easily counter that it was the public sphere—rather than the private sphere—that occupied a sham existence in the GDR, at least until the very last few years of the regime. In fact, it was precisely the relative absence of any public sphere of open debate and genuine civil society that rendered the private sphere so important and politically potent. While no one could overlook East Germany's unforgiving authoritarianism and 'will to total power,' the private sphere as such hardly disappeared, and actually played a key role in East German everyday life and social politics. Indeed, one of the main contentions of this book is that private life—generally associated with liberal society—assumed its most political power and personal value under authoritarian regimes.

These hypotheses were corroborated in more formal interviews held with East Germans between 2005 and 2007 about the shape and significance of the private realm. Around forty-five people took part, and another forty filled out questionnaires on the topic. Most answered the questions fully, though a number expressed some difficulty, incomprehension, and even outright hostility toward the very concept of a private sphere. Some responded cynically that the Stasi 'knows best about private life', or that 'since I haven't checked my Stasi file, I am not able to say how private my private life really was'.[2] Others intoned that the term 'private sphere'—variably designated as *Privatsphäre, Privatleben, Privatbereich,* or *Intimbereich*—was itself commonly associated with 'petty bourgeois vulgarity' (*kleinbürgerlich-spiessig*), thus something 'under suspicion' that one 'wanted to hide'. Still others clearly felt uncomfortable about describing their private lives, since communicating about it perforce undermined its very nature. One interviewee responded to the question of whether there were additional aspects of the private life worth mentioning this way: 'No, because private life is indeed private life. What can one say about additional aspects of private life, apart from that it was private? Otherwise, it is no longer private.'[3] Still, almost all of them confirmed that private life was extremely dear to them and to their fellow citizens. By the late 1970s and 1980s it seemed to trump all public identities and associations. For them private life provided a sense of equilibrium (*Ausgleich*), calmness (*Ruhe*), a 'place of trust', a 'counterworld to the official one', and/or a space to pursue what many called 'one's own life' (*eigentliches Leben*). Christians tended to portray private life in terms of 'Rüstzeit', 'refuge' or 'spiritual home' (*geistige Heimat*), and they generally spoke more openly about the defensive quality of the private sphere, since it was for them a precious shelter of retreat for religious devotion in a nominally atheistic state.[4]

How these people defined private life of course varied, though most referred in one way or another to a world outside of work, usually synonymous with home and friendships. Many cited dachas, hobbies, family celebrations, holidays, book reading, listening to Western radio, or their beloved automobiles as the very symbols of private life.[5] Almost all of them saw the private sphere as something that grew with time—generally seen as a function of the reduced work day and the regime's praised delivery of socialist security in the form of a steady job, stable rents, and subsidized prices, factors that contrasted dramatically with the dangers and disappointments of life after 1990.[6] Large political events, interestingly enough, rarely matched up with their memories of private life. On the whole, these people did not see the Uprising of 1953 or the erection of the Berlin Wall in 1961 as all that important for them personally, and scarcely commented on how they related to their own life. These political watersheds were apparently not internalized, apart from them recalling what they were doing when they heard the news. Occasionally someone remarked that 1961 was a big blow, since it cut them off from Western media, culture, and music.[7] Private life was invariably associated with weekends, especially the oft-quoted phrase: 'Freitags nach eins— jeder macht seins', wherein one's real life began Friday afternoon after work. Opinions differed about where the private sphere began or ended, but most insisted on their boundaries. One Berlin woman described the borders this way: 'Privacy basically ends with those other people who should not impinge upon one's circle of friends and family, and that goes not only for the state.'[8] But for the overwhelming majority, the private sphere was neither a place nor experience of isolation, but rather was closely connected to a profound sense of shared intimacy. It was often painted as a kind of a 'needs-based community' (*Notge-meinschaft*), in which people used private networks of informal barter exchange to cope with the notorious bottlenecks of state socialist production.[9] Likewise, it was the arena 'where one could exchange views on the absurdities that one had experienced over the course of the day'.[10] One questionnaire respondent went so far as to say that what reigned in the GDR was a kind of 'collective feeling of privacy'.[11]

These sentiments were by no means isolated cases. Interest in private life has emerged as a key dimension of post-1989 histories of the GDR, as the 1990s saw a flood of first-person narratives and autobiographies about people's subjective experiences as 'private citizens'. The first wave of post-Wall personal recollections was written by dissidents and civil rights activists aiming to bring to light shocking tales of Stasi tyranny and citizen–citizen betrayal. In this atmosphere, the old Marxist revolutionary slogan of 'expropriating the expropriators' was transformed into frenzied rounds of 'denouncing the denunciators'.[12] Not long thereafter this impulse to write, or rewrite, one's own past fanned out to more general recollections about 'life in the other Germany'.[13] The ironic title of a 2000 Berlin exhibition about a clutch of idiosyncratic characters from the GDR past neatly summed up this desire to rediscover lost private lives beyond the clichés of trumpeted collectivity: 'The Collective Is Me.'[14] The shattered SED monopoly over the articulation of East German cultural identity, national history, and official memory has given rise to alternative, more personalized forms of commemoration and memory-work.[15] Emphasis on the private side of history has also worked its way into popular reappraisals of a world that is gone for good. Not only were behind-the-scenes biographies of state leaders Walter Ulbricht and Erich Honecker written with a particular accent on their intimate lives; there was also real appetite for gossip about what exactly Ulbricht, Honecker, and Stasi Chief Erich Mielke did behind the high-security gates of the East German government's leafy residential compound of Wandlitz, as told by former butlers, chauffeurs, and bodyguards.[16]

These trends raise several questions. Was this dizzying 1990s 'memory industry' simply an effect of cultural liberalization, as East Germans had learnt to see themselves in brand new ways in the aftermath of Reunification? Or did these impulses reflect older patterns of subjectivity acquired under state socialism? More broadly, to what extent did the supposedly 'bourgeois' distinction between public and private have any meaning in the GDR? These were the preliminary questions that inspired my research, and I went back to the archive to find answers.

Some readers may find this departure point somewhat puzzling, not least because privacy was apparently another one of those East German commodities forever in short supply. The late Gerald Feldman, one of the leading historians of modern Germany, probably spoke for many when he half-jokingly responded to my research topic with the comment, 'Privacy in the GDR? Sounds like a very short book.' Granted, private life and state socialism have long been assumed to be antithetical by definition, insomuch as that the private person has no legal identity or political standing outside the socialist community. Privacy, so goes the logic, is the natural and exclusive offspring of liberalism, not least because privacy is theoretically grounded in individual liberty and a distant relationship between state and citizen. For Marx and Engels, any notion of the private sphere must be anachronistic, in that people—once freed from capitalist oppression— would then regain their nature as social beings. Small wonder that for socialist regimes the word 'private' was fraught with unwanted and toxic associations, and used very sparingly in official parlance. The German word for privacy— *Privatheit*—did not even appear in the SED's official political dictionary, the *Kleines Politisches Wörterbuch*; the only entry related to privacy at all was 'private property', which predictably was included as a negative foil against which to define—and justify—the very existence of the GDR in the first place. For its part, the SED devoted a huge amount of state energy to integrating the private individual into the full machinery of GDR state and society, endeavouring to fully fuse I and We. The state's myriad surveillance techniques, best evidenced in the well-known exploits of the Stasi and its reserve army of 'unofficial collaborators', further dramatized the full penetration of the state into the private sphere. Yet it is misleading to interpret these well-known developments as merely proof of the absence of privacy in the GDR; for if privacy really did not exist, then the state would hardly have gone to such extraordinary lengths to investigate it. The deeper question is rather: why did the private sphere matter so much?

Such a question is crucial to understanding socialist culture more generally. After all, it was the state's overbearing presence itself that made a relatively private home life all the more necessary and valued among its citizens. As noted in a range of published recollections, this was certainly the case with the much-loved dachas and small country garden houses, where citizens felt freer and more private than anywhere else. A cherished sense of private identity was also something that people cultivated at home. In a world in which most social interaction was heavily monitored, the private sphere functioned for many citizens as an outpost of individuality, potential dissent, and alternative identity-formation. It became a place where religious conviction could be openly expressed and nurtured, or where non-worker class identities—as noted in furniture and housewares betraying bourgeois or even aristocratic family backgrounds—could be displayed. It was also the main location where artefacts from the West (foodstuffs, objects, and even books) were to be found. The domicile thereby acted as a semi-permeable refuge from public life and prescribed collective identities, as well as giving form to more private understandings of the self.

To date there is very little empirical work on the private sphere in non-liberal regimes. It is remarkable how much scholarly energy has gone into investigating the genesis and impact of the private sphere's historical spin-off, the public sphere. Most are aware that the emergence of civil society (and what later became known as the public sphere) has been a hallmark of bourgeois politics since the Enlightenment, and became a perennial subject of transatlantic political thought over the course of the last two centuries. Back in the early 1960s West German philosopher Jürgen Habermas famously traced the development of this bourgeois public sphere through coffeehouses and a new merchant-driven print communication culture, inspiring a vigorous cottage industry of scholarship on the subject ever since.[17] In recent years the public sphere's gender and class dimensions have been the subject of sustained scholarly criticism, especially insofar as the public–private divide was strongly encoded as masculine and feminine from the very beginning.[18] In any case, it is often forgotten that the private sphere has been equally prized in Western political thought as a sign of 'enlightened' political development in its own right. So much so that the very distinction between public and private became a distinguishing feature of Western political society,[19] and even one of the fundamental indices of civilization itself.[20]

But studies of the private sphere are few and far between. Part of the reason for this neglect is that privacy is tricky to define. In ancient Greek the word for private is *idios*, meaning 'one's own, pertaining to one's self', that is, the realm of the personal. By contrast the word for public is *demios*, which denotes 'having to do with the people'. A private individual was someone not holding public office, a layman, or someone without technical skill. Privacy in Greek thus carries negative overtones, since it implied someone not involved in the social order.[21] Emphasis instead was on public obligation, not private rights.[22] Privacy possessed a similar connotation in Latin with the word *privatus*, which means the withdrawal from public life, and *privare*, to bereave or deprive. In both cases, there was a close etymological and conceptual connection between private and privation.[23] The German word *privat* emerged in the middle of the sixteenth century, having the same meaning as the English 'private' and French 'privé'—all designating 'the exclusion from the state apparatus'.[24] In a modern sense, however, private became increasingly associated with secrecy and concealment. Over the course of the sixteenth to the nineteenth centuries, privacy took on the more favourable quality of privilege, in that its limited participation was no longer a deprivation but an advantage, as seen in private house, private education, private view, private club, and private property.[25] Privacy is generally seen to have had its golden age in the nineteenth century, after which it has been relentlessly under assault from twentieth-century technologies, expansive states, and brutal social engineering projects of all stripes.

Yet the private sphere enjoyed a remarkable ideological comeback in the aftermath of the Second World War. The cold war was decisive in this respect. By the early 1950s the place—and defence—of privacy became a common ideological yardstick with which to measure the differences between the 'free West' and the 'totalitarian East'. Some saw communism as having destroyed private life altogether in its sphere of influence, while others saw the shrivelled private sphere east of the Iron Curtain as the last refuge of humanity for those living under red rule. In her 1951 *Origins of Totalitarianism*, Hannah Arendt wrote: 'Totalitarian governments, like all tyrannies, certainly could not exist without destroying the public realm of life, that is, without destroying, by isolating men, their political capacities. But totalitarian domination as a form of government is new in that it is not content with this isolation and destroys private life as well.'[26] Other so-called totalitarian theorists saw private life as the last respite from the all-controlling Stalinist state. Only within the shelter of a fragile private sphere composed of small circles of family and trusted friends, so Carl Friedrich and Zbigniew Brzezinski argued, could individuals living in totalitarian states be their 'true' selves.[27] A free private life was now elevated as a very marker of liberal democracy.

A generation of Western legal theorists extended these claims, as the invasion of privacy was interpreted as an affront against the individual's dignity, civil rights, and even human rights. As part of the effort to overcome the Nazi legacy, Article 12 of the 1948 Universal Declaration of Human Rights stated that 'No one shall be subjected to arbitrary interference with his privacy, family, home or correspondence, nor to attacks upon his honour and reputation.' Such language was reproduced almost verbatim as a fundamental right for Europeans in the 1950 European Convention on Human Rights.[28] While the legal roots of privacy in modern liberalism hark back to Samuel Warren and Louis Brandeis's landmark 1890 *Harvard Law Review* article, 'Right to Privacy', American courts first codified the 'right to privacy' in 1965, partly because this newly hallowed value of privacy was seen as not being respected in American life. In his 1956

Organization Man, sociologist William Whyte wrote about the 'lack of privacy' and mutual surveillance of suburban life, while Betty Friedan, in her 1963 *Feminine Mystique*, voiced similar alarm about the invasion of privacy both at home and at work for women. A range of best-selling sociological studies published in the USA in the 1950s and 1960s—such as Morris Ernst and Alan Schwartz's *Privacy: The Right To Be Let Alone* (1962); Vance Packard's *The Naked Society* (1964); Myron Brenton's *The Privacy Invaders* (1964); and Alan Westin's *Privacy and Freedom* (1967)—were all animated by what they identified as the perilous 'death of privacy', a theme that became one of cold war America's favourite subjects of anxious political commentary.[29] With time, the 'sanctity of the private sphere' became a fundamental point of reference distinguishing West from East,[30] and was a standard view in Anglo-American jurisprudence.[31] Not surprisingly such logic applied to the two Germanies as one of the main theatres of cold war confrontation. By the late 1950s West German courts placed more premium on post-fascist 'private rights' guaranteed in the Basic Law as fundamental to West German civil liberties.[32] One writer baldly summed up the cold war polemic: 'In the West you had freedom of speech and private life. In the East you had the language of slaves (*Sklavensprache*) and assaults on private life.'[33]

Even so, we need to be careful about assuming an elective affinity between liberalism and the separation of public and private spheres. In fact, there was another tradition of linking the public sphere to absolutism, to the extent that the Roman idea of sovereign power created the 'public' by virtue of forging a coherent collectivity that united otherwise particular interests. This idea of the public sphere as coterminous with the sovereign was the guiding principle of Frederick the Great's eighteenth-century *Polizeistaat* Prussia and Catherine the Great's Tsarist Russia.[34] Less well-known is that serious discussion of the place and legal significance of the private sphere—with calls for new civil rights such as postal privacy and the inviolability of the home—also emerged under late eighteenth-century absolutism. While these civil protections from the long arm of the state were not formally enshrined in the German lands until the 1848–9 Constitution, the point is that 'private sphere talk' was not solely limited to liberal countries.[35] For their part, Bolshevik theorists picked up this absolutist model of rule to build an all-powerful party-state a century and a half later,[36] including the place of the private sphere. Even if Marx and Lenin paid little heed to privacy, dismissing it as a bourgeois residue that would die off with the overthrow of capitalism, Stalin saw things differently. A number of 'bourgeois' rights and liberties (such as the protection of private property, inheritance, and personal copyright) made their way into the Soviet Union's 1936 Constitution, and there was a marked shift toward the glorification of the family and domestic life as the bedrock of Stalin's 'neo-absolutist' social order from the mid-1930s on.

Scholarship on the Soviet Union has addressed this theme in various ways. This is certainly evident in Orlando Figes's 2007 book, *The Whisperers: Private Life in Stalin's Russia*, which aims to illuminate the 'inner world of ordinary

Soviet citizens living under Stalin's tyranny'. Of primary interest to him was how people internalized the values and social engineering projects of the regime, creating a world in which 'the walls have ears' and where everyone should 'watch your tongue'. As a result, citizens 'learned certain rules of listening and talking' and how to cultivate 'double lives', as private matters were often conducted in the form of whispering.[37] By contrast historians like Sheila Fitzpatrick, in her 1999 *Everyday Stalinism,* has persuasively shown that citizens were hardly silent at all, but rather were speaking out in many ways—complaining, pleading, and cajoling authorities—to advance their personal interests.[38] This was even more the case after 1945. Others have shown that a kind of Soviet private sphere emerged in the 1960s among the Moscow intelligentsia as a retreat from politics and the 'system of public compromise', and flourished across the Eastern bloc as well.[39] The coming of socialist consumerism accelerated the development of the socialist private sphere even more so, as citizens during the late Khrushchev and Brezhnev eras agitated quite loudly against the state to make good on its promise as the provider of private material well-being.[40]

The growing gap between public and private identities became common in Eastern Europe in the 1970s.[41] By that time the figure of the apolitical, withdrawn Eastern European became a kind of stock character in histories of the region.[42] While such trends were a source of government consternation (and later resignation) in Eastern Europe, they were greeted in the West as welcome signs of the collapse of socialist community, political fatigue, or the liberalization of communist society. By the late 1970s and 1980s the public–private split was embraced among Eastern bloc dissidents as a source of political resistance and moral renewal, most notably in dissident Czech playwright Vaclav Havel's notion of 'living in truth'.[43] With it Marxism seemed to be turned on its head. After all, Marx himself lampooned such an alienated civil society as typical of nineteenth-century bourgeois politics. In an excerpt from his 1842 article on 'The Freedom of the Press', he wrote that 'The government hears only its voice. It knows that it hears only its own voice and yet deceives itself that it hears the people's voice and demands of the people that it is also deceived. For its part the populace sinks partly into dissent, partly into skepticism, and turns entirely away from public life.'[44] Marx's target here was Prussia's overbearing governmental control of the *Vormärz* public sphere and its suppression of dissent; yet the passage ironically spoke to the sorry fate of freedom of speech, 'thinking otherwise', and political engagement under Eastern bloc socialism too.

East Germany remained an extreme version of these wider developments. By the early 1980s the GDR was deemed by observers to be the most 'privatized' country in the Eastern bloc, in terms of apolitical attitude and individual retreat from public life.[45] This is where Günter Gaus's classic description of the GDR as a 'niche society' comes into play. Gaus popularized this idea in his 1983 book, *Wo Deutschland liegt,* and it has been a key term used to denote East German society ever since. Gaus of course was no ordinary observer; he was the Federal

Republic's first official representative to the GDR, serving as a quasi-ambassador in a world of warming East–West German relations. In his assessment Gaus all but 'went native' in praising the once-rival socialist republic for having retained an authentic sense of German *Volkskultur* and *Gemütlichkeit* long absent from a hyper-modernized, consumer-oriented West German society. The 'other Germany' was a world characterized by domestic comfort, gardening, do-it-yourself projects, and private pastimes. In Gaus's rendering, East Germany's 'real existing socialism' emerges as a land of petit-bourgeois values, with pride of place going to the joys of private life far removed from collectivist pressures and demands. As he put it: 'What is a niche in the society of the GDR? It is the preferred place for people over there, the place in which the politicians, planners, propagandists, the collective, the great goal, the cultural legacy—in which all of these depart so that a good man, with his family and among friends, can water his potted flowers, wash his car, play [the card game] Skat, have conversations, celebrate holidays.'[46]

No less important was that Gaus argued that East and West Germans were very much alike, despite geopolitical division and intense political rivalry. Each society has its 'central point of existence in the private sphere'.[47] Gaus's account thus closed the gap not only between dictatorship and democracy, but also between East and Western Europe (and North America) in terms of 'privatized' civic culture and social values.[48] The withdrawal from politics (and nationalism) was common across Europe in the aftermath of the Second World War, as people 'rediscovered democracy's quiet virtues—the space it left for privacy, the individual and the family'.[49] Still, Gaus's 1983 book signalled a turning point in East–West German understanding, written as it was in a spirit of détente. Both German societies, in his view, were earmarked by depoliticized individualism and a turning away from public life, animated by the same 'pretty virtues' that Ralf Dahrendorf mocked so savagely in his 1965 classic *Society and Democracy in Germany* as the dangerous (and unwelcome) comeback of the 'unpolitical German'.[50] What transcended divided Germany as a residual shared *Kulturnation* was ultimately an updated cold war Biedermeier on both sides of the Berlin Wall.

Gaus was firmly in keeping with 1970s and early 1980s revisionism, which sought to challenge earlier cold war views of communist society as a kind of Stalinist concentration camp dominated by an all-pervasive state and extensive security apparatus. More sympathetic accounts were part of the sea change of *Ostpolitik*. What was described for the 1970s East German family became emblematic of the niche society in general by the early 1980s—'a safety valve, a place where one can let one's hair down, grouse, and complain uninhibitedly and not worry what others may think of you'.[51] At times this meant that the GDR became a soft touch for West Germany's leftist and liberal critics (and politicians) over the course of the 1970s, many of whom tended to close their eyes to the Stasi and the regime's human rights abuses in an effort to build better bridges to their cold war arch-rival.[52] In this climate, Gaus's book became standard by the mid-1980s.[53] Just a few years after its publication a team of journalists from the leading West German weekly, *Die Zeit*, journeyed to the GDR, painting an equally rosy picture of the 'other Germany' in an Era of Good Feeling.[54] In some measure this West German romanticization of the GDR as a kind of (semi-modernized) idyll of 'authentic' Germany served as the forerunner to the fabled East German nostalgia for their lost republic (*Ostalgie*) of the 1990s. In any case, the notion of a niche society, once rejected as firmly anti-socialist, was more and more accepted within the GDR itself. By the late 1980s the 'withdrawal into the private sphere' was openly acknowledged in East German publications, wherein the family was portrayed as an affective 'counterworld' of 'private being' (*Privatsein*) that remained largely 'outside societal forms of activity'.[55] Not everyone was so uncritical. In the early 1980s Timothy Garton Ash mocked East Germans for their political lethargy, unwilling to put their cars, apartments, and holidays at risk in pushing for Polish Solidarity-style reforms.[56] A few years later East German peace activist Freya Klier lamented that the GDR reform movement was losing steam, as a 'niche society was threatening to return'.[57] Indeed, it was widely joked that deep down East Germans loved their dachas and garden gnomes far more than civil or human rights.[58]

In this context it is worth remembering that the 'niche society' concept has a long history before Gaus. In the mid-1960s West German sociologists identified what they called the 'ventilative character' of the GDR private sphere as a 'protective community' (*Schutzgemeinschaft*) of family and friends.[59] In its anti-communist guise the notion can be traced back to Czeslaw Milosz's 1951 classic, *The Captive Mind*. Here Milosz astutely analysed the East Europeans' double game of public conformity and private individuality that characterized Stalinized societies made over by the 'New Faith'. But one could go back even further, for there seems to have been a kind of niche society in the Third Reich too. This may seem strange in light of common perceptions of the regime. No doubt the Nazi regime reached deep into the personal lives of its citizens and subjects with lethal ferocity, apparently doing away with the private sphere as yet another casualty trampled beneath the jackboots of the New Order. As one Nazi jurist argued in 1934, 'the so-called 'private sphere' is only relatively private; it is at the same time potentially political'.[60] At one point German Labor Front leader Robert Ley was reputed to have remarked that the 'only people who still have a private life in Germany are those who are asleep'. But even the arms of Morpheus were apparently no respite. According to some analyses, the fear of denunciation and surveillance entered the nightmares of ordinary citizens in Nazi Germany in the form of a world 'without walls'.[61] And yet, the private sphere apparently did play a role in the regime. The clandestine Social Democratic Party morale reports (SOPADE) from the mid-1930s recounted the way in which the mass mobilization of the populace paradoxically led to a 'withdrawal into privacy' for many citizens.[62] Such attitudes were of course typical among Jews targeted by the Third Reich in the run-up to the Second World War.[63] And as Ian Kershaw has recently written, the war seems to have encouraged a 'retreat into the private sphere' as regards political opinion in general and the Jewish issue in particular. Such a retreat into concerns of private interest and welfare to the exclusion of all else in conditions of crisis and danger is neither specific to Germany nor to societies under dictatorial rule, but the level of repression and the increasingly draconian punishment for politically nonconformist behavior enhanced this trend in the German population during the war.[64]

This book seeks to address some of the blindspots in Gaus's 'niche society' idea. First, Gaus assumes that this 'exit to niches' started sometime in the 1970s, with no explanation as to why or to what extent it related to the GDR's earlier decades. There were interesting continuities with the 1950s and especially the 1960s, and for this reason this book covers all four decades of the GDR's existence. Such an approach bucks recent trends which treat the regime as a tale of two halves, with Erich Honecker's ascent to power in 1971 conveniently serving as either the starting or end point in the analysis. Yet most of the key developments regarding the shifting private sphere—and this is one of my principal arguments—actually straddle the GDR's middle two decades. The 1960s play a pivotal role here. From the beginning of the decade the SED acknowledged the formal existence of a private sphere as a vital dimension of the state's social contract with its citizens, which included the protection of personal property and a well-ordered residential life. Patrolling, protecting, and providing for its charges was fundamental to SED paternalism, what Konrad Jarausch calls the regime's 'welfare dictatorship'.[65] Indeed, enclosure was one of the founding concepts of East German society. This idea was readily picked up by pop psychologists after 1989, who endeavoured to diagnose the confusion and disappointment felt by many East Germans in the wake of Reunification. East Germans were portrayed 'as walled in emotionally as our country was blocked off physically from the outside world by the Berlin Wall'.[66] Yet this was an older concept. As Greg Eghigian has shown, the understanding of the East German citizen as a *homo munitus*—a sheltered, defended entity—became a central metaphor for SED social scientists for conceptualizing East German state, society, and the self. As a consequence, the policing of borders and behaviour derived not just from 'Cold War fears and communist paternalism', but also from a broad understanding from the 1950s on that the East German subject 'required education, rearing, and consciousness-raising, and needed to be protected from dangerous diversions and detours'.[67] The 1960s were thus the GDR's real age of social reconstruction.

Things changed significantly a decade later. By comparison the 1970s was more of a 'Thermidor reaction' after the energetic social experiments of the previous decade, a cooling off of ideals and reform zealotry. There was a noted trend towards individualism, and people tended to turn away from public life. What political culture did exist was more a matter of formal obligation and politically correct observance. Why did the socialist private sphere blossom during the Honecker era? For one thing, citizens enjoyed more leisure as a result of shortened workdays, giving them more time to spend outside of work, at home and/or with their families and friends. This was the GDR's high period of Socialist Biedermeier with its emphasis on gardening, family camping trips, and evenings with loved ones, which reportedly served as compensation for a decline in the emotional connections to socialist ideals, alienation at work, and the lack of self-determination in public life.[68] Secondly, this emphasis on private life was also a result of SED successes. What Tocqueville observed for *Ancien Régime* France was equally true for SED-run East Germany: centralization and bureaucratization inadvertently smothered and suppressed political life.[69] In other words, it was precisely the state's overbearing presence itself that made a relatively free home life all the more necessary and valued among East German citizens. Thirdly, the new cultural legitimacy of the private sphere was increasingly acknowledged by the SED as a vital dimension of the state's social contract with its citizens.[70] A pleasant and peaceful domestic life was seen as a reward for hard work, and the state relaxed its demands and buttoned-up imperatives in a number of ways. A more accepted devotional life and youth subculture became oft-cited evidence of the state's new reform attitude. Nonetheless, the growing gap between state and citizen characteristic of the 1970s also saw the Stasi's stepped-up surveillance of private life as a reaction to Honecker's 'liberalization' of GDR society. What follows will explore these issues in detail, charting the very ways in which the domestic sphere played host to protracted tensions between state and citizen over the expression of personal liberty and alternative social identities.

Within Walls takes issue with another one of Gaus's limitations, namely that these niches were effectively removed from the realm of politics. While he did say that 'niches are not external [to the socialist system], but rather are niches inside GDR socialism', much of his analysis went on to assume the niches' removed quality. Private life, however, was never a world apart, but was always shot through by the forces of state and society. In this I am building on Mary Fulbrook's suggestive notion of the 'honeycomb state', as articulated in her 2005 social history of East German society, *The People's State: East German Society from Hitler to Honecker*. In it she rightly asserts that, far from 'withering away', as Marx had predicted, the state ballooned enormously under the conditions of 'real existing socialism'. As a result, there was really no pure 'outside' in this world. Instead, the lines demarcating state and society—or public and private—had been blurred beyond recognition in a 'multiplicity of little honeycomb cells of overlapping and intersecting elements in the GDR networks of power and social organization'.[71] Various 'limits to dictatorship' did exist, but they were not absolute, and were less at points outside the state's reach than within the very terrain of politics itself.[72] What remains unclear in her analysis, though, is how this model changed over time; these pockets within the 'honeycomb state' were never fixed or static, but mutated according to political issue, generational outlook, and special interest.[73] The fate of the church and the battles over the Christian home in the 1960s and 1970s are also good examples of how these honeycomb hideouts of relative privacy were at times transformed into highly politicized confrontations with the state. Defending one's private life under shifting circumstances was part and parcel of the GDR's own 'changing boundaries of the political'.[74]

For this reason, I decided to retain the older vocabulary of public and private to analyse the dynamics of East German society. Others have chosen different binary oppositions, such as individual and collective, social and personal, or domination and self-reliance.[75] At first glance these terms may appear more apt. In official documents 'individual' and 'personal property' was invariably preferred to 'private property', as was 'personal rights' to 'private rights'. Nevertheless, private remained a popular word used by virtually everyone in the GDR in one form or another. Of course its meaning shifted greatly according to context and period, but the term's very semantic slippage is what makes its story so interesting. Some may object that the public–private dichotomy is itself conventional and even obsolete. After all, challenging this dualism has been central to the feminist political struggle from the very beginning, punctuated by 'the personal is the political' slogan that served as one of the great feminist rallying cries of 1968 and beyond. But things were different on the other side of the cold war divide, and these terms—despite propaganda to the contrary—lived on in compelling ways in East Germany and elsewhere in Eastern Europe. How private life was perceived and understood by state and citizen alike is what concerns me.

It is tempting to argue that private life became a form of resistance in the GDR. This was sometimes true, as people used the intimate spaces of their private lives to hide away or resist Stasi infiltration.[76] This argument is supported by oral histories that claim that the retreat into the private sphere was especially rife among non-SED members.[77] Private life also shaded into resistance for churchgoers, for example, and was effectively used by Christians as 'weapons of the weak' against the encroachments of the state.[78] But such a model is too simple, since private life could mean very different things. The well-documented penchant among East Germans for a removed, quiet private life was perhaps a fitting desire for a country characterized by the 'absence of both revolutionaries and counter-revolutionaries'.[79] For most people, private life became a key instance of what historian Alf Luedtke has perceptively called *Eigensinn*, or doing things one's own way. One's private life is a relatively secret realm that contains our most precious and personal possessions, and is a place or circumstance where we are often most unguarded and 'ourselves'. Private life, like *Eigensinn* itself, is a matter of 'expressing longings and desires as well as anxieties', whose activities constitute a 'distinct experience of autonomy as well as of collectivity, perhaps even of homogeneity'.[80] Privacy is thus both personal and social, and East German private life ran the gamut from apoliticism to political resistance. The point is that private life possessed no determinate political meaning in itself, but very much depended on the situation and inhabitant, as noted in the interviews summarized above. In the East German case, its meaning could not be contained by its etymological origins—privation and/or privilege. The premium was put instead on intimacy, action, and self-development. Not for nothing were the two best-selling books in the history of the GDR explicitly geared toward the cultivation and enjoyment of private life—one was a sex self-help guide, Siegfried Schnabl's *Mann und Frau Intim*, while the other was a primer on gardening tips, *Ein Rat für jeden Gartentag*.[81]

Privacy, paradoxically, can also be seen as a social practice. Indeed, this book challenges the notion of private life as simply a terrain of repression and withdrawal, secrecy and silence. State socialism may have severely curtailed the limits of permissible talk, patrolling the borders of public discourse as much as it policed its state borders. Nonetheless, East Germans were by no means silent. They grumbled and groused and sometimes resisted, and used the pressing problems of their private life not simply to defend a private sphere. Instead— and this is another principal argument of the book—people constructed and staged a private sphere for various purposes. In this sense, the private sphere was less a zone of immunity than a social assertion and even political claim. Precisely because privacy was never rooted in law as in the West, and thus not actionable in court,[82] those civil rights linked to privacy, like the right to free conscience, had to be fought for with other means. Yet citizens found ways of carving out personal space through various strategies, such as arguing that the private sphere was a key element of the social contract between citizens and the state, usually in the form of agitating for a safe, clean, and quiet domicile free of undue state interference. Civil court records registered how residents often challenged state authority by forging a new rhetoric of socialist justice and even human rights in their defence of private life. And the state was listening. In its capacity as provider of security and prosperity, the state had a vested stake in maintaining its image as guarantor of domestic order and citizen material happiness. In so doing the GDR regime 'seemed to conspire in the growing preoccupation with private life'.[83] How the socialist state paradoxically acted as both the foe and guardian of the private sphere is one of the main themes of this book.

Moreover, my book shows how central gender is to the understanding of private life in the GDR. After all, women wrote most of the citizen complaint letters; were usually the ones who filed for divorce, at least by the early 1960s; submitted the majority of residential Dispute Commission 'moral injury' cases; campaigned as working mothers to secure better social services from the state; dominated local religious networks and parents associations; and were the GDR's most prominent writers and photographers documenting the private sphere over the decades. In this *Within Walls* builds on the work of historians such as Donna Harsch, who persuasively argued in her 2006 study, *Revenge of the Domestic*, about how the domestic sphere—the blindspot of traditional socialist theory and practice—came back with a vengeance in the 1960s and 1970s, as citizens (led by female activists) campaigned for more state welfare assistance.[84] What is so useful about Harsch's argument is that she shows that the domestic sphere was no *fait accompli*, but had to be fought for by engaged citizens pushing the state to make good on its promises of equality and prosperity for all. In the end, it was the East German answer to the 1968 feminist slogan in the West that 'the personal is the political'. Men too, however, also put a great premium on private life. A range of late 1970s and early 1980s questionnaires confirmed the extent to which East German linked their identities to family life and domesticity, apparently valuing the private sphere much more than West German men did.[85] By the 1980s, both men and women ranked a 'harmonious family life' as their primary (albeit often unrealized) life goal and confirmed a 'notable home-centeredness in defining their lives'.[86] However, the private sphere took on a broader meaning for many citizens beyond the campaigns for shopfloor equality, reproductive rights, and family assistance. Expanding the scope to include secret police surveillance, religious conflict, marital relations, and property disputes shows how citizens politicized their private lives in manifold ways.

This book is quite experimental in theme and approach. Given its subject matter, it makes no pretensions to being definitive—much of what makes the private sphere private is precisely that which resists archival collection and cataloging. It is thus neither a monograph in the traditional sense, nor a book exclusively devoted to chronicling the private lives of a select number of people in the GDR. Memoirs, diaries, Stasi files, court cases, photography, and citizen letters have all been integrated along the way, but more with a view towards casting some light on the making of the socialist self more generally. This study is thus indebted to a wide body of interdisciplinary scholarship on East Germany that touches on citizens' private life in various respects, including their consumer habits and even sexual activities.[87] Moreover, I have opted to drill down to the local level to study the very negotiation of private and public at the neighborhood level, in this case East Berlin. In this I am following other studies that have pioneered work at the grassroots to investigate socialism in action on the ground.[88] And given the capital's fascist legacy and geopolitical location at the 'frontiers of power',[89] it is little wonder that privacy and the private sphere acquired special meaning in East Berlin. While some of this had to do with East Berlin's special status as a cold war showpiece of 'socialist modernity', it was also closely connected to the common notion of the domicile as a cherished arena of individual freedom amid an otherwise heavily regulated social order. Even if the most empirically grounded research of this book is largely based on East Berlin archives, developments were seemingly not all that different in other large cities, or even in the countryside. Detailed comparative research will have to await future researchers; but in each chapter I have tried to provide comparative remarks in both directions—westward towards Federal Republic and eastward towards the Eastern bloc and the Soviet Union, and even back to the Nazi and Weimar periods as well. It should be added that such a project—based as it is on numerous civil court files and secret police dossiers—could only have been undertaken on a country like the GDR, marking the second time in half a century that a defunct German state's most classified and sensitive files have been made available for public scrutiny. The GDR lives on as a kind of archival Pompei, an 'extinct volcano' ideal for studying the dreams and delusions of creating 'socialism in half a country'.[90]

The book is divided into two parts, featuring seven chapters altogether. Each one addresses a specific theme that provoked considerable concern (and controversy) about the very place and power of private life in the GDR.

In Part I, 'Secret Societies, Public Institutions, Private Lives', the three chapters discuss those institutions straddling the threshold of public and private. Chapter 1 takes on the notorious Stasi as the exemplary case of the state's clandestine effort to bear down on citizens' private life, with a view towards how the Stasi was less a secret organization hovering above society than one firmly enmeshed in it. Chapter 2 concentrates on the Stasi's rival secret society, the Church. Historically the right to privacy came out of the Reformation, and the Evangelical Church in the GDR forged its identity around the constitutional 'right to free conscience'. Particular attention is paid to local battles between believers and the state in East Berlin over religious devotion, the Christian home, burying the dead, and children's education. Chapter 3 shifts discussion to another semi-private social institution bridging the individual and collective, namely marriage. Divorce court records will be used to analyse the inner workings and pressures of private life within GDR families, revealing the ways in which gender relations and intimate life changed markedly over the decades.

Part II, 'Domestic Ideals, Social Rights, and Lived Experiences', turns to the domestic sphere as a new site of social reform in the 1960s and 1970s. Chapter 4 considers the issue of interior design and the construction of an East German *Wohnkultur*, or domestic 'living culture', as both ideal and lived reality. Attention will also be paid to the flourishing cottage industry of East German etiquette books as further efforts to stylize the socialist self and to 'deprivatize' home life as an outpost of socialist civilization. The next two chapters explore the relationship between law and private life. Chapter 5 addresses the relationship between the individual, neighbourhood life, and popular justice. How norms of socialist domestic life were understood, presented, and adjudicated in residential communities—as seen in minor disputes regarding private property, noise, and honour—by residential dispute commissions (*Schiedskommissionen*) is the main thrust of this chapter. Chapter 6 continues in this vein, taking up the politicization of individual civil rights regarding the private sphere. Central here is the individual's right to petition, or *Eingabenrecht,* wherein GDR citizens were permitted—and encouraged—to write to the state as private *Bürger* with specific individual grievances. Chapter 7 moves in a new direction, exploring how private life was presented in the visual arts and in particular professional photography. How and why a new generation of GDR photographers saw themselves as maverick social historians recording the private lives of ordinary East Germans is the subject of this chapter.

The epilogue tackles 1989 and its aftermath, mostly in terms of the manifold forms of the reassertion of private life in the 1990s. How and why private life has featured so prominently in post-1989 memory-making is the main focus of this final section. It dovetails with the book's overall aim, which is to investigate the changing meaning of the private sphere across a variety of fields, ranging from law to photography, religion to interior decoration, family life to memoir literature, and to point to the myriad ways that private life was articulated and presented by citizens living in communist society. In the end, these issues are hardly GDR-specific, and hopefully this book will cast some new light on Eastern European social life in general. In his essay on twentieth-century French private life as part of well-known five-volume edited collection, *A History of Private Life*, Antoine Prost wrote that 'the twentieth century may be seen as a period during which the differentiation of public and private, at first limited to the bourgeoisie, slowly spread throughout the population. Thus, in one sense the history of private life is a history of democratization.'[91] This particular aspect of democratization was not limited to the Western world—in fact, similar forces were at play east of the Berlin Wall, and constituted a key dimension of 'Socialist Modern' there.[92] This book is an attempt to bring East Germany back into this broader European development by sketching the precarious yet persistent presence of private life under state socialism.

I
SECRET SOCIETIES, PUBLIC INSTITUTIONS, PRIVATE LIVES

1

The Tyranny of Intimacy

The Stasi and East German Society

FAUST: Do you spend much of your free time in spying?
MEPHISTOPHELES: I'm not omniscient yet—but I keep trying.

Goethe, *Faust,* Part I[1]

In the beginning was the Stasi. This perspective has long been a staple of popular appraisals of the German Democratic Republic, serving as Genesis 1 in chronicles of the trials and tribulations of Germany's first socialist state. The GDR's infamous Ministry for State Security—the Stasi for short—encapsulates the jealous dominion of a highly developed 'police state' that kept its captive population under rapt attention and control for four decades. In the aftermath of 1989 the Stasi's reputation has only grown as the world's most elaborate surveillance outfit, brimming with 'spy-tech' intelligence-gathering gadgetry and subtle psychological warfare techniques that shamelessly preyed on the fears and foibles of a cowed society.[2] The 'House of 3000 Rooms' (referring to the Ministry's massive compound in Berlin-Lichtenberg) stands in as the epitome of East German Stalinism long after the death of the Soviet dictator in 1953. So extensive was its reach that commentators have described the East German secret police as the 'centre of the most extensive spy organization in world history' and the 'most pervasive and efficient secret service in history'.[3] For many observers, the Stasi was the grim realization of Jeremy Bentham's infamous Panopticon, wherein 'a permanent, exhaustive omnipresent surveillance' had 'transformed the whole social body into a field of perception: thousands of eyes posted everywhere'.[4] Florian Henckel von Donnersmarck's 2006 box-office hit, *The Lives of Others,* further fuelled this fascination with the Stasi's dark empire for an international cinema audience. No wonder that Orwell's 1949 dystopian novel *1984* was repeatedly invoked as the ready reference for making sense of East Germany's defunct 'totalitarian' regime in the aftermath of Reunification. That Orwell's book was banned in the GDR as 'trash' that 'discriminates against the conditions created by the state and the political and economic situation in socialist society' only hastened the association.[5] In this sense, Mirabeau's well-known quip about Hohenzollern Prussia ('other states possess an army, Prussia is an army which possesses a state') seems to have found its East German correlative: a secret police in possession of a state.

Exaggerated as some of these views are, they contain a certain amount of truth. There is no denying that the Stasi was a massive organization with tendrils stretching deep into East German state and society. By the end, it had amassed some 180 kilometres of files, one million pictures, and 200,000 tapes to monitor its citizens. There were over six million dossiers in a country of only seventeen million inhabitants. So large was the sheer quantity of data produced by the secret police that Klaus-Dietmar Henke, who headed the Research Department of the Stasi File Authority (BstU) in the 1990s, likened it to 'the equivalent of all records produced in German history since the Middle Ages'.[6] But the Stasi's presence went far beyond file production. It was a pivotal part of the criminal justice system, ran its own prisons and internment camps, operated terrorist training programmes for foreign insurgents (such as the West German Red Army Faction), and possessed its own postal network, university-style training centre, supermarket, soccer team (Dynamo Berlin), and even a barber shop.[7]

Nonetheless, it was its ability to penetrate the very fabric of everyday society that caught the public's imagination after 1989. The ears and eyes of the state were seemingly everywhere. The Stasi lorded over a world in which mail was routinely opened, houses bugged, citizens harangued, and dissidents imprisoned for 'hostile negative' attitudes and nonconformist activities. Six hundred Stasi agents were responsible for checking mail in East Berlin alone.[8] Tiny holes were drilled in the walls of apartments and hotel rooms to watch suspects, and even bathrooms were secretly videotaped by Stasi voyeurs.[9] Confidentiality between doctors and patients was routinely breached, as medical information about suspect citizens (including their psychiatric files) was passed to the secret police.[10] One journalist's account of the Stasi's surveillance of citizens laid bare the state's outsized obsession with the private lives of troublesome residents:

The Stasi knew where Comrade Gisela kept the ironing board in her apartment . . . and how many times a week Comrade Armin took out his garbage and what color socks he wore with his sandals while doing it . . . The Stasi kept watch on trash dumps and lending libraries—the names of those who checked out books on hot air balloons or rock-climbing equipment were of particular interest—and tapped the booths of Catholic confessionals and the seats at the Dresden Opera. Stasi cameras monitored public toilets. The Stasi photographed every slogan found scrawled on a wall and wrote down every rumor. Some of its dossiers on East Germans had a hundred categories of information—even the number, location, and design of tattoos. The Stasi kept a library of smells: a few hundred glass jars containing bits of dissidents's dirty underwear, so trained dogs could sniff and match the smell to an antigovernment pamphlet found on the sidewalk.[11]

Hannah Arendt's assertion, in her 1951 classic, *Origins of Totalitarianism*, that both the Nazi and Soviet systems created worlds of 'ubiquitous spying where everybody may be a police agent' and where 'each individual feels himself under constant surveillance', seems to have found supreme expression in Orwellian East Germany.[12] Not for nothing was the Stasi nicknamed the *VEB Horch und Guck*, or 'The People's Own Listen and Look Company'.

Harrowing revelations of husbands spying on wives and children informing on their parents drove home the extent to which the lines between state and society, public and private, had seemingly been effaced in the GDR. The shocking discovery of the millions of Stasi files in January 1990 by various citizen groups—including the 'complete smell collection' of the Leipzig opposition—has furnished some of the most disturbing images of East Germany's homegrown 'tyranny of intimacy'.[13] While no one could deny the secret police's power and presence, it pays to recall that the Stasi grew quite slowly and unevenly. In fact, its heyday was actually in the 1970s and 1980s, paradoxically during a period of détente and relative liberalization. Retrospective reinventions of Stasi omnipotence from the very beginning were often quite self-serving efforts to deny complicity after the fact. The shopworn characterization of the Stasi as a kind of 'state within a state' by the likes of state leaders Erich Honecker and Egon Krenz helped to mythologize the agency's untouchable conspiratorial subculture as well as to exonerate their own responsibility for its actions in the face of post-1989 accusations of governmental abuse.[14] Such Stasicentric views of the GDR are really a post-cold war invention. Until the 1990s, the main books on East Germany scarcely addressed the secret police. As a consequence, the Stasi remained all but invisible in the historiography of the 1970s and 1980s, precisely when the state security organ was at its zenith of power.[15]

This chapter endeavours to take a different tack, namely to reread the Stasi as an institution embedded in socialist society rather than hovering above it.[16] Even if the Stasi became a latter-day secret society in its own right, it could never have achieved its wide influence without the participation and compliance of hundreds of thousands of people, often in the form of a reserve army of voluntary informants. It was also part of a social world whose covert tactics and public image changed over the years. What primarily interests me is how, and to what extent, the secret police bore down on people's private lives. The first part of the chapter will address the historical emergence of the Stasi's secret surveillance society and how it affected those under scrutiny. The second part looks at the Stasi's transformation in the 1970s, as it developed new duties, strategies, and networks of informants to monitor the private lives of ever-more citizens. A central theme of this chapter is how the secret police's targeting of private lives as a haven of secrecy and danger created its own limits and backlashes. In effect the Stasi's secret machinery of power both undermined and in turn inadvertently created a sense of privacy among GDR citizens.

THE STASI AS 'SCRATCHY UNDERSHIRT'

The East German Stasi was modelled after its Soviet forerunner and counterpart, the Cheka and KGB, and functioned for almost four decades as the fabled 'sword and shield' of the ruling Socialist Unity Party. As Mike Dennis has noted, the construction of a secret apparatus within the Party was an integral element of communism from the very beginning. Indeed, secrecy was a mandatory condition of membership into the Communist International only a few years after the Russian Revolution, as articulated by the Comintern's Second World Congress in 1920. This was the birth of communism's identity as a conspiratorial confraternity, an identity that only intensified during the experience of the Second World War.[17] After 1945 every Eastern bloc country created a secret police force along these lines. The clandestine dimension was central to the Stasi as well. Stasi agents, for their part, were forbidden any contact with foreigners, sworn to secrecy, and prohibited to discuss their work with family or friends. Dozens of disguises were used—dressing up as refugees, gas station attendants, waiters, tour guides, train conductors, and even West German tourists—to coax coveted information.[18] The statutory basis of the Stasi was also secretive—the 1950 law creating the ministry consisted of one vague paragraph. No history of the Stasi was ever published in the GDR for security purposes. Its power lay precisely in its clandestinity. Over the decades the Stasi provided the regime with a kind of *arcana imperii*, uniquely exploiting the power of mystification to stifle independent action and the emergence of a public realm.[19]

But despite its secret fraternal subculture, the Stasi was heavily involved in wide-ranging state affairs. It commanded substantial state funding, absorbing some 2 per cent of the country's entire budget. The Stasi even had its own separate banking system, along with some 2,000 properties across the country. It was the GDR's largest employer, with 1.5 times more people than the country's standing army. By 1989 the number of paid Stasi employees was estimated to be 91,000, with a budget of over 4 billion marks.[20] In a country of seventeen million inhabitants, the density of the Stasi translated into roughly one operative for every 180 citizens. By comparison, there was one secret police officer per 595 citizens in the USSR, and one in 1,574 in Poland.[21] The Third Reich's notorious Gestapo, by contrast, had only 7,000 employees in a population of sixty-six million by 1939, and its informer network was also relatively small. As for the Soviet secret police, the NKVD, 366,000 people were working for it by 1939, translating into one secret service operative per 500 citizens, or roughly twenty times the size of the Gestapo. Yet the Stasi network easily dwarfed them all, especially if we factor in the vast network of 'unofficial collaborators'. The number of informers active during the closing years of the GDR varied from 110,000 to 180,000, which meant that about one in thirty citizens had served at one time or another for the Stasi. All told, it is estimated that some 800,000 people worked for the Stasi over the decades.[22]

While large secret police organizations were certainly hallmarks of twentieth-century politics, their historical roots stretch back much further. The formalization of political policing had its origins in the absolutist monarchies of the eighteenth century, most notably in the reign of Habsburg emperor Joseph II (1780–90). In Central Europe political policing intensified in the conservative backlash following the French Revolution, as police forces were established during the Napoleonic Wars and their aftermath to combat new political threats.[23] National police and intelligence services were further beefed up in the wake of the 1848 revolutions to maintain public order, as nationalists, reformers, and radicals of all stripes were kept under a close eye by all European states.[24] But it was really the First World War that gave birth to the modern national security state in Europe, as all wartime governments became increasingly preoccupied with the moods and morale of its citizenry and soldiers. This was the first blush of government-level war propaganda departments, organized postal censorship, and citizen surveillance in the modern sense, as information was used to sculpt and mobilize a fighting body politic. This found heightened expression in the Soviet Union, in part because its war experience lasted until 1921 and in part because Soviet communism built its identity on a siege mentality about hostile enemies. Elaborate surveillance cultures were developed among all of the belligerents during the Second World War as modes of knowledge and administration; so common were they that even wartime oppositional groups—such as White Russian intelligence networks in the Great War or German Social Democratic morale reports compiled from exile in the Second World War—drew on the same surveillance techniques of mass observation.[25]

Such trends continued after 1945, especially in Soviet Occupied Europe. Nowhere was this more important than in war-torn Germany. That the armed enemy was just across a porous makeshift border—defended only by barbed wire and low-level checkpoints until 1961—made security a pressing concern. For the Soviet authorities, the top priority was to set up a ruling Communist Party equipped with an effective German security service. It was justified as a necessary response to the threat of the West. The presence of the US-sponsored Gehlen Organization in the American Zone, an anti-Soviet intelligence agency led by a former Nazi general who just a few years before had headed the intelligence operations of the Wehrmacht's foreign auxiliaries on the Eastern Front, gave credence to Socialist Unity Party accusations of Western subversion. In 1947 the Soviets created a special department of the East German People's Police, the so-called Komissariat-5, to carry out de-Nazification measures in the broadest sense. It built a sizeable base of information-gathering and surveillance in its zone, patterned on KGB methods. All three of the GDR's Ministry of State Security directors—Wilhelm Zaisser, Ernst Wollweber, and most famously, Erich Mielke—had previous careers as Soviet intelligence officers. Early secret police activity—as noted in the activities of the so-called People's Control, or *Volkskon-trolle*—centred on combating extortion, black marketeering, and hoarding across the Soviet Zone. Intelligence was vital for its success. According to the agency's founding document, the aim was to 'form a comprehensive and as seamless as possible network of confidants and informants' in order to help the communist cause. Thousands of Social Democrats were imprisoned for opposing the Party's merger with the KPD in forming a new Socialist Unity Party, or SED, as were hundreds of Christian Democrat adherents.[26] With it the union of the SED and secret police was consecrated.[27]

The official creation of the Ministry of State Security in February 1950 followed the founding of the GDR state a few months before.[28] For justification, the SED claimed that the new security force was part of the great revolutionary tradition dating back to the abortive Spartacist uprising in Berlin in 1919. From the outset there was a high degree of integration between Stasi, Party, and state organs of coercion, and it recruited heavily among former Gestapo, SS, and Wehrmacht officers, apparently so as to prevent them from going over to the West.[29] Many of them had been persuaded to enlist in Soviet-run antifascist schools for POWs, and thereafter invited to form part of the new police force in the Soviet Zone.[30] The Stasi's early task was to protect the 'people's property' and communally owned businesses from banditry; to fight against hostile agents, saboteurs, and spies; as well as to defend the country from outside threat. But until the June 1953 Uprising of nationwide wildcat strikes, the Stasi was relatively small, employing only 601 full-time staff in 1949. The seismic 1953 revolt was construed as a massive intelligence failure,[31] after which the Stasi swelled to 9,000 agents by 1955, adding more again in the wake of the 1956 Hungarian Revolution. The 1961 construction of the Berlin Wall unleashed a wave of Stasi repression against potentially hostile citizens: 18,297 people were sentenced for crimes against the state in the second half of 1961,[32] and the Stasi leapt to over 19,000 staff members by the end of 1962.[33] While the Stasi at this point mostly concentrated on foreign threats, it was preoccupied with domestic issues too. By the late 1950s full-time Stasi officers were posted in all industrial plants, and in every apartment building one tenant was designated to report on residents to the local *Volkspolizei*, or People's Police.

This is not to say that GDR citizens were without rights. In the 1949 GDR Constitution, for example, people enjoyed the right to express opinions freely and publicly, the right of assembly, and even the privacy of post. However, these classic liberal civil rights were rarely respected. Whereas liberal law was built on protecting individuals from the state, socialist jurisprudence presumed that the state was the people. Law was invariably subordinated to power. As Stasi Chief Mielke put it: 'Power is the most important position from which to fulfill the historical mission of the working class, to establish Communist society . . . Socialist law is an important instrument of exercising, enhancing and consolidating power.'[34] To this end the definition of 'negative hostile' behaviour was left deliberately vague for maximum exploitation. In a 1958 official guide, for example, the Stasi's central role was so defined: 'The Ministry of State Security is entrusted with the task of preventing or throttling at the earliest stages—using whatever means and methods may be necessary—all attempts to delay or to hinder the victory of socialism.'[35]

But the Stasi was neither the only—nor even the most significant—repressive organ in East Germany during the country's first decade and a half of existence. That dubious honour went to the GDR's People's Police. It was the first institution created by the new East German state, and even predated the formation of the government by four years, having been created by the Soviet Military Government immediately after the ceasefire in the summer of 1945. The Stasi was essentially an offspring of the People's Police. By 1952 the People's Police expanded its reach by creating a new voluntary system of *Abschnitts-bevollmächtige*, or Auxiliary Police, which helped strengthen the power and presence of the police at the residential level. Local 'sectional commissioners' worked alongside other police branches in patrol and criminal investigation. They were required to move into their residential jurisdiction, keep office hours, be available by phone, and make regular visits to all households. This often meant keeping track of nonconformity in whatever guise. Homosexuals for example were often singled out as dangerous citizens by these Auxiliary Police officers. One gay East Berlin worker recalled his experience from the early 1950s: 'I moved into my apartment in the early 1950s. Just before I moved in the Auxiliary Police officer went from household to household where young people lived, and informed them: in the first courtyard, second floor on the right one of them is about to move in. Beware.'[36] After the construction of the Berlin Wall in 1961, the police began to adopt a less confrontational line. Regular police officer meetings with wayward citizens were considered a key part of the regime's expansive notion of re-education, in that the Auxiliary Police used a non-conflict model of citizen improvement as a means of governing at the local level.[37]

The state used other networks to intervene more directly in people's private lives. The lack of any real avenue of unregulated popular expression—be it uncontrolled mass media, alternative culture, or of course voter choice—meant that the state was always unsure about citizen loyalty. In fact, the SED created a secret Institute for Opinion Research in 1963 to ferret out popular attitudes towards economic policy, work life, internal political changes (such as the revised constitution of 1968), international events, and general satisfaction in the Party so as to rule more effectively. Still, there was much that the SED had a hard time finding out, and morale within residential communities was one of the most impenetrable.[38] The state thus felt compelled to organize networks of intelligence, snooping, and supervision in order to scout out potential wellsprings of dissatisfaction. The home was routinely singled out as the most worrisome cell of secrecy and dissent. After all, GDR citizens had long made clear that their homes were places where they discussed all sorts of problems, ranging from mismanagement at work and at school, the lack of people's voices as well as encounters with the police and Stasi, often in 'crass contradiction to what the classic doctrines of communism envisaged for a proletarian state'.[39] Private life needed to be kept under close supervision.

The socialist state's fear and suspicion of private life was nothing new, having become a staple of communist ideology ever since the Russian Revolution. Lenin's wife, Nadezhda Krupskaia, made no bones about declaring that 'a distinction between private life and public life will lead sooner or later to the betrayal of Communism'. In 1927 Anatoly Lunacharsky, the Soviet Union's Commissar of Education, wrote that '[t]he so-called sphere of private life cannot slip away from us, because it is precisely here that the final goal of the Revolution is to be reached'. On this theme Stalin reportedly said that 'A true Bolshevik shouldn't and couldn't have a family, because he should give himself wholly to the Party.'[40] Here and elsewhere private life itself was viewed with great trepidation by communist authorities, and the GDR was no exception.

Monitoring private life in East Germany increased dramatically in the wake of the June 1953 Uprising. A good deal of this was linked to the perceived (and sometimes real) threat of Western espionage, as reports of American spy activities were routinely published in East German newspapers.[41] One of the earliest state incursions in the private sphere was the so-called *Hausbuch*, or 'Housebook', programme. While this initiative started in the early 1950s, it was expanded considerably after 1953. In this case, every GDR citizen was required to register all house guests in a *Hausbuch* kept by an elected housing supervisor, significantly named the *Hausvertrauensmann*, or Residential Confidence Man. It not only enabled the government to keep track of who was entertaining visitors (especially foreign ones) on a regular basis; it also helped create a new cadre of so-called 'confidence men' (and they were nearly 90 per cent men) to keep tabs on tenants. Not surprisingly, the West German press made much of this 'invasion of the private sphere' as the 'realization of Orwell's sinister vision of the dictatorial state', with overtones of Nazi terror.[42] Even so, such measures were introduced to help monitor what civil society existed and to inspire citizen confidence in the state as the guardian of public order.

Likewise, new 'housing communities', or *Hausgemeinschaften*, were set up in the early 1950s to help 'rationalize' residential life and instil it with a new developed sense of community. Historical precedents could be found in the Kaiserreich's *Ehrenämte*, which were late nineteenth-century agencies of neighbourhood-based urban administration, as well as in Lenin's ideal of small cells of local self-government to help train citizens in the tasks of democratic political life. Such housing communities continued to exist through the Weimar Republic, but were expanded considerably after 1933 as part of a new *Blockwart* system of neighbourhood associations to better bind the Nazi Party and German society. By the late 1930s some two million residential block leaders across Germany (as well as in Austria and the Sudetenland) were elected as 'confidence men' to oversee residential concerns, and after the outbreak of war were even entrusted with organizing civil defence against bomb attacks. They kept card catalogues of all residents, and routinely visited people in their homes to gather opinion, information, and advice, keeping an eye on any untoward activity or behaviour.[43] These neighbourhood block leaders were often more effective than the Gestapo in making the regime present in the lives of ordinary people.[44]

The Soviets built their East German intelligence network on the Third Reich's old neighbourhood-based *Blockwart* system of social surveillance, appointing block and house leaders to report to Soviet authorities.[45] After 1949 the SED continued this policy by strengthening these organs of neighbourhood order and control. In Ulbricht's eyes, the 'housing communities' were to help raise 'national consciousness' and mobilize the masses in the collective construction of genuinely socialist residential culture.[46] Housing community leaders drafted innumerable reports on communal housing life, material problems, and 'uncooperative citizens', and were key representatives of the state in neighbourhood life. In close cooperation with the National Front, they helped build common rooms, create inter-housing sports leagues and organize parades in connection with 1 May festivities. By early 1953 there was already much talk within the National Front about using these housing communities to extend patriotism 'into every house' and to root out the influence of Western 'warmongers and their agents'.[47] While this was already evident in the early 1950s,[48] this campaign was accelerated in the wake of the 17 June Uprising. The 'housing communities' were used to make sure that everyone knew that the 'provocation' engineered by 'foreign powers' in Berlin and elsewhere had been successfully suppressed, and to help ensure 'loyalty to our government' by keeping a 'watchful eye on our residences and families'.[49] One pre-Wall Berlin National Front report registered the cold war rhetoric: 'we must strengthen our persuasion tactics, since the enemy is trying to beat us in a war of nerves. They want to confuse our people and to precipitate a mass exodus from our republic. Every house must be a defense... If we don't succeed in bringing such progress to every home and to pull together all residences in this common fight, we will be lost.'[50]

Such tactics were intensified after the construction of the Wall a few months later. In one December 1961 report it was stated that

many negative habits of small segments of the population, such as shiftlessness, listening to RIAS [Radio in the American Sector], watching West German television and black marketeering, are being practiced by families in the home. In these residences such issues must be confronted and discussed, since the formation of politically-functioning housing communities is of uppermost significance. The educative role of the housing community is to complement the citizen's broader socialist education received at work and in the factory.[51]

Scattered evidence indicates that there was a widespread perception about the glaring contradictions between public conformity and individual behaviour.

This disjuncture was not even limited to private life, but occurred in public institutions as well. A good example can be found in a 1954 letter to Queen Elisabeth-Hospital in Berlin-Lichtenberg, in which the complainant was shocked to learn of the blasé attitude on the part of hospital authorities toward the 'constant playing' of the supposedly taboo RIAS in a public building. She brought the matter to the attention of the director, who concurred that it was 'forbidden to listen to it in a public building'. Yet, so she reported, he concluded by saying that 'privately one can do as one pleases'.[52] This vignette illustrates the common perception that public and private behaviour were two different matters altogether. Home life was seen as a particularly troublesome refuge of non-compliance. Even if the early 1950s dream of 'having a housing community representative on every single East German street' never came to pass, some 30–40 per cent of GDR communities were involved in the programme by the mid-1960s. Older residents looking back on those years recall that 1961 marked stepped-up state interest in people's private life, as well as 'increased spying on friends and families'.[53] Its general success of course is difficult to gauge with any certainty, as some local authorities were more zealous and engaged than others. East Berliners interviewed in 2005 and 2007 had very different recollections of the *Hausbuch* and *Hausvertrauensmann* system. While some remember them as unobtrusive, others recall the tenant life as riddled with nosy neighbourhood authorities. Whatever the case, these initiatives did represent powerful state interventions into the private lives of GDR citizens in the Ulbricht era.

Certain people were routinely targeted by the authorities as dangerous. In the housing communities' effort to 'restore confidence in the government', particular social groups—non-SED members, artisans, *Mittelständler*, and farmers—were seen as recalcitrant and in need of special scrutiny. Youth were also identified as potentially unreliable and resistant, and in need of close observation.[54] Yet no group was subjected to more overt pressure than Christians. The Party viewed them as reactionary and dangerous fifth columnists, whose loyalties lay outside the GDR. From the outset the SED's ultimate objective was a state without churches, a society without Christianity. There were a range of pre-Stasi police reports from 1948–9 on church activities, and many of them pointed out the menace of the pastor's house as a cell of alternative culture.[55] Numerous Stasi reports were written about house searches of suspect pastors, accusing them of 'politically negative' and even 'decadent' behaviour, especially toward their young charges.[56] Christian student groups were regularly placed under Stasi surveillance, and a great deal of attention was paid to young Christians who opted out of the communist youth group, the Free German Youth.[57] By the 1960s the Stasi had created a special 'Section XX/4' responsible for the observation and subversion of the churches, showing the extent to which private matters of conscience were issues of serious state concern.[58] This was especially so when it came to the so-called *Bausoldaten*, pacifist 'civil construction soldiers' who refused armed service from the mid-1960s on, usually under the aegis of the

Church. Countless files were compiled on these conscientious objectors, with tabs on background and activities through the 1980s. The persecution of Christians became a favourite topic of cold war tension, as the West German press eagerly published many a report about life in GDR jails by East German Christians who eventually fled to the West.[59] Through the 1970s and 1980s the Stasi continued its assault on the churches, often working to discredit pastors by 'outing' them as alcoholics, homosexuals, or libertines. At the behest of the Stasi one 1973 'unofficial collaborator' organized sex parties for churchmen in order to scandalize and ensnare them, and did so all the way until 1989.[60]

Even after the construction of the Wall in 1961, anti-socialist behaviour of all kinds was considered as dangerous as ever, and systematically targeted for 're-education'.[61] The 'confidence people' and 'housing communities' were now entreated to play more active roles in this regard. Housing administrators were urged to devote more attention to the private life of its citizens, as evidenced in the new 'housing community leader' handbooks.[62] Calls for expanded communal control were largely fuelled by growing fears of violence and crime, particularly among youth, which spurred wide discussion in the 1960s and 1970s among GDR sociologists, educators, and social workers. For them, a great deal of the problem lay in identifying the roots of deviant behaviour within state socialism, especially since traditional Marxist sociology maintained that crime essentially sprang from capitalist sources (economic inequality, material misery, and social alienation), all of which the GDR supposedly had overcome with its successful revolution. Residential life was thus increasingly singled out as largely responsible, giving rise to widespread interest during the 1970s in studying 'socialist personality', 'socialist lifestyle', 'socialist living conditions', 'socialist childraising', 'socialist family life', and above all 'asocial behavior' as new targets of social reform.[63] While some of these problems were patently quite old, the state approached them in new ways. Over time the GDR explicitly adopted a range of Western social science models in developing socialist psychiatry, behavioural psychology, criminology, and urban sociology. Socialist selfhood and character became favourite new subjects of research and policy-making.[64] These trends were not perforce bad in themselves, as they often brought great benefit to suffering citizens. The cumulative effect, however, was that the private life of citizens became a growing state concern. In this sense, the state's preoccupation with the private sphere was a marriage of old ideology and new science, as the dwelling was viewed as a key testing ground for socialist education and good citizenship.

As a consequence, the Stasi was not merely interested in dissident activists. Often they spied on ordinary people who were seen as nonconformist in a broad sense. One late 1980s Stasi file in Leipzig is quite revealing in this regard. It featured a report on Erdmuthe P, a young woman 'without Party affiliation' who apparently was uninvolved in any 'mass organization', outside of her Free

German Youth membership. Stasi reports on her political views didn't turn up anything, and her attitude toward the West was vague:

Her political position cannot be ascertained, she apparently has not expressed any opinions about political problems. Numerous conversations with house residents have also revealed nothing . . . She does not decorate her home for festival days and does not participate in neighborhood activities. Whether her parents put out a flag for festival days is also not known . . . Whether she receives West German radio and television cannot be determined, since she has never spoken about it with her neighbors.

She was apparently a Lutheran, but even this—along with her musical interests— was kept private: 'Occasionally Family P makes "house music" together, and the mother or father is active in the church choir. But in the residential community the family never speaks about confessional activities, nor do they seem to have any Christian visitors. According to the neighbors they pursue their confessional activities outside their residence.' But it was her attitude towards her neighbours that was singled out as suspicious. Although commended for being 'friendly and polite to her neighbors', she was also 'very quiet and withdrawn', without 'any close or friendly contacts to her neighbors. She does not seek any conversations with them, and only engages with them when spoken to, and then does so only with great economy and superficiality.'[65] There may be little of great drama here, to be sure, but the Stasi report is significant in several respects. First, it reveals how the Stasi operated at the local level, gathering intelligence from 'numerous conversations with neighbors'; secondly, it reflects the state's preoccupation with nonconformity and those apparently opting out of socialist society. Thirdly, as we shall see later, it also points up the Stasi's frustration with 'non-transparent' characters and limited intelligence in the face of wily citizens' ability to protect their privacy.

Yet Stasi harassment was not just aimed at so-called 'asocials'. In fact, it devoted a good amount of energy spying on its own agents. During the first five years of the regime the SED undertook a number of expulsions and purges of its members, often using forced confessions and brutal interrogations. This changed over time, though, as repression turned into disciplining. With it the functionary's lifestyle became increasingly important. It is worth recalling that, apart from clear oppositional groups, the Stasi's early targets were mainly those sectors entrusted with physical violence—the military, the defence industry, border security, and the police. Once these groups were brought to heel, the Stasi moved on to scrutinize the reliability of the functional elites and the so-called *nomenklatura*.[66] Nowhere was this more evident than in the work of the SED's Control Commission, or *Kontrollkommission*. This commission was explicitly created to vet the suitability of young SED Party cadres (such as police officials and Stasi agents) for government service, which included prying into their private affairs in the name of 'socialist morality' and proper comportment.[67] Such puritanical communist standards had their roots in the early Soviet Union. As early as 1920 a Communist

Party Control Commission was established as a modern-day ecclesiastical court to 'civilize' the private actions of wayward Party brethren. In these quasi-legal 'comradely conversations', fellow Bolsheviks were admonished for alcohol abuse or sexual misconduct, and reminded how far short they fell from the lofty 'monastic ideals' of Bolshevist morality.[68] This kind of communist asceticism and moral policing was typical across the Eastern bloc after 1945. As Czeslaw Milosz observed about 1950s Poland: 'The higher one stands in the Party hierarchy, the more attentively is one's private life supervised. Love of money, drunkenness, or a confused love-life disqualify a Party member from holding important offices. Hence the upper brackets of the Party are filled by ascetics devoted to the single cause of Revolution . . . The general ideal of the New Faith is puritanical.'[69]

In the GDR this took on an extreme form. The pressure to maintain upstanding private lives was considered important as they were instances of 'socialist personality', and the private lives of government officials, police officers, and Stasi agents were often placed under severe scrutiny.[70] As a testament, the words of Feliks Dzierzynski, the founder of the Soviet Cheka, were conspicuously displayed on Stasi office walls: 'Only a person with a cool head and a warm heart and clean hands can be a Chekist. A Chekist must be cleaner, more honest than anyone—he must be as clear as a crystal.'[71] Notably, these were often understood as particularly male codes of conduct. Indeed, the Stasi was one of the last bastions of East German patriarchy. For a society that prided itself on the equality of the sexes at work and in public life, the Stasi was a remarkably traditional male preserve of power and privilege. It was often ridiculed by GDR feminists as a 'men's club' that directed its misogyny at 'alternatively-thinking and independently-minded women'.[72] Women working at the Stasi were generally relegated to traditional gender ghettos, such as secretaries, cleaners, and cooks. As one female agent recalled in the 1990s: 'The functions associated with a lot of work but little honor were always filled by women. Because they had children, women were not put in functions which were really important.'[73] Wives and daughters of Stasi employees were often recruited for service since they were presumed to be particularly loyal. The percentage of women in the Stasi's foreign intelligence unit was higher (around 18 per cent), but this seems to be because they were often used as so-called Juliets—'romantic decoys' or prostitutes.[74] Early Stasi recruitment guidelines stated that 'young, good-looking female unofficial employees with good manners, the ability to pick things up quickly and who are able on account of their professional position to form connections to specific social groups' were considered a great advantage.[75]

The Party's Control Commission files were predominantly about male officers. They noted if SED members married Christian partners, since they were suspected of being 'without an honest connection to the GDR'.[76] Drinking habits and sexual behavior of Stasi officers were also favourite subjects of comment and investigation.[77] The expectations of marital solidity were especially high for the aspiring SED elite. If married functionaries were caught in adulterous relationships, for example, they were often forced to confess all before the commission, express contrition, and recommit to their spouses at the next Party forum.[78] No less interesting is that it was often the wives of functionaries who initially brought the cases before the quasi-court, as citizens looked to the Party as a moral arbiter of private domestic conflict.[79] And these commissions took their task seriously. They kept track of subsequent behaviour, and there was little chance of career advancement in government if the Party functionary in question was divorced.[80] In the despondent words of one Stasi officer interviewed in the mid-1990s, when recalling the Stasi's control of private life: 'You couldn't marry without the Ministry' approval. If your wife' father or even uncle had been in the SS, you would have to choose between her and your job . . . Why, you weren't even allowed to grow a beard.'[81] The Stasi subculture was one built on a severe code of conformity, superiority, and model citizenship, whose repressive politics were geared towards itself as much as to 'asocials'. So whereas the occupying Red Army maintained a segregated subculture, rarely mixing with the larger East German population, the Stasi very much reflected—and helped maintain—East German social norms and ideals.

How ordinary people reacted to this network of surveillance is not easy to gauge with any precision. No doubt the Stasi, along with these other quasi-state networks such as the 'housing communities', cast a wet blanket over GDR society, making open discourse risky business. In the mid-1970s a number of GDR residents who had recently fled to the West were interviewed by a West German journalist. Here they recalled their abiding fear of speaking too frankly at work or around the neighbourhood.[82] Others interviewed remarked that they were apprehensive to talk about their personal problems outside a small circle of friends and family.[83] How draconian or repressive this actually was of course depended on the individual person. In the twenty-five interviews and thirty questionnaires on private life that were conducted for this book over the period 2004–7, I was surprised how few people communicated any real conflict with either the Stasi or the *Hausvertrauensmann*. Invariably they all knew who these people were in the neighbourhood and residential building, and that they had to be very careful and discreet in their dealing with them. Many recounted an atmosphere of fear and mutual surveillance. Yet those who kept their heads down and never fell foul of the state's purview—probably the vast majority of people— rarely encountered any real problems, and even dismissed the state's security presence as more akin to an accepted annoyance. One questionnaire respondent likened the confidence men and Auxiliary Police to 'bothersome stairwell terriers' (*lästige Treppenterrier*) in tenant life.[84] For most citizens, the Stasi was less a repressive organ than a constant irritant, what publicist Jens Reich described as an irremovable 'scratchy undershirt'.[85]

Experiences certainly were very different for dissidents, though. Christians, as noted, suffered greatly in the face of Stasi persecution. But so did other dissident activists. Writer Jürgen Fuchs, who eventually emigrated to the West in the early 1980s, chronicled how he had been constantly victimized by Stasi terror.[86] Theatre director Freya Klier kept a diary about the octopus-like reach of the Party, as well as her constant fear of the next police visit.[87] Dissident Robert Havemann was the subject of constant Stasi harassment and eventual house arrest, and his activities (visitors, phone calls, and intimate relations) filled dozens of dossiers at the Stasi office.[88] In her 2003 collection of short stories *Meine Freie Deutsche Jugend,* Claudia Rusch, whose mother was close to the Havemann family, recalls how she and her family lived under constant surveillance from Stasi 'cockroaches' from the late 1950s onwards.[89] This had profound psychological effects on those under observation. As Joachim Gauck, the Rostock pastor who headed the Federal Government's 'Gauck Authority' charged with overseeing the Stasi files after Reunification, asserted in 1991, '[t]o be caught in Stasi crosshairs normally meant years of psychic pressure and the need to put up with a constant feeling of being observed—even more [it meant] the experience of impotence and being unable to carry on with one's life'.[90] As a reaction, 'most withdrew into whatever privacy could be carved out' to cope with these conditions.[91] But this did not always work. People dreamt of being followed and observed by the Stasi.[92] Some internalized fear to such an extent that the Stasi were believed to be able to spy on their dreams.[93] One East Berlin photographer recorded in his diary that Stasi agents dominated his recurring nightmares in the 1980s, often imprisoning him in a cage to prevent him from escaping to the West.[94] Such internalized fears were also common during the Third Reich, as nightmares about the regime were often characterized by a world 'without walls', with the eyes and ears of the state everywhere.[95] As one GDR interviewee laconically remarked, 'We were a large collective . . . to be private was not looked upon kindly.'[96]

DIARY WRITING (OR NOT)

Such anxieties found their way into secret East German diaries. Some registered unpleasant encounters with the Stasi. One East German banker for example wrote how he was accused by the Stasi of extortion, and how he had to fight to restore his reputation and post before eventually migrating to West Germany in 1982.[97] Pastors recorded rough Stasi harassment, while others recounted how they were spied upon by the Stasi in their residential areas or elsewhere.[98] Several women chronicled violence within the home, whether in the form of rapes from Russian soldiers or physical abuse from their husbands.[99] (Domestic violence will be discussed in Chapter 3.) One Potsdam actress wrote in the 1970s about her 'flight into a so-called private life' as a retreat from state surveillance and the atmosphere of mistrust. In one of her diary entries from 1979, she penned that it was widespread disillusionment towards GDR state and society that spurred the desire for 'private, soft love' among friends and partners as a 'protest against violence'.[100]

Drawing on diaries as historical sources is certainly not new, and has been used by historians for years as unique—if not necessarily representative—insights into the past.[101] In recent years the study of diaries has offered fresh perspectives on the study of the Third Reich, as noted with the 1998 publication of Victor Klemperer's two-volume eyewitness testimony, *I Will Bear Witness*, as well as Saul Friedländer's landmark two-volume, *Nazi Germany and the Jews*, published in 1997 and 2007.[102] Yet one of the most interesting—and rarely remarked—aspects of GDR society is how few East Germans kept diaries. This is extremely striking to anyone researching at the two research archives for modern German diaries, namely the Deutsches Tagebuch-Archiv in Emmindingen and the Walter Kempowski-Archiv in Berlin. Both contain a good collection of German diaries from the late Wilhelmine period to the 1960s, but comparatively little on the GDR. To say however that this is a natural result of authoritarian regimes is not very useful. After all, the lion's share of both archives focuses on the Third Reich, as people kept diaries in various forms by the tens of thousands across the country. And this went for the victims as well. For their part, Jews tirelessly chronicled the transformation of Germany and Germans during these years, often at their great peril, writing in circumstances far more threatening than anything any East German diarist ever encountered.[103] And yet private diary-writing was rarely done in the GDR, and if so with great trepidation. As several interviewees noted to me, East Germany was 'no diary culture'.

The lack of diaries was apparently due in part to a Stasi-inspired culture of fear. As noted in interviews, the main thing that inhibited people from keeping a diary was the possible consequences of what would happen to them if it were discovered by the police. They recounted many personal stories—especially from those affiliated with the Church or any dissident group—of burning letters or diaries in moments of anxiety about a possible house search. Gustav Just, the former editor of *Sonntag* news magazine and the GDR's first Secretary of the German Writers Union, expressed his fear of keeping a diary in the 1950s in his secret notebooks at the time: 'I don't write this diary at home. Because I am fearful . . . fearful that suddenly the doorbell could ring, and outside six men could be standing there, with an arrest warrant from the state court due to "urgent suspicious activities," and while searching the house they could find this journal with my true thoughts.. To this I should say where I write this journal: at my parents house in Bad Schmiedeberg.'[104] Such anxiety was registered by others too. Another diarist put it this way in an entry as late as May 1989: 'I hate this diary! Nobody here in the "East" may ever be allowed to find it, while in the "West" I can't go public with it.'[105] Diary-writing in the GDR was at once isolated and isolating, endangered and dangerous.

Of course diary-writing was not strictly taboo in the GDR. Heroized accounts of exemplary antifascists—such as Ernst Thälmann or East German Spanish

Civil War veterans—were standard references within East German official culture.[106] Pupils were required to write diaries to document school trips to the Soviet Union and other Eastern bloc states. From the late 1950s diaries were even promoted, but in state-sponsored ways. An initiative took wing with the pivotal Bitterfeld Conference in 1959, after which workers were entreated to pick up their pens to chronicle the heroic and world-historical construction of socialism in the form of so-called 'brigade books'. The aim was to integrate workers into GDR literary culture with the catchphrase 'Grab Your Pen, Mate!' and to write 'collective diaries' of labour achievement and socialist solidarity. Workers were encouraged to contribute to them at their workplace, and many did so by the thousands in the 1960s and 1970s. The opening of one 1969 Leipzig collection of worker short stories commemorating the country's twentieth anniversary was typical: 'The members of the writing circle [of this collective diary] would like to express their thanks that they have grown up in this republic. The republic has always been a homeland to them, and has shown them the good way, a way to the future in which the small happiness of the individual is embedded in the great happiness of our socialist community.'[107] But such collective diaries were predicated on eradicating the distance and singularity of individual diary-writing. This was precisely the antithesis of bourgeois diary-writing, as one's private views and feelings were to be incorporated into the collective framework of common enterprise and historical optimism. Perhaps this was why that there was such great attention paid to—and popular interest in—those writers who published diaries or tales of 'subjective authenticity', like Christa Wolf, Brigitte Reimann, and Maxie Wander, since the presence of uncensored first-person subjectivity had relatively little place in GDR culture.[108]

In the few GDR diaries one can find, there is a noticeable disinclination to communicate anything really intimate, revealing, or judgemental, reflecting a deep and widespread fear of discovery. It is not that people were uncritical; but they were reluctant to commit their private thoughts and feelings to paper. This was certainly true of writing and sending letters. Everyone knew for example that the secret police closely monitored all correspondence, especially if it involved contacts in the West. But such self-censorship continued on even in their private diaries too, as East Germans whom I interviewed reiterated.[109] The result was that state and society—along with the whole world of ideology—hardly figured at all. I never encountered one diary that chronicled socialist life with the enthusiasm or excitement encouraged in the 'brigade books', or anything like the proud private chronicles linking personal triumph and national achievement so common among German diary-writers in the Nazi years. Instead, entries were almost exclusively shaped by personal or family concerns, with society itself as quite distant or non-existent. Work life rarely entered either, nor was there much material or references to the Stasi, residential authorities, community life, or neighbours, aside from the exceptions discussed above. Basic quotidian concerns—material shortages, consumer acquisitions, love stories, Christmas celebrations, births and deaths of family members—served as the main pivot points. While some might see such 'apolitical' diaries as denoting the limit of the state, others could counter that they represented the remarkable internalization of Stasi censorship even at home. As writer Jurek Becker averred:

One of the Stasi's greatest strengths lay in the fact that one often presumed its representatives to be present when in reality this wasn't the case. Many telephone conversations only took place for the benefit of the person listening in. Letters contained empty phrases which were not meant for the person they were addressed to but for the person monitoring them, and at public gatherings (everyone's life was full of public gatherings) you even made yourself sick with your applause at certain points.[110]

Fear and self-censorship were not just limited to public behaviour, but seemed to have found expression even in the most private activity of all—diary-writing. The famed 'double life' of East German citizens, built on the split between public and private self, outward conformity and inward dissent, was infrequently registered in the most bourgeois of all genres of selfhood. That privacy in the GDR was rarely recorded in this traditional cultural form may attest in some measure to the perceived power of the Stasi in the lives and imagination of East German citizens. As we shall see in subsequent chapters, East German citizens were not shy about narrating their private lives, but they used different forms.

'OPERATIVE PSYCHOLOGY' AND PRIVILEGE

The ascension of Erich Honecker as Walter Ulbricht's successor in 1971 augured a spirit of change and even liberalization in the country. Not so with the Stasi. In fact, the Stasi grew both in numbers and importance under Honecker. Almost immediately Stasi Chief Erich Mielke was named as a full member of the all-powerful twelve-man Politbüro, underscoring the Stasi's central role in the Age of Détente.

At first this may seem odd, not least because the potential threats from West Germany and the West more generally had been clearly mitigated by both the 1961 construction of the Wall and the advent of Ostpolitik, or Eastern Policy, a decade later. National security, international recognition, and domestic stability had all been achieved, while the economy was posting quite satisfactory results overall. The signing of the Helsinki Accords in 1975 also reaffirmed the sanctity of borders of Stalin's Europe. It signalled that the West's original outrage towards the Soviet intervention in Czechoslovakia in 1968 was a thing of the past, to the extent that the Yalta partition was now given international blessing. A growing sense of normalization reportedly pervaded the country, as the state effectively relaxed its reformatory zeal toward the vast majority of its law-abiding citizens. But it seems that it was precisely this new distancing of state and citizen that fuelled renewed state apprehension about citizen conduct.

Key international events shaped East German domestic policy. For instance, the Stasi's expansion under Honecker was in part a reaction to the potential repercussions of the ill-fated 1968 'Prague Spring' reform movement in East Germany. The international diplomatic recognition of the GDR as a separate state five years later also spurred increasing Stasi activity. It was not just that Western diplomats in East Berlin needed to be kept under increased surveillance. The home population also had to be kept under closer watch, given the country's increasing contact with and influence from the West as a result of Ostpolitik. The Helsinki Accords in 1975 were viewed as a worrisome Trojan Horse in this respect.[111] By 1977 the Stasi expanded to over 10,000 employees.[112] It generated countless nervous reports about the changing domestic situation, especially regarding the churches' assertive political role both in GDR society and across the Eastern bloc.[113] Files were kept on the East German signatories of the Czech human rights declaration, Charta 77, along with any dissident who had contact with the churches.[114] The blossoming of new human rights groups in the GDR in the 1980s was duly noted by the Stasi.[115] Indeed, the major spikes in Stasi activity were directly linked to destabilizing international events—the 1968 Prague Spring, 1975 Helsinki Accords, and the declaration of martial law in Poland in 1981.[116] There was also stepped up surveillance after Gorbachev's takeover in 1985 against the ever-elastic term of 'subversives', since Moscow was no longer seen as willing to exercise military intervention to quell disorder.[117] The SED's hard-line repudiation of Gorbachev's glasnost and perestroika only complicated things for the Stasi, as dissidents increasingly looked to Moscow to challenge GDR authority.[118]

The 1970s were thus the golden age of the Stasi. It was at this time that Mielke's empire developed its full spectrum of technological wizardry, including secret video equipment, recording devices, invisible ink, automated letter-opening machines, smell samples, and fluorescent 'spy dust'. By the 1970s secret cameras were installed in all big city hotels. The Bellevue in Dresden, for example, supposedly had all of its telephones tapped and rooms bugged, with video observation set up in select suites. Stasi-paid prostitutes were hired as 'honey traps' to seduce unsuspecting Western politicians and businessmen into divulging secrets and intelligence.[119] Specifically designated 'safe houses' were installed with ubiquitous cameras and audio equipment—even in the bathroom—to debrief defectors or monitor agent groups.[120] Such activities were a far cry from the first two decades of the GDR, when the Stasi showed comparatively little interest in the private lives of its citizens. As late as 1957 the Stasi did not even possess its own telephone network.[121] But all of this changed in the 1970s and 1980s, as the opening of the GDR to permeation from the West only intensified state surveillance. Mary Fulbrook captured the paradox thus: 'As time went by, and the very existence of the GDR appeared less under threat, the paranoia became, in a sense, more institutionalized.'[122]

As the Stasi got bigger, it also changed in outlook. By the 1970s the agency relied less on violence and imprisonment, using instead more sophisticated 'subversion' and 'distraction' methods. The new approach went by the name of *Zersetzen*, roughly translated as 'decomposition'.[123] According to a confidential State Security document, the goal of this decomposition was 'splitting up, paralyzing, disorganizing and isolating hostile-negative forces in order, by means of preventive action, to foil, considerably reduce or entirely stop hostile-negative actions and their consequences, or, where possible to win them back both politically and ideologically'.[124] Such a strategy saw the application of 1960s 'operative psychology' and its preventative 'milieu theory' of deviance, one that necessitated a more robust regime of close observation and record keeping.[125] The new approach was in part due to the growing perception that terrorist methods were counterproductive, and that a more brutal style of extracting information would undermine the legitimacy of the regime, especially after the signature of the Helsinki Accords in 1975. Indeed, the international reputation of the regime was always very important to the government, and the SED learned to couch its activities in terms palatable to an international audience. The 1969 Stasi statute, for example, spun its task as above all 'to investigate criminal offenses, especially those against the sovereignty of the GDR, peace, humanity and human rights'.[126]

A 1976 Stasi directive spelt out what this 'decomposition' strategy meant more concretely. Its aim was the

[s]ystematic discrediting of public reputations, appearance and prestige on the basis of combining true, verifiable discrediting facts with false, but believable and unverifiable discrediting claims; systematic orchestration of career and social failures in order to undermine the self-confidence of individual persons . . . the instigation of mistrust and mutual suspicion within groups of personal circles and organizations; instigation, exploitation and intensification of rivalries within personal circles, groups and organizations through the use of personal weaknesses among individual members; occupying groups, circles and organizations with their own internal problems while limiting their negative-hostile actions.[127]

Particular target groups included those who applied to leave the country, activists and artists, 'reactionary' clerics, dissident Christians, and 'negative' groups of youth.[128] Women were typically targeted more frequently than men.[129] Such psychological repression aimed to undermine the suspect's self-worth and confidence by inducing fear, panic, and confusion. Methods not only included telephone tapping, mail control, and routine house searches,[130] but also breaking down suspects, sowing disagreement among opposition groups, and restricting movement, such as the withdrawal of driver licences.[131] Often this took the form of Stasi collaborators entering the suspect's place of residence and doing small things to puzzle the resident. Pictures would be rearranged slightly, spice jars would be displaced, and favourite teas would be replaced with other brands.[132] Agents often sent compromising photographs and anonymous letters with false allegations to friends and neighbours to undermine citizens, as chronicled in writer Reiner Kunze's 1990 exposé of his own Stasi file, *Deckname 'Lyrik'*.[133] No private issue was off limits. Measures even included trying to sow discord between married partners by sending doctored photographs of insinuated trysts and extramarital activities. A classic case was that of the dissidents Gerd and Ulrike Poppe. Upon reading through his 12,000 page file after 1989, Gerd Poppe learnt that the Stasi had hired a young male agent provocateur to try to seduce his wife as a means of undermining their marriage.[134] In so doing the Stasi had expanded into new territory. Such repressive psychological methods meant that there was 'no inaccessible spheres for these decomposition strategies', as 'incursions into intimate life' shattered any sense of a 'protected private sphere'.[135]

The Stasi was moving into other areas well beyond its former sphere of political security. Over time its 90,000 paid operatives did much more than simply open mail and monitor telephone calls. By the mid-1980s the Stasi had accumulated twenty-seven separate divisions entrusted with matters ranging from party loyalty to economic surveillance, whose annual budget actually exceeded that of the Interior Ministry. The Stasi became more and more involved in safeguarding the economy in myriad ways. This included protecting the vital sectors of microelectronics, energy, the chemical industry, and foreign trade; uncovering graft, corruption, and sabotage; and/or investigating fires and accidents much like an insurance agency. It even fell to the Stasi to keep the GDR's infamous sports doping programme running.[136] It is no exaggeration to say that the Stasi was the only real growth industry in Honecker's Germany, baldly reflecting the priorities of the state. Another statistic puts Honecker's understanding of socialist welfare in perspective: whereas there was one doctor per 400 GDR residents in 1988, one in 165 citizens worked for the Stasi.[137]

By the 1970s the Stasi tended to wield its power with inducements. It made sure that those who were loyal to the Party got good or important jobs, and those who were disloyal did not. The Stasi could—and did—influence who did or did not go on to study at university, as well as who was appointed university lecturer or professor. Indeed, some 80 per cent of professors were SED members, and many of them saw it as their duty to report to the Stasi if asked. Doctors too were recruited as informers. In part this explains the febrile production of six million citizen files, to the extent that the Stasi 'was as much a massive system of vetting as it was an apparatus of simple persecution'.[138] But it was also a dispenser of precious privileges. Here it pays to recall the Stasi's long-forgotten world of rare GDR status and luxury, one that diverged markedly from the bland uniformity of most people's lives. Stasi agents were relatively well-paid, had privileged access to special shops with Western goods, and could travel abroad more freely than others. They often lived in the best apartments and villas, and enjoyed a vast network of vacation spas, exclusive hospitals, and sports complexes. To be sure, this rarified world of socialist indulgence was the preserve of only a lucky few, and access to such luxuries greatly depended on internal rank, length of service, and function within The Firm. Lower-ranking Stasi agents, for example, often griped about the poor quality of their housing, showing that they were hardly immune from the problems affecting the rest of society.[139]

But such a world—the extent of which was only made fully known after 1989—did draw attention to a ticklish theme of GDR life: status and class differences. Class privilege was rife across the Eastern bloc and Soviet Union, and East Germany was no exception.[140] Given the bottlenecks of production and chronic shortages of desired consumer items, GDR society featured a flourishing—if officially non-existent—black market of goods and services. Access to them often depended on luck (such as family members in the West), extended social networks, or a good relation with the authorities. One's ability to get scarce goods was popularly known as 'Vitamin B' for *Beziehungen*, or connections.[141] It was well known that Party cadres, government officials, and top athletes got better housing, consumer goods, telephones, and travel rights than others, while white-collar workers generally enjoyed better housing than manual labourers. In fact, the Party often used decent housing to lure new recruits as SED functionaries, or to bribe valuable scientific experts to stay in the country. When luxury boutiques Intershop and Delikat were opened in the 1970s to attract Western currency and allay pent-up East German consumer frustration, the 'unsocialist' inequality of income and access to highly coveted Western commodities became apparent to all, and was widely criticized by the public.[142] So strong was this resentment that in the political demonstrations of 1989, placards against the injustice of consumer goods distribution took their place alongside others demanding political change and free elections.[143]

The Stasi played a pivotal role in this regard, as people often turned to the secret police for personal concerns and favours. Some wrote letters to the Stasi about poor work conditions and widespread corruption, and fully expected that the secret police would act on their behalf.[144] Stasi agents were thus perceived as social workers as much as secret policemen. The point is that these citizens believed that the Stasi could and should set things right. What the Stasi administered, however, was less social justice than private privilege. In this socialist world of scarce resources and rationed privileges, the Stasi ruled the roost. It sat atop an East German clientele system in which favours, privileges, and status were bargained privately in exchange for information and cooperation. Privilege became a standard and effective way of controlling the distribution of what people wanted most and, just as importantly, keeping its rewards arbitrary.[145]

THE INFORMANT

This brings us to perhaps the most notorious aspect of Stasi activity, the remarkable network of so-called 'unofficial collaborators'. The explosion of informants in the 1970s and 1980s can well be understood in relation to this rationed world of privileges in East Germany, as people were tempted by the Stasi's material enticements. Denunciations were of course crucial to the success of the Stasi, in that they served as secret link between the Stasi and society. Informers became the agency's eyes and ears, and were highly sought after for their effectiveness. So much so that agents actually competed with one another over the number of recruited collaborators—those who did not bring in twenty-five new informers a year were frequently criticized.[146] In the Stasi imagination, the world was characterized by a kind of friend/foe mentality. There was a constant fear of 'fifth-columnism', as all nonconformity was seen as the work of 'class enemies' and 'hostile-negative forces'. Of utmost concern was the need to encourage what was called 'antifascist alertness' among the citizenry. Article 6 of the GDR 1949 Constitution, which railed against the danger of *Boykotthetze*, provided cover for turning unfavourable opinions against the state into treasonous 'hostile negative' activities.[147] Marxist-Leninist principles underlay the Code of Criminal Procedure, which stated that citizens should play a key role in developing 'the socialist state and legal consciousness' by helping the police solve crimes and keep socialist society socialist.[148] Identifying 'asocials' and other suspicious characters was then interpreted as an act of patriotism, justice, and social welfare. Informants were hired to help identify and root out deviance, which covered anything from 'petty bourgeois egotism', careerism, criminal behaviour, excessive grumbling, as well as sundry anti-social(ist) attitudes.

Denunciations are notoriously difficult to define, but at the very least they constituted accusations of wrongdoing by other citizens or officials, usually—though not always—delivered privately to the authorities. Denunciations as a social practice enjoy a long tradition, stretching from the Inquisition to Calvin's Geneva through to the Venetian Republics and the French Revolution. The Napoleonic Penal Code of 1810 imposed severe penalties for not denouncing infractions against the security of the state, while Russian tsars had long used the 'duty to denounce' as an effective means to expose corruption and cultivate subject loyalty. The Bolsheviks may have at first despised these traditions, but they soon recognized that denunciations were useful and even affirmative. Similar trends could be found elsewhere. In Vichy France, for example, French citizens wrote three to five million letters of denunciations during the Nazi Occupation, and the US Congress's House of Un-American Activities Committee incited its own 'culture of denunciation' as part of a McCarthyite witch hunt for internal enemies of the state at the height of the cold war.[149] Even so, the Allies condemned such destructive social practices as characteristic of tyrannical states and an affront to civilization itself, and discouraging them was seen as a necessary condition to building a model civil society in post-fascist Germany. In fact, Article 2 of the Allied Control Council Law 10 of December 1945 even made denunciation a human rights violation.[150]

While denunciations were practised across all twentieth-century regimes, they were most common in authoritarian regimes. Two stand out in the flagrant use of denunciations as a means of consolidating government power over their citizens. The first was the Soviet Union. As Sheila Fitzpatrick put it, the Bolsheviks viewed denunciations with a particularly sectarian zeal—there can be 'no secrets in the community of saints'. The ideal was the self-policing collective, based on vigilance and mutual surveillance. No coincidence that the explosion of denunciations was linked to periods of social upheaval and new ideals of social mobility. It was during the period after the abolition of peasant serfdom in 1861 and then again after the 1917 Revolution that denunciations reached their height, as many of them were fuelled by envy and moral injuries resulting from perceived inequality. That the distribution of dachas to the Party elite was to be kept strictly forbidden belied this sentiment about keeping social inequalities within the communist regime hidden.[151] Issues of 'class morality' became even more important under Stalin. Children were encouraged to inform on their parents, as the playground became a 'breeding ground of informers'.[152] In this sense, denunciations played an analogous role to Stalin's 'second economy' of black marketeering.[153]

The other regime was of course Nazi Germany. Recent scholarship has revised the long-dominant popular image of leather-clad Gestapo standing on every corner, fastidiously keeping tabs on a subjugated German society. In fact, the Gestapo was a relatively small organization, perhaps 7,000 officials in a country of sixty-six million inhabitants. Given its relatively small size, the Gestapo needed a great deal of help from citizens. Even before taking power in 1933, the Nazi Party had developed a certain 'culture of denunciation' in its press, most notably in Julius Streicher's notorious Nazi rag, *Der Stürmer*, which routinely featured zealous denunciatory letters from readers about Jews, racial defilement, current affairs, and local scandals.[154] After 1933 the Gestapo's mission to combat 'political criminality' was given broad scope, as dissent and criticism were criminalized. People denounced their neighbours for various personal ends, often invoking the elastic term *Volksgemeinschaft* (racial community) for their own self-interest.[155] But there were pre-1933 roots of such activities. Building networks of informants and citizen surveillance was a hallmark of modern policing, and took on new importance after the First World War. Given the unstable political situation after 1918, criminal police forces in the Weimar Republic encouraged and relied upon an extensive world of 'mutual surveillance' to carry out their work. Even communist cells in interwar Berlin enforced discipline in their ranks by soliciting reporting on fellow Party members. The point is that German citizens had grown accustomed to serving as the eyes and ears of the police long before 1933.[156]

This intensified in new ways after the Nazi seizure of power. Local cases involving the identification of those listening to foreign radio broadcasts or the enforced isolation of Jews relied to a large extent on voluntary denunciations. Private motives (a better apartment, a neighbourhood grudge, or marital conflict) were usually at the root of these denunciations.[157] Many, for example, were advanced by women who sought protection from physical abuse and sexual violence.[158] The Gestapo became an instrument for resolving sundry private disputes from the very beginning, helping to shore up Party legitimacy at the local level by serving as 'the petty power of the Volksgenossen'.[159] Since denunciations and petitioning were a 'zero-sum game', in that one's welfare came at the expense of another's, the Gestapo therefore emerged as a key instrument of popular justice.[160]

However, there were fundamental differences between the Gestapo and the Stasi in their attitude towards collaborators. Nazi leaders were actually quite uncomfortable about fostering too much denouncing, to the point of publishing verdicts in the press when suppliers of false information were exposed in court. By 1934 the Reich Minister of the Interior actually demanded that steps be taken to reduce the number of denunciations filed with the police.[161] But even if the Gestapo voiced concern about the 'objectivity' of voluntary informers, it depended heavily on volunteers to help identify potential 'enemies of the state' and keep order at the local level. Conversely, the Stasi was more suspicious of voluntary informers. In part this was because they were seen as possible enemy agents and 'imperialist spies', or that their aggressive zeal might prove useless in supplying reliable information. The 1953 Uprising proved crucial in this respect, in that the new Stasi interpreted this intelligence failure as a consequence of relying too heavily on volunteers. After 1953 the emphasis shifted towards formalizing a network of reliable informers. The Stasi much preferred to select its own candidates and to initiate them into the values and practices of The Firm. The Stasi had effectively 'professionalized' its network of informants, and voluntary, extra-Stasi denunciations played virtually no role in intelligence-gathering and criminal prosecution.[162]

As for figures, the scholarly consensus is that some 500,000 citizens worked as 'unofficial collaborators' for the Stasi. If part-time informants are included, there were reportedly as many as one informer for every 6.5 citizens. According to statistics, 80–90 per cent of informants were men, aged between 25 and 40.[163] (In Nazi Germany, by comparison, roughly three-quarters were male.[164]) Recruitment started early. While numbers were comparatively small by 1950, estimated at well below 10,000,[165] by 1952 the Stasi had won over some 30,000 citizens as 'secret informers'.[166] This increased twenty-fold over the decades. To maintain control and to assure the good running of the system, around 10 per cent of 'informal collaborators' were 'retired' every year, making way for a new crop of recruits to take their place.

Typically potential informants were approached at home or work by Stasi agents with quite innocent requests.[167] They were then given more intense assignments once their trust and competence had been demonstrated. New recruits often met Stasi officers in so-called 'conspiratorial apartments' to disclose their findings. Before they were accepted, background information was gathered from other informants, close relatives, work colleagues, neighbours, and friends about the candidate's political views, habits, organizational membership, sexual behaviour, and contacts with the West. Once he or she had passed, the new recruit was given a cover name, and a file opened. A pact of cooperation, loyalty, and secrecy was then signed. Tellingly, the labels used to describe such covert actions changed over time. Until 1968 collaborators were known as *Geheime Informatoren,* or secret informers. But this designation was changed to 'IM'—*inoffizielle Mitarbeiter,* or 'unofficial collaborator'—on the grounds that the new moniker appeared less invasive, conspiratorial, or morally reprehensible. (The Stasi was also keen to avoid the word snoop (*Spitzel*), for fear of its Gestapo association.) The informer's private life was considered an important part of the relationship, and Stasi agents routinely offered moral advice to them about maintaining proper standards of behaviour at home. According to Stasi protocols, the informer was to be treated with 'utmost respect', and agents were encouraged to cultivate 'genuine human bonds' with them. Trust and reliability were the favorite watchwords used, and it seems to have succeeded with many. A number of former informants interviewed in the 1990s asserted that the Stasi 'gave me roots' and 'comfort' in the world.[168] Others referred to their personal Stasi contact as 'my Stasi', adding that 'no one else came as close to me as my Stasi officer'.[169]

The Stasi even exploited children as spies and collaborators. In fact, around 20,000 informers were under the age of 18.[170] While their influence was exploited over the decades, young informants became especially valued in the 1970s and 1980s. Secret opinion poll data at the time revealed that GDR youth were more and more disaffected, and thus needed to be watched more carefully.[171] The Stasi used young informants to penetrate circles of 'decadent youth' (punks, Goths, skinheads) otherwise resistant to standard surveillance tactics. Children were also cajoled into spying on dissident adults or 'hostile negative youth' who resisted the heavily regimented world of school, socialist youth groups, and military training. Many teenage informants were babysitters, who reported on family discussions. Children from broken homes were easy recruits, as the Stasi provided them with structure, protection, and badly needed esteem. Enticements were dangled before them as well—guaranteed university places, coveted jobs, or a better apartment were standard carrots of inducement.[172] For criminal youth, their sentences were commuted if they cooperated. The children of Stasi agents were particularly favoured recruits for restocking the ranks of informers, since they were seen as being already inured to the cardinal virtues of trust and secrecy.

Motivations for collaborating with the Stasi varied. Often it came about from political conviction—be it Marxist-Leninism, humanism, patriotism, religious views, and/or anti-capitalism. Others wanted to make good on their compromised pasts. Many SED members were former Nazis or had incriminating political pasts, and were desperate to make amends in demonstrations of loyalty and service. Still others were motivated by career ambition, petty revenge, and/or the desire for social privileges.[173] One 1967 internal Stasi report listed citizen motives for cooperation as ranging from 'recognition of societal demands', 'ethical obligation', 'personal advantages', and various desires, such as love of secret adventures.[174] However, the idealism that motivated earlier denunciations tended to drop off in the 1970s and 1980s both in East Germany and across the Eastern bloc; rather, material considerations—and in particular the allure of privileges—mattered most with time.[175] Such material benefits included visas to the West, better apartments, higher publishing runs, rare consumer goods, and financial bonuses.[176] There are many files on Christian informants who spied on fellow Christians in exchange for various favours (improved housing and guaranteed university places) from the state.[177] East Germans were thus bought off, blackmailed, or intimidated into serving the Stasi in one way or another. For them, collaboration was thus a mixture of pressure and temptation, idealism and materialism.

The Stasi–informant relationship was not just transactional. In fact, the personalization of contact was considered quite important for many informants. The informer's altruism and idealism was often encouraged by the Stasi officer, and personal needs and interests were exploited to cultivate loyalty. Gifts and benefits, while not the sole motivational factor behind collaboration, did have a decisive bonding effect.[178] Through the 1970s and 1980s the Stasi also became more savvy about deploying psychotherapeutic language to nurture their charges, effectively blending care and control. For many the relationship became a form of communication and communion in a world in which these things were scarce commodities. As one informant recalled in the 1990s, the 'chat' with the Stasi officer made up for the absence any democratic public sphere: 'This type of discussion was for me the last modest remnant of a public discussion that society was capable of.' The emphasis on a genuine interpersonal connection was the soft face of this 'operative psychology' discussed above, in that this was designed to 'decompose' the informant into loyal service to the Stasi. As another informant confessed: 'I had the impression that my officer wanted to help me in my private life.'[179]

A good insight into the making of an informant can be found in writer Reiner Kunze's bestseller, *Deckname 'Lyrik'*. This was one of the first books published about the Stasi after 1989. In it Kunze used his own Stasi file as a historical document to expose the reach and strategies of the secret police. In one entry from 1972 the Stasi agent recounted his success in getting Kunze's neighbours on board:

For surveillance of Kunze in his residential area one can make use of: Comrade R, who lives next to the doorway of Kunze's flat, and can look into his apartment while opening his window. Comrade H...68 years old, retired, lives diagonal from Kunze and has condemned (*verurteilt*) him...in my presence. H is often at home and evenings can observe Kunze's doorway at any time...The comrade couple F...approximately 65–70 years old, live just across from Kunze...

Another Stasi interview in 1976 with a husband and wife team asked to spy on Kunze was even more revealing. According to the Stasi records, the main objective of the meeting was to test the loyalty of the wife as a possible informant against Kunze. Comrade B (the husband) agreed that certain listening devices could be used, and, given his proximity to Kunze, he could easily bore a hole in the suspect's wall to listen in on his 'intimate sphere'. However, the comrade's wife expressed initial reservations, saying that it

was somewhat awkward for her to spy on someone whom she highly respected, and that afterwards she could no longer look him in the eye. With the support of her husband it was made clear to her that what we do in defense against attacks against our humanist social order is nothing compared to measures taken against us by the capitalists. K[unze] is involved in antisocialist activities against our socialist society and thus does deserve to be so highly respected by his wife. Her husband added: 'We should not share in the guilt of what Kunze does. He is not a member of society, and with such people we should not have any scruples.' I could see that the informant's wife was in agreement. . . . Both gave their support and permission to avail their apartment of necessary measures. They were told in no uncertain terms that this discussion must be kept strictly confidential.[180]

The effects of Stasi complicity and the world of mutual surveillance were widely commented on after 1989. Most tended to see its destructive legacy in the breakdown of solidarity. Even the most resistant alternative subcultures—the Church, artists, dissidents, and punks—were riddled with Stasi informers. One historian registered this widespread shock by saying that 'the most appalling aspect of the system of IM was the breakdown of the bonds of trust between officers and men, lawyers and clients, doctors and patients, teachers and students, pastors and their communities, friends and neighbors, family members and even lovers'.[181] Upon reading her Stasi file dissident Vera Wollenberger lamented how Stasi agents (in her case, her husband) had ruined 'her joy in life, her health and private sphere', and with it had destroyed the 'moral foundation' of 'human social life'. Writer Günter Kunert, after reading his own Stasi file, asserted that the Stasi had killed off any sense of communal life by corrupting basic interpersonal relations: 'In the defeated system we lived in deformed interpersonal relationships and conditions. We did not act freely in casual encounters with others—like with the neighbors. We automatically blocked our reactions, we turned away as soon as a look seemed too curious to us, a question too probing, an interest in us not sufficiently justified. We lived in many respects like oysters.'[182]

In conclusion, pulling away the curtain of Stasi activities is important for a number of reasons. First of all, it exposes the limitations of crude models based on the idea that the state acts and citizens simply react. Publicist Klaus Hardung may have overstated the case when he wrote that the Stasi 'was not only the largest civil war army that has ever arose on German soil; it was also a part of East German everyday life, a society within a society'.[183] But he is right in taking issue with this self-serving image of the Stasi as an ominous 'state within a state' with little connection to people's lives. The elaborate network of informants makes plain that citizens actively participated in this state security system, often voluntarily. Or put differently, the state's repressive powers were dependent on the actions of individual citizens. This was not so much a Panopticon as a world based on private bargains in exchange for cooperation and complicity. Over time GDR citizens learnt to 'speak Bolshevik' in the GDR, both internalizing and mastering the language (and practices) of power offered to them by the regime.[184] Denunciations were therefore a kind of citizen activity in their own right, one of the few powerful forms of agency available to them.

Secondly, the Stasi undermined socialist cohesion even despite itself. While the Stasi sought to build a sense of community by defining it against dangerous 'asocials', the effect of its activities was to pit citizens against citizens. Much is known on how modern states classify and control its citizenry, how governments 'see like a state' in an effort to transform people into a legible body politic based on the concept of 'a uniform, homogeneous citizenship'.[185] But the Stasi story shows something different, namely how citizens were trained to view each other suspiciously in a world of mutual surveillance. This was the dark side of the social contract between GDR state and its citizenry, but it is one that went far beyond the classic bargain of exchanging freedom for security. In this case it was a strictly private agreement between the state and its citizens, based on material rewards for snitching and snooping. What the Stasi story reveals in this regard is how the SED personalized 'conflict-management' in the name of paternalism and stability. Simply put, the Stasi was both a repressive organ and a mediator of private conflict.[186] And yet the expansion and transformation of the Stasi into a sprawling welfare organization of sticks and carrots did not make ruling any easier. In fact, it created more problems, not least because it bred rising expectations of what the state could and should do for its citizens.[187] This eventually opened up the real problem of governability for the GDR's 'welfare dictatorship'. The result was that the regime ultimately undermined its own touted virtues of solidarity through its own social politics of divide and rule.

Thirdly, the Stasi story points up the limits of Hannah Arendt's 'atomization thesis' about social breakdown under authoritarianism. In fact, social cohesion became polarized. It may have eroded in the wider 'public' sense, but it was reinforced in smaller, more private networks. The Stasi's concerted efforts to break down the family through surveillance and denunciation actually tended to strengthen—not undermine—family solidarity. The well-publicized revelations in the 1990s about Stasi betrayal by family members were in fact quite rare. Generally, the Stasi was most successful in secondary circles—that is, among one's work colleagues, housing residents, dacha neighbors, sports team members—rather than within families.[188] Despite the Stasi's best efforts, there was a low rate of success in getting children to spy on their own family members.[189] In this way, the family still functioned as a kind of protective refuge for most people.

Fourthly, people became more skilled at protecting aspects of their private lives by means of dissimulation and outward conformity. Denunciation may have been a way of making the private public, but it also steeled resolve to protect what little privacy existed even more so. Put differently, the Stasi's secret power was met by citizens' own developed sense of secrecy and masked identities. As one Leipzig diarist put it: 'The [state's] incursions in the world of leisure and private life led to stronger private bonds among people.'[190] It is perhaps no accident that it was precisely former prisoners, deportees, and POWs—many of whom were victims of denunciations—who were most concerned with keeping clear lines between public and private life.[191] This possesses far-reaching implications for our understanding of the private sphere under communism. Whereas most observers have interpreted such wily dissimulation as a shield to protect the citizen's pre-existing private sphere from state interference, one can go further in saying that the socialist private sphere actually came into being under these very authoritarian conditions.[192]

Finally, the Stasi story also requires us to revise our traditional ideas of public and private. Certainly it is true that it effectively eliminated any real social enclaves that might have allowed people to gather, discuss, and organize resistance. This jibes with more traditional understandings of the private sphere as a defence against state incursion, something that had been undermined in the East German case. In his highly influential *Seeing Like a State*, James Scott has argued that the 'idea of a private realm has served to limit the ambitions of many high modernists, through either their own political values or their healthy respect for the political storm that such incursions would provoke'.[193] But this doesn't go very far in understanding socialist societies like the GDR, where notions of public and private were distorted and remade by citizens living within authoritarian conditions.

The next chapter takes this story into the broader field of social conflict, focusing on how the Stasi's secret society clashed with its great rival secret society, the Church.

2

East of Eden

Christian Subculture in State Socialism

The relationship between religion and socialism became one of the defining features of East German history. Over the decades this latter-day conflict between the rival claims of *sacerdotium* and *imperium* furnished plenty of sound and fury, touching as it did on the very identity of East German state and society. The GDR's homegrown 'clash of civilizations' attracted a good deal of scholarly attention from the 1950s on, and became a pet issue among Western critics of state socialism as proof of the sham nature of civil rights in what was known as the 'Soviet Zone'.[1] The events of 1989 predictably sparked renewed interest in church–state relations, as many archives were opened for the first time. While some claimed that Lutheran political opposition paved the way for the 'Protestant Revolution' of 1989, others denounced the Evangelical Church as too accommodating, self-serving, and compromised by Stasi infiltration. Over the course of the 1990s tracing the lines of control, complicity, and resistance in GDR church–state relations became a subject of heated public debate in newly unified Germany's painful effort to 'come to terms with the past'.[2]

The aim of this chapter is not to reopen the case on the fate of the 'church in socialism', however. It seeks to explore how state–church conflict centred on another idea of privacy, in the form of 'freedom of conscience', or *Gewissens-freiheit*, a civil liberty enshrined in the GDR's 1949 Constitution. While the state crusade against organized religion affected all faiths, my discussion mostly will be confined to the Lutheran Church, since it was by far the largest and most powerful confession in the GDR. In fact, the GDR was the only country in the Eastern bloc where a communist regime faced a largely Protestant population and political culture. Given its size, influence, and soul-caring mission, the Church also represented what one scholar called the 'last structure' charged with mediating the public and private spheres.[3] To date there is much literature on church–state relations in the GDR, especially regarding the role of the churches as 'fifth columns' within state socialism.[4] Most of it, however, approaches these questions in terms of official policy and high-level exchanges between church and state authorities. Attention in this chapter will be paid instead to how 'ordinary' Lutherans reacted to heavy governmental pressure, and how this affected their personal lives. As such it gives some voice to agitated citizens—besieged pastors, Christian parents, and zealous state officials—so as to cast some light on the private side of religion in a communist country. Of chief concern will be to analyse local battles in East Berlin between Christian parents and state authorities, particularly with reference to the GDR's national campaign to introduce in 1954 the infamous Jugendweihe, a socialist version of Christian confirmation that was intended to curb religious influence and better bind young people to the atheistic state. This 'youth dedication' was a uniquely German tradition stretching back to the late nineteenth century, without equivalent anywhere else in Europe, East or West; what is more, its undeniable success— over 95 per cent of East German teenagers underwent the socialist rite of passage by the late 1960s—made the Jugendweihe a key 'lieu de mémoire' of GDR culture in its own right.[5] While there is a sizeable literature on the Jugendweihe as a decisive moment in East German history,[6] it usually tends to discuss events at the national level, paying little attention to how these church–state conflicts were expressed locally. Indeed, the individual Christian household emerged as a battleground of this new Kulturkampf, as the campaign to implement the socialist rite of passage for East German youth became a key litmus test of private rights and religious liberty under state socialism.

A NEW REFORMATION

In a published 1950 letter entitled 'God's Beloved East Zone', the popular long-time University of Halle pastor and former prisoner of war Johannes Hamel painted the problem facing Christians in the GDR in the early days of new republic:

Typical was the remark of a first semester theological student recently: 'We reject this Leninism which is being forced on us, of course, from something within us. But we really don't know what we have to say against it.' In the face of continual public resolutions, most keep silent. Many vote simply the desired 'Aye.' Others withhold their vote, which in our situation requires already a certain courage. But rarely does anyone rise in the discussion and openly refuse to sacrifice his conviction. So it is that many lead a dangerous double existence: on the one side in the Bible Study hour, in public worship, communion and cell group; on the other side in the public life of a student. With time one becomes accustomed to this double life and one finds it no longer unbearable; or one emigrates spiritually in secret, to the West, and hopes for the Americans, i.e. for American bombers and tanks—a strange hope for us in Germany! Alongside this runs a deep, only too understandable, human bitterness and national hate, which longs for the day when the foreign tormentors will be beaten and the German tormentors will hang from the gibbet. Under the so uniform surface of our social life smoulders a dangerous fire. One can only shudder to think of the time when it may break forth.. Every Christian shares in some way the guilt of this unhealthy development, just as does every East Zone resident as well. The shame of our sin is visible in everyone, so that it is only the most honest who freely say to me in private: 'I know that I lie, but I cannot find the inner strength to speak the truth openly, for what would become of me then?'[7]

On one level, this seemed perfectly in keeping with the long Lutheran tradition of a subservient state church, one that respects political authority and does not mingle happily in temporal affairs. It is a complex message mixed with feelings of resignation and assured power ('the dangerous fire'), guilt, shame, hatred, and sin, as well as longed-for liberation from political persecution ('foreign tormentors', 'German tormentors') and the consolation of spiritual suffering. Hamel's statement is an anguished inability to reconcile his private conscience and political circumstance, one in which Christians in the 'East Zone' were yet again set against a regime in which free fellowship and Christian service were under totalitarian threat. Hamel's subsequent sermons made clear that this endangered Christian conscience must adapt to the situation, and even must learn to work with the communists, since they too were 'God's instruments'. He ended one of his 1957 sermons thus:

Let us pray: We thank thee, our Heavenly Father, that we may receive our rulers of power from thy hands, for thou hast set them over us. We commend our government to thee, our President, Wilhelm Pieck, his Prime Minister Otto Grotewohl, his deputy and General Secretary of the SED, Walter Ulbricht, the Ministers and all who rule over us. We pray thee for the government in Bonn as well. Let them perceive thy truth so that they may govern righteously in godly fear. Deliver them with us from sin, death and Satan, and we together with them may praise thy name in all eternity. Amen.[8]

Hamel's 1950 sermon can also be read differently. After all, his words easily accorded with what Polish dissident Czeslaw Milosz, in his widely read 1951 *The Captive Mind*, famously called *ketman*. It is an Arabic word and Islamic concept that means 'hidden', and for Milosz captured the behaviour of Eastern bloc inhabitants and their 'customs cultivated in the country of the New Faith'. As he put it: 'Ketman in its narrowest and severest forms is widely practiced in the people's democracies. As in Islam, the feeling of superiority over those who are unworthy of attaining truth constitutes one of the chief joys of people whose lives do not in general abound in pleasures.' According to Milosz, Eastern bloc citizens thus lived in a world based on lying, duplicity, and masks, leading double lives of public conformity and private opinion. Ketman 'brings comfort, fostering dreams of what might be, and even the enclosing fence affords the solace of reverie'.[9] Nowhere was this attitude more pronounced than among Christian believers in the Eastern bloc, who sought to balance their split existence by means of 'inner emigration', 'inner sanctuary', invisibility, and 'as if' thinking. It was precisely this dramatic difference between public behaviour and private conviction that Hamel identified as central to the Christian's 'dangerous double existence'. Now, it is easy to dismiss such sentiments as the rhetoric of powerlessness or even the last refuge of the cowardly, particularly in light of the more politicized Lutheran Church of the 1970s and 1980s. But it was the power of secrecy (as well as the arrogance of truth, as Milosz suggests) that nourished the Church in the face of communist assault, as its public role and mission had all but been banished to limited religious service and modest domestic gatherings. Hamel's comment thus affords an illuminating glimpse into the existential 'smoldering' under 'the so uniform surface of life' that defined a certain Christian self-understanding in a world not of their making.

If nothing else, Hamel's letter reflects the troubled place of Lutherans in the early years of the new socialist republic. The tension between the Church, family, and the state had been a perennial one in German history, but it took on special significance in the GDR. After 1945 the two political losers of Hitler's seizure of power—Christian conservatism and communism—were vying for power across the occupied zones. But whereas the communist leaders needed to be parachuted in from Russia to revive the crushed communist movement and remake (East) Germany in Moscow's image, the churches were in an altogether different situation. They emerged surprisingly intact after the collapse of the Third Reich, and nimbly recast themselves as both the persecuted opposition of Nazism and the rightful moral architects of post-Nazi German society. They were well-placed to do so, as German war survivors flocked back to the churches for solace and comfort. In a 1946 poll, for example, over 90 per cent of Germans declared themselves Christians, and a high percentage of them attended church on a regular basis. The churches' close contacts with Allied authorities and strong social networks beyond Germany—combined with the absence of organized political parties—strengthened their position even further. Some even saw the German churches of the early postwar period as their most influential since the Reformation. Not only had the 'churches alone survived the collapse of three Reichs, several catastrophic wars, an accident-prone republic, foreign occupation and the dismemberment of the country', they were more united than ever about the moral reconstruction of postwar Germany.[10] Their insistence on acting as brokers of postwar moral justice did not always go down well with Allied occupational authorities, especially in light of the churches' penchant for exonerating their parishioners of any wrongdoing during the Third Reich. One American Military Government officer noted that 'in one community almost every person summoned for investigation of his Nazi activity arrived equipped with a certificate from a minister or a priest attesting to his fine Christian character'.[11] In any case, the political gravity and popular appeal of the churches after 1945 were undeniable. This was especially true in West Germany. There, church leaders—especially Catholic ones—played a decisive role in the reinvention of Christian democracy, and exercised surprising control over political appointments, media, and school education into the 1950s and beyond.

In the Soviet Zone, things were different. But the clash between Christian and communist ideology did not lead to political conflict from the beginning. A kind of truce born of 1930s Popular Front antifascism coloured the relationship between the two foes in the first few years after the ceasefire. In fact, the official communist position on religion harked back to the German Communist Party's 1935 Brussels Conference, in which the illegal and repressed party sought to win over potential Christian comrades against fascism by proclaiming 'freedom of belief and conscience' as a fundamental right, and pledged to work for its restoration after the defeat of Nazism. Toleration and plurality emerged as the new communist watchwords of post-Nazi recovery and cooperation, as Lenin's famous comment that religion should be tolerated as a private matter unrelated to socialist life became postwar communist policy. Soviet leaders were well aware that their support in war-torn Germany was shallow and unreliable, and they hardly wished to risk further alienation by offending local beliefs and sensibilities regarding religion. In a 1949 census some 81 per cent of East Germans identified themselves as Lutherans, and another 12 per cent as Catholics; only 5 per cent declared themselves 'confession-less'.[12] Of the seventeen million people in the Soviet Zone, fifteen million were nominally Protestants and one million Catholics.[13] For this reason the Soviets sought reconciliation with the churches in the name of peace and stability. The clauses of religious freedom in the GDR's 1949 Constitution, which echoed similar guarantees in both the 1919 Weimar Republic Constitution and 1945 Potsdam Accords, reflected this early postwar spirit of openness and cooperation. This was taken quite seriously. While church property was summarily confiscated by the Soviets across the Eastern bloc, it remained untouched in the sweeping land reform and nationalization measures in East Germany.

But as the Soviets began to tighten their grip on the Eastern half of the former Reich, hostilities toward the Church grew. By the late 1940s, Christian Democratic leaders in the Soviet Zone were purged as Western spies, church activists were intimidated and occasionally imprisoned, and the churches' access to the media severed. Christian publications were drastically curtailed, allegedly due to paper shortages, promised state subsidies to the churches were scaled back, and Christian meetings blocked. That the Evangelical Church retained its all-German institutional structure despite cold war geopolitical division only fuelled the SED's suspicion towards Protestants. The widely publicized decision by the leadership of the All-German Lutheran Church to minister to NATO soldiers (the so-called *Militärseelsorgevertrag*) only fed the regime's fears about the presence of a Western-oriented 'NATO-Church' operating within the country. Young people were seen as particularly vulnerable and in need of defending. In 1951 the Central Committee promulgated that all GDR teachers must propound the 'materialist, atheistic worldview' of Marxist-Leninism in their classrooms, as agitation spilled from the classroom into residential communities. Most of the reports written by the newly established Stasi in the 1940s and early 1950s, for example, centred on the behaviour of Christians in neighbourhoods, including spying on pastors' houses as cells of subversive activity.[14] Pastors commonly recounted the difficulties of establishing youth congregations, or *Junge Gemeinde*, in churches and in residential areas, since they were deemed threatening to the only permitted organization for East German young people, the communist Free German Youth (FDJ). Junge Gemeinde members who wore their religious insignia were bullied by the FDJ, often expelled from school, and routinely discriminated against across the GDR. The SED blocked their conferences, tarring them as 'enemies of the republic' and Western spies.[15] Harassment intensified after the June 1953 Uprising. Pastors recalled how the state often sent local teachers as informants to Junge Gemeinde evening gatherings, and how they lived in constant fear.[16] In 1954 the SED founded the Department of Church Affairs, or Abteilung Kirchenfragen, to keep a close eye on church activities. Across the country Stasi agents and informants were assigned to attend Sunday sermons, taking notes on any possible subversive content.[17] Even SED members who married Christians were kept under close watch.[18]

THE 'YOUTH DEDICATION' CONTROVERSY

What outraged the churches most were the state's incursions into the world of primary and secondary school education. At first such an attitude may seem anachronistic, given the broader trend of secularization across the Western world since the late nineteenth century. But Germany represented an exception to this story, especially in the world of children's education. Perhaps the most well-known example is Bismarck's ill-fated Kulturkampf against the Southern German provinces to root out the influence of the Catholic Church in the world of primary and secondary school education; Catholic leaders there successfully resisted this Prussian campaign as an infringement upon their religious liberties and civil rights. The collapse of the Second Reich at the end of the First World War certainly signalled the historic end of 'throne and altar' rule in Germany. But for all of the political importance associated with the formal separation of church and state in the Weimar Republic's 1919 constitution, the old union persisted in the area of education. On the eve of the Nazi takeover in 1933, for example, over 80 per cent of German elementary schools were still confessional, and religious instruction remained central to Nazi era schools as well. Article 23 of Hitler's infamous 1933 Reichskonkordat with the Vatican guaranteed confessional schools everywhere in Germany, attesting to the power and influence of the churches. After the war the churches clamoured for the re-establishment of these confessional schools as post-Nazi moral renewal and a defence against communism.[19] They succeeded in the Western Zones, but failed in the Soviet Zone. For the Soviets, religion was to be privatized as part of the campaign to create a new communist culture, beginning in the sphere of children's education. By May 1946 the Soviet authorities passed the Law for the Democratization of German Schools, stating that 'the education of children in schools is exclusively the prerogative of the state. Religious instruction is the prerogative of religious associations'; there was strenuous church opposition, as the churches presented opinion polls showing that over 85 per cent of Berliner parents wanted religious instruction in schools.[20] Nonetheless, denominational schools were formally abolished across the Soviet Zone in 1947 and in East Berlin in 1948.[21] A broad humanist-based curriculum was introduced in primary and secondary schools by the late 1940s and early 1950s, as the SED was keen to tread lightly for the sake of political order and popular support. Yet the SED had bigger plans.

By the mid-1950s, the churches were again up in arms about what they saw as the state's infringements upon their newly guaranteed civil rights. In the wake of the arbitrary rule and totalitarian reach of the Third Reich, church leaders across the zones successfully campaigned for legal provisions recognizing the churches' independence from the state, individual freedom of conscience, as well as the special protection of the family under law. Both the new West and East German states honoured these claims in their respective 1949 constitutions.[22] But these rights were soon subject to revision in East Germany. In large measure GDR lawyers were embarrassed by the fact that the new republic was still governed by the old Civil Code of 1900, which was liberal in origin, bourgeois in tone, and, worst of all, the cherished legal framework for the hated Federal Republic. As a liberal guidebook, this Wilhelmine civil code was built on a distant relationship between state and citizen in the form of a raft of private rights and 'negative freedoms'. The GDR's Minister of Justice Hilde Benjamin was looking to create a new civil code more in keeping with socialist dictates and the desired fusion of citizen and state. In 1954 a Draft Proposal for a Socialist Civil Code (EFGB) was announced and widely distributed. The Church reacted very angrily, partly owing to the proposed code's lenient divorce criteria and firm assumption that wives could and should work. (These issues will be discussed in more detail in Chapter 3.)

Other aspects of the family law section of the proposed code alarmed the churches. Of special concern was that the long-standing constitutional guarantee of 'parental authority' (*Gewalt*) over their children had been replaced by 'parental care' (*Sorge*). This apparent minor semantic mutation effectively meant that parents were to surrender their autonomy to the state. They were to practise their 'rights and duties toward the state, society and children' precisely in that order, with the aim to 'raise "independent and responsible children of the democratic state who love their homeland and stand for peace"'.[23] Just in case anyone was left in any doubt, Benjamin boldly averred that all parents were to raise their children 'in the spirit of the socialist worldview and morals'. Christian parents who did not comply, she threatened, only ended up cheating themselves of the state-provided educational system offered to their children from kindergarten to university. The Draft Proposal galvanized the Christian community in protest, filling parish churches, and inspiring numerous petitions to the state.[24] Thousands of open meetings were organized across the GDR to discuss the proposed code, and after months of surprisingly open citizen debate the SED decided to shelve it for further revision. The churches felt vindicated, having beaten back the encroachments of the state upon what they saw as the private sphere of everyday citizens. Yet the state's withdrawal of the proposed civil code was neither a defeat nor a real retreat. Later that same year the SED drove forward another initiative against Christian tradition: the introduction of the infamous Jugendweihe.[25]

Briefly, the Jugendweihe introduced in 1954 was conceived of as a youth dedication ceremony that East German 14 year olds of both sexes would undergo to mark their coming of age in socialist society. Officially the Jugendweihe was to be a milestone event in the 'process of imparting to young people useful knowledge in basic questions of the scientic world-view and socialist morality, of raising them in the spirit of socialist patriotism and proletarian internationalism, and helping them to prepare themselves for active participation in the construction of developed socialist society and the creation of the basic preconditions for the gradual transition to communism'.[26] A key influence came from the Soviet Union, which had already devoted great energy to replacing Christian traditions with newly minted communist ones. Back in the 1920s the USSR had set up new socialist 'name-giving' ceremonies to replace Christian baptism, along with 'red marriages' and 'red funerals'.[27] After 1945 this was continued, as Leningrad opened a huge communist 'wedding palace' in 1959 as well as a large hall for socialist 'name-giving' ceremonies in 1965.[28] The East German Jugendweihe plainly borrowed its liturgical form and spirit from Christian confirmation. It followed a similar format of music, speeches, and pageantry. April was selected for its symbolism of awakening nature, but also because it was the season of Easter and confirmation services. Boys and girls were even advised to wear dark blue suits and white dresses, which had been long associated with confirmation ceremonies.

But the Jugendweihe far predated the 1950s. Its roots extended back to the mid-nineteenth century and the practices of so-called 'free-thinking religious congregations' across Western Germany, whose dissident Protestants and Catholics created a new youth dedication as an alternative to the rigid formality of Christian confirmation. For them, it was more an 'Enlightened' event for liberal Christians celebrating personal religious dedication and communal solidarity. By the late nineteenth century, however, the banned SPD worker movement adopted the religious ritual for its own purposes, secularizing it as a subcultural rite of passage for adolescent socialist youth. It was recast as a political christening that signalled a personal commitment to the leftist cause, and after 1918 became a fixture of German worker culture through the Weimar Republic. Under the Nazis the youth dedication was racialized as a ritual of adolescent allegiance to the Third Reich, whose shift in tone was registered in the fact that the term 'Jugendweihe' was replaced by 'celebration of commitment', or *Verpflichtungsfeier*; it was therefore under the Nazis when the dedication rite finally lost its oppositional character and became an inclusive national event for all German youth.[29]

After 1945 efforts were made to reinvent the socialist tradition for a new postwar generation. As early as 1947 2,500 Berlin children underwent the Jugendweihe as a means of reconnecting with the interwar proletarian heritage.

While the SED reversed course in 1950 by banning the ceremony for two years lest it might offend the Christian majority and threaten the new country's tolerant pretensions, the initiative was reintroduced a few years later with renewed vigour. By 1952 the SED had decided to direct more political energy towards securing the 'foundations of socialism', and the June 1953 Uprising was in part blamed on Christians as unreliable 'enemies of the state'. The Eastern bloc's first real political crisis thus became a pretext for driving the Jugendweihe forward as a means of doing away with Christian 'superstition', isolating the Christian community, and challenging church authority over the education of the young. The SED reckoned that they could never build a popular base without first undermining the strength of its main 'worldview' rival.

As a consequence, the Jugendweihe was retooled to serve SED ends. For one thing, the GDR's version of Jugendweihe would no longer be an emblem of alternative culture, as it became a full-blown propagandistic affirmation of socialist victory, communal life, and state belonging.[30] Great communist luminaries who had undergone the ritual themselves—such as Karl Liebknecht, Rosa Luxembourg, Wilhelm Pieck, Ernst Thälmann, and of course Walter Ulbricht—were lionized as antifascist inspiration and for emulation.[31] For the SED, the Jugendweihe was viewed as an Enlightenment version of confirmation, initiating young people into socialism's secular, scientific, and materialist philosophy. Atheism was to be the cornerstone of humanist education. In the SED's own literature, the point was repeatedly made that religion began where science ended, and thus further research and knowledge would dispel the consoling need of such 'mysticism'. Ulbricht himself polemicized against religion and religious education in a 1954 *Jugendweihe* article, insisting that the GDR 'will carry on its campaign against superstition, mysticism, idealism and all other unscientific worldviews'.[32] Even the term 'Christian faith' (*christliche Glaube*) was replaced by the derogatory moniker 'superstition' (*Aberglaube*) in SED official language.[33] East Berlin Mayor Friedrich Ebert captured the moment when he opened the 1958 school year with the words: 'Therefore we are not educating [pupils] to believe in imaginary powers and the existence of transcendent spirits. We are educating youth to believe in themselves and in the power and energy of the working class.'[34]

The Jugendweihe aimed to educate the East German adolescent as a well-rounded young citizen on the path to socialist adulthood. It was to separate the child from the parental home and to transform the 14 year old into a mature member of the socialist community. Fourteen was a symbolic age in the GDR: it was the year when GDR citizens received their own passport, were addressed by their teachers in the formal grammatical address (*Sie,* instead of *Du*) as a marker of their new status, were deemed old enough to be punished in court, and were eligible for membership in the Free German Youth.[35] Preparation materials underlined that the main task was 'to promote the development of the valuable qualities of the socialist personality'.[36] Included among them were cultivating good relations with parents, developing deep friendships (Marx and Engels were hailed as exemplars), as well as encouraging the virtues of respect and loyalty to the state.[37] In the nationally circulated Jugendweihe preparation materials, young people were entreated to help combat petty crimes such as 'the destruction and damage of flowers, lawns, trees, park benches, etc.', to help the People's Police to do their work, to 'refrain from excessive noise in public spaces and streets, to avoid truancy and shiftlessness, practise financial responsibility and respect the People's Property', as well as to be on the lookout for any racism, violence, or anything that 'undermines the state order'.[38]

Jugendweihe education usually consisted of ten special classes over the span of several weeks. Emphasis was placed on modern science and a materialist *Weltanschauung*, with a strong dosage of astronomy, evolution, technological development, progressive socialist human relations, and even good manners.[39] A monthly journal, *Jugendweihe*, was founded in 1954 with the motto 'Knowing is Better than Believing', with a view towards instructing teachers on how to initiate their charges into modern socialism. In-class political discussions and excursions to factories, farms, museums, and theatres were arranged to reinforce the message. Speeches from Nazi era resisters and visits to Buchenwald were included to dramatize the stakes of socialist triumph.[40] The actual ceremony itself generally took place in cinemas, schools, or factories, and featured a solemn processional entry, formal address, presentation of a commemorative gift book, *Cosmos, Earth, Man* (*Weltall, Erde, Mensch*), a collective oath of loyalty, and flowers from the Young Pioneers. The message was usually wooden and repetitive: one adolescent recounted in 1964 that the featured speaker used the word 'socialism' sixty-four times in his twenty-minute oration.[41] The ceremony was to reaffirm proletarian tradition, socialist patriotism, and classical humanism, as the likes of Goethe and Johannes Becher were invariably read out as inspirational poets.[42] Shostakovich's 'Für den Frieden der Welt' and Beethoven's Egmont Overture provided musical accompaniment.[43] The visual representation of the rite also bespoke its solemn and confirmation-like character. Figure 1 features East German youth gazing at Jugendweihe certificates and gift books, while Figure 2 captures the stiff pageantry of adolescent initiates on stage. The whole event was typically followed by a family meal and party, at which the teenager received gifts and blessings from family, friends, and relatives.

But the SED knew that such a pledge of allegiance would be a hard sell to Christians. Spies who had infiltrated Christian parent meetings reported that they would reject outright 'any purely Marxist perspective for their children'.[44] To soften the impact, the SED announced in December 1954 that the Jugendweihe 'is neither a state initiative nor one of any single organization. Youth of all worldviews can take part. Confirmation is not touched by it, and the freedom of belief and conscience reigns supreme ... Participating in Jugendweihe is voluntary.'[45] What is more, the SED portrayed the churches themselves as on the side of exclusion and the constitutional abrogation of freedom of conscience.

Figure 1. East Berlin Youth Examining Youth Dedication Certificates and Gift Books, 1958.

Local Jugendweihe committees were instructed to appear conciliatory, relaying to concerned Christian parents that the Jugendweihe 'would in no way offend the religious feelings of your children', and that the 'freedom of conscience guarantee in our constitution will be respected'.[46] SED publicists shamelessly cited the GDR's own constitution for justification, including Article 41 ('Every citizen enjoys full freedom of belief and conscience') and Article 42 ('Private and citizen rights and duties are neither conditioned nor limited by religious practice'[47]). In a great ironic turn, the SED even presented itself as the guardian of private rights: 'The state and the Party are dedicated to protecting the freedom of belief and conscience. It is the free and democratic right of parents to decide with their children, whether the child goes to Jugendweihe or confirmation or both. This right is protected by the constitution. No child or parent will incur any disadvantage if they do not send their child to Jugendweihe.'[48] Conversely, so argued the SED, the churches should be more 'tolerant' towards the 'transconfessional' Jugendweihe, and should therefore desist from terrorizing 'the conscience of parents and children'. The SED went so far as to accuse church leadership of 'disturbing the peaceful relations among the citizens of our republic, and not for the first time furnishing ammunition for the Western "war press" in their crusade against the GDR'.[49] 'Reactionary clerical circles' were pilloried

Figure 2. Jugendweihe Ceremony, Britz bei Eberswalde, 1957.

for using the 'Westpresse' and RIAS to sow youthful agitation and 'malicious campaigns' against the republic.[50]

It was no great surprise that the churches would have none of it. The Lutheran Church had already made clear back in the Weimar Republic that Jugendweihe was incompatible with confirmation, and now the GDR state's backing of it only stiffened resistance.[51] Lutheran authorities sternly rejected SED propaganda, especially the state's novel self-image as the guardian of tolerance and constitutional freedom.[52] Pastors not only cited numerous passages from the *Weltall* commemorative book for its 'aggressive atheism' and belittling portrayal of religion as antiquated and obsolete; they also reiterated that confirmation was a voluntary act, and that the state was wrong to portray it otherwise.[53] For Christians the stakes were extremely high, and both the Protestants and Catholic churches took a firm line on Jugendweihe. According to church leaders, SED actions had forced everyone to make a stark choice, and they typically cited Luke 11: 23 ('Whoever is not with me is against me') and Matthew 6: 24 ('No one can serve two masters') for biblical justification.[54] Letters written from the church leadership to all Berlin congregations at the time were unwavering in tone that 'Christian belief and a Marxist worldview is an insuperable contradiction.'[55] The official Catholic stance was equally severe.[56] Distraught parents were urged to take part in Christian support groups to find strength and solidarity with other believers.[57]

Now the state stepped up its campaign. Already by November 1954 the SED had formed a new Central Committee for the Jugendweihe to spearhead the campaign, as hundreds of thousands of paid employees and volunteers were enlisted for the cause, including local Jugendweihe committees, school organizations, parents' associations, Free German Youth leaders, and local enterprises.[58] Pressure was put on teachers to comply with state policies in the classroom, and those who didn't—including numerous Christians—were removed from their posts. A few years before the SED promised that religious groups could use school grounds for after-school religious study as a gesture of compromise; but they rarely made good on this agreement, sometimes citing health and safely issues as reason for denying Christian assembly after hours. Pastors complained that the state was thus in violation of their constitutional freedom of conscience, particularly Article 34 ('Art, scholarship and teaching are to remain free') and Article 44 which held that 'The right of the church to provide religious instruction in school spaces is guaranteed.'[59] Such conflict even spilled over into quarrels over children's holidays, as church leaders claimed that school trips were really Marxist indoctrination sessions championing atheistic teaching, designed to separate children from their parents' home and to weaken religious belief.[60] More aggressive tactics were also devised to break Christian resistance. By the late 1950s Junge Gemeinde were routinely broken up as 'agents of Anglo-American imperialism'; theological work was carefully scrutinized for any seditious content; and Christian families were subject to routine police harassment. Police and Stasi files from the period show that informants regularly sat in the back of church services, penning short summaries of the sermons and noting any suspicious views regarding the Jugendweihe, West Germany, or international political events, such as the Hungarian Revolution of 1956.[61]

THE CHRISTIAN HOME

GDR state authorities realized that the socialist remaking of society would not take root unless the campaign was carried into the family home. For this GDR pedagogues led the charge, often taking their cues from the Soviet Union. In particular Russian pedagogue Anton Makarenko was commonly cited as guidance for socialist 'domestic education'.[62] What they valued from his work above all was his assertion that 'the bourgeois family was and is considered as a private world (*privater Lebenskreis*), in whose sphere neither the state nor other societal forces are allowed to penetrate. Many parents believe that it is exclusively their business how they raise their children.' Conversely, 'family life and childraising in the Soviet Union are closely linked to the political destiny of the Soviet people as a whole'.[63] GDR authorities strove to follow his lead in dissolving the walls of the family home. In practical terms, this meant closer relations between school and the parental home by means of more active parent associations and obligatory visits from teachers to the homes of pupils, often in the name of rooting out juvenile 'egotism and indifference'.[64]

As early as 1952 the monthly journal *Elternhaus und Schule* was founded as a means of better linking society and the family home. The first issue neatly announced its intentions, reprinting a telegram from Minister for People's Education Paul Wandel. In it he stated that the magazine 'should help all parents and teachers realize a democratic, engaged education for peace. It should help bind school, parental house and youth organization.'[65] Issues were filled with short stories of happy school children in the Soviet Union; model households, schools, and parent associations; profiles of famous teachers; tales of youth from the heroic biographies of Lenin and Stalin; as well as tips on which films to see, books to read, and toys to buy. Featured too were articles on pedagogy and renewed calls for teachers to visit their pupils' homes more often.[66] Occasionally articles even touched on 'atavistic' domestic violence, for example, driving home the point that child-raising was no longer a private matter.[67] While the journal's general understanding of parent–child relations softened over time in the GDR and elsewhere across Europe in the 1960s and 1970s, as more relaxed attitudes and demonstrative love towards children became more prevalent from the early 1970s onward,[68] the overarching objective was to deprivatize family behaviour by undermining the authority of the family as an autonomous social unit.[69]

But against this the Church put up great resistance. The primacy of the Christian household as the foundation of church life emerged immediately after the defeat of Nazism as a precondition for Christian renewal. A 1945 report from the Evangelical Bishop of Berlin stated that

any true school reform as well as the revival of the Church begins with the parental household. With God's will it must be realized in what we call the 'church in the house' (morning, evening and mealtime prayers; Christian artefacts; recounting biblical stories from the mother, religious instruction from the parents) . . . The way of our people back to God begins with the engaged Christian teaching of our children at home and school.[70]

Other sources from the period expressed the urgent need to strengthen parent associations in order to maintain Christian communities, and in this regard the Christian household was fundamental.[71] A 1951 report of an assembly of 150 Christian parents stated that they were in agreement with Pastor S that 'parents are the stewards of God in the education of their children. The responsibility of the parents (in relation to the children) most immediately takes place at home.' This inevitably led to a split existence in GDR society, as 'children experience contradictions between what is taught at school and what is experienced at home'.[72] This 'war of position' ideology continued through the 1960s, even at the official church level.[73] Catholics espoused a similar view towards the family home as the refuge of private religious devotion; indeed, they were duly instructed to decorate their homes with crosses and images of Mary to cultivate religious Christian sensibility at home.[74] For Protestants and Catholics, faith-based homes played a key part in the Christian archipelago of tradition, dissent, and solidarity in the midst of a hostile Marxist state. As New Forum activist Jens Reich recalled of his 1950s Christian household, 'we learned, in accordance with Matthew 22: 21, to give to Ulbricht what was Ulbricht's and to give to God what belonged to God'.[75]

Interviewees make this plain in their recollections about Christian life in the GDR. For them the Christian home was a vital 'counterworld', a place of respite ('*Ruhepol*') and rejuvenation over against the hostile world outside. It was a counter-culture composed of family homes and the Church, sustained by a network of solidarity and service that they often called a 'Christian private sphere'. They fondly recalled evenings and weekends spent with family and friends, enjoying Bible study, hymn-singing, prayers, Christian celebrations, and relaxed conviviality. Pastors even termed the Christian domicile a 'geistige Heimat', or 'spiritual homeland'. The home itself was often decorated with traditional Christian symbols—crosses, Bibles, pictures, religious magazines, and hymnbooks—though others said that the open display of Christian objects in the house varied considerably. They consistently spoke of the 'double life' of being a Christian, and the unpleasantness of being 'dishonest' at socialist school. Both Protestants and Catholics made clear that it was best to keep to themselves; for Christians the private sphere, as one Catholic put it, was 'a secret, not something that was ever supposed to be made visible to the outside world'. Most recollected some personal encounter with the Stasi resulting from their 'alternative lifestyle'; almost every one of them pointed out that they were under 'constant surveillance' from neighbours, colleagues, and the authorities, and that their mail was routinely 'controlled.' This was unavoidably the case if they had any contacts with 'the West', especially West German churches. But this Christian subculture found other expressions as well. For example, a surprising number of people interviewed claimed that they could immediately identify a Christian home upon entrance. However, the telling signs were not what one would predict—Bibles, crosses, songbooks and sundry Christian accoutrements within sight. What distinguished a Christian home, according to these interviewees, was also a strong rejection of the GDR's typical standardized furniture (*Massenmöbel*) and uniform interior décor as 'hideous' and 'lifeless'. Instead, they tended either to build their own furniture or decorate their homes with eclectic styles that celebrated what they all called the resident's 'individualism'.[76] If nothing else, these recollections underline that the Christian faith was closely linked to—and nurtured by—a whole material habitus of nonconformity and alternative behaviour at home.

Such attitudes predictably met with consternation from the authorities, and were seen as an impediment to the building of socialism. The Christian home was thus increasingly identified as a key locus of secrecy, tradition, and subversion, harbouring anti-socialist attitudes and bourgeois tendencies.[77] This was certainly true of the pastor's own house, which traditionally had served as a locus of alternative culture and a magnet for outsiders.[78] Yet ordinary Christian households were also viewed suspiciously. In one high-level 1954 discussion among Free German Youth secretaries, the task of conquering the walls of recalcitrant residences was deemed necessary on the grounds that they supposedly hid unwanted egotistical and 'petty bourgeois' attitudes: 'Dear Friends! Our task is to win over all German youth to our cause. You know what difficulties we encounter. To a large extent they are the result of the petit bourgeois household. Let me remind you all of all of the individualistic inclinations that pupils carry from their parental homes, such as the instincts of private property and other foreign influences, that they first learn in their parental homes.'[79] Their 'reactionary milieux' were seen as vitiating the ethos and mission of the state's youth policies, whose ideal of 'planned childhood' began with effacing the boundaries between the public and the private spheres. Non-compliant 'low cultural level' households were identified as the source of asocial and 'republic-hostile' behaviour, juvenile delinquency and even youth crime, since children growing up there were not being properly socialized as responsible members of the socialist community.[80]

The years 1957–8 saw the intensification of the state crusade to break the Church's secret power by promoting the Jugendweihe with renewed vigour.[81] By this time the gloves were off, as the SED made no qualms about using the dedication ceremony as a weapon against the stubborn churches. Until this point, the SED had argued that support for the event had come from 'society' with no direct links to the state. By 1957 this had changed. That year the Department of People's Education, or Abteilung für Volksbildung, was established to universalize the Jugendweihe. The national flag gracing all Jugendweihe ceremonies was now joined by the international worker's movement flag and the Free German youth banner. The change of tack resulted from two things. First, the 1956 Hungarian Revolution impelled the SED to stamp out all potential dissent in the country, beginning with the churches. Christians were accused of fomenting revolution in Budapest, and the SED used the revolt to suppress church activity. Secondly, the success of the 1957 Sputnik launch emboldened the state to accelerate its atheistic, science-oriented school education as the way forward into the socialist future.[82] With relish the GDR press quoted a Radio Moscow broadcast that year, which brazenly crowed that 'the Soviet spaceship has penetrated outer space, and neither God nor Heaven was discovered there'.[83] A pamphlet called *Dear God and the Sputnik* was quickly published to ridicule religious creationism in the age of science.[84] This was the dawning of the great Soviet era of 'moving mountains' with science and technology, so Ulbricht prophesied in a 1957 speech, and Christian doctrine was only in the way.[85] There was now more of an effort to link Ulbricht and GDR leaders to the ceremony itself, as noted in Figure 3. In 1958 Ulbricht re-emphasized the link

Figure 3. Walter Ulbricht Delivering Jugendweihe Address, Dessau, 1957.

between the Jugendweihe and Germany's proletariat tradition 'under the rising star of Sputnik,' and for the first time explicitly called the socialist dedication requisite political education.[86] A number of propaganda parades were organized to publicize the Jugendweihe (Figure 4). New posters were designed, as noted in Figure 5, emphasizing the connection among youth, science, and a sunny socialist future. Such ideology was dramatically on display in a 1958 placard, which featured a young East German girl struggling to choose between the black, backward world of the Bible and the literally enlightened path of Marx and the Free German Youth (Figure 6). That same year he announced his 'Ten Commandments of Socialist Morality', a post-Christian code of ethics calling for more worker solidarity; workplace discipline; cleanliness; as well as respect for socialist property and family.

Such actions confirmed Christian suspicion that the constitutional right to freedom of conscience was under threat as never before. Many recounted constant Stasi surveillance, wiretapping, and People's Police browbeating, adding to the widespread feeling of fear and anxiety among church leaders.[87] Even those Christians who had all but withdrawn to their homes for religious cultivation were subjected to Stasi haranguing. One Berlin Christian wrote how he, like many others, had set up *Hausbibelkreise* in the 1950s, and for this was harassed by some twenty agents because of the group's contacts with the West, 'freedom-seeking lifestyle', and 'critical attitude toward state and society'.[88] One long-time minister from Berlin-Weissensee recalled how he once told a SED 'church mediator'

Figure 4. Propaganda Parade for the Jugendweihe in East Berlin, 1958.

Figure 5. Youth Dedication Placard, 1958.

Figure 6. East Berlin Placard on the Irreconciliability of Marxism and Christianity, mid-1950s.

(*Kirchenreferent*) who had dropped by his house that he would never send his children to any communist school that preached revolution and war. State authorities were sent to his residence, searched his home, 'seized' (that is, wiretapped) his bedroom and his children's room, and then briefed the neighbours about reporting any untoward behaviour. The pastor sought legal counsel for the affront, but was told that pursuing the issue 'would only make matters worse'.[89]

Engaged pastors faced the special wrath of the state. Frequently they were singled out in police reports as politically dangerous, and were threatened with detainment. Some were accused of wooing young people to resist the Jugendweihe by giving them chocolates from packages they received from the West.[90] Trumped-up stories of pastors' 'violence and abuse' towards non-believers and socialist youth were rife, and satirical accounts of their 'medieval' nay-saying to progress and Enlightenment were widely circulated in the GDR press.[91] Defamation campaigns were also common.[92] At times the crusade against pastors got even uglier. One Catholic priest recalled a 1957 incident in which a town meeting in Nossen was organized by the National Front against a Pastor K because of his outspoken views against the Jugendweihe. The rally outside was crowded with 'police wagons and many Stasi people in cars with megaphones at the marketplace'. A chosen speaker apparently exclaimed that he had proudly ripped a church magazine out from the hands of a visitor who was leaving the pastor's residence, brazenly concluding to great cheers that "I chased him away! I shit on Lord Jesus!," to which the Christians in the hall 'held their breath in shock, while the teenagers found it all entertaining'. A flurry of press articles were published against the pastor, after which he received numerous protest letters from all corners of the GDR denouncing him as a 'dog', 'shit', 'scum', and 'asshole', along with several death threats. The besieged pastor was subject to repeated house searches, and even jailed on one occasion.[93]

Many Christian families were caught in the crossfire of state–church conflict. 'Sideline-standing' parents were constantly cajoled at work, in their neighbour-hoods, and at home to relent in allowing the dedication rite for their children. It was made clear to them that non-participation would effectively penalize them and especially their children, in the form of job demotion and blocked university education.[94] University admission in the GDR was not easy in itself, as the state lacked sufficient resources to admit more than a fraction of qualified students. Refusing to take part in the Jugendweihe was duly noted by the school, and—while not official—made university matriculation all but impossible. (The only avenue of university study open to devout Christians was theology, but these degrees were also limited and carefully monitored.) Many parents wrote bitter letters to school directors, charging that their child's constitutional civil rights were abrogated in being discriminated against for reasons of religious conviction. By the same token, a great deal of pressure was exerted on Christian parents by the Church itself.[95] Pastoral letters were sent to Christian parents entreating them to stay the course, threatening that those children who took part in the Jugendweihe would not be confirmed. More, parents who refused their chil-dren's confirmation would not be allowed to stand as godparents, serve as (or elect) local church leaders, or celebrate mass, and may even be denied a Christian marriage. The Church ratcheted up the rhetoric in a 1955 circular to all congregations, admonishing that 'any Christian parents who allow their baptized children to attend Jugendweihe are guilty as Christians' and 'may God help you in facing up to your guilt'.[96]

Christian parents were in a difficult spot. Many wished to stay true to their religious beliefs, but they did not want to jeopardize the lives and careers of their children. In these circumstances, parents often sought compromise, pleading to their superiors that their children should have the right to undergo both Jugend-weihe and confirmation.[97] One 1956 letter from a desperate Berlin mother to her local provost took the Church's supercilious inflexibility to task: 'The representa-tives of the Lutheran Church stress again and again that Christians should know only love, not hatred. But how do these words square with actions? . . . Are you aware that in Bad Elster a young man hanged himself because he was terrorized by the local Christian circles for undergoing the Jugendweihe?' For her the Church had needlessly put Christian parents and children in a 'great conflict of conscience'. As she wrote: 'Do you wish to punish children simply because they and their parents *as Christians* also believe in the progress of our republic?' She concluded her letter by shaming the Church for its dogmatic obedience to misguided church policy: 'We expect of you that you break your slavish obedience to Bishop Dibelius and assume your Christian responsibility before God and challenge his unchristian position regarding the spiritual well-being of our children.' Other parents followed suit, arguing that 'We progressive parents see this [either/or doctrine] as a grave error on the part of the Church,' and that 'many parents feel alienated' in the face of the Church's intransigence.[98] Most however stayed somewhere in the middle, seeking compromises and occasional desperate measures. So tortured by the dilemma were some East Berlin Christian parents that they pushed for 'emergency confirmations' (*Notkonfirmationen*) in West Berlin churches until 1961 to square the ideological circle.[99]

Christian children were harried from both sides. Like parents and pastors, many were subject to police bullying. There were numerous accounts of young Christians lending catechism material to other pupils at school, and it was common that a People's Police officer would then pay a visit to the child's residence, abruptly seizing the material from them.[100] West German journalists took great relish in publishing accounts of how the SED hectored parents into sending their children to the Jugendweihe,[101] and violated people's civil liberties by harassing Christian children in their home.[102] To counteract these West German accounts, GDR newspapers carried short stories or letters to the editors attesting to the supposedly aggressive nature of Christian children so as to undermine their image as persecuted victims.[103]

The pressure went in the other direction as well. One 1958 exchange of letters between state authorities and a pastor over the fate of a wavering Berlin girl was quite revealing in this respect. It was reported that once her mother had registered her daughter for Jugendweihe celebrations the following spring, her pastor arrived at their door, spewing 'hatred toward the Jugendweihe'. Pastor S apparently threatened that if the girl went to the socialist ceremony, he would deny her religious confirmation and thereby bar her from the Church. The pastor finished by appealing to the girl's conscience and family history, sniffing that the 'grandmother and great-grandmother would never have allowed a member of the family to be excluded from church services'. A school representative who got wind of this visited her house soon thereafter. He countered that taking part in the Jugendweihe would enable R to learn about her world scientifically, deepen and broaden her knowledge of the real world that she was already learning at school, and would allow her to discover her homeland through excursions. He concluded by saying: 'No one in later life will ever ask what you remember from catechism or about the Ten Commandments or the content of the Bible; instead, the emphasis will be on what one needs to know: how one masters nature and society.'[104] The pastor then complained that the school director's wife had slyly visited R's sick mother, promising that her daughter could undergo both the socialist event and Christian confirmation. Angered, he then demanded to return to the house, insisting that this was wrong and that the family must ultimately choose. After long family discussions the girl eventually opted for confirmation. But whatever the outcome, this case amply illustrates how this church–state battle over the soul of children was carried into family residences.

Children of pastors were put in an unusually awkward position. The state was well aware that the pastor's house often served as a kind of 'core and crystallization point of an "alternative culture"',[105] a place where critical discussions against the regime commonly took place.[106] While all believing Christians felt compelled to lead double lives in the GDR, maintaining one identity at home and another in public, this split existence was even more pronounced for the families of religious leaders. Sometimes this led to a degree of freedom, since the regime knew that these kids could not be won over to the socialist cause.[107] Still, children of pastors were thus put under special scrutiny. As one pastor recollected: 'We explain to our children that they must live in contradictory worlds: "At home we have to conceal the difficulties we have with school instruction so as not to make problems, and at school we have to hide our true attitudes toward the state."'[108] As children of pastors they suffered because of their social position, most notably in education. One East Berlin pastor recalled investigating why his own daughter, who was top in her class, was denied a university place: 'I submitted a formal complaint, and during the conversation with a member of the school council he said that "We didn't reject the daughter, but rather the father." At that point the cat was out of the bag, and I then petitioned the city council, but only got a formulaic confirmation of the rejection.'[109] Other pastor memoirs recounted the obstacles awaiting those children who came from the 'wrong parental home', even in the 1980s.[110]

By the mid-1960s the tide had turned very much in favour of the state. Ulbricht had succeeded in 'privatizing' the Church and driving it out of public life. The implementation of the new GDR Family Law Book in 1965, eleven years after the Draft Proposal was withdrawn, stressed the links between family and state in the 'active construction of socialist society', mainly through building up its network of creches, kindergarten, schools, youth organizations, and Free German Youth. The same logic informed the GDR's 1968 Constitution, whose Article 38 stated that the most important task of the family was the education of the next generation in terms of nurturing the 'socialist personality' and 'state-oriented citizens'.[111] By that time too the Jugendweihe was fully integrated as 'an integral pillar of state education in our general schools'.[112]

The statistics were startling. In Berlin the 1955 Jugendweihe ceremony was attended by only 15–18 per cent of 14 year olds, as some 7,000 Christian children opted out. By 1958 Jugendweihe participation was up to 40 per cent, and by 1959 was experienced by 80 per cent of East German youth across the country.[113] Meanwhile, Christian confirmation dropped dramatically from 75 per cent to less than 33 per cent by the second half of the 1950s.[114] A similar trend occurred with weddings and baptisms.[115] By the mid-1970s the percentage of pupils who underwent the Jugendweihe never dipped below 95 per cent.[116] In one North Berlin district with 35,000 14 year olds, over 96 per cent of the children had undergone the Jugendweihe that year, while there were only twenty-one confirmations; and all but one of these had also gone to Jugendweihe. A 1969 survey carried out for the SED found that only 14 per cent professed themselves religious, whereas 43 per cent declared themselves atheists.[117] By 1975 the Jugendweihe was fully enmeshed into the thirtieth anniversary of the end of the Second World War, closely connected with 'the world-historical victory of the USSR over Hitler-Fascism and pride in our successful socialist path'.[118] Every spring some 200,000 East German teenagers took part in the 'youth dedication', accompanied by some 2,000,000 guests in attendance, thus making it an increasingly important fixture of GDR national culture. Massive propaganda and political bullying were having their effect, as the state successfully generated an atmosphere of anxiety among churchgoers, not least because church ties were seen as hindering educational and career opportunities. This was the fruit of two decades of concerted state effort, which included over 100,000 voluntary and 200 paid functionaries working for the cause. With time bigger venues needed to be found, as the spring ritual frequently took place in factory hallways, movie theatres, or university auditoria. It took on broad cultural currency, whose presence in East German public life—as seen in display windows full of its clothing articles, gift ideas and commemorative books, press and media coverage—shaped GDR family life every April. This was not only important as a marker of GDR visual culture; it also signalled the Jugendweihe's passage from an officious loyalty oath to a key episode of GDR popular culture. So whereas the state's introduction of secular rituals to supersede religious ones may have famously failed in Revolutionary France, the Marxist version of the Cult of Reason triumphed in East Germany.

Church leaders were hardly caught by surprise. Internal church reports had long confirmed fears that they were losing the battle, detailing how pastors felt tired, under siege, and overwhelmed in the face of relentless state pressure.[119] Parents were losing their will to transmit Christian values to their children in an increasingly hostile environment,[120] and were putting up less resistance to the state's crusade. Above all they did not want to endanger the lives and careers of their children, and they themselves tended to de-emphasize their religious conviction at home. As one 1968 Erlangen report put it, these 'unchurched parents' were abandoning the formidable power of the Christian home.[121] In response church leaders began softening their stance by renouncing earlier views that the Jugendweihe and confirmation were incompatible; the compromise solution was to recommend that Christian children wait a year after the Jugendweihe to be properly confirmed.[122] Even so, West German articles reported how religious life in GDR was dying out by the late 1960s.[123] Churches were apparently so empty by the late 1960s that 'pastors had to preach in people's homes' in order to reach out to believers.[124] The *Volkskirche* had apparently lost its *Volk*.

BURYING THE DEAD

The undeniable success of the Jugendweihe did not mean that the state had vanquished all domains of church influence. While the state had taken much from the Church in terms of rituals and symbolism, having also effectively de-Christianized baptisms and weddings in the 1960s and 1970s, one area remained quite immune from socialist politicking: burying the dead. To the state's chagrin, surprisingly few inroads were made in the world of Christian funerals. Fifteen years after the founding of the GDR, and a decade after the trumpeted introduction of the Jugendweihe, merely 16 per cent of Berlin funerals were conducted in a socialist manner.[125] Pastors often used the prospect of an undignified socialist burial as a popular deterrent against the Jugendweihe. In 1955 a kindergarten teacher in Neubrandenburg persuaded a school girl not to go to the Jugendweihe by reminding her that when she dies she 'will not be buried in the churchyard, but rather will be thrown into the ground like a dog on the other side of the cemetery walls'.[126]

The question of how to bury the dead was always a ticklish one for the SED. Officially there was a clear Marxist rejection of the Christian notion of an afterlife as simply false consciousness intended to stabilize the unjust 'capitalist system'. The dominant view was that 'Whoever lives in socialism needs no consolation of an afterlife.'[127] What afterlife existed was limited to the remembrance of this-worldly achievement and exemplary service. Lenin's monumental embalming in Moscow is an obvious example, designed as it was to bestow upon him—and his socialist ideals—a kind of immortality among the living, to inspire and guide new generations of socialists to follow his lead. State funerals for fallen socialist heads of states and communist heroes were laden with cold war gravity, creating a new pantheon of socialist luminaries for the communist cause in the USSR, the Eastern bloc, and of course China.[128] Ordinary people were also to be linked to the greater cause, in that their lives were seen as emblematic of collective purpose in the great communist cosmology. The task was then to devise a fittingly dignified 'this-worldly' (*weltliche*) ceremony that stole the thunder from the Church in the same way that socialist 'name-giving' ceremonies, marriages, and the youth dedication were designed to do.

The windfall of the Jugendweihe inspired the SED to direct similar energy toward breaking the Church's grip on the administration of last rites. A massive propaganda campaign was organized to publicize the importance of these new socialist funerals from the mid-1950s. It borrowed classic Christian rituals in its use of music, oratory, and silent commemoration, all the while making it difficult for people to arrange Christian interments.[129] But it was not only the link of the individual to the wider secular community that mattered for the SED; just as crucial was the connection between the living and dead. For those who were left behind 'were extorted to close the ranks, and move forward according to the example established by the fallen hero, to the ennobling of life and the perfecting of the only true reality, the socialist society on earth'.[130]

Despite the state's efforts, socialist funerals remained unloved. In the period 1961 to 1971, for instance, Christian marriages were halved in Berlin-Brandenburg and Mecklenburg, while baptisms were reduced to about a third of their 1961 numbers. And yet Christian burials declined by less than 10 per cent.[131] For this reason, the SED deemed it necessary to change tack. A new attitude could be seen in the 1972 publication of G. E. Freidank's *Everything is Worth it in the End: A Manual for This-Worldly Funerals*. In it Freidank began by toeing the Marxist line:

As materialists we know that nature makes no sense. Death and life 'in themselves' are meaningless, like the sun and the snow. There is neither God, nor is Spirit the originator of the world. Instead, laws keep stars and atoms in motion. Not 'God's mysterious will' but the workings of objective laws govern creation and demise in nature, as well as life and death in humans. This knowledge of the relationship of things however cannot comfort us in the face of tragic situations of painful loss, such as the death of a young person from a traffic accident or fatal illness; death is and remains beyond meaning.[132]

However, this clearly was not enough, as the communists had no real viable alternative to the sacred canopy of Christian comfort and eschatology. There was of course a tradition of honouring socialist martyrs and heroes, but this was essentially elitist. The question of how to lend meaning to the death of ordinary people went largely unaddressed. It was this problem that accounted for widespread popular resistance to communist funerals in the Soviet Union from the 1920s onwards, and it bedevilled East Germany as well.[133]

In consequence, the SED sought a new strategy for a decent socialist funeral. German socialists (and Protestants, though not Catholics) had long championed cremation and short funerals as a more modern death rite since the late nineteenth century,[134] but the SED was well aware that it was the ceremonial aspect that people found so lacking. Socialist burials were never made compulsory, but they continued to attract a good deal of propaganda. Freidank's booklet featured instructions on how to conduct a proper socialist funeral, complete with detailed musical recommendations, suggested poems, and model condolescence speeches. Organizers were to engage more directly with the bereaved, taking care to be sensitive to their needs. Of chief concern was how to square a standardized event with painful individual loss. The passage from Heine's *Reisebildern* was hailed as especially apt: 'Is not the life of the individuals just as worthy as that of the whole species? For every single person is an entire world that is born and dies with him. Under every gravestone lies a history of the world.' Such passages were selected precisely because they helped deprivatize death, stripping it of undue 'individualist meaning' by integrating the deceased with the collective.

Leaving nothing to chance, and making sure that private grief remained tied to the community, an Association of Funeral Orators was founded to see off the dead in a professional manner.[135] These salaried orators were to deliver their speeches in a 'thoughtful and emotionally convincing' manner, using 'clear, good German without excessive pathos'. They were explicitly instructed to provide individual touches by 'taking into consideration the individuality and personality of the deceased, in both his life and work'. To this end socialist orators duly recounted the milestones of the deceased's life, including dates of birth, weddings, family relations, occupation, special work achievements, party affiliation, service to society, and personal pastimes. The emphasis was on giving thanks for a life in service to the community, honouring the deceased as closely tethered to the living through deeds and remembrance. This was evident in the language of 'our colleague' and 'our comrade', who 'untiringly devoted his work to the service of socialism'. And even if the brochure explicitly stressed that such funerals 'in our society' have 'not been exclusively "private" affairs for a long time', it did acknowledge that the 'destiny and development of citizens are understood as individuals, especially in families'.[136] National flags were draped on the coffins, and usually the orator strewed earth on the descending casket with the words: 'For peace, for the unity of our fatherland, and for socialism.'

Still, the SED's efforts to de-Christianize death met surprising resistance. Why this is so is not easy to ascertain. Some of it no doubt had to do with the persistent influence of Christian customs among East Germans, even secular ones. Sending your child to the Jugendweihe was one thing; burying the dead in such a modern and stark manner was quite another. In this way the GDR was consonant with broader trends across Europe in the twentieth century, in which burial rites remained the most stubborn holdover of Christian culture. What apparently also contributed to the lack of popular interest in socialist funerals was their delivery. From the 1970s on there were numerous citizen complaints about the shabby and depersonalized form of socialist send-offs. Many of these professional socialist orators delivered five or six funeral speeches per week, and citizens bristled at their empty, formulaic quality. In part this was the result of dwindling finances and inadequate facilities. Indeed, some 60 per cent of all GDR cemeteries remained church-owned as part of the SED's concessions to the Church after the introduction of the Jugendweihe.[137] Conditions were so poor sometimes that family members had to dig the graves themselves for lack of any state support. Citizens also criticized what they perceived as incompetent and indifferent local staff; Christians were particularly sensitive to state insouciance toward the dead. In 1980 an angry Berlin Christian took issue with the way that the SED newspaper *Die Volksstimme* had changed the biblical passage in the death announcement of one of his relatives. In it the word *Gott* was substituted with *Herr*, and 'called home' (*heimgerufen*) was changed to 'went home' (*heimgegangen*). He charged that 'as a Christian I demand that the original text be reinstated'. Vexed, the state representative shot back that 'it is hardly customary for biblical passages to appear in the press of the SED', and dismissed the citizen's complaint as unduly 'dogmatic' and 'provocative'.[138] Though aggregate percentages tipped in favour of the state, Christian burial continued as as a strong cultural practice through the 1980s.[139]

TURNING OUTWARD

But this is not to say that the Church faded away in the 1970s. It continued its presence, but did so differently. For one thing, the Church played a surprisingly large public role in welfare activities, such as care for the elderly, orphans, the mentally ill, and physically infirm. By 1973 the Lutheran Church had around 6,000 parishes, 4,230 parsons, 5,000 catechists, and 5,000 social workers, and ran institutions staffed by more than 15,000 officials, including 51 hospitals, 89 convalescent homes, 21 orphanages, 226 nursing homes, and 326 kindergar-tens.[140] The Church continued to run some fifty agricultural enterprises on half a million acres of land, in effect functioning as the only 'private landowner in the GDR'.[141] Indeed, its status as alternative welfare agency for many at-risk citizens became even more important with time. In the 1980s, for example, the churches received numerous petitions from citizens asking them for help with housing issues or public order matters, as people now turned to the Church as a kind of ersatz city government all the way to 1989.

But there were other changes as well. By the mid-1960s the Church sheltered a number of young people who for reasons of conscience did not wish to serve in the military following the introduction of conscription in 1962. The Lutheran Church played a key role in the establishment of an alternative civil service called *Bausoldaten*, or 'construction soldiers'. The GDR was the only country in the Eastern bloc where one could refuse military service in this way. A very high percentage of these *Bausoldaten* was Christian, and remained so through the 1980s. Church services were also modernized to attract more young people. These so-called 'blues services', or *Bluesmessen*, often featured jazz, blues, and 'beat music', and were very popular among young people, as noted with great consternation in numerous Stasi reports from the mid-1960s onward.[142]

Moreover, the Church's initial strategy of hibernating until Reunification was increasingly viewed as impolitic and impracticable. The all-German organiza-tion of the Church was outlawed in the 1968 Constitution, making clear to East German Christian leaders that its links with the West were becoming a serious political liability. In 1969 the East German Lutheran Church therefore broke away from the all-German Evangelical Church of Germany (EKD) to form the East German Federation of Evangelical Churches in Germany, or *Kirchenbund*, to signal its independence. The new policy was essentially a peaceful cohabita-tion of church and state in the spirit of Ostpolitik. The organizational separation of the East German churches from their West German brethren was immediate-ly welcomed by the GDR state as a step towards rapprochement by accepting the status quo. With it the SED eased off on its atheistic propaganda and allowed more church autonomy. Monies from West German churches, slated for the restoration of crumbling church buildings across the country, were now authorized, not least as a means of attracting Western currency. Further concessions were made to the Church over the ownership of church property and cemeteries in the name of securing political loyalty. Old-style confrontational language against the Church was also curbed. The new 1974 pedagogical handbook for Jugendweihe organizers, *Handbuch zur Jugendweihe für Jugendstundenleiter*, did not mention religion at all, while the new Jugendweihe commemorative book, *Du und Deine Welt*, even featured positive passages about religion. In it the Bible was quoted favourably, and early Christianity was praised as an early form of utopian socialism.[143] By the mid-1970s bishops were appointed without state interference, and the *Bausoldaten* option as a 'kind of legal conscientious objection to military service' was permitted and expanded. Even religious minorities—above all Jews—were given surprising state support by the early 1980s.[144]

The growing partnership between church and state culminated in the celebrated March 1978 Agreement. Much of this was the result of Bishop Albrecht Schönherr's famous formulation of the 'Church within Socialism' coined a few years before. At the 1971 *Kirchenbund* synod he articulated the position by saying that 'it is not our intention to be the Church against socialism, nor the Church beside socialism; we want to be the Church in socialism'. It was a turn away from Hamel's 'two-world doctrine' so as to bring the Church out of isolation and overcome the Lutheran tendency towards 'inner emigration'.[145] While there had been gestures of church–state amity in the 1960s, this new 'church in socialism' concept marked a sea change. For its part the state saw it as a means of consolidating socialism and ending the Church's sympathies and contacts with the West once and for all. The churches, by contrast, understood the idea as a call to bring churches out of the ghetto and homes, renounce its 'niche status', and reclaim its Reformation era theological commitment to living in the world.[146] This included expanding the Church's social and media presence. In fact, the key negotiating points for the Church in the Agreement were closer ministerial contact with prisoners; the construction of new churches; pensions for clergy members; and perhaps most importantly, increased access to television. The SED conceded all of these demands, even granting television time to the churches six times a year.[147] Church media presence had long been limited to small Christian journals and sacred music concerts, so this new policy meant that the state had surrendered its monopoly over the press and media to its long-standing enemy.[148] Such changes could be seen in film as well. While GDR films produced in the 1950s and 1960s studiously avoided religious themes to avoid offending religious sensibilities after the introduction of the Jugendweihe, religious figures were recast as sympathetic figures over the course of the 1970s.[149] Luther himself went from being a 'traitor against the peasants' in 1950s television to a symbol of unified German history.[150]

The 1975 Helsinki Accords marked a watershed in these developments. While much of their discussion was on international security, cultural exchange, and travel rights, religion played a key role too. The Basket III agreements, which covered human rights issues, boosted church resistance, in that they now had a new language to couch and defend their freedoms. Progressive pastors frequently invoked the 'right to freedom of conscience' in Article 7 of the Accords to justify their criticisms, endeavouring to shame the state into honouring its signed pledges.[151] The Jugendweihe was now portrayed as a human rights abuse,[152] as was mandatory military service.[153] Church leaders took issue with the GDR's official line that human rights were basic social rights (such as the right to work and education) granted by the state as a reward for fulfilled socialist duties and obligations. Instead, they countered that human rights were not contingent on the social system, as argued by the SED, but were in fact 'God-given' natural rights. Other reformers argued that, since socialist states concentrated exclusively on social rights, the Church should be more involved in protecting individual rights. The galvanizing effect of the Helsinki Accords on the churches was duly noted by the Stasi, especially in terms of the church leaders' new interest in intensifying contacts with international networks and expanding the political role of the churches in society.[154] The Stasi was not wrong to see that the Accords signalled a pivotal moment in the Church's effort to 'pluralize' GDR society by gaining more latitude and public presence, often in the form of exchanges with Christian scholars, Christian reading clubs, etc. While the Stasi had been reporting on the dangerous invocation of human rights language in church sermons and circulars since the early 1970s, this rhetoric multiplied after 1975.[155] By the early 1980s the Stasi nervously observed that the Accords had provided the Church with the chance to position itself as the guardian and promoter of human rights in the GDR as never before.[156] This effort to create a stronger Christian public sphere went hand in hand with renewed claims to moral universalism, subjecting the state to a moral trial on issues ranging from Christian constitutional rights to environmentalism. As a consequence, the Church was growing as a political force, having been transformed from an enclave of internal exile to a new centre of public moral authority.

With time the churches felt more emboldened to criticize the state, and did so with the issues of censorship, the environment, and the peace movement. The GDR green movement flourished under Lutheran auspices, and the expansion of a non-military *Bausoldaten* programme was a major Christian initiative of the 1980s. By that time the Lutheran Church had become the umbrella for various dissident activities, as it addressed the concerns of young people in terms of sexuality, alcoholism, popular music, and the militarization of society. There was also great concern about 'nonconformist' pacifists and *Bausoldaten*.[157] Progressive pastors took pains to take in homosexuals and other social outsiders, who were otherwise shunned by GDR state and society.[158] The churches often agreed to host events for 'longhairs' and disgruntled youth, turning over the church to rock and punk venues. As one leading East German punker reminisced, the GDR was the only place in the world where punk rock was played before the crucifix.[159] The Church was also stepping up its media presence, founding new journals (*Streiflichter*, or Searchlights) and libraries (Berlin's Umweltbibliothek, for example) to link dissident groups across the country.

But while the official relationship between church and state thawed considerably over the 1970s, the situation on the ground remained largely unchanged for ordinary Christians. Many Stasi reports were filed on 'non-cooperative' pastors, and house searches continued to seize subversive material (books, music) on suspicion of wrongdoing.[160] Pastors and their wives were prohibited from serving on Parent Associations, lest they criticize the treatment of Christians in the education system. Anxiety towards Christian believers was still palpable, most notably in the Church's supposed 'anticommunist tendencies, especially among youth gatherings'.[161] The state also stepped up its campaign of taking the Jugendweihe campaign into family households, to the extent that the goal was 'that no family goes without reading and discussing the commemorative book *Weltall, Erde, Mensch*.[162] Pressure on parents went unchanged, as those pupils who didn't participate in the Jugendweihe (and this included both Protestants and Catholics) were ostracized by teachers and other pupils as unwanted outsiders. Moreover, the SED continued to hassle aspiring party members, forcing them to leave their congregations and to remove their children from church influence if they wished to advance in their careers. They were also discouraged from taking Christian partners. In the early 1970s youth magazines such as *Junge Welt* devoted discussions to whether Christian and Marxist 'worldviews' could be reconciled, often recommending that love and happiness were 'almost impossible' as a result of the 'clash of exclusionary worldviews like the materialist and religious ones'.[163] In the following issue, *Junge Welt* published a flurry of letters from readers, most of which confirmed the article's claims about not taking up serious relationships with Christians.[164] West German journalists expressed outrage about the GDR state's incursion into the private sphere of love and friendship,[165] though it hardly stopped similar articles from being published in the 1980s.

The Christian household remained a key battleground between state and church. By the 1970s the situation had become a kind of war of position, in which the Church had to defend its spaces of freedom. Bishop Schönherr made this explicit at the time, claiming that the home needed to be defended as a 'relatively free space for Christian education'.[166] Pastors often conducted regular house visits to their parishioners to discuss their concerns (and fears) about how to sustain their Christian identity in an increasingly hostile Marxist society.[167] With it came a trend towards the privatization of faith. By the early 1970s the churches' one-time adversarial ethos seemed moribund. As one Zurich reform pastor who frequently visited the GDR caustically noted: 'In the claim that religion is a private affair, Eastern bloc communisms and Western bourgeois society are united.'[168] One West German reporter wrote that the withdrawal of Christians to small niches (*Raum-Erleben*) was especially notable in the GDR, wherein Christians lived in a 'holy Christian world consciously set against the unholy world outside'. For him, these believers behaved like the middle classes in the 1930s, nursing 'fantasies of yesteryear' (*Heimatsträume*) for compass and comfort, taking shelter 'behind the Christian tradition of belief, teaching and activity'. There was 'little missionary steadfastness' any longer, as the Church had become a protective *Rüststätte*.[169] If nothing else, it points out the tenor of much of Christian life at the time, as Christians often retreated into dreamworlds of tradition and defensive ritual. But all were not so resigned, as some greeted the privatized world of the Church as a kind of virtue in itself. As one pastor put it, the 'space of the church can function as a kind of refilling station, an oasis. It allows for an attitude of responsibility toward the world in which he or she lives.'[170] Other pastors remarked on the positive side of this 'retreat into the private' for its 'honesty' and idealism.[171] By the early 1980s there were even reports of rising numbers of baptisms and confirmations across the GDR;[172] 'religiosity' was apparently back on the rise, especially among young people who often joined the Church to overcome social alienation.

Just as religious life was changing, so too had the Jugendweihe. By the 1970s the youth dedication was becoming a convivial *Volkssitte* family celebration drained of its former solemnity and ideological verve. For most people it was an event associated with gifts for the initiates: bicycles, leather bags, jewelry, mopeds, new clothes, and stereo equipment, often costing parents a month's salary. The symbolic imminent departure of the child from the parental home was accompanied by the accumulation of new capital, usually in the form of household goods (linens), consumer toys, and/or money.[173] The state conceded this crass commercialization of the Jugendweihe, issuing yearly recommendations on what to wear for the event.[174] Annual fashion shows were held for the event at Berlin's Kongresshalle from 1966 onward to showcase new looks for the event.[175] One 1975 *Stern* article, cheekily entitled 'Marx on the tongue, Moped on the Brain!', mocked the once-hallowed Jugendweihe as a 'great consumer show', what 'people have long deemed the 'mini-wedding'. With relish it noted that 'the gifts, especially cash, had much more meaning than the ritual's ideological content'.[176] A similar sentiment could be found in the GDR press as well: in one 1977 'diary extract' from a 14-year-old boy published in a leading pedagogical journal, the pupil freely admitted that the Jugendweihe was ultimately about gifts and drinking, 'since one is allowed beer and schnapps as a new member of society'.[177] Not that such views were warmly greeted in all quarters: articles sternly reminded parents about the larger socialist ideals of the Jugendweihe.[178] Nevertheless, the materialization of Jugendweihe, as one 1984 article coyly put it, was a sign of the times of the 'secularization of socialism', a telling symptom of the decline of the ascetic ethos that had sustained the postwar generation.[179]

Figure 7. *Eulenspiegel* Magazine Cover, 16/1979.

The changes could be noted in the visual representations too. As already noted, the solemn, public, and socialist aspects of the ritual were always foregrounded in the GDR press in the 1950s and 1960s. This shifted markedly in the 1970s. In a special 1974 issue of *Für Dich* commemorating the twentieth anniversary of the Jugendweihe, it was not only the showy appearance—and fashion—of the event that was highlighted. The issue was also characterized by more intimate shots of pupils among friends spending time together in anticipation of their coming of age rite of passage, recalling a US high school yearbook-style aura of relaxed informality and budding adulthood.[180] The materialist dimension of the Jugendweihe was now openly acknowledged, even finding its way to a 1979 cover cartoon of the GDR's leading satirical weekly, *Eulenspiegel*. Figure 7 makes no bones about revealing the main meaning of the event for most people, as it depicted people queuing up in line to give the new initiate cash and gifts for his rite of passage. Furthermore, the changing visual imagery could also be seen in the way that the significance of the event lay in its private family celebration at home, not in public ritual performance. The official celebration at the town hall still went on with its weary speech-giving, to be sure, but this was generally dismissed as the wooden Orwellian language of SED state-speak. The transformation of the Jugendweihe as essentially a family event with little connection to the state reflected the large trend towards to the retreat from collective culture already under way since the 1970s across the GDR. This was registered in 1970s press photographs, as seen in Figure 8, as the event's political aspects—including links to socialist mission and leadership—had dropped away

(a)

(b)

Figure 8. Jugendweihe Celebration at Home, 1973.

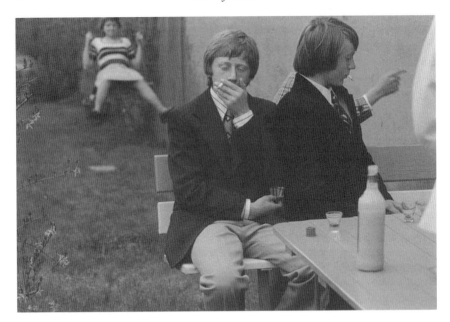

Figure 9. Werner Mahler, *Jugendweihe*, Berka, 1978.

in a spirit of teenage intimacy and conviviality. The unflattering reality of the Jugendweihe was best captured in a 1978 photograph by Werner Mahler, who depicted the fest as essentially one of debauched drinking and smoking among East German youth (Figure 9). If nothing else, such images confirm the extent to which the GDR's socialist coming of age rite, originally conceived of as a ritual to better bind youth and state, had taken on a life of its own, having been remade as a milestone of personal passage, material acquisition, and family solidarity.

The privatization of social life only increased in the 1980s. This was widely remarked on at the time, most famously by West German writer Günter Gaus in his 1983 *Wo Deutschland liegt*. In the GDR death too was becoming more and more of a 'private affair'.[181] On one level, this could be seen in the fact that church burials remained disproportionally high in relation to church membership. While only 7 per cent of East Berliners remained members of Protestant Church by 1986,[182] some 30–40 per cent still received church funerals until 1989.[183] Notable too is that the 1980s saw a new trend toward individualizing death, as families had vases embossed with the deceased's name and dates of birth and death as surrogate gravestones. Apparently this spoke of a popular disenchantment towards all collective rituals of death, be they socialist or religious, as more and more people opted for silent funerals.[184] Similar trends towards the 'silencing' of death rites were also noted in West Germany as well.[185] The de-Christianization of West German society thus went hand in hand with the decommunization of the GDR, as both societies were turning away from their collectivist cold war cosmologies of order and meaning. In this regard, the persistence of the Jugendweihe in East Germany long after the demise of the GDR betrayed a similar trend. In 1990, for example, 75 per cent of GDR 14 year olds still underwent the Jugendweihe, despite the collapse of the state,[186] and such rates continued through the 1990s. At the very least, this showed that the socialist coming of age ritual had long shed its prescribed socialist meaning, having been recast as a cherished folk festival and privatized family celebration.

In the end, the GDR's church–state conflict revealed a good deal about changing values in Europe. The new clamour for rights may be seen as part of a larger sociological shift across North America and Europe as a whole in the late 1970s, as new levels of prosperity brought in its train a shift of social emphasis from material interests (physical reconstruction, work, performance, diligence) to the pursuit of 'post-material' values (freedom, rights, self-realization, etc).[187] Such trends took root in Eastern Europe as well, as the Helsinki-inspired 'rights culture' there surely attests. But this had serious implications for socialism. After all, socialism began historically as a materialist philosophy and remained so through to the end, as its zealous oppositional ideology and ascetic ethos faded in the face of spiralling citizen demands for consumer comforts and material improvement. Indeed, it is worth noting that the Church had most trouble keeping its parishioners when state ideology competed with it as an alternative worldview in the 1950s and 1960s, when the SED offered a brave new world of devotion, self-sacrifice, redemption, and even eschatology beyond the demands for food and shelter. The heady invention of socialist customs to replace traditionally Christian rites of passage (marriage, baptism, funerals, and of course the Jugendweihe itself) betrayed this broader vision of socialist world-building. But this effort to sustain a new socialist cosmos had faded markedly by the 1970s, and socialist welfare was all but reduced to discussions about services and stuff. The state's victory in introducing the Jugendweihe was thus a Pyrrhic one, in that it pointed up how its worldview had been hollowed out by rote routine, spiritual indifference, and material desire. After 1989 it was often pointed out that the supposedly secular East Germans were the ones who 'still adhered to the classic "Christian" values of nonmaterialism, care for others, and concern about social justice'.[188] Such an irony may testify to the limits of communist ideology and the persistent power of Christian values in East German society. But it also goes some way in revealing how the citizenry was good at remaking both socialist and Christian customs to their own ends.

Secondly, this chapter sheds some light on the nature of the so-called 'niche society' in the GDR. Given its status as an unwanted tradition and alternative subculture, the Evangelical Church served as the GDR's original niche society long before it was labelled as such. Its career under communism shows that even this relatively closed-off subculture was never removed from public life and the directives of socialist society, but rather was significantly shaped by them. It was never sealed off from the outer world, and remained in constant dialogue with the atheistic state, as even its rituals and messages were shamelessly pirated by the state to serve socialist ends, as the Jugendweihe neatly illustrates. If anything, the Church served as a kind of semi-permeable institution that occupied an awkward but crucial place in GDR state and society, a Christian archipelago of churches, homes, and private networks. No other body mediated public and private sphere in this way, as the 'right to free conscience' furnished the Church with its *raison d'être* and secret moral authority. Ultimately it embodied the paradoxical nature of the niche society itself, and nowhere was this more dramatic than with the churches.

Finally and perhaps most importantly, a good deal of the historiography written after the fall of the Berlin Wall has tended to evaluate the Church's role in society in terms of how it contributed—or not—to the events of 1989. Much of the early focus after 1989 was on judging the Church and its leaders, particularly in terms of just how much the Stasi had penetrated its organiza-tion.[189] But this has led to a simplification of church–state history in the GDR, which has often romanticized the more politically engaged church of the 1970s and 1980s, while consigning its pre-1969 phase to a sad tale of persecution, withdrawal, and even cowardice in face of an overbearing state. After 1989 the Church's more visible 'turning out in the world' during the 1970s and 1980s was heralded as the roots of a nascent civil society in the GDR, showing how this powerful NGO eroded state sovereignty through the use of a new language of rights and morality.[190] According to this logic, the closed-off possibility of 'exit' (the building of the Wall in 1961 as well as the 1969 abandonment of formal ties to the West German Evangelical Church) gave rise to more 'voice' (increased political presence and post-Helsinki civil rights engagement on a number of fronts). Looking at religious life at the local level, however, reveals that these large changes did not affect ordinary Christians all that dramatically, as their lives were in fact characterized by greater continuities over the decades.

What this chapter reveals is that the concepts of the niche society and civil society are not inherently contradictory, and that it is misleading to suggest that civil society begins where the niche society ends. After all, the privatization of faith was itself a political stance to build a new niche society as a defence against socialist state and society. Much of its power therefore lay in its invisibility, as it was all but driven from the public sphere into private homes and behind church walls. But this turn inward did not necessarily mean that the Church had become apolitical, only to 'rediscover' its mission in the world in the 1970s and 1980s. It was precisely this relationship between secrecy and liberty that sustained the Church, as it provided a world of 'as if' moral universalism for its members from the very beginning. Linking secrecy and freedom is not all that strange histori-cally, as recent research on the Freemasons, for example, has made clear.[191] After all, it was in the absolutist political cultures of the seventeenth and eighteenth centuries where these secret societies first flourished as the germs of civil society.

As Reinhart Koselleck cogently put it, 'freedom in secret became the secret of freedom'.[192] As a consequence, the assumed elective affinity between civil society and the public sphere does not obtain in non- or anti-liberal societies, and the career of the Evangelical Church in the GDR is a good reminder of the need to move beyond this liberal prejudice. Indeed, one could argue that the 'outward turn' of the 1970s and 1980s was only possible because the Church had sustained itself by turning inward in the 1950s and 1960s. The 1975 Helsinki Accords may have provided a new lexicon of grievances, and the pivotal 1978 agreement certainly helped propel the Church back into the public sphere. Yet the widely noted privatization of faith made later developments possible, and fuelled the moral universalism born of persecution and a relatively closed community. The career of the church as the GDR's original 'niche society' illustrates the effective coping strategies of organized religion amid the Stalinist neo-absolutist regimes East of Eden. The communist crusade against religion may have forced it into the private sphere, but in so doing, the socialist state, as Engels warned long ago, inadvertently helped 'it to martyrdom and a prolonged lease on life'.[193] However, the Stasi and the Church were not the only social organizations straddling the border of secret society, public institution, and the private sphere; the next chapter addresses perhaps the most intimate one of all: marriage.

3

Intimacy on Display

Getting Divorced in East Berlin

Welt-niveau, or 'world-class,' was one of the most cherished adjectives in GDR parlance, conveying the regime's abiding obsession with trumpeting the regime's global accomplishments in economics, politics, and culture. But despite the state's repeated boasts of global arrival and achievement, the GDR's much-coveted world-class status was unfortunately only attained in a few dubious areas: competitive sports, suicides, and divorce rates.[1] This chapter will focus on the last one, as the frequency and ease of divorce became one of the distinguishing traits of GDR socialism. From the 1950s to the 1970s, divorce rates rose 20 per cent across the country, and leapt 35 per cent in the capital.[2] Roughly one-third more divorces occurred in East Germany than in West Germany over the decades;[3] internationally, the GDR ranked fifth in the world in divorces per 10,000 inhabitants, lagging only behind the US, the USSR, Cuba, and Great Britain.[4] It is tempting to read these startling divorce rates as proof of a kind of 'special path' development for East German socialism. Yet this is not very tenable. For one thing, research has shown that German divorce statistics actually reflect older regional patterns long before the Second World War, as religion, class, and urbanization remained the key determinants for the comparatively high occurrence of East German divorces from the late nineteenth century onward.[5] For another, the two rival republics experienced quite similar trends in the intensity of (and stated reasons for) divorce from the early 1950s to the late 1980s, betraying what is sometimes called a shared ideology of 'egalitarianism in private life' on both sides of the Berlin Wall.[6]

Over the years, much has been made of interpreting divorce as a key indication of secularization, modernization, and the 'desolidification of society' in international perspective.[7] European society was affected in similar ways across the cold war divide, and East Germany was no exception. But this chapter is not a macro-level discussion of the frequency and causes of marital breakdown in the GDR.[8] Rather, my focus is on the public presentation of private domestic problems in court, based on the analysis of some 1,500 never before used East Berlin divorce records. They reveal a great deal about the intimate nature and conflicting expectations of East German family life. While East Berlin was not exactly typical—the capital's divorce rate was twice the national average—the city's divorce court records afford insights into common trends across the country. My approach also parts company from other studies of East German divorce in allowing those involved—judges and spouses—to articulate their views in court. What makes these divorce court records so valuable is the way in which they cast light on the shifting articulation of the 'private good', showing how the moral sphere of the family served as a crucible for the changing understanding of marriage within socialism.

MARRIAGE AND MODERNITY

In 1982 a West German journalist made the following observation about GDR social life: 'Socialist society is increasingly oriented toward marriage... "True life" takes place in the family, in the private sphere. A person's work life and individual development are of secondary importance, as the harmony of the couple is of uppermost concern. Men and women are tired from work as well as from the battle of the sexes, and thus seek in their partners protection from the hard demands of everyday life.'[9] At first glance such a comment seems hardly new, extending many of Günter Gaus's widely circulated views at the time—as noted in the Introduction—about East Germany's cultivated 'niche society' and remarked retreat into the private sphere. The telling difference in this instance, however, is the accent placed on marriage and the couple's intimate life as the main refuge from the demands and directives of socialist collectivity. This is something that is borne out in the literature on the 1970s and 1980s, and something I frequently noted while conducting interviews about people's family lives in the GDR.

Historians have long understood that the family was often closely bound up with the formation, maintenance, and self-image of the state, even to the point of serving as a principal metaphor of its ideal of intimate community. This logic was hardly unique to Germany, shaping as it did the political thought and cultural imagination of modern states everywhere. Even so, the family–state nexus has been a powerful one in German history. At no time was this more pronounced than after 1945, especially in West Germany.[10] During the first decade of the Federal Republic, the reconstruction of the state was closely linked to the reconstruction of the family as a key instance of the 'search for normality', as a strong and stable family was hailed as a bulwark against the Nazi past and a potentially communist future.[11] But this was not just state ideology. Oral histories conducted later confirmed the extent to which the family emerged for postwar survivors—especially women—as 'an obligation, a fantasy, and a project', a 'concrete utopia' that promised 'warmth, understanding and help, simplicity, fairness and protection' after the war.[12] The same went for war victims; in displaced persons camps, for example, there was a rush to get married and have children as a 'conscious affirmation of Jewish life' and the 'reconstruction of collective, national and individual identity' based on family and reproduction.[13]

Such attitudes are not commonly associated with the East, however. After all, was it not precisely the private family sphere that was supposedly undermined by the all-pervading state? Many GDR initiatives aimed to break down the distinction between public and private life, and marriage was no exception. Citizens, for example, were entreated to get married within enterprises as a way of better linking work life and family,[14] and wedding speeches often made plain the relationship between marital union and larger socialist goals.[15] Marriage was thus by no means seen as a sphere closed to society and larger political imperatives, but in fact was a key instance of them. In this conception, marriage was as much about service and debt to society as it was about private affection, wherein the partners were just as linked to the state as to each other.

This may not seem all that surprising. From the very beginning, the notion that the family served as the bedrock of socialist society and happiness was broadcast as one of the foundational elements of the new socialist state. As opposed to the early Soviet Union, which crusaded for the dissolution of the family as a precondition for building up communist society, the GDR never strayed from its insistence on marriage and family as the true building blocks of socialism. The GDR's 1950 Mother and Child Protection Law, for example, stated that 'a healthy family is one of the fundamental pillars of a democratic society. Its fortification is one of the most important tasks of the government of the GDR.'[16] The GDR's 1968 Constitution continued in this vein, proclaiming in Article 38 that 'marriage, family and motherhood stand under the special protection of the state. Every citizen enjoys the right to the respect, protection and promotion of his/her marriage and family.' Not that this was unique to East Germany: Article 6, paragraph 1, of West Germany's 1949 Basic Law stated that 'Marriage and family stand under the special protection of the public order (*staatliche Ordnung*)', illustrating the degree to which the wartime geopolitical dream of *Lebensraum* (living space) in Eastern Europe now gave way to what West German Family Minister Franz-Josef Würmerling revealingly called the 'inviolability of the *Lebensraum* of the family'.[17] In the GDR, however, the family was to assume its place alongside the workplace as the primary site of socialist personality formation.

The extent to which the family was actually an extension of the regime is still a matter of dispute. While some have argued that the family became a real locus of privacy, a kind of 'counterworld' respite from the collective demands of socialist public life, others have maintained that socialist families were nothing but the 'instumentalized life sphere' of state control.[18] The truth is naturally somewhere in between. Given their long workdays, social demands, schooling and childcare arrangements, GDR families may have spent less time together than their West German equivalent, but this is not to say that their families were somehow less meaningful. Families there too were places of intensively felt experiences, the primary location of love, intimacy, and private emotions. This is something the GDR state cultivated as distinctive of socialism. Indeed, the ideal of marriage based on love and mutual respect harked back to Engels's 1884 *Origins of the Family, Private Property, and the State*, in which he argued that marriage under capitalism was always an economic arrangement of exploitation that would cease in a world of post-capitalist property relations. Only then would it be freed of economic motives, and returned to the world of emotions, morality, and social values.

Traditional German marital law did not see things this way. While Germany's legal understanding of marriage derived from ancient Germanic law, the Protestant Reformation ushered in fundamental changes. With it marriage was no longer recognized as a sacrament but rather a worldly union, what Luther called a 'weltlich Ding' protected by the state. Yet it was the French Revolution that most fundamentally changed German marital law, recasting marriage as a secular civil contract. By 1794 Prussia led the way in redefining marriage accordingly in its Allgemeines Preussisches Landrecht; other German lands, too, rewrote their marriage laws along the lines of Napoleon's 1804 Civil Code, legislating French-style family law reforms in the first decades of the early nineteenth century.[19] The legal notion of marriage as a civil contract remained in place until the passage of the landmark German Civil Code (BGB) in 1900, which was the first attempt to standardize marriage and divorce law at the national level. It echoed a strong Protestant tradition, and sought to ground marriage as the main pillar of moral and social order. The Civil Code was a distinctly patriarchal document, one that reflected the distinctively middle-class gender expectations of the time. In it men featured as free citizens, while their wives were subject to almost feudal constraints.[20] Husbands were 'heads of household', while their wives were expected to 'manage the common household'.[21] As a result, the 1900 code made plain that women's legal and economic standing mostly depended on their marital status. In terms of divorce law, it introduced the principle of the 'guilty spouse' (*Verschuldensprinzip*) as the central criterion for divorce, which shaped German divorce proceedings for the next two generations.

With time the marital code was criticized as reactionary and out of step with the modern world, especially after the outbreak of the First World War. After 1914 marriages were often hastily arranged and frequently estranged due to wartime problems, thus vitiating the moral and legal basis of the newly established 'fault-principle.' Divorces skyrocketed to record levels, as marriages collapsed under the strain of the war and its immediate aftermath.[22] In the 1920s leaders from both the Union of German Women's Associations (BDF) and the Communist Party found common cause in agitating for reform of the BGB's divorce law in the Reichstag, calling for more flexible notions of divorce in the form of a no-fault 'breakdown principle'. Unhappy unions, so they argued, could and should be dissolved if both parties consented, sparing their private lives from public court scrutiny. However, their parliamentary reform campaign foundered in the face of strong resistance from the churches, which felt that such 'modern' principles would undermine the moral sanctity and social meaning of marriage in German society.[23]

The Nazi era radicalized marriage in fundamentally new ways. Above all the Third Reich placed marital union under the sign of racial hygiene and the state's protection and promotion of the vaunted 'national community'. Overseeing the quantity and quality of German offspring became a mandate of the Third Reich, effectively undermining the nineteenth-century division between public and private.[24] In so doing it effectively 'deprivatized' marriage by subordinating an autonomous contract between two people to the ideals and dictates of the 'racial state'.[25] Divorce in the Third Reich was more complicated, however. After 1933 there was a huge spike in divorces in spite of the regime's family values rhetoric. This was partly the result of the state's effort to disband 'racially defiled' marriages or childless unions for reasons of race.[26] To expedite matters, the infamous Nazi Marriage Law of 1938 rewrote divorce law according to eugenic considerations, removing the reigning 'fault principle' from the 1900 Civil Code in favour of a new no-fault marital 'breakdown principle', or *Zerrüttungsprinzip*. While the 'breakdown principle' was the brainchild of leftist parliamentarians during the 1920s, the Nazis reformulated this idea to their own ends. Even 'Aryan' women who had fulfilled their duties as a wife (including having had children) could find themselves divorced if the courts believed that more children could be had in a new marriage.[27] As a consequence, divorce was easier to obtain after 1938, as couples who had not lived together for three years could be divorced, just as childless marriages could be dissolved in the name of the regime's population policy.[28] Moreover, adultery, traditionally the main criterion of divorce, was no longer recognized as an automatic ground for marital dissolution, but now depended on circumstances and above all the judge's discretion.[29] The point is that the Third Reich untethered the 'breakdown principle' from its original 'individual-liberal' spirit by linking it instead to racial politics.[30] So for all of its propaganda about upholding the traditional family, the regime actually undermined it almost beyond recognition.

THE INTERREGNUM

After 1945 there was a concerted effort to break from this Nazi legacy. In postwar marital law all references to racial hygiene were duly expunged, as was childlessness as actionable grounds for divorce. Hitler's assertion that 'marriage cannot be an end in itself, but must serve the one higher goal, the increase and preservation of the species and the race' was rejected out of hand, even if the call to produce more babies for the state lived on long after the demise of the Third Reich.[31] After 1945 divorce law essentially reverted to the 1900 German Civil Code, though its traditional 'fault' ideology was in practice slowly abandoned in the face of postwar physical destruction, social dislocation, homelessness, poverty, and widespread misery.[32] The no-fault principle was also seen as the most effective means of dealing with the fallout resulting from countless marriages made hastily during the war. After 1939, for example, the regime permitted soldiers on the front line to marry their fiancées simply by letter or formal declaration, since it was often difficult in wartime to make arrangements for the couple to be together. This was sanctioned to encourage as many couples as possible to marry for both morale and the production of (legitimate) offspring, and 40 per cent of German couples married in this way in 1939 and 1940.[33] In 1941 a Führer's decree consecrated these so-called 'postmortem marriages' after the fiancé had died in battle; some 18,000 women (many already mothers) applied for this so as to qualify for widows' benefits and legitimize their children,[34] in effect making widows out of women never before married.

In the wake of war it was no surprise that the reasons for marital breakdown were legion. Millions had died or were badly injured; homes were destroyed; and partners who hadn't seen each other in years were often traumatized by war violence and defeat, sick or maimed, and were fundamentally changed people, mostly for the worse. But this all paled in comparison to the violence visited upon women at the end of the war. In fact, it is estimated that a third of Berlin women—out of population of 1.5 million—were raped by Soviet troops,[35] apparently as a 'weapon of revenge' for Wehrmacht actions in the USSR.[36] Mass rape traumatized women's lives, and often alienated their husbands, especially returning POWs. Resuming relationships under these circumstances was difficult and troubling, to say the least. Physicians and social workers drily reported that 'wives often rejected the sexual advances of unsightly husbands, and husbands refused to live with violated wives'. Many had also taken comfort in new lovers during the war, adding to marital strain.[37] Such a legacy did not disappear quickly. One Leipzig physician described the aftereffects of war in GDR private life as late as 1952: 'The wreckage field of the Second World War stretches into that region where interhuman relations are most frequently realized . . . namely into that of sexual life.'[38]

Scattered divorce court files also reveal harrowing pictures of Berlin in 1945, complete with burnt-out buildings, broken families, and the desperate struggle for food and shelter. There was an overwhelming sense of emotional stress and fatigue from all parties, including the judges, all of whom sought a speedy and peaceful resolution. Under these conditions, there was little in the way of remaking character and using the divorce court setting as a forum to shore up social values and the community. In the wake of war, little state effort was made to keep marriages together at all. Cases were full of stories of returning soldiers who found their wives living with other men; wives who discovered their husband's wartime love letters to other women; disputes over ration cards, as angry husbands often kept food vouchers from their wives as blackmail; or of spouses finding their partners living rough amid the ruins of the city, often alone, sometimes with others, ill, violent, and mentally unbalanced.[39] Testimonies of violence and abuse were rife, as the traumatic effects of defeat and its aftermath found expression in intimate marital relations and on women's bodies, sometimes so bad that the 'marks of abuse could be seen days later all over her body'.[40] At times Russian soldiers found their way into the proceedings, especially if the wife had taken up a relationship with one of them.[41] While stories of the rape and abuse of German women at the hands of the Red Army have come to light in recent years as a tragic effect of the endgame of the Second World War, it is less known there was a good deal of German–Russian fraternization.

In light of 1945 circumstances, it is no great surprise that divorces were quickly dispatched. There were some 29,494 divorces in the Soviet Occupied Zone in 1947, rising to 49,860 by 1950. Adultery, abandonment, mental abuse, domestic violence, and neglect were catalogued as the formal reasons for 'marital injury' or breakdown claims, and were listed as the principal criteria for granting divorce under the terms of the 1900 German Civil Code. Aggrieved partners even hired detectives to spy on accused spouses to strengthen their cases.[42]

Striking were the patriarchal attitudes among those involved in divorce proceedings, including the judges. Returning soldiers were not shy in voicing their anger at unfaithful wives, often drawing on war service as moral support. One August 1945 case, in which a returning soldier discovered love letters at home from four different soldiers, emphasized that while he 'unflaggingly stood down the enemy', his wife by contrast 'was enjoying herself in relations with other men'. No doubt this was a common refrain from returning German soldiers, who often claimed that while German men held out against the enemy for five years, German women, faced with exotic and attractive Allied Occupation soldiers, surrendered after only a few minutes.[43] But here the problem concerned other German soldiers. In this case, his wife insisted that these were mere friendships, though she admitted that she kissed one of them at the movies. The judge issued the verdict in almost Victorian language: 'If the defendant during her marriage has on several occasions gone out with another man and permitted herself to be kissed several times, she has long ago trespassed the limit of maintaining her marital duties.'[44] Another 1945 case lodged by an aggrieved husband condemned his wife's allegedly 'anti-marital behaviour', meaning that she 'was not fulfilling her obligations as a housewife' in cooking and cleaning for him.[45]

In fact, the incidence of husbands suing for divorce owing to the dirty condition of the home and the wife's failure to care for them accounted for roughly 15–20 per cent of cases between 1945 and 1950. Clearly wives and husbands brought with them certain expectations based on conventional codes of behaviour. The problem of the 'asocial' wife and bad housekeeper, for example, found wide reception during the Nazi years, drawing on nineteenth-century ideals of propriety and femininity.[46] Such traditional images were especially pronounced among returning POWs, whose ideals of home and domesticity were shattered on returning home.[47] Cut off from Germany and unaware of conditions back home, German war prisoners in the Soviet Union often 'dreamed of the wealthy, orderly and comfortable surroundings they recalled from their civilian days'.[48] They were rudely shocked when they managed to make it back to Berlin. In one 1948 case, a husband filed suit because his wife had 'neglected her duties as housewife in the most offensive way. She is completely untidy and lets the house get totally dirty . . . She puts little effort in cooking and does not attend to washing my clothes.' The husband's brother, mother, and niece were brought in to testify to the unkempt quality of the home. His wife tersely replied that it was difficult to maintain the household when it was so badly bombed, and that she was doing her utmost to 'keep things in order', even bringing in her own mother to attest that the place was tidy and that she was looking after the children properly.[49] Household negligence was not sufficient grounds to win a divorce claim, and at best was used as supplementary evidence of the marital state. But the strong presence of the theme in postwar courtrooms illustrated that patriarchal notions of marital order very much survived the war, and were only intensified by wartime experience and suffering.[50]

DIVORCE IN THE NEW REPUBLIC

After 1949 East German divorce proceedings were a mix of old and new. To the mid-1950s, men submitted slightly more divorce claims than women, but by 1958 women filed the majority of divorces, and this increased with time. After 1945 the main criterion was still adultery, proven by the fact that one partner was living with a new partner, or that the act of infidelity had ruined marriage to such an extent that the 'restoration of the essence of marriage as a healthy living community (*Lebensgemeinschaft*) was no longer possible'. Insults, defamation, and domestic violence were frequently mentioned as key causes as well.[51] Numerous early 1950s cases pivoted on men not paying rent and driving the family into debt, thus making life impossible for the wife and family.[52] Judges generally would not hear cases unless the couple had 'attempted reconciliation' at a counselling centre (*Sündestelle*), reviving a German tradition stretching back to the late nineteenth century.[53] But there were signs of change too. For one thing, religious affiliation—always noted in pre-1949 cases—was replaced by work designation. The GDR also broke from the German tradition (which continued in West Germany through the 1970s) of designating female spouses simply as *Ehefrau* or *Hausfrau*; in GDR divorce cases, women's professional standing was consciously noted, so that the files read for example Carpenter K versus Tailor K, Telegraph-Inspector Hermann B versus Seamstress Hertha B. Included in the file was a one to two page statement summarizing the facts and plaintiff's grounds for action, sometimes with accompanying personal letters and counterstatements. The public hearing took place with a judge, two jurists, and a stenographer. Witnesses were often summoned, and *Jugendhilfe* visits to the home (often by the jurists themselves) were accompanied by short reports. In the proceedings, the judge commonly asked the traditional question of when the last marital intercourse ('letzte eheliche Verkehr') had occurred as evidence of marital health, but this practice faded over time, and stopped being asked in the early 1970s. The verdict 'In the Name of the People!' appeared at top of the first page, with a brief summary of the facts, grounds for decision, legal justification, and relevant marital law cited. The plaintiff had the right to resubmit his/her case if the divorce was denied, upon which the case was reopened and rejudged. In fact, many divorce claims had been filed at least once before.

One thing that distinguishes the 1950s files from their 1945–9 predecessors is that they were thicker, and there was more concerted effort to reach reconciliation. There was a great deal of discussion about the state's obligation to protect and promote 'healthy' marriages and families. To be sure, health itself emerged as a key symbolic battleground in the cold war struggle between East and West Germany over which state actually offered its citizens the best living conditions. The GDR, for its part, never tired of broadcasting its welfare policies and universal health system as a sign of political legitimacy.[54] For East German authorities, health was often closely connected to productivity,[55] and this found its way into 1950s divorce proceedings. A partner's disinclination to work was duly noted as a key criterion of marital dissolution, for example.[56] In court plaintiffs often argued that the stress of a failing marriage was taking a heavy toll at work, underscoring the social effects of conjugal problems on their capacity as labourers. And it often proved a successful strategy. In a 1957 case a divorce was granted on account of a Berlin wife's serial philandering: 'The plaintiff's [husband] job as a locomotive driver is a heavy and responsible undertaking. For the replenishment of his work capacities it is necessary that his family relations are in order. It is not acceptable that he constantly must be confronted with the fear that his wife is conducting various affairs.'[57]

Yet it is not always so clear what 'healthy' meant exactly, as judges and jurists themselves were often unsure how to evaluate divorce claims.[58] Given the elasticity of these criteria, judges were given great latitude in weighing evidence and determining the health of the marriage. In a very real sense, these courts were understood as tribunes of moral education, and the judges as front-line social workers.[59] Just as the priest or pastor emerged as the key social player in mediating the intimate domestic life of couples in the late nineteenth century, to be replaced by the family doctor in the Nazi period, judges and social workers assumed this function in the GDR.[60] The code's ambiguous language granted a good deal of discretion to judges, whose decisions often varied considerably; for instance, it was easier to get a divorce in big cities, and divorce claims were filed more frequently in densely populated areas.

Such elasticity of terms effectively empowered courts to inquire into the intimate life of the couples in crisis. According to paragraph 8 of the 1955

Eheverordnung (Decree on Marriage and Divorce), a marriage could only be dissolved 'as a result of serious problems, and only after the court has conducted a thorough investigation into the personal and societal worth of the marriage, and has come to the conclusion that the marriage can no longer function as a foundation of communal life'. Often in the name of protecting children, the courts assumed a broad role. This often meant summoning neighbours, lovers, work colleagues, and even children to step forward and provide information about conflict, violence, and/or the character of those involved. Work colleagues were considered especially valuable witnesses, in that judges needed to know whether the problem marriage was exerting a deleterious effect on the estranged spouse's ability to work well. The intrusion into the intimate lives of couples was justified insofar as their marriage was of vital social interest, rendering the private sphere behind closed doors fair game for the court's inquisitive gaze. No doubt divorce courts everywhere are entrusted to investigate the roots of domestic conflict, often for the sake of the children; but the wide powers granted to these divorce courts was particularly socialist, and found real presence in the GDR. Such licence departed markedly from West German divorce courts, where spouses were given more latitude in deciding their marital fate before the judge. As a rejection of Nazi family policies, the Basic Law (Art. 6, para. 6) stated explicitly that spouses enjoyed 'a subjective public right of defense against the state's interference into their marital community'.[61] The GDR may have jettisoned race as the pretext for intervention, but 1950s GDR divorce courts saw the family as closely bound up with East German state and society.

By the mid-1950s, the GDR did move towards a more articulated set of criteria on divorce. The 1955 Eheverordnung, for instance, enshrined the more liberal 'breakdown principle' in GDR family courts, which had already become common practice since the late 1940s. It also emboldened courts to seek reconciliation of the partners whenever possible, reflecting the GDR's strong sentiment towards fruitful marriage as the very bedrock of the socialist state. The standard line that '[i]n the GDR and democratic sector of Berlin marriage is a consecrated community (*geschlossene Gemeinschaft*) for life between a man and woman' was taken very seriously. To this end it was not unusual for judges to call in many witnesses—sometimes up to eight—to look for reasons to keep couples together, especially if they surmised that the foundation of marriage seemed sound. Such attitudes were on display in one 1957 case in which a wife had grown estranged from her husband. She made clear that she never enjoyed sex with him, eventually had a short affair with a work colleague, and even was pregnant with his child; the husband forgave her, said that he would try harder to improve their sexual life, and was willing to help raise the child. As a result, her claim was denied by court on the grounds that such an affair—though not to be condoned—was not 'of such a serious nature to justify the claim for divorce', since this marriage 'had by no means lost its sense for the spouses or for society. The court expects that the plaintiff can bring her good will to the problem, and can work to stay together with her husband. If she has the will, this marriage can be restored in a completely harmonious manner.' A good dosage of will and a visit to the marriage counsellor, so went the logic, could fix whatever problems they faced. What is more, the judge continued, both parties had responsible posts and were members of the SED, suggesting that their 'worldviews were also in unison. Equality of the sexes is also respected, and there is evident mutual respect between the partners.' The wife's two additional appeals for divorce were denied, and the final verdict concluded by appealing to her role as a future mother: 'The difficulties that the plaintiff sees in her marriage are by no means insuperable. To overcome them—and this must be repeated and reemphasized—is an earnest obligation, which the plaintiff—in the interests of her expected child, whose upbringing in the family is to be assured—is to fulfill.'[62]

This impulse to intervene was also related to how the courts viewed the causes of social problems. Not unsurprisingly, they typically did not locate the roots of marital strife in the material conditions of the GDR. The SED's social policy and in particular the country's poor housing stock were rarely—and only obliquely— mentioned. (This was different for citizen complaint letters, as discussed in Chapter 6.) Everyone knew that young people usually got married and had children to try to secure a residence of their own, but even that did not always guarantee a couple their own place. Many thus were forced to continue to live with their parents, even after having children, which fuelled domestic tension. Moving from damp, ill-equipped homes to better, bigger residences was also very difficult. The lack of adequate childcare and state services in the 1950s also exacerbated marital problems. But such pressing material issues were largely ignored in the proceedings, as they were in the official literature. Instead, domestic strife was placed squarely on the shoulders of the individual, whose shortcomings were largely attributed to personal failures of character, underdeveloped (socialist) socialization, and residual 'capitalist values' of egotism and irresponsibility.[63] The difference, however, was that such 'anti-socialist' behaviour was seen as reformable, and the divorce courts saw themselves as crucial instances in the re-education of negligent spouses and irresponsible citizens.

Older marriages in particular were targeted for special protection. In 1957 the GDR's High Court added a new guideline to the 1955 Marriage Decree to discourage disbanding long marriages.[64] There were many cases in which the courts 'reminded' the couple in crisis about their long-functioning marriage, and that 'older marriages must be protected by the state'.[65] One 1957 case featured numerous problems for a couple who had been married for eighteen years—the last sexual act was recorded 'six or seven years ago', and the husband was now living with his new lover, who was pregnant with his child. Nevertheless, the husband's divorce application was rejected. The deciding factor was the moving speech given by the couple's daughter, who testified that she loved her father and wanted him to come home. In the end, the judge concluded that:

The existence of their long marriage [since 1939] alone speaks for the fact that the marriage is in need of protection. Their daughter B. made a good impression on the court . . . Our Workers'- and Peasants' State fights for the interests of children to maintain older marriages. Karl Marx had this in mind when he wrote that nobody is forced to get married, but when one does, then one must respect the rules: 'Whoever decides to get married cannot subordinate his marriage to his will, but rather his will to his marriage.' The complaint before us contravenes this notion.

While a lack of 'corporal contact' since 1950 was cited as proof of alienation, it was not deemed decisive, as was common in pre-1949 cases. The husband then filed a counterclaim, with a long written statement that his wife frequently insulted him with 'unspeakable expressions' in front of the child, which have undermined his paternal authority at home. Moreover, he contended that their daughter was misused in court, presenting letters from his daughter in which she called him a 'Lump' and did not really want to see him any more. With this new evidence, divorce was granted on the grounds that the husband was practically living elsewhere with someone else, was expecting a child with her, no longer wanted to be with his wife, and whose child was not as committed to her father as she testified in court. Whatever else can be said about it, the case did reveal the lengths to which courts were willing to go to keep couples together.[66]

Conversely, unhealthy marriages were quickly dissolved with the standard criterion that 'the restoration of the essence of marriage and its corresponding communal life can no longer be salvaged'.[67] This was especially true of cases marred by domestic abuse, even if the root causes and frequency were rarely taken up beyond the courts. Domestic violence was practically a taboo subject in the GDR, and found little public acknowledgement.[68] If anything, domestic violence—and criminality in general—were dismissed as residues of the pre-1949 past and the negative 'effects of the imperialist world',[69] and domestic violence cases were usually attributed to 'aberrant'—but not criminal—comportment. Not that this is unique to East Germany: for a century characterized by the full expansion of the state into all recesses of society, it is remarkable how little we know about the history of violence within families.[70] Still, violence did make its way into divorce proceedings. A mid-1950s case featured a desperate wife who, having filed unsuccessfully for divorce twice before, kept a running diary over months of when her husband went out, disregarded family life, and came home drunk, pleading that 'my nerves are so stretched that I beg you to free me from this person immediately, who has caused me so much suffering and depression'. Three home visits from the court representatives made no difference, and after 'hours-long discussions' with the defendant about his unemployment and alcoholism, the judge concluded that there was nothing to be done apart from granting the divorce.[71]

'Unhealthy marriages' often included conflicts of lifestyle. In some incidences, the cleanliness issue was reversed. Whereas many husbands returning from the war complained that their wives did not provide an orderly home for them, others in the 1950s claimed that their partners were neurotically clean. One estranged husband filed for divorce by saying that his wife was 'overly clean (*übersauber*), and drives me out of the house. I can't sit down anywhere; she is so clean that she makes me sick ... I can't wear my street shoes in the house ... We always argue about this at home ... and sometimes I go to Friedrichsstrasse train station to sleep so as to have some quiet.' At first glance this may look similar to the patriarchal claims made by husbands in the late 1940s; but this case pivoted less on expected wifely duties than her actions to undermine a 'marital community' based on mutual care and consideration. In this instance, the divorce was granted, as the judge declared that 'the marriage was sick', since seven years of marriage had produced no harmony.[72] The suitability of partners also exercised the courts, particularly in cases of glaring differences of age. In one 1957 case, the husband was 64 years old, the wife 23. The wife's claim pivoted on their growing incompatibility, and the judge in his verdict seemed disgusted by the 'severe age difference'. As noted in the verdict, the aggrieved young wife's colourful testimony of her much older husband's 'perverse sexual demands' (oral and anal sex) only confirmed the judge's strong moral views about the wrongfulness of this union.[73]

THE INTERVENTIONIST 1960s

Things shifted markedly in the 1960s. By this time the social revolution propagated for women was beginning to take hold: more married mothers were working full-time, and women were undergoing more vocational training and education for a lifetime of work. Indeed, women's employment became one of the defining issues in the cold war battle between the Germanies about which republic was delivering the good life. In 1950 GDR President Otto Grotewohl made this plain, declaring that 'When people say that women's honour is injured by their integration into the production process, then I'd like to say: one can impose nothing more dishonourable on a woman than to expect her to be her husband's unpaid maid.'[74] While divorce claims filed by men in the 1960s still occasionally betrayed patriarchical expectations about 'wifely duties' of care and consolation,[75] significant changes were afoot. After 1958, most appeals were filed by women, and this increased with time, going from 53 per cent in 1958 to over 64 per cent by 1972.[76] It is also more likely that marriages would end in divorce. Whereas in 1958 the chances that a suit would end in divorce were almost 60 per cent, they increased to 68 per cent by 1969.[77] In 1960s court proceedings, the majority of cases had to do with drunken husbands, many of whom were violent, adulterous, or living with new partners. (Violence was often noted with a red x in the margin of the judge's deposition.) Of the cases that I read, some three-quarters had to do with alcohol, while a third to a half reported physical abuse. By the 1960s domestic abuse started to be more reported in GDR records, even if obliquely, prompting more open discussion of such matters.[78] Naturally, it is hard to tell if the 1960s actually saw more domestic violence, or if only women felt more comfortable citing abuse as immediate grounds for divorce. Doubtless many women did not. Court records contained many cases of wives changing their minds and abandoning their claims. In the period 1958 to 1970, nearly 25 per cent of divorce claims were withdrawn without stated reasons.[79] In many cases this was most likely due to domestic pressure from their partners to do so, not least to avoid the shame and humiliation of exposing one's unsavoury private life to neighbours and co-workers. In one 1960 case of wife-beating, a Berlin wife terminated the proceedings with a handwritten letter to the court announcing 'My husband regrets everything, and has pledged to be a more reasonable man by above all giving up alcohol, which is the root cause of it all!', to which her husband added his own apology, laced with a barely veiled threat to his wife: 'From now on I will conduct myself in marriage as befits our state, and as a husband will behave in such a way that my wife will not come before the court again.'[80]

But this is not to suggest that divorces were easy to obtain. Even more so than in the 1950s, the 1960s witnessed redoubled effort to rehabilitate partners and to save marriages at risk. The new stepped-up intervention of the state into problem marriages was in part spurred by the passage of the landmark 1965 Family Law Book. It was the GDR's most far-reaching statement about the relationship between the family and the state, as well as that between family members. The preamble made clear that the family in the GDR was to serve as the 'smallest cell of society', one supposedly based on 'mutual love, respect and trust between all family members'. More concretely, the main thrust of the new family code was to link the family more with the state's creche, kindergarten, and school system; youth organizations; as well as housing communities, work environment, and collective existence more generally, as law would help bind people better with society and its standards of 'socialist morality'.

For 1960s divorce courts, their task was to apply these principles in the name of holding families together. Dossiers were noticeably thicker and casework more extensive, exhibiting a clear wish on the part of courts to get to the bottom of problems in order to solve them. Many neighbours were called as witnesses of marital estrangement, counselling centres were recommended, and great judicial energy was expended in investigating domestic conflicts and re-educating wayward citizens. Instead of looking away from the private troubles of friends, work colleagues, and neighbours, people were encouraged to get involved in their lives.[81] This was the great era of what Dorothee Wierling has called the 'didactic dictatorship' in the GDR, and divorce courts served as key welfare institutions to redress social problems at the most intimate level.[82]

Even the most cursory leafing through the divorce files makes plain just how communal these divorces often had become. Party organizations, trade unions, work collectives, and residential 'housing communities' were all entreated to get involved to help repair marriages in crisis. Cases commonly reported fifteen to twenty discussions with work colleagues and authorities on the theme of marital stability and social order.[83] Family disorder, to be sure, was a favourite cold war propaganda weapon in the 1950s and 1960s. The 'epidemic' of so-called latch-key children, for example, was publicized in both Germanies as evidence of the other rival republic's failed social system, whether as a symptom of absent mothers in the work-obsessed and callous East or as a symbol of parental neglect, moral insensitivity, and rampant egotism in the West.[84] The social danger and moral fallout of rising divorce rates in both countries in the 1960s attracted similar concern across the cold war divide, but the rates of failed marriages took on heightened gravity in the GDR. While courts in the 1950s were encouraged to 'take issue with citizens of our worker-and-peasants' state who do not under-stand how to maintain a proper and moral attitude toward their marriage and family',[85] this anxiety was dramatically intensified a decade later. A mid-1960s case was revealing in this regard. It involved alcohol abuse, insults, and repeated misbehaviour towards a Berlin wife. After hearing the initial complaints, one of the jurists paid a house visit, submitting a handwritten report stating that the husband did not come home at least one or two nights a week, and, from what he gathered from neighbours, was having an affair with a work colleague. The court convened a meeting at work between the husband and his colleagues to discuss his family life. In the minutes the factory foreman, personnel manager, and jurist concluded:

The factory foreman made it very clear to him [the offending husband] that the enterprise had a great deal of interest that co-workers are not only professionally sound, but that they also lead orderly lives outside the enterprise ... The participants in the meeting informed the husband that he should fundamentally reconsider his life, and finished by saying that he must bring some order and cleanliness to his private affairs if he hopes to enjoy the respect of his colleagues at work. Herr M countered that his marriage, which was irrevocably broken down, should be ended by divorce and reiterated his insistence on this position.[86]

After further deliberation, the divorce was granted; but it does give some sense of the social machinery of pressure, re-education, and social shaming put in place to combat marital breakdown in 1960s East Berlin.

The courts relied on other administrative organs to mend marital problems, such as family, marriage, and sex counselling centres. In fact, the expansion of sex and marriage counselling was even stipulated in the 1965 Family Code, thereby ushering in a new era of professional assistance in domestic matters. German marriage counselling centres were originally creatures of the Weimar Republic's political conservatives, who believed that public health and well-being trumped individual interests, a view that often dovetailed with the advocacy of eugenics and racial hygiene at the time. By the early 1930s over 200 such marriage clinics existed across Germany.[87] After 1933 Weimar marriage counselling centres were replaced by new National Socialist versions, which 'racialized' marital life and procreation more radically. After 1945 a few marriage counselling centres were re-established to help men cope with sexual dysfunction following war and psychological disability,[88] but the boom really started in the 1960s. By 1966 there were some 100 centres across the GDR, rising to 242 by 1977.[89] People flocked to these centres, and seemed unfazed by their possible intrusive function. Consultations were apparently confidential and anonymized, as these centres supposedly built their credibility on respecting the private sphere of estranged citizens.[90] For these social workers, the centres became key institutions of information-gathering about the problems of everyday life, especially during an era in which GDR sociology was exclusively concerned with productivity, work conditions, and labour relations.[91] Experts penned numerous reports on variable class behaviour in an allegedly classless world, maintaining for example that domestic violence and hasty marriages were more typical among 'proletarian' couples, while 'incompatible' lifestyles issues were more common among intelligentsia and white-collar workers.[92] In this sense, the counselling centres served as vital outposts for the regime's 'moral mission' as well as instructive sources about the private side of 'real existing socialism'.

The boom in counselling centres was also accompanied by the golden age of sex manuals. Though not officially acknowledged, the burgeoning field of sexology revealed the ways in which the GDR was being influenced by its cold war rival. Just as GDR sex therapy was influenced by American sexologists, such as Masters and Johnson, this new GDR self-help literature was explicitly borrowed from the West. Siegfried Schnabl's runaway 1969 bestseller *Mann und Frau Intim* (Man and Woman Intimately) explicitly cited Simone de Beauvoir's notion of individual engagement in society as a precondition to female emancipation akin to men's.[93] But even if the studies of sexual liberation were being pirated from the West, the blossoming of a new GDR sexual culture based on sensual pleasure was something that supposedly distinguished it from the uptight and prudish West. Already by the late 1950s less conservative GDR publicists began to discuss sex more frankly. In one 1959 guide, not only was sex described as 'the quintessence of being alive', it also stated that 'we as free people know that intercourse does not just serve the propagation of the human race, but also furthers pleasure very significantly'.[94] At stake was more than simply disconnecting sexual pleasure from reproduction. What these guides hoped to show—buttressed by numerous journalistic articles in the magazines *Für Dich* and *Das Magazin* from the mid-1960s on—was that 'socialism, in short, was not just about better love; it was about better sex'.[95] With time there were even efforts to publicize Marx's amorous affection for his wife Jenny as a new image of Marx the sensualist for a younger, more pleasure-seeking generation.[96]

In light of these cultural changes, 1960s divorce courts increasingly saw their role as part of the country's modernization drive to confront patriarchal attitudes and male 'egotism' at home. This could be seen in a number of ways. First, slander and verbal abuse became more decisive as criterion of marital breakdown, as respect and equality within marriage now grew in salience as never before. By the 1960s women appealed more frequently to the equality of the sexes guaranteed in the 1949 GDR Constitution as grounds for divorce, citing Article 7 that 'men and women are equal. All laws and proclamations that contravene women's equality are null and void.' Similar trends were evident across Eastern Europe at the time, as women learnt to exploit the language of socialist legality and civil rights to individual ends.[97] And the courts followed, increasingly taking umbrage with the 'selfishness' of 'traditional' husbands. Law journal articles stressed the need for a 're-education of the husband to fully responsible cooperation in the household'.[98] In one revealing mid-1960s case, the judge decided that the wife did everything to make the marriage work in the face of the husband's 'non-recognition and non-respect of the dignity of women (*Frauenwürde*)'. In the verdict the judge surmised that the marriage 'was not built on love, respect and confidence. The accused does not respect the equality of sexes and the dignity of the plaintiff as a woman.'[99]

Such language was a dramatic departure from husbands taking their old-fashioned ideals of domesticity into court as cause for divorce in the 1940s and 1950s, often with sympathetic (male) judges. To be sure, Ulbricht himself had signalled the change at the beginning of the decade. In an oft-cited 1960 speech, the SED's First Secretary defined marriage as a life-long relationship between husband and wife, uniquely based on 'mutual love and consideration between equal partners devoted to the education of children in the spirit of socialism'.[100] The gender composition of the bench was also changing. By 1953, one-third of *Volksrichter* were women; by the end of the decade, women comprised 23.3 per cent of prosecutors, 26.8 per cent of judges, and 34.6 per cent of lay judges (the German variant of a jury). Still, female judges tended to cluster at the lower levels of the system, and disproportionately entered the family and divorce court system.[101] By the 1960s, the courts made clear that traditional attitudes were no longer acceptable in a socialist state that prided itself on the full equality of its citizens at work and at home. It was precisely the equality of the sexes that emerged as the distinguishing feature of socialist marriage.[102]

In the courtroom, it became more and more common to scold recalcitrant husbands for their outdated and 'unsocialist' sexist attitudes. In one 1966 case a wife claimed that her husband 'subordinated' her by seeing her main role as 'serving him and putting up with his every mood', making it impossible to 'build a proper and orderly marriage'. This was patently unfair, countered the husband, since 'long before the marriage he made it clear to his wife—and she agreed to it—what the relations would be in the marriage. When I say no, it's no, and when I say yes, it will be yes. I made this clear to my wife before getting married.' The judge upheld the wife's claim, on the grounds that the accused did not see his wife as 'an equal partner'.[103] Common claims from the late 1940s and 1950s that wives did not do enough to make their husbands happy were now slapped down as 'egotism', unmodern, and unjust.[104] In another particularly sad 1960 case, a wife filed because her husband 'had constantly mishandled her for months', beating her at least three times a week. In court, the husband nonchalantly admitted that

'I have forbidden my wife to go to work, since she should stay in the kitchen. I have given her 470 Mark monthly, and for it I expect my breakfast and warm dinner prepared. This she has seldom done, and she has often refused marital intercourse. I have told her repeatedly that she should change her behavior. Since she hasn't done so, I have hit her on occasion, especially since she has provoked me.

The judge seethed that such an attitude had no place in the GDR, and finished by saying that the divorce was justified on account of the husband's 'uncontrolled and tempestuous character', his abuse of his wife's equality, and his conduct 'unbefitting a reasonable person'.[105] Here and elsewhere, the courts voiced great concern that strong patriarchal attitudes were still all too present in many homes, and that their mission was to eradicate this social poison and to support aggrieved female citizens.

Another new yardstick of marital dysfunction was divergent lifestyles. This ranged from differing cultural tastes (the wife liked to go dancing, while the husband preferred to stay home to watch television) to 'worldview' differences, such as religious devotion. In one 1960 case, a wife filed that the husband was neglecting his family duties to the extent that he 'only came home to eat and sleep, demanded occasional sex, but otherwise the accused showed no interest in the family whatsoever'. In the hearing, the wife complained that he never brought gifts or sweets from West Berlin, where he worked in a bakery, nor was she ever taken to the Botanical Garden or cinema. The husband retorted that he was in fact not 'egotistical', since he purchased all the furniture and household 'luxury items' like the refrigerator and television. Six witnesses were summoned to testify, one of whom remarked that 'nobody ever saw the man pay attention to his wife, to say nothing of bringing her gifts like sweets and chocolates; he did bring herring on occasion, but ate it all himself. He also called her many names, such as "dirty pig," slut, etc.' In the verdict, the judge cited the credibility of two witnesses (including the son) that the accused was 'extremely egotistical' and was mostly concerned 'with enlarging his own personal property' at the expense of his family. The cold war dimension came into play, as the husband was chided for exploiting his 'parasitical lifestyle' in West Berlin for himself at the expense of his family.[106] In another case a few years later, a wife complained that she and her husband were incompatible. She cited his excessive love of sports and his disinclination to help around the house as causing marital unhappiness and their 'not 100 per cent harmonious' sex life. The husband sheepishly concurred, emphasizing their lack of common interests as the root of the problem. The judge's verdict found that the marriage indeed 'had lost its meaning', mainly 'since the parties have no common interests, they have become alienated from one another, and the plaintiff especially registers this misunderstanding in her emotional attitude toward the intimate sphere of the marriage'.[107] This was a relatively easy divorce, and there was little effort to save the marriage.

Lifestyle differences often shaded into political issues. This usually pivoted on notions of what were seen as clashing worldviews. In one mid-1960s case, for example, a husband charged that his wife constantly mocked him for his SED activity, especially in front of the children. Witnesses were brought forth to attest that his wife 'ridiculed [him] in rough fashion about his Party membership', and the judge concluded that the defendant was not capable 'of raising the children in a socialist manner. I thus draw the conclusion that the defendant has a negative stance towards our socialist social order.'[108] There were apparently no further repercussions as a result of her anti-SED attitude, and the divorce was granted. Ideological conflict often centred on religion. The dossier of one 1960 case is instructive here: 'The husband belongs to the SED, while the wife is a believing Catholic. Although these divergent viewpoints were long known to the plaintiff, he hoped that he could succeed in bringing her around to a Marxist worldview.' Things deteriorated, and the husband confessed to having had two affairs. In her counterstatement, the wife admitted to having insisted on a church wedding, though she found exaggerated his complaint that their church wedding was responsible for his exmatriculation from the university and even the Party. To cover herself, she added that she was employed in the 'state apparatus', enjoyed the trust of her co-workers, had been singled out at work for her exemplary industry, and had been 'engaged fully in building up socialism', even taking courses in Marxist philosophy 'in order to loosen my beliefs'. To her the real reason for the divorce plea was not 'political disharmony' but rather his extra-marital affair only six weeks after the wedding: it was the 'immoral and charac-terless behaviour of my husband in his *private* life that continually destroyed the foundations of a happy marriage'. Consequently she took her husband's insinu-ation that she was an 'enemy of our republic' as an affront 'to my honour and as working member of our society'. In the verdict, politics—to say nothing of the fact that the husband was an enthusiastic Party member—exerted no bearing on the case, underscoring how civil courts were often quite removed from heavy-handed state ideology. The judge ultimately came down on her side, granting the divorce because the husband's 'inconsistent behaviour' indicates that 'despite his socialist worldview' he was entering into 'marriage-undermining relations with other women'. Socialism was not just about political conviction and public service, but was just as concerned with private comportment.[109]

Perhaps the most telling shift of the mid-1960s was the accent on sexual problems as grounds for divorce. In 1950s divorce cases, court interest was usually limited to the routine question about the 'last marital intercourse'. While some sexual history was discussed in late 1940s cases, there was a discernible move away from such questions in the 1950s. By the mid-1960s, though, a couple's sexual life became a key part of the court hearing. In 1959, sexual problems as grounds for divorce were recorded in only 6 per cent of cases, yet they tripled to almost

18 per cent by 1972. And while some sexual dysfunction cases were put forward by men, most were filed by women. Naturally, this does not denote necessarily less satisfying sex than before; instead, it registers a new language of sexual problems over the course of the 1960s, as divorce cases became a locus for women in particular to stake their broader claims about personal dissatisfaction on a range of levels. Sexual incompatibility thus blurred into broader issues of lifestyle differences. In one 1966 case, the husband's drunkenness and occasional violence were cited, along with the fact that he was 'not prepared to go with her to the theatre or to a concert, or to show Berlin to her'. Yet their sexual problems were put at the centre: 'In a sexual sense there exists no harmony between the parties. The defendant [the husband] is absolutely egotistical, and only thinks of his own satisfaction. Over the course of the whole marriage the plaintiff has never enjoyed fulfilment in their intimate life. Because of it she has become nervous, and has developed a disinclination to engage in further sex with her husband.'[110] In another 1966 case, an unhappy wife complained that their marriage was 'constantly in danger' since 'we do not understand each other sexually, are never satisfied, and I must say, my nerves suffer because of it'. Recommendations to see a marriage counsellor made little difference, as noted in the verdict: 'Despite many consultations the parties have not been able to overcome their misunderstandings in the sexual sphere, and the medical counsel over the last year [seemingly to treat the husband's chronic erectile dysfunction] has not been effective.'[111] More and more these courts saw marriage as an arena for freedom and enjoyment, and granted divorce if these expectations were not satisfied.

The doubling of 'sexual grounds' as a reason for divorce over the decade also had to do with the changing nature of the East German family itself.[112] By the 1960s the GDR family was becoming what some describe as an island of consumerism and care, as the more traditional functions of the family—production, education, and even child-raising—were increasingly assumed by the state.[113] This resulted in what has been called a 'privatization of marriage', in that marriage was being recast as a respite of comfort, intimacy, and close-knit family life. Which meant that marriages were often saddled with higher demands of emotional and sexual fulfilment.[114] One might conclude that such decisions reflected a new-found pessimism about the limits of counselling and reformability of dysfunctional relationships; yet one could just as easily interpret this spike in divorces by the end of the 1960s as driven by rising expectations of marriage as truly based on mutual respect, love, and satisfaction.

This shift can also be seen in the way that the 1965 Family Law Book was interpreted in courts. According to the famed paragraph 24 of the law, a marriage could only be dissolved if 'it has lost its meaning for the spouses, the children and therefore also for society'.[115] Compare this language with the 1955 Marriage Ordinance, which held that divorce could only be granted if the marriage 'had lost its meaning for the spouses, the children and for society'. The semantic difference at first may seem negligible, yet the clause 'therefore also for society' (*und damit auch für die Gesellschaft*) was quite novel and far-reaching. For it implied that the primary meaning of the marriage rested with the couple itself, not with society, thereby challenging the subordination of marriage to social imperatives found in the 1955 Marriage Ordinance. Legally, it suggested that the concerns of the spouses trumped that of the state, opening the door towards separating private domestic problems from state expectations.[116] To be sure, the state worked hard to spin these developments in a positive light. For example, the high divorce rates were sometimes interpreted as the internalization of the norms of socialist civilization. One 1962 *Neue Justiz* article argued that 'divorce rates are rising because social relations in the GDR have been fully remade, and socialist morality has penetrated [the fabric of everyday life] more and more'.[117] The high divorce rate was even given a distinctive cold war dimension, celebrated as it was as an indicator of socialist liberty that symbolized 'just how much the [elevated] societal position of the citizen in the GDR departs from that of people living in yesterday's and today's imperialist states'.[118] Nonetheless, the net effect was eased divorces and more autonomy for the private sphere, as the both the state and its citizens lost interest in maintaining marriages devoid of personal happiness, emotional satisfaction, and/or sexual pleasure.[119]

CREEPING PESSIMISM: THE 1970s AND 1980s

In the 1970s things accelerated in this direction. For one thing, the 1975 Socialist Civil Code made it even easier to divorce. It stated boldly (para. 1564) that a 'divorce can be granted when the marriage is ruined. A marriage is ruined if the domestic community (*Lebensgemeinschaft*) of the spouses no longer exists, and if it cannot be expected that the spouses will restore it.' If both sides agreed, the divorce only took three weeks after filing a joint application. If not, divorce could be granted if the couple had lived apart for at least one year, or if one spouse found the marriage undermined by what was called 'unzumutbare Härte', literally 'unreasonable hardness'. Though the courts were still required to investigate the causes of 'unreasonable hardness', their reform zeal flagged dramatically in the face of spiralling divorce requests. There were also more cases of multiple divorces: in 1950, only 4 per cent of marriages featured partners who had both been previously divorced; by 1970 the percentage had doubled.[120] This meant that there were both more marriages and more divorces.[121] Divorce record testimonies make clear that marriage and love life became an important place for GDR citizens to assert some sense of individuality and personal liberty in a world where such freedom was severely circumscribed.

The 1970s files were not as thick as they had been in the 1960s, and there was less desire and confidence on part of the courts to fix failing marriages. Even 'older' marriages (defined as more than twenty years old) were dissolved more readily. Egotism, selfishness, and dishonour were upheld as justifications for divorce in ways that departed from common verdicts a decade before.[122] In the 1970s there were still many cases that pivoted on sexual disharmony, but the details were not as lovingly noted.[123] There was a more tacit acknowledgement too from the state from the mid-1960s onward that domestic problems were related to GDR life, especially the poor housing stock and the material challenges of everyday socialism.[124] The old idea that domestic conflict was simply a holdover from capitalism and 'imperialist thinking' was taken less and less seriously, as judges more openly admitted that state socialism generated its own sources of marital strife.[125] There was also a marked drop in the moral language about who was at fault, as things moved toward an expeditious 'divorce on demand' model. Nor was there much language about socialist marriage, the importance of socialism, or the virtues of socialist comportment in comparison to the 1960s. And whereas in the 1960s the 'Collective' tended to plead for the maintenance of the marriage, the opposite was truer in the 1970s, as friends, work colleagues, and neighbours commonly pleaded for the ending of unhappy unions.[126] Moreover, professional *Jugendhilfe* social workers replaced representatives from the Collective as mediating figures between the estranged couple and the state's judicial organs.[127] Little wonder then that there was a rash of publications on the 'family in socialism' calling for closer links between families and society, since it was quite clear to many observers that family life was less and less linked to socialist concerns.[128]

In part these changes were constitutive of larger shifts in GDR culture. For one thing, there was a widely noted 'privatization of leisure' in the 1970s, whose prevalence was even more pronounced in the GDR than in the Federal Republic.[129] By the end of the decade, GDR sociologists were aware that the 'enclosure of family life against the outside world' was becoming a distinctive feature of the 1970s.[130] This was the beginning of what Günter Gaus later called the GDR's infamous 'niche society', and was something that had become a staple of GDR official literature by the mid-1980s.[131] Yet this notion of the GDR family as the 'synonym of leisure, freedom and privacy' had its downside too, in that it put increased pressure on marriages to make up for the slow deterioration of positive communal life. As one sociologist put it,

family became compensation for the collapse of meaningful activities and possibilities in public life that one sought but rarely found. The phrase 'privacy precedes catastrophe' (*Privat geht vor Katastrophe*) conceals the fact that families could not deliver what was expected of them: harmony, happiness, meaning, personality, spice and excitement. It was no great surprise that the overburdening of the family with hopes and expectations led to high divorce rates.[132]

To be sure, the heightened emotional burden placed on conjugal relationships from the 1960s on was hardly unique to East Germany, or even socialist lands, but found wide echoes across the West as well at the time.[133] But it took on acute expression in the GDR as symptomatic of the growing gap between individual and collectivity.

No less significant is that sexual issues were out in the open as never before. It is well-known that the GDR's ease with nudity and sexual liberty became hallmarks of East German socialism, arguably the result of a non-commercialized sex culture comparatively free of prostitution and pornography.[134] What was new about the 1970s was the frank openness of sexual dissatisfaction. Granted, the theme of women's discontent had emerged as a theme of GDR literature from the late 1960s onward, most famously in Christa Wolf's *Nachdenken über Christa T* (1968) and Brigitte Reimann's *Franziska Linkerhand* (1974). But nowhere was the issue of sexual discontent more directly dealt with than in the 1977 publication of Maxie Wander's oral history of GDR women, *Guten Morgen, Du Schöne*, which loudly bespoke the deep reservoir of dissatisfaction at the core of GDR domestic life. In it nineteen anonymous GDR women spoke candidly about their personal lives, complete with graphic details about their sexual experiences, desires, and disappointments. As Reimann noted in her preface, this was 'unresearched territory' into women's 'new lifestyles, both in private and in society'. In her introduction, Christa Wolf went further, arguing that what distinguished the book was its demonstration of how the 'private had become public' and how the 'private life and feelings of many women in the GDR have transformed'.[135] The book inspired a new genre of realist documentary literature, and similar 'realist' voices found expression in the magazines *Für Dich* and *Das Magazin*, often in the form of letters from female readers about their unsatisfactory sex lives.[136] Behind-closed-doors exposés of the GDR's own intimate 'private sphere'—including people's experiences of love, marriage, and sex—even attracted West German curiosity in the mid-1970s.[137] And although the GDR never witnessed anything equivalent to the West German feminist movement, the issue of sexual inequality did enjoy wide public discussion across the country in the 1970s.[138] New sociological studies were commissioned on the inequality of the sexes (including the disinclination of East German men to do housework), many of which were not shy about calling for a social transformation of values and attitudes towards women and the family. One sexologist writing in the mid-1970s went so far as to say that 'the fidelity concept is closely related to a private property mentality (*Besitzdenken*). "My wife" means "my property." . . . Increasing education, economic independence and sexual equality challenges the property mentality of men.'[139] If nothing else, such commentary reflected the state's growing admission that the constitutional guarantee of sexual equality was not taking root in everyday socialist life, especially at home.[140]

In the 1970s GDR divorce courts stepped up their campaign against patriarchal behaviour within families and even in the bedroom. In hearings husbands were routinely chastized for regressive attitudes.[141] Even so, there was a creeping pessimism that such behaviour could really be changed. The words of one exacerbated female judge hearing a late 1960s case of domestic violence was quite typical for the 1970s as well: 'It is still quite common among the male citizens of our state to beat their wives. It shows that this bourgeois lord-of-the-house mentality has not yet been overcome ideologically, and in the heat of the moment the path of least resistance is taken.'[142] By the 1970s, however, there was less political correctness of the part of judges to issue pat statements that such chauvinistic attitudes were simply a holdover from a 'bourgeois world-view', or could be overcome through re-education and effective counselling. The one-time enthusiasm about the reform and reformability of sexist behaviour had all but evaporated amid the mounting claims of marital discord and private unhappiness.

A 1978 judicial report called 'A Study on the Causes of Divorce' reflected these shifts. It began by praising the state of marriage in the GDR, arguing that under socialism marriage had been freed of old bourgeois baggage, not least because it was no longer linked to private property. A secure material life, good income, and social welfare, so the report continued, meant that people were more open to seeking better relationships, making new demands upon society and partners as never before. A 'certain egotism' was now seen as the natural by-product of economic independence—and not capitalism—and thus a contributing factor to rising divorce claims. Furthermore, women at work were exposed to many other potential partners as well as available 'modern contraception', which made 'extramarital contact' 'largely risk-free'.[143] Perhaps most striking was the conclusion. It in no way lamented the rise of divorces as perforce negative, but actually contended—in classic Marxist fashion—that these changing social structures had simply found their reflection in 'the subjective sensibilities' of everyday citizens. That is, the socialist liberation of marriage from bourgeois constraints had brought in its train a range of good and bad effects, something—and this is the key phrase—that could not be 'resolved by juridical means'.[144] At the very least, the report acknowledged the limits of the 1960s social engineering crusade, and that the courts could not be expected to carry out the moral re-education of the couple in crisis. There was more open admission of the common social factors behind divorce, such as very early marriages and 'increasing alcohol consumption'. High divorce rates were thereby interpreted as an inevitable effect of modernization. They were a 'sign' of the growing social status of women in socialist society, insofar as their desires and expectations marked their 'equal and economically independent personality'.[145] So whereas West Germany tended to denounce the GDR state and divorce courts for intruding too much in the private affairs of East German citizens,[146] or to attribute the country's high divorce rate to working mothers,[147] the GDR increasingly viewed divorce as a species of women's liberation.

Courts still endeavoured to keep couples together, but the reasons were different. With time the legal notions of 'in the interest of society' and the 'societal meaning of marriage' were reduced more and more to the interests of the child. The importance of children in marriage had always been a central plank of the GDR, and even as late as 1976 the SED 9th Party Conference promulgated that 'children are constitutive to the meaning and happiness of marriage'. In court there was constant discussion of the welfare of children caught in the maelstrom of marital discord, reaching back to the nineteenth-century German tradition of family courts entrusted to protect and promote the young. By the 1970s there was growing public discussion—albeit indirect—of domestic violence in the press (like *Wochenpost*) as a means of raising awareness and helping at-risk children.[148] In fact, many GDR divorce claims were denied for the sake of the children; about a third of the cases involving adultery—once automatic grounds for divorce—were rejected to keep the family together. One typical early 1970s verdict stated that 'for child-raising reasons both parties are expected to overcome their existing problems with fullness and consistency . . . The marriage has thus not lost its meaning for society, and thus the divorce criterion of Para 24 has not been fulfilled.'[149] In one 1971 case, a wife brought charges against her husband, who constantly insulted her 'in the most ugly manner'. In it the effect on the children was construed as more grave than its negative impact on the plaintiff: in the end the judge claimed that the marriage 'offered nothing in the way of positive education for the adolescent son, and gave no other member of the family a feeling of safe comfort (*Geborgenheit*) and familial harmony'.[150] Similarly, a 1974 divorce claim was denied on the grounds that 'the maintenance of the marriage for small children is extremely important, and that the dissolution of a family for the sake of the child is only justified when all possibilities of creating a home in which the child can thrive are no longer to be expected. In this case the marriage still had meaning for the children'.[151]

   No less interesting is that the 1970s were marked by a new disinclination on the part of jurists and social workers toward treading upon the privacy of comrades. To be sure, there were traces of this in earlier periods; in the Nazi era, for example, the state's insistence on making marriage certificates mandatory was viewed by local officials as an 'unnecessary, undesirable intrusion into their private lives'.[152] Misgivings were common in the GDR in the 1970s and 1980s. Often to the irritation of state officials, such sentiment was even shared by 'leading functionaries', who still 'harbour the old belief that family and marriage problems exclusively belonged to the personal and intimate realm of the individuals'.[153] One January 1970 case was quite revealing in this respect. In it Monika D. filed against her former husband, who was still living in her residence after the divorce. She felt threatened by him, maintaining 'that she no longer felt safe in her own apartment'. The case included an appended letter from the Housing Community Leader, who said that he felt uncomfortable intruding into the couple's business. In his words: 'Among other things a housing community (*Hausgemeinschaft*) in our state carries a certain responsibility, which in this case extends into the private sphere (*Privatsphäre*) of Herr and Frau D, however unpleasant and unjustified this may at first seem.' However he justified getting involved in the following way:

But in the end we cannot permit that these domestic rows over the most fundamental private things (*ureigenste Privatdinge*) between two partners exerted its damage on the work life of the couple, as well as on the child, who suffers from the effects of these scenes played out by his parents. Not least it seems to us that such behaviour is undignified for a SED member, in the way that Herr D tramples upon the dignity of a woman.[154]

Notable was the explicit assumption that there was indeed a private sphere, and that it was neither his role nor the role of the state to get involved in it unless necessary. In the end, the pretext for intervention was of its time: the adverse effect on labour capacities, the child, and the 'dignity of women'. But so too was the new inclination to avoid doing so whenever possible.

By the 1980s, there were further changes. Not only did the number of divorce claims keep rising, but divorce claims were more successful—nearly 80 per cent according to one study. Only 15 per cent of estranged partners were referred to counselling centres, in stark contrast to the 1950s and 1960s. In the 1980s there was also a significant drop in the number of marriage counselling centres as well as recorded visits to them,[155] as people relied on sexual manuals for their information and tended to keep their private lives to themselves.[156] This was especially the case among younger people.[157] In large measure, divorce claims were dispatched quickly and without much hope of reconciliation. This could be seen in the fact that there was remarkably little paperwork in the files, compared to the 1960s and 1970s. Scant details were entered in the record, and few witnesses were called; instead, judges seemed content with dissolving marriages on account of the partners' own testimonies of incompatibility. Not much effort was expended to save marriages, as questions about accommodations and child custody usually took precedence. The thickest files concerned the division of property and personal effects, as battles over motor boats, cars, and housewares filled the dossiers. Indeed, some 20–30 per cent of the 1980s East Berlin divorce court casework concerned property disputes after the dissolution of what was revealingly called the 'property-community' (*Eigentumgemeinschaft*) of marriage. That this will to rehabilitation was much less prevalent in the 1980s may be attributed to understaffing problems, or simply exhaustion on the part of judges in the face of so many divorce claims. Most cases were characterized by formulaic decisions, with little colour. The typically dull and matter-of-fact bureaucratic language was noted in a 1988 verdict: 'The cause was ascertained that the parties harboured incompatible ideas on the issue of how to live together, which ultimately led to quarrels and conflicts.'[158] Judges no longer saw love and marital relations as amenable to legal control. The new stress on individualism was also palpable. By that time the freedom of each partner was paramount, with much less attention paid to the duty and sacrifices of marriage, even older ones.[159] To be sure, the necessity of maintaining 'a clear, stable and quiet domestic environment for children'—as one 1987 verdict put it—remained a key refrain from the courts, and a chief cause for action.[160] Yet the once-central idea that children functioned as the 'glue' in a marriage started to fade, as parents increasingly acted for themselves and sought divorce accordingly.[161]

Such changes may also reflect a new attitude towards the private lives of conjugal partners. By the 1980s courts were less keen to investigate people's marriages in much intimate detail, perhaps because they were no longer convinced that they could get to the root of the problem or could solve things for the future. There were even instances—first starting in the 1960s, but present in the 1970s and 1980s—in which citizens voiced their objections about having their colleagues and neighbours involved in their painful private lives.[162] The effect was to leave couple's private lives relatively alone, implying a new respect (or perhaps indifference) towards the private sphere. This may be strange to read, especially given the common perception of the East German family as a field of social and state security surveillance. Doubtless some did remember the 1950s and 1960s in the GDR as the intrusive supervision of private lives in the name of conformity and collective community-building.[163] But this was not all that typical later, to the extent that the state—as reflected in the court records—largely backed off from its citizens over the course of the late 1970s and 1980s.[164] Overall, there was manifest fatalism about the causes of divorce, and little blaming any longer of either the West or even the litigants. With it the era of 'didactic dictatorship' had all but ended, as divorces were both routine and routinely dispatched.

In conclusion, divorce court records are revealing sources for studying how issues of tradition and modernity were grappled with in East German everyday life, in this case behind the closed doors of dysfunctional marriages. Just as marriage counselling centres became places 'to mediate between the private realm of sexuality and the more public function of families in the socialist state',[165] the courts sat at the intersection of intimacy and society. Of course it remains debatable whether the increase in divorces was a sign of pessimism or optimism on the part of people, but the court proceedings did betray changing notions of liberty and union in the most intimate settings. One thing is certain: given the constitutional guarantee of sexual equality as the very basis of 'communist ethics', women seized on this to their own advantage. With it the social understanding of marriage had changed as expectations of duties were gradually replaced by a new language of rights. What first showed up in the 1960s divorce court proceedings as actionable breaches of women's 'right to individuality' and 'right to pleasure' spilled over into mainstream GDR public life by the end of the decade, as the enjoyment and control of bodies (seen in easier access to contraception, abortion rights, and relaxed attitudes towards unmarried parenthood) became more widespread.[166] And the state followed suit. Lynn Abrams has shown how nineteenth-century German divorce courts 'became the last line of defense for the state in its attempt to reinforce masculine and feminine roles' in an era of great instability.[167] GDR courts by contrast moved in very different directions, targeting patriarchal attitudes and sexism for eradication as part of the larger effort to build a modern form of socialism at home.

Secondly, the records show how East Germany was both different and similar to its Western rival. In the end, GDR divorce courts intervened in family issues for precisely the same reasons that they did in the West, as both cultures developed their own versions of the 'therapeutic state'. The private sphere may never have been sacrosanct in the GDR, but it did begin to matter more to more people over the course of the 1970s and 1980s, precisely at the moment that the state lost faith (or interest) in remaking people. Such trends emerged in various ways, not least in the GDR's sex culture. As Dagmar Herzog has argued, 'sex eventually became a crucial free space in this otherwise profoundly unfree society'.[168] But it also surfaced in the understanding of women's liberation as a fundamental aspect of socialist culture, supposedly marking East Germany's superiority to its bourgeois rival's 'regressive' and 'patriarchal' society. To be sure, the 1960s liberalization of divorce as a constitutive element of a rejuvenated women's movement found expression across the industrialized world at the time.[169] But given the cold war setting, the lack of any real public sphere, and the SED's ideological support of sexual equality, GDR divorce courts became the arena in which the feminist crusade of the 'personal is the political' took on its most popular and potent expression.

Thirdly, court records tell us a great deal about the shifting meaning of the private sphere. It was not only different from West Germany, but it was unlike the Third Reich too. Elizabeth Heineman is certainly correct in saying that the Nazis' 'politicization of and incursions into the family make it impossible to speak of the family as a "private" sphere, distinct from the "public arenas of politics, work and war"'.[170] But even in this most totalitarian of all regimes, there was a certain cultivation of the private sphere as a place of pleasure, relaxation, and respite.[171] A similar phenomenon took place in the GDR, especially after the state's social engineering projects cooled off in the 1970s and 1980s. Indeed, it was the growing expectation—and claim—that the private sphere should serve as a locus of personal freedom and sexual equality that fuelled many of these divorce petitions in the first place, especially by women. More than anywhere else in the GDR, divorce courts brought the private sphere to public attention, revealing both the hopes and limits of the socialist project as a full-scale revolution of social relations, as well as the determination on the part of East German citizens to define and defend private life. Citizen testimonies of despair (especially from aggrieved wives) not only anticipated the 'realist' genre of 1970s feminist literature and documentary interest in closed-off domestic worlds, they also gave voice to common tales of personal discontent and abandoned social ideals at the most intimate level. Looking at families merely as objects of social policy, as most scholars do, is quite limiting in this respect. For it is the changing language of the participants—wives, husbands, and judges—that is so instructive and historically valuable, as the lexicon of rights—the right to equality, the right to pleasure— reflected changing perceptions of self-worth and social justice.

II
DOMESTIC IDEALS, SOCIAL
RIGHTS, LIVED EXPERIENCES

4

Building Socialism at Home

Remaking Interiors and Citizens

The last decade has witnessed growing academic interest in material culture as a particularly rewarding approach to reinterpreting the German past. New studies on monuments, architecture, museums, urban landscapes, and 'commodity culture' have greatly enriched the ever-expanding field of German cultural history.[1] That Germany served as one of the twentieth century's busiest construction sites of political experimentation and utopian ventures of all stripes meant that the built environment was crucial for conveying new dreams of political power, place, and possibility. Two world wars, revolution, full-scale physical destruction, and cold war division only intensified the primacy of symbolic artefacts, as buildings and public spaces were enlisted by each twentieth-century regime to broadcast desired historical ruptures and restored traditions, fresh political starts as well as images of continuity.

Less well-known is that the twentieth century placed great premium on the domestic interior. At first this may seem a little surprising, given that the twentieth century is commonly viewed as an 'age of extremes' marked by brutal projects of social engineering that often began by doing away with the traditional boundaries between public and private. Over the decades many an observer has interpreted the state's assault on the private sphere as one of the defining elements of the last century. Nowhere was this more pronounced than in Germany. While usually associated with the Third Reich and the German Democratic Republic, these developments were also present in both the Weimar and Bonn Republics. Indeed, the private sphere and the idealized domicile were central to each German government over the course of the last century, not least because decent housing was so closely tied to political legitimacy.[2] This was especially the case in the GDR, and this chapter will turn towards domestic space as a key instance of the private sphere in East Germany. It will focus on interior design and the construction of an East German *Wohnkultur*, or domestic 'living culture', as both ideal and lived reality. Attention will also be paid to the flourishing cottage industry of East German etiquette books as further efforts to stylize the socialist self and to 'deprivatize' home life as an outpost of socialist civilization.

THE NEW CULT OF THE DOMESTIC

After 1945 the home attracted a remarkable amount of public attention across Europe, ranging from national governments to municipal policy-makers, welfare workers to women's organizations, architecture and design circles to advertisers and consumer activists. It was the centre of social policy in every European country after the war, despite extremely divergent experiences of material decimation, housing shortages, social dislocation, and refugee crises. Common to all, though, was a powerful desire to begin things anew. So much so that for many Europeans securing 'a home of one's own' signalled the real conclusion of the war and its subsequent 'hunger years', as noted in the period's memoirs and oral histories across Britain and Europe.[3] At first glance, the primacy of the home and home life after 1945 may seem a recycled version of developments and sentiments following the First World War. There is no doubt that homes took on new-found political significance during the interwar years. This is particularly true of worker domiciles. Even if worker housing first emerged as a new pet issue among social reformers, architects, and city planners in the late nineteenth century, as international schemes about improving worker housing made their debut at the World Exhibition in Paris in 1851, the German reform movement did not really take wing until the 1920s.[4] Housing then moved to the centre of social politics and often served as a critical testing ground of the new Weimar welfare state until its demise in 1933. The Nazi accession to power may have announced the state's assault against Weimar modernism and its 'cultural bolshevik' conspiracy to reduce the hallowed German dwelling to mass-produced 'living machines,' as gabled housetops and völkish appliqué replaced flat roofs and unadorned surfaces in at least the Third Reich's high-profile building projects. But the ideological centrality of decent worker homes—significantly renamed the 'Volkssiedlung'—carried on through the 1930s, even if the Nazis never actually built as much housing as their hated predecessors.[5]

Needless to say, the massive destruction of the country during the Second World War ensured that housing would remain top priority in postwar social policy. Yet this went far beyond simply physical reconstruction. A key element in building a post-fascist culture was the new accent placed on private life. So much so that the postwar period may even be characterized as a new 'culture of privacy' in its own right, one that began by reinstating the boundaries between public and private life. This was especially pronounced in West Germany, where the restored nuclear family, domestic stability, and the 'private virtues' of individual propriety and decency were commonly lauded as the bedrock of a post-fascist social order.[6] Housing then assumed heightened significance as a symbol of peace and recovery, freedom and prosperity. The urgent task of providing shelter for the millions of refugees after 1945 further intensified the primacy of housing after the war, and in turn the state's credibility in delivering adequate accommodations to its homeless masses. The upshot was that the private sphere assumed unprecedented political gravity during the postwar period, as Hannah Arendt and Jürgen Habermas perceptively observed. Now, whether or not this led to the vitiation of the public sphere or the ironic reversal of public and private in postwar life is debatable.[7] What is beyond doubt, however, is that the private realm moved to the centre of social policy and public discussion in the postwar years. It then is no surprise that the home became a favourite theme of exhibitions in the immediate postwar period. Across Europe there was renewed interest among state officials, industrial leaders, educators, and museum curators to mount numerous housing shows as markers of national recovery, social improvement, and aesthetic education. While the 'cult of the private' played a key—and still underestimated—role in wartime life in both the Allied and Axis countries,[8] it acquired new vigour and authority after 1945. This found cultural expression as well, as there was a discernible shift in aesthetic focus from the grandiose and spectacular (political pageantry, monumental building, and epic films) toward the stylization and showcasing of domestic interiors and home furnishings. Even if this trend was everywhere apparent in the West, it was especially commended in 're-educated' West Germany, Italy, and even Japan as manifestations of post-fascist progress and liberal culture.[9]

The stylization of the private sphere was equally manifest in the GDR. Yet it took place under different conditions. After all, the revival of monumentalist architecture and statuary, the regularity of state pageantry, the politicization of public space and the workplace, the celebration of martyred heroes, the state policing of literature and the arts, the religious iconography and pop culture memorabilia glorifying the SED, as well as the cultural elevation of the united 'community of workers' all underscored the kinship with 1930s style 'aestheticization of politics' and the GDR's unwitting continuities with both Soviet and Nazi culture.[10] Nevertheless, the private sphere took on great symbolic importance there too. From the late 1940s on, the importance of the home as an emblem of personal security, socialist achievement, and postwar prosperity emerged as a primary concern in the GDR and across the Soviet Union. There too the much-touted 'standard of living' and the visual markers of material comfort played a decisive role in the larger 'soft power' cold war struggle for ideological legitimacy.[11]

To date there has been plenty of ink spilled about GDR urban planning, workplace design, housing policy, and architectural forms. Yet we still know relatively little about the material dimension of the private sphere in GDR life. It is all the more unfortunate, given that the home played host to such potent political dreams and desires. From the very beginning the ruling SED recognized its potential in buttressing the party's shaky political authority, wasting little time in making decent housing and a secure domestic life its chief campaign promise to the new republic's war-weary citizenry. Already by 1946 such sentiments were enshrined in the new *Wohnungsgesetz*, or Housing Law, which made affordable housing a right of every socialist citizen. The GDR's 1949 Constitution proudly proclaimed the state's guarantee of a 'healthy and need-fulfilling dwelling for every citizen and family'. Not that this promise was new; the SED was paying homage to this key feature of the 1919 Weimar Constitution. The Weimar heritage could be seen in other ways too: indeed, the SED followed the interwar SPD and KPD in making the reorganization of domestic life a vital step in raising socialist political consciousness and brokering the vaunted peasants' and workers' state.[12]

Cold war concerns also came into play. In part this was fuelled by cold war competition to build more and better dwellings than its Western counterpart, not least because adequate worker housing was seen as a key litmus test of 'people's democracy' and can-do socialism. Justification, as always, was found in Marxist ideology. For its part, the SED never tired of quoting Friedrich Engels's conclusion to his 1873 essay on the 'The Housing Question', where he wrote that the 'housing question' was inseparable from the 'social question'. Only once the 'capitalist contradictions' of society had been overcome, so he argued, would housing problems be truly resolved. The 'true humanism of the socialist order' would then bring in its train the 'well-being of people, the happiness of the nation as well as the interests of the working class and other workers'.[13] Solving the housing problem was therefore seen as the very fruit of a centrally planned economy and socialist victory. But there was another ideological element at work. Since the revolution of the economic base had already come to pass, then—following classic Marxist theory—a new socialist *Wohnkultur*, or 'domestic culture', must necessarily arise as the corresponding cultural expression of such economic transformation. Decisive here was the old chestnut of consciousness: for if it was true that the home was the citizen's first and most influential material environment, then the actual form and habitus of the home were instrumental in properly educating socialist citizens. This of course was hardly novel: many Soviet designers and ideologues grappled with similar concerns in the wake of the Russian Revolution, as did their counterparts in interwar Germany, Austria, Holland, and elsewhere.[14] Yet the stakes were higher in East Germany, especially in view of the SED's wish to rid the population of both the remnants of fascist culture and the allure of the West.

Building a model socialist culture at home was neither easy nor obvious. Given that socialist victory in East Germany was really born of fascist defeat and Soviet intervention, and not popular demand, and given that much of the old Weimar worker culture had been irreparably destroyed by the Nazis, the SED was forced to create a new national material culture virtually from scratch. The devastation of the bombings also forced planners to rethink German material culture from the bottom up. This chapter aims neither to rehearse Soviet cultural influences, nor reiterate the heated 1950s and 1960s debates about what exactly constituted proper social domestic culture. Rather, it focuses on how the reform crusade largely set its sights on the home and its inhabitants as targets for aesthetic and political makeover, precisely because domestic living was identified as a critical dimension of 'socialist education'. The slew of housing exhibitions, interior design shows, and trade fairs, to say nothing of the symbolic authority of Stalinallee as a model of future socialist dwelling and urban community, all bespoke this reform spirit to re-engineer both private spaces and private citizens.

In the cold war rivalry between West and East Germany, each government used housing reconstruction to trumpet its democratic credentials and ability to meet its citizens' most pressing needs. Such propaganda tactics were especially rife in the newly formed socialist republic. Countless newspapers editorials, pamphlets, and books aimed to expose the false gods of the West, arguing that its apparent affluence was really the privilege of the happy few. Lurid journalism about the misery of the masses under capitalism was never in short supply. In his oft-cited 1954 book significantly entitled *The Rental Barracks of Capitalism, Living Palaces of Socialism*, Herbert Riecke described the squalor of capitalist worker life from New York to Nuremberg. Repeatedly the connections between 'dollar domination' (*Dollarherrschaft*), militarism, oppression, and domestic despair (complete with photographs) were presented as the true face of the West. The second half of the book was then given over to extolling the virtues of socialist life in general and East German housing in particular. The high-profile East Berlin worker housing project, Stalinallee, was singled out as a 'foretaste of the good life to be found in socialist residential quarters of the future', one that both 'enriched and beautified everyday life'.[15] In it a well-built, comfortable, and affordable dwelling was heralded as material proof of the new regime's rupture from the class-based inequalities and woeful working-class life found in 'Western fascist society' and the 'capitalist-imperialist' powers. The 'ennoblement' of everyday life was seen as a trump card in winning over citizens to the socialist cause. As Riecke put it: 'The noble traits of communist citizens, including their compassion, joy, openness to the world, love of beauty and cultivation must find appropriate cultural expression in their surrounding architecture... The high task of architecture is then to ennoble the everyday life of workers, and to promote communist education about the ideals of humanity.'[16]

But what exactly was 'socialist domestic living culture'? Was it to be a complete break from the past, or did certain traditional styles and historical influences count as positive legacies? Was GDR domestic culture only to be an imitation of Soviet models, or was there to be something fundamentally German, or for that matter East German, about it? Questions such as these invited great controversy over the decades, especially since the successful revolution of the economic base necessitated a revolutionized domestic life.[17] The outfitting and arrangement of domestic space was therefore both cause and effect of socialist change and stability. Given its importance, it is no surprise that this debate resonated across wide political terrain. Various viewpoints and ideological stances about 'socialist lifestyle' surfaced in a wide variety of sources, ranging from government committee papers to design journals, social policy to home decoration magazines like *Kultur im Heim* (Culture in the Home).

While the politicization of housing began immediately after the ceasefire as a cherished symbol of peace and recovery, the cold war dimension was a creature of the early 1950s. In fact, the East German campaign to convert housing into political capital was in no small measure a response to similar developments in West Germany. From the late 1940s onwards, the American Occupying Government was keen to exploit housing exhibitions as a means of showcasing the 'American way of life' to destitute West Germans and especially West Berliners. Already in 1949 the US Office of the Military Government for Germany (OMGUS) sponsored the show 'So wohnt Amerika', or 'How America Lives', in Frankfurt as a supposed forerunner of coming American-style modernity and future prosperity. A spate of additional housing exhibitions of idealized domestic life followed, complete with the latest consumer appliances made in America. That many of these early cold war shows—such as the 1952 'We are Building a Better Life' exhibition, which started in West Berlin and then travelled to Stuttgart, Hanover, Paris, and Milan—were sponsored by Marshall Plan administrators makes plain the perceived connections between reconstruction, re-education, and domestic happiness. For the East German government, the most troubling aspect of these shows was their incontestable success. It was bad enough that this West Berlin 'Better Life' exhibition—which included a model family of local actors inhabiting the space as living evidence of 'Atlantic Community' material comfort and democratized luxury—attracted over half a million visitors in its three-week run. More awkward, however, was that an estimated 40 per cent of them were East Berliners who travelled across town to see what the West had to offer.[18] The SED did not take long to realize that these shows were perhaps the most effective propaganda weapon of all, and that the East German government needed to respond in kind quickly and forcefully.

This was all the more grave given the deplorable state of East German housing at the time. While precise statistics are difficult to come by, the housing situation during the 1950s was sobering: 52 per cent of residences were one or two rooms only, while 31 per cent had three rooms. Central heating was available in less than 3 per cent of residences; less than 30 per cent of residences had a toilet and only 22 per cent a bath. Some 11 per cent of housing had been built since 1945, whereas 45 per cent of GDR housing had been constructed before 1900. The only thing that saved housing from becoming a truly explosive political issue was that the exodus of some two million East Germans to the West over the course of the 1950s opened up housing for those who stayed.[19] Even so, the regime needed to provide some sort of indication of where the future lay.

By 1950 the issue of developing a distinct vision of 'socialist lifestyle' at home became a hot topic of discussion among government officials, architects, and interior designers. Much of the sound and fury grew out of the question of whether Germany's interwar modernist heritage or Soviet-style neo-classicism should be embraced as the most apt expression of 'national in form, socialist in content'. At this point there is no need to revisit the ideological battles between East German modernists and anti-modernists, much of which pivoted on assessing the value of the Bauhaus legacy for postwar building and design practice.[20] What was clear is that, by the early 1950s, official ideology clearly swung in favour of Soviet neo-classicism.[21] Nowhere was this more evident than in the construction of the famed Stalinallee, hailed as 'Germany's first socialist street'. It was the GDR's grandest and most documented housing project ever, comprising some two miles of worker housing along East Berlin's Stalinallee boulevard. The ensemble, overseen by East Berlin architect Hermann Henselmann, perfectly captured this new postwar ideology. Paramount here was the firm rejection of Western ideas of dispersed, decentralized urban planning (as codified in the 1933 Charter of Athens) in favour of a more centralized integration of the citizen's work life and home life, production and social reproduction. As such Stalinallee was a kind of miniaturized version of the GDR's ideal community, one that integrated residence, shopping, and communal activities in a tightly organized architectonic whole.[22] Even the use of monumental decoration, as stated in Principle 6 of the GDR's Bauakademie (Building Academy) sixteen-point programme of 1950, was part and parcel of this new desire to overcome the alienation of capitalist urban life by building new 'worker palaces' befitting the new citizens of a new worker state.[23]

The same went for the model domestic interior. Official ideology was plainly on display in the pronouncements during the 1951 'Battle for a New German Interior Architecture'. Here the objective was to apply a more local variant of Soviet-style socialist realism to the realm of East German visual culture, most notably in the fields of painting, crafts, and architecture. Interior design was trickier, though, not least because 1930s neo-classicism offered little in the way of guidance for furniture and household prototypes. Equally worrisome was that Western modernism—often derisively called the 'Bauhaus style'—was still very much present in East German material life. In one newspaper article covering the Central Committee's 1951 'Battle Against Formalism in Art and Literature' Congress, the unnamed journalist reported that not only was true architecture hindered by the 'so-called "Bauhaus style" and its underlying constructivist, functionalist philosophy', but that this style was particularly pronounced in 'mass-produced furniture and household utensils'.[24] Yet it was not just formal pluralism—and potential cultural decadence—that prompted such concern. High ideological stakes were also at play, since remade East German interiors were to be publicized as emblems of a victorious socialist culture, and as such would help assure its uncertain citizenry that the future—despite present problems—still belonged to socialism. In this respect, the interior was viewed as vital in educating socialist citizens. SED Party Chairman Walter Ulbricht himself often weighed in the debate. As a trained furniture maker, he repeatedly stressed the power of well-designed domiciles in raising 'socialist consciousness'.

In one 1959 speech, for example, he remarked that properly designed residential architecture 'will promote social life, as well as the unity of personal and societal interests...The principal task is to bring family life and social life closer together. The arrangement of socialist living quarters should harmonize the inhabitant's material and cultural daily needs'.[25] For him, such socialist consciousness would naturally result from bringing socialist citizens in closer contact with beauty. By this Ulbricht meant a more traditional arts and crafts style, one that patently rejected the anonymity and industrial boxiness of modernist furniture. The SED premier made the point explicitly a few years before in his keynote speech at the two-day 1952 conference on 'Questions of German Interior Architecture and the Design of Furniture' held at East Berlin's House of Soviet Culture, when he said that 'furniture manufactured in the Bauhaus style does not correspond to the sensitivity to beauty among the new Germany's progressive human beings'.[26] The main task, however, was to design and decorate homes so that dwellers, as Ulbricht promised, 'felt happy and fortunate'.[27] A new domestic culture based on a distinctive national cultural tradition, so went the logic, would be both the precondition and proud fulfilment of a new 'socialist humanism'.

THE INVENTION OF TRADITION

What these ideals of 'national cultural tradition' and 'socialist humanism' meant changed with time. To illustrate, I would like to focus on two well-known exhibitions from the 1950s and 1960s. The first is East Berlin's 'Besser Leben-Schöner Wohnen' (Living Better, Dwelling More Beautifully) exhibition from 1953. The idea of this show grew out of SED debates the year before on the specific theme of 'realism and formalism' in domestic architecture and furniture design. Its goal was to help instil and popularize a new 'progressive, national living culture' based on a newly celebrated 'realistic interior design'. The exhibition was supposed to combat the dangers of 'culture-destroying formalism', while at the same time serving the 'spiritual and material necessities of our workers'.[28] Once again the main bugbear was the infamous 'Bauhaus-style', whose 'cult of the ugly and the immoral' was denounced for having perversely deformed postwar German architecture and industrial design in the name of the 'profit-seeking economy of imperialism'.[29] According to internal documents about the preparations for the exhibition, 'Bauhaus machine-furniture is Enemy Number One', with 'eclecticism' and 'kitsch' not far behind as 'Enemy Number Two'.[30] Such sentiments were nothing new, having been enshrined as official ideology in the 'Formalism Debate' two years earlier when modernism was summarily condemned as toxic and degenerate Western influence. But in this case the danger went well beyond painting and literature; given the basis of industrial mass production, these 'degenerate' architectural forms were everywhere. Even worse was the fact that these mass-produced 'alienated forms' had penetrated the private sphere. This was all the more perilous, since interior design supposedly determined the very form, actions, and even understanding of home life. As Jakob Jordan, the director of the Bauakademie Research Institute for Interior Architecture, put it, 'the domicile and its interior design (*Innenarchitektur*) indeed play an especially active role in the development of a progressive consciousness among our workers. The necessity of a realistic orientation is a vital precondition for a new German living culture.'[31]

In this instance the way forward was to look back to tradition, which was interpreted as the very font of cultural identity, aesthetic education and psychological ballast. As Jordan concluded:

there can therefore be no disregarding of our own national cultural heritage. Let's show each other in a dignified manner how to carry on this crusade into our consciousness, how to build a beautiful life that summons our energies for the still greater successes of our Five Year Plan to come. In this way, we architects are helping the state to achieve its goals faster. We are consequently meeting the challenge of giving form to a new interior design style that will help develop and raise the nation's taste, while at the same time enthusing our people with new progressive ideas.[32]

Design's importance thus went well beyond style wars; instead, aesthetics was viewed as instrumental in binding state and citizen.

Some 67,000 visitors flocked to the show to glimpse the future, and to see what the regime had in store for its hallowed 'working community'. Not surprisingly the exhibition catalogue began by praising Stalinallee as the guiding star for East Germany's new 'domestic culture'. Its harmonious 'architectural ensemble' supposedly reflected 'the humanism underlying our democratic order in connection with a progressive national architectural heritage'.[33] Not that Stalinallee boasted any pure pedigree: it harked back to the more conservative architectural style of the Kaiserreich, while at the same time paying homage to the official style of postwar Soviet architecture of the early 1950s. The problem, however, was that most East German interiors were seen to be grossly at odds with this new spirit. To help bring exterior and interior into a new unity, the show's organizers mounted thirty small exhibition rooms featuring both positive and negative models from the late medieval past down to the present. As such the show functioned as a kind of history lesson of German home furnishings from the state, one that made clear which traditions were acceptable and which were not. Each room included short commentary condemning or praising the particular style on display. Little surprise that Gründerzeit eclecticism, Jugendstil subjectivism and above all Bauhaus functionalism invited special ire. The catalogue was also not timid in singling out certain hotels and restaurants in the capital and other large East German cities as fifth-column 'capitalist monuments' (for example, the Dresden Hotel in Berlin) in their midst.

More interesting perhaps is the way that certain styles—namely Schinkel neo-classicist furniture, English Chippendale, and early nineteenth-century

Biedermeier—were routinely lauded for their simplicity, taste, and proportion. In fact, postwar furniture makers were encouraged to take their cues from these older styles. As Figure 10 indicates, every attempt was made to draw connections between past and present—in this case, between eighteenth-century English Chippendale styling and 1950s Building Academy-designed chairs, or between early nineteenth-century Biedermeier and the always-celebrated reception room of East Berlin's Soviet Embassy. More traditional German *Volkskunst* and rustic styles—presumably as part of the effort to distance the GDR from Nazi 'blood and soil' ideology—received scant attention. What emerged as the venerated 'realistic living culture' were to a large extent recycled models from the early 1930s. As seen in Figure 11, it was a style expressly rooted in tradition, whose artisanal materials and hand-crafted appearance were explicitly counterposed to the hard-edged world of steel and concrete outside. The implicit notion was that East Germany was the true guardian of German culture and tradition, not least because the Federal Republic was supposedly in the process of sacrificing its venerable national past on the altar of naked American-style economic interest and spiritless functionalism. So much so that the exhibition organizers crowed that this 'new blossoming of our national living culture' will doubtlessly 'win more and more friends in West Germany' as they too will appreciate the socialist republic's cultivation of Germany's common cultural heritage. The goal was to help build 'a life of happiness and prosperity in a united Fatherland through the design of beautiful dwellings'.[34] The irony of course was that this East German

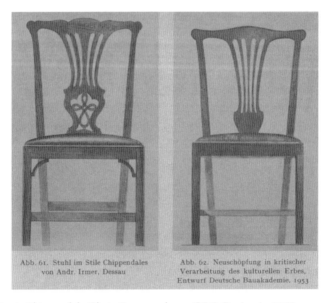

Abb. 61. Stuhl im Stile Chippendales von Andr. Irmer, Dessau

Abb. 62. Neuschöpfung in kritischer Verarbeitung des kulturellen Erbes, Entwurf Deutsche Bauakademie, 1953

Figure 10. A Chippendale Chair Compared to a GDR Design in 1953.

Figure 11. Inspirations for GDR Interior Design, from *Besser Leben, Schöner Wohnen* (1953).

'national style' was really a makeover from selected international styles of the past, and even bourgeois ones at that (i.e. Biedermeier). But such inconsistencies hardly troubled the regime overmuch, largely because such internationalism could be safely rediscovered under the umbrella of the broadly defined 'socialist style'. East German domestic furnishings were to be distinguished by heightened artistic value and stylistic continuity, reflecting the proud craftsmanship, *Lebens-freude,* and technical achievement allegedly characterizing socialist culture. Not that the show yielded cultural dividends. Many of the prototypes on display were unavailable to consumers; those that were were often beyond the financial reach of most citizens.[35] Many visitors were reportedly disappointed, and continued to buy some of the more modernist furniture styles if for no other reason than that they were readily available and cheaper.[36] Still, the show was of great cultural importance, to the extent that it captured the Party's idealized union of classic bourgeois culture and communist private life. It was also revealing in the way that it sought to provide cultural ballast for a new republic with shallow historical roots, all while giving form to the regime's promises of 'worker palaces' and domestic comfort for all.

MODERNIZATION AT HOME

The second selected exhibition took place almost a decade later. This was the famed 1962 'P2 Wohnung' (P2 Dwelling) show, which marked a dramatic shift in East German ideology and outlook. In the intervening years, much had

changed. The thinly disguised threats issued from the 1953 show were heeded
less and less by East German manufacturers and the public. The demonized
Bauhaus style and functional forms continued apace—albeit under new mon-
ikers such as 'good form'—in the name of cost-cutting industrial production.
This was especially true in the sphere of interior design, where Soviet models
lagged behind technical developments in East German furniture production
and consumer goods technology.[37] The modernist cause also enjoyed increasing
patronage from new official Soviet ideology, as Khrushchev to everyone's surprise
now changed tack in his 1954 speech at the Moscow University Conference on
Soviet architecture. In it he rejected the Stalinist penchant towards monument-
alism and *Baukunst*, arguing that such expensive decorative styling ultimately
hindered the construction of badly needed housing. He even went so far as to
make the ironic point that Soviet architects were themselves in danger of
becoming more 'constructivist' than their Western enemies, in that they had
unduly subordinated all considerations to outward form. Instead, Khrushchev
commanded architects, engineers, and planners to modernize the Eastern bloc's
building industry and appearance by 'building better, cheaper and faster'.[38] Only
such a modern industrial building programme, so argued the Soviet premier,
could help redress the catastrophic housing situation bedevilling the Soviet
Union. Many East German observers were perplexed by Khrushchev's dizzying
ideological pirouette. Rearguard warnings about the pitfalls of such modern
styles were issued by the East Berlin Bauakademie,[39] while Ulbricht himself
condemned East German 'technoid' domestic modernism ('black coffee cups,
black souls', as he put it once) for being spiritually bankrupt.[40]

Nonetheless, the portals of modernization were now wide open. There was a
new interest in learning from the West, and modernism was slowly being
rehabilitated across the GDR. In 1957, as architecture historian Greg Castillo
has shown, the Bauakademie Research Institute for Interior Architecture dispatched a model East German home to a Munich design show on 'How Does
Europe Live Today?', and was praised in a West German journal for its progressive design and 'sense of European standard'.[41] The changes quickly made their
mark on the world of industrial architecture and housing construction. In 1958,
for example, only 12 per cent of new housing units were built with prefabricated
components. By 1963 this figure had leapt to 63 per cent.[42] Of perhaps more
relevance here is that the shift also helped unleash a new crusade to make over
East German interiors in this new modern style. A raft of new interior decoration
and industrial design journals were founded in the mid to late 1950s, including
Kultur im Heim (1957) and *Form und Zweck* (1957), to serve as pacesetters for
East German domestic modernism.

The famed 'P2' Berlin exhibition of 1962 was born of this spirit. It pivoted on
a new design for East German 'domestic culture'; it derived its name—P2—from
the new five-storey residential housing block design (Figure 12). It was fully
prefabricated and standardized according to new industrial techniques, and was,

Figure 12. Prototype of a P2 Standard Dwelling, Exterior.

as one of its chief designers recalled in a 1995 interview, the realization of old Bauhaus dreams.[43] The design was publicized as a symbol of the regime's renewed commitment to improving the material life of workers, as well as further evidence of socialism's cultural progress.[44] No doubt the 1961 construction of the Berlin Wall loomed in the background, to the extent that the 1962 show aimed to stem growing internal criticism about socialism's backwardness and material misery. The SED looked to the wonders of science, engineering, and technology to transform socialist life in new and exciting ways.[45] It was during the early 1960s that the SED decided to embark on its daring experiment in 'consumer socialism'—complete with state advertising agencies, colorful product packaging, modern furniture, household decoration magazines, mail-order clearinghouses, and even state travel bureaux—as a kind of Great Leap Forward in the modernization of GDR material culture. Passages from Marx and Engels's *German Ideology*—in particular the one stating that 'Life however involved above all eating and drinking, a dwelling, clothing and other things. The first historical act is thus the production of the means to satisfy these needs'—were repeatedly cited to illustrate the SED's firm commitment to meeting the consumer needs and desires of its citizens.[46] Yet it was housing that held centrestage in this reform initiative, and it was this P2 design that fundamentally remade East German domestic life. In fact, it became the standard

Figure 13. Kitchen in a Model P2 Dwelling.

model of East German residential building construction from 1962 all the way until 1990. Already by 1965 over 80 per cent of all new dwellings were built along these lines.

   The design's real innovation was in the interior. First, it explicitly rejected the Bauakademie-inspired 'realistic living culture' concept espoused at the 1953 'Living Better' show. This time there was virtually nothing about tradition or the past; even the once-obligatory references to the USSR were muted. In fact, inspiration for these ideas actually came from Scandinavia and West Germany.[47] Special emphasis fell on the more practical issues of the home's ground plan: it was a more integrated use of tighter spaces, including built-in bookshelves and wall-units; it was also relatively open in plan, featuring large windows, central heating, small efficient kitchens and bathrooms for its users (Figure 13). What is more, the living room was foregrounded as the real centre of domestic life. Such a design represented a fundamental departure from traditional worker housing, which tended to make the enlarged kitchen (*Wohnküche*) the worker domicile's real centrepiece (usually because it was the warmest room).[48] The new plan reflected the idea of the home as primarily a respite of leisure and relaxation, one that put family life as the heart of socialist solidarity. Its novelty is more striking if we contrast it with Stalinallee residences. There the worker apartment was not dominated by the living room; relatively generous space was given to the kitchen and bedrooms instead. Even more revealing is that the guiding logic of Stalinallee was one of socialist community, of a kind where housing units, common rooms, grocery stores, bookstores, sports facilities, and cafes were all integrated into a larger architectonic whole. In this case the aim was to create a semi-enclosed socialist world based on organized community and collectivist living.[49] In the P2 interior, by contrast, the modern technology of the large communal kitchens had been integrated into each individual apartment, while the living room was enlarged to enable family members to spend more time together. The large collective spaces (common rooms, state-run *Handelsorganisation* shops, etc.) were either located elsewhere, or reduced in size and importance.

The P2 model was thus both a departure and continuity with the 1953 exposition. In the 1953 show, for example, the task was not simply to educate East German citizens into bourgeois taste and style. It also featured a bourgeois conception of the home itself, one in which the home was seen as a respite of familial socialization and repose. The world of technology, production, and rationalization was noticeably absent. There were no traces of the interwar fascination with bringing Fordist factory ethics—much of which was based on the disciplining and rationalization of the female homemaker—into the home. Indeed, housework and domestic labour—let alone its work station, the kitchen— hardly figured in this show at all. Housework, in the forms of communal laundries and kitchens, was to be taken out of the private domicile altogether. By contrast, the 1962 show marked the full-scale introduction of the world of industrial technology and rationalization into the home.[50] The socialization of household services still continued apace, but there was increasing clamour from women's groups for more labour-saving appliances to ease their double burden of work and domestic duties. This was especially pressing in light of the fact that the late 1950s witnessed the massive influx of women into the GDR workforce.[51] Such design changes were thus in large measure propelled 'from below' as the state worked to address the plight of women and working families under duress.[52] Yet policy—and interior design—still assumed that women were and would be the primary homemakers. The P2 show—to say nothing of the gendered literature and advertising surrounding the exhibition—made this plain. In this sense, the 1962 show was a mixture of nineteenth-century ideology and mid-twentieth-century socialist demands, and became the guiding image of GDR domesticity for decades to come.

Such a ground plan was also a boon to modern furniture designers and decorators. The small spaces made larger, representational furniture almost impossible; newer styles—including Scandinavian and West German Modern—were considered more appropriate for this kind of modern living. Gone was the accent on preserving the German arts and crafts tradition, or any efforts to close off the dwelling from the technological world outside. Exterior and interior were again to be harmonized, but this time in the spirit of industrial modernity. But this was not just an urban phenomenon. Design and home advice journals, women's magazines (*Für Dich,* 1963) and Regional Home Advice Centres played a decisive role in popularizing East German modernism far beyond the capital.[53] Not that East German designers ever completely abandoned the 1950s rhetoric of the elevated artistic and even spiritual quality of things. While it is true that the new stress upon austerity, rationality, and functional use-value was seen as the perfect expression of the larger GDR effort to create a controlled socialist consumer culture ('each according to his needs') that did not fall prey to capitalist decadence and commodity fetishism,[54] modern interior design was still seen as possessing formidable affective powers.

At the Fifth German Art Exposition in 1962, for example, design moved to the centre of the SED's crusade to modernize socialist culture. Given that design was considered an 'applied art' endowed with the 'spiritual qualities' that could move and win its subjects, designers were now summoned alongside writers and artists to provide new sources of affective identification with the state. As noted by East German Design Council director Martin Kelm, the new socialist designer's chief task was to 'contribute to the development of the socialist lifestyle and character'.[55] Such views lay behind the state's motivation to introduce more zip and excitement in socialist furniture and product design, not least because the SED feared that functionalist socialist goods looked too ascetic and cheap.[56] The 1960s explosion of colourful plastics in GDR interiors registered the shift, as plastics were now championed as a vital element in modernizing and beautifying GDR interiors, what Ulbricht called 'an essential element of the socialist cultural revolution'.[57]

As a consequence, the picture of the modern socialist family relaxing together amid the latest design goods and consumer technology—like in West Germany—became a mass-produced symbol of normality, security, and prosperity in GDR lifestyle journals. This was a common cold war emblem across divided Europe. While disputes continued over what counted as proper domestic form, it is clear that the home and the restored nuclear family it housed served as Europe's romanticized sphere of postwar moral and aesthetic idealism. There were thus real similarities between West and East European domestic cultures in terms of the cultural representations of happiness and the good life. Admittedly, the favourite West German image of the modern middle-class home complete with elegantly dressed (that is, non-working) housewives and high-tech kitchens was a distinguishing self-representation of the leisured, affluent West.[58] But even here, the 1950s and 1960s ideals of East German home life—despite SED rhetoric about the full equality of the sexes—betrayed its own myth of the 'new woman in socialism', based to a large degree upon old bourgeois assumptions of proper female behaviour and duties. Not only were images of the cheerful nuclear family touted as the very embodiment of fulfilment in East German media; women were photographed at home (and at work) in such a manner that underscored a more traditional feminine identity.[59] In this way, both Germanies shared a common perception about the elective affinity of traditional family and domestic modernity as a key hallmark of post-fascist culture.

By the end of the 1960s, the state's growing preoccupation with the private sphere also found expression in a new guise: market research. Whereas the SED concern with private life in the 1950s usually centred on issues of housing safety and hygiene, social welfare and family stability, it took on a decidedly new twist in the 1960s. The Institute of Market Research now routinely sent market researchers into people's homes, asking them about furniture preferences, design ideas, and aesthetic predilections. Officially market research was to encompass 'the full scope of conditions under which the realization of use-value and the satisfaction of national economic concerns' could best be met.[60] But there were other issues at work. A surprising number of painstaking analyses on East German domestic interiors, decorative tastes, and consumer habits were drafted and sent to various government committees. Included among them were elaborate consumer questionnaires detailing deep-seated gender, generational, and even class differences in East German taste and consumer spending.[61] Frank and quite unfavourable comparisons to West German consumer trends were surprisingly common in these papers. These reports on generational and class distinctions became even more detailed in the 1970s, as modern furniture styles were increasingly attributed to the young, educated, urban, and upwardly mobile; disproportionate dissatisfaction with available decorative items and housewares was also recorded among students.[62] These marketeers served as veritable foot soldiers in the wider crusade to modernize East German material culture and to bring the country along the path of 'consumer socialism'.[63] But it was also true that these marketing scouts were valued for their role in gauging private dissatisfaction and identifying the 'psychological barriers' obstructing the full development of socialist domestic culture. Often seemingly trivial issues about domestic lifestyle attracted considerable attention from these officials. One 1963 Institute of Market Research report on upholstered furniture, for example, conceded that many GDR families were forced to use the living room as a makeshift bedroom, and the sofa as a bed. Poorly designed sofas, so the report concluded, are thus leading to a dangerous 'physical and moral wear and tear on our workers', since the 'gap between the supply and demand' of modern, well-made furniture is deepening resentment and criticism towards the state.[64] Another 1971 market research report underlined its task in helping build a sustainable national 'living culture' in stating that 'the dwelling is no counter-world to the sphere of labour, no so-called "private retreat tower," but rather is more and more an integrated element of a comprehensive socialist everyday life'.[65] From this perspective, the interior design crusade takes on a decidedly more political dimension.

The housing exhibitions reflected these larger impulses. One architect affiliated with the 1952 Berlin 'Besser Leben' exhibition, for instance, made it quite clear that this 'new living culture infused with progressive elements' would entail more than just cosmetic changes; for him, it also necessitated the full dissolution of the boundary between public and private:

We know that political consciousness is for many not sufficiently developed to enable citizens to distinguish beautiful and good from ugly and bad. Such a faculty is analogous to an adopted child. Only when such material education penetrates [the citizen's] most inner being, including the world of his dreams and fantasies, only when we have fully recognized how intimately and indelibly connected the substance of life is with the form of life, will such changes bear fruit.[66]

At the very least, such statements cast these exhibitions in a different light, revealing the extent to which they were partly inspired by the impulse to remake the relationship between citizen and state.

ETIQUETTE AND SOCIALIST CIVILIZATION

The effort to redesign domestic space was also accompanied by the drive to make over its inhabitants. A revealing example is the East German cottage industry of etiquette books. The immediate postwar period saw a remarkable flourishing of etiquette books across Europe (and North America), beginning in the late 1940s and reaching its apogee in the late 1950s. To the extent that these books are usually read as symptomatic of 'recasting bourgeois Europe' after 1945, the postwar boom in etiquette books has been considered almost exclusively as a Western phenomenon. Yet these manuals were equally prominent in the East, and went through numerous editions there too as popular guides to helping people behave and stylize their lives according to new postwar principles.[67] Fewer guides may have been published in East Germany than in West Germany, but those that were enjoyed robust circulation and full state backing. Karl Smolka's 1957 *Gutes Benehmen von A bis Z* (Good Behavior from A to Z), went through ten reprintings by 1974, whereas W. K. Schweickert and Bert Hold's 1959 *Guten Tag, Herr von Knigge! Ein heiteres Lesebuch für alle Jahrgänge über alles, was 'anständig' ist* (Good Morning, Herr Knigge! A Humorous Book for Everyone about What is Proper) was already in its twentieth reprint by 1969.[68] East Germany was a particularly fertile ground for these guidebooks, not least because there was so much concern about the moral makeover of Germany and Germans after 1945. This is not simply a story of relearned table manners after the war, however. Central was to re-educate the self, retrain the body and mind to live in a new post-fascist world, as well as to reschool a thoroughly militarized society in the values of peace, dignity, and personal honour.[69]

These texts captured the SED's mission to build a new socialist culture on a new concept of selfhood. It was one in which the gestures and small coin of everyday life—eating, drinking, dressing, and conversing—were key elements of this new crusade to correct the 'crooked timber of humanity'. In their estimation, practising good manners was inseparable from the grand historical triumph of socialist civilization itself. Smolka's *Good Behavior from A to Z* heralded the new dawn of socialist civility thus:

The vast majority of the population has been excluded from the rules of good form and the opportunity to apply them, just as they have been excluded from justice and education. For the first time in German history, in the Workers' and Peasants' State, our GDR, the working population is setting the tone. It is now in a position to acquire those things that were withheld for so long: education, knowledge—including knowledge of the rules of good form, which help to determine how people live together.[70]

For Schweikert and Hold, this new socialist morality represented nothing less than the great liberation of the twentieth century's real protagonist, the 'kleiner Mann', or common man. East German etiquette book authors routinely condemned their West German counterparts as brazen egotism dressed up as personal cultivation, whose main message was primarily about gaining a competitive edge and using manners for personal career advancement.[71] Traditional etiquette books, so they continued, had been infused with the sensibility of the underling, reflecting a strict social hierarchy built on hypocrisy and injustice. Socialist society in turn was hailed as its very antithesis, insomuch as it ushered in a 'new humanity' based on the values of equality, solidarity, and mutual respect.[72] In this setting, correct table manners took their designated place in the utopian dream of a post-capitalist world of peace and probity. Manners, morals, and Marxism were seen as inextricably linked, as perfectly expressed in the following passage from Schweiker and Hold's book: 'Man in socialist society, when it is in full bloom, will have neither the opportunity nor the desire to behave badly. He will not dissemble, bow, scrape, or swindle, neither will he eat fish off a knife, or drink champagne out of red wine glasses, any more than he will rob or exploit others.'[73]

Such sentiment was part of the regime's broader preoccupation with radical social transformation, uprooting previous class structures and traditions and replacing them with a new Soviet-style society. State officials had no qualms about intervening in the sphere of manners and decorum. As we saw in Chapter 2, Ulbricht propagated his normative 'Ten Socialist Commandments' in 1958, with their emphasis on performance, loyalty, cleanliness, and decency. Workers were encouraged to make 'personal pledges' to their colleagues about good socialist comportment: 'I shall endeavor to enthuse my wife for our good cause' or 'take the Ten Commandments of socialist ethics and morality as the guiding principles by which to act within the family in a socialist manner'.[74] These commandments were widely published in the media, and mass-produced in card form to be carried around in wallets or to display on the mantelpiece at home. Functionaries and school teachers were to preach the virtues of pursuing a career, founding a family, and working diligently and uncomplainingly for the good of the country.[75] In his keynote speech at the 11th Plenum in 1965 Erich Honecker proclaimed that 'Our GDR is a clean state, in which there are unshakable standards of ethics and morality, of propriety and decorum'.[76] As such these views dovetailed with the incessant discussion of creating new 'socialist personalities' for socialist state and society.[77] But like in Stalin's Soviet Union, the new virtues of socialist behaviour also implied a transformation of public values, effecting the transition from militant revolutionary asceticism to individual consumption based on a prosperous private life and civilized conduct.[78]

These manners manuals betrayed a mixture of new and old. Despite all of the rhetoric about socialist difference, the GDR guides to eating and greeting expressed a discernibly similar tone and message to their Western rivals. They too were concerned with detailed instructions on how to sit, walk, and shake hands, when to take off your hat and use the informal (*Du*) grammatical case, how to set the table and dine properly, how to behave in trams or at the doctor's office, and when and which gifts should be brought to dinner parties. There were however some distinctive features: the world of work received surprisingly little coverage in East German guides, while a good amount of space was devoted to the theme of how to get on with rude civil servants and bureaucrats. In the realm of home decoration, modern personal touches were everywhere praised, to the extent that 'everyone wishes to be tasteful, comfortable, unostentatious and functionally-decorated, so as to keep in step with the living conditions of our social order'.[79] The same went for encouraging a more relaxed, informal, and 'modern' attitude in terms of getting along with comrades in everyday settings. Still, these manuals harboured plenty of traditional attitudes, and often were criticized for not being modern enough. While it is difficult to gauge the wider reception of these books beyond sales statistics, since the state control of the media did not permit a critical book review culture, the reader reports solicited by the presses give some indication of what people felt at the time. Interestingly, reviewers assessing Smolka's *Good Behavior* book judged it too conservative. One complained that the book was too old-fashioned in discussing 'completely obsolete' themes such as women's clothes and 'bridal showers'; specifically East German features of modern life—such as having weddings take place in the factory—were to be encouraged instead.[80] In another, Smolka was taken to task for including a section on confirmation and baptism, while ignoring the newly instituted 'rite of socialist name-giving' as its secular substitute. On this score, the critics pointed out these books' 'petit bourgeois attitude' in propagating a buttoned-up socialism that preached moderation and propriety above all else.[81] In this way, these books had more in common with late nineteenth-century bourgeois manners guides than with the more radical *proletkult* pronouncements propounded by the early Soviet Union or the communist subculture of the Weimar Republic.[82] These socialist courtesy manuals reflected what German philosopher Ernst Bloch derided as the GDR's 'dictatorship of petit-bourgeois taste in the name of the proletariat'.[83]

These petit bourgeois sensibilities were patently on display in their attitudes towards women and girls. That the socialist world in general—and the GDR in particular—harboured strangely traditional views of women and family after 1945 is well known.[84] Scholars such as Ina Merkel and Donna Harsch have noted the ways in which the promotion of socialist family values—much of which assumed that the wife/mother would bear the responsibility for housework and child-raising—flew in the face of vaunted socialist ideology about the full equality of the sexes.[85] GDR women's magazines, such as *Frauen von Heute, Für Dich,* and *Junge Welt*, went to great lengths to argue that women needed to maintain their femininity at work, often in the form of make-up and 'womanly attitude'. Etiquette books mostly concentrated on the world after work, and it was here that they championed a host of petit bourgeois ideals, not unlike their West German counterparts. It was precisely at home and on the town where women and girls were to cultivate their femininity with grace and charm. In this sense, GDR guidebooks ironically indicated how 'bourgeois rules of deportment had been adapted to the new society'.[86]

No less striking was that the intended audience for these books was often young men. Karl Smolka's widely circulated 1964 *Junger Mann von heute* (Young Man of Today) is a good example of this socialist dispensation.[87] Smolka's book aimed to educate the socialist young man as a civilized member of the community, taking pains to provide detailed advice on the importance of working well, serving in the military with honour, being a good friend, choosing a compatible partner, and enjoying sports. Individual chapters were devoted to personal hygiene, nutrition, moderate drinking, clothing, interior design, sex education, and even cooking. A wealth of illustrations were included to help readers visualize how best to open doors for women, dress smartly, decorate the living room, comb your hair, and even wash your face. Where these books departed from West German equivalents was not only in the 'softer' form of masculinity, replete with tips on sewing and attractive hairstyling. It was also distinguished by a more comprehensive approach to the young man's life. West German guides by contrast tended to limit their advice for young men to work, dress, and decorum for the public sphere—the private sphere of home life was more or less confined to table manners. This was certainly the case with sexual intimacy, which was rarely discussed in West German manners guides until the late 1960s. In the East German books, sexual education was a common topic, and enjoyed relatively extensive coverage from the mid-1950s on.[88] Scholars have argued that this East

German emphasis on bodily pleasures became an important expression of individual liberty in a world where citizens enjoyed few political freedoms.[89] That may be so, but what I find especially noteworthy is the extent to which these East German etiquette guides were explicitly concerned with regulating intimate rituals of personal self-care. The subtle need to erase the boundaries between 'private life and collective life under socialism without overdoing it, since it is much better if done unobtrusively' animated the confidential reports to the press about these etiquette books.[90] With this in mind, one could say that the pith of *Young Man of Today* book lay in the passage: 'It is a calming feeling to be bound to a collective. An isolated individual can go in false directions, while the collective will always be there to help rescue the individual from the labyrinth of errant ideas, beliefs and decisions. A single individual can be weak, but his power only grows in tandem with others. Everything should go toward collective life.'[91] To the extent that this book was about socializing the young person into the ways of adulthood, ranging from love to ironing, its thrust was toward deprivatizing private life in the name of 'socialist community'.[92] Here and elsewhere the emphasis fell on remaking citizens at home as an extension of the broader communist project to refashion citizens in the workplace, at school, and in public life.

For this reason, it is mistaken to dismiss these GDR manners books as simply traditional and petit bourgeois. Like the exhibitions and decoration advice literature, there was a very modern sensibility at work in this etiquette book industry, and this was the notion of social engineering. It is worth taking Karl Kleinschmidt's foreword to his 1961 *Don't Be Afraid of Good Manners* quite seriously as part of the GDR's radical reconstruction of East German society: 'So much must be conceived of anew, since socialist society has developed new relations between people, and this must be reflected in good manners.'[93] In the early 1960s the advice books took on a more urgent tone. By that time, there was growing anxiety in the guidebooks that, despite the eradication of capitalism and liberal political structures, East German citizens had not been sufficiently changed in terms of everyday life. This was no cultural trifle, since it implied that Marx's classic formulation that the revolution of the base would necessitate a transformation of the superstructure (values, culture) had not come to pass as predicted. The survival of 'petit bourgeois attitudes' seen in increasing youth crime, vandalism, and domestic violence all pointed up that 'socialist civilization' was not automatically emerging, and thus the superstructure (including domestic life) needed more robust state intervention. It was becoming plain to all that passages from the courtesy manuals about the GDR's 'special consciousness of togetherness and community' and that 'socialists really are friends in the private sphere as well' were little more than wishful thinking.[94] As will be discussed in the next chapter, the impolite nature of GDR society was patently on display in the proceedings of the so-called residential dispute commissions (*Schiedskommissionen*) about neighbourhood conflict. The unavoidable conclusion was that 'socialist civility' was not all that visible in everyday residential settings, and needed more state attention.

1970s LIFESTYLE

Particularly revealing are the shifts in the 1970s in this regard. By now it is common to emphasize the standard line about the relative liberalization and normalization of the Honecker years. Many observers have noted the ways in which the ascent of Honecker marked a significant relaxation in GDR social engineering, as the SED moved from intense cold war antagonism and internal political transformation towards more accommodating ideas of cohabitation and domestic stabilization. A widely distributed poster commemorating the thirtieth anniversary of the GDR in 1979 captured the spirit of the time, showing a happy family living in a house drawn as if by a child, with the caption 'Here we're at home.'[95] By then the socialist state had supposedly eased its demands on and scrutiny of its citizens, mirroring trends across the Eastern bloc.[96] One British journalist reported the sea change in the GDR in 1977:

People withdraw into the privacy of their homes after all the collective activity of the day. In the period after the war, a social worker said, the authorities found it suspicious if someone stayed too much at home and declined to take part in communal activities. The party leadership felt threatened and unsure on many grounds. A citizen's refusal to take part was interpreted as a sign of passive resistance. In some cases it was. Now the party accepts that there is a legitimate sphere for private life and a human need for people to recharge their batteries at home. 'Respect and protection of the family' are laid down in the Constitution.[97]

For many people, the family became 'synonymous with leisure, freedom and privacy'.[98] By the early 1980s such sociological trends were common knowledge, and even openly admitted in state publications.[99]

This was certainly noticeable in the GDR home advice literature. Everywhere was the new term 'diversity,' as the Ulbricht Era campaign to standardize East German domestic culture gave way to a celebration of stylistic difference. The 1970s saw a new emphasis on imaginative varieties of decorative styles and upholstered interiors, even if most of the furniture models themselves remained virtually unchanged from the 1960s (Figure 14).[100] The trend towards more 'individual forms' and personalized expression was noted in market research as well.[101] Arts and crafts objects now made a comeback, and existed in easy cohabitation with East German industrial modernism.[102] Revealingly, the prescriptive industry of etiquette book writing all but disappeared by the early 1970s. All of this was interpreted as part of the Honecker era's accommodationist attitude towards the domestic sphere, as citizens increasingly used their homes (or rooms, in the case of teenagers) as theatres of pent-up individuality and

(a)

(b)

Figure 14a–b. Sibylle Bergemann, Various P2 Interiors, 1970s.

subcultural pursuits.[103] This too found expression across the Eastern bloc, reflecting a more general relaxation of policies that demanded cultural homogeneity and conformity.[104] By the late 1980s the home decoration magazine *Kultur im Heim* was even doing features on various social group styles and subculture designs, as their once strictly normative ideals of a uniform national domestic culture dropped away.[105] One East German sociologist summarized this view when he wrote that

[t]he withdrawal of the regime from the private sphere created a new free space for the development of materialism, pleasure-seeking and individuality. The one-time identification with the system, with official public life and ideological commitment, eventually gave way to a decline in the legitimacy of the system, to a turning away from publicness and idealism altogether ... The 1970s was then a period of retreating to new private and individual free spaces, in which one could take refuge from the large events outside, which went hand in hand with the draining of all idealism.[106]

Interviewees confirmed these trends. As one questionnaire respondent recalled in 2005: 'The private sphere was important to me [as a place] where the confrontation between prescribed attitude and one's real feelings were openly provoked', and a place 'where thinking differently was not excluded'.[107]Domestic life may have remained communal, but it had become less and less collectivist.

Such retreat could be seen in other ways. One was the popular penchant toward spending weekends at country cottages, small garden plots, or dachas outside the city. The phenomenon was most famously described in Ulrich Plenzdorf's 1973 novel, *The New Sorrows of Young W*, in which the protagonist, Edgar Wibeau, takes refuge in a shack outside Berlin as relief from the general pressure of industrial life and the patronizing attitude of his foreman at work. Such activities were not just common among young people, but had become a widely practised pursuit by the mid-1970s. While the SED was initially concerned about this popular weekend exodus to the countryside, it grudgingly accepted it as a sop to popular culture.[108] With time the state even made it easier for people to build bungalows around Berlin and other cities, and magazines featuring home improvements, fashion, and leisure activities flourished in response.[109] The love of country cottages was of course extremely common across the Soviet Union and the Eastern bloc,[110] though East Germans cultivated their gardens with particular gusto. Published recollections make clear that dachas and small country garden houses were cherished in large measure because people felt more private there than anywhere else.[111] As one East Berlin diarist put it in 1977: 'the dacha was a Russian word for a German desire', a place where 'a certain individualism ruled'.[112] For many interviewees and questionnaire respondents having a dacha was a potent symbol of the private sphere. One went so far as to call it 'his own individual piece of the people's property',[113] whereas another confessed that it was the only place where one felt 'unobserved, naked and free'.[114] An East German woman spoke for many when she remarked 'We had a little dacha, and this is where we talked and complained and got angry. And it this is exactly how every other GDR citizen did it as well. Everybody had a niche in which he sat and quietly complained.'[115] It was a world in which informal sociability thrived, as East Germans 'disappeared on weekends and evenings into a "Bermuda triangle" of home, car and allotment garden'.[116]

Another form of retreat was of course television. In the 1970s and 1980s television-viewing, especially watching West German programmes, became far and away the most popular pastime for many East Germans.[117] It served as 'nightly collective political anesthesia' for many.[118] By that time the percentage of East German citizens who owned television sets was nearly as high as that of the US. What is more, the 'noctural migration via the airwaves' offered a 'cherished window into the "nonsocialist world"'.[119] While the SED initially outlawed and then tried to limit the reception of Western media, it eventually caved in to popular practice in the name of peace and stability. In fact, the GDR permitted the reception of West German television in the 1970s in the hope that if East Germans could watch West German television at home, then they would feel less inclined to emigrate.[120] By 1987 some 85 per cent of the population admitted to watching these 'enemy channels' on a regular basis.[121] For many citizens television also represented 'the desire for an element of private life', a rich repository of alternative news, trans-Wall fantasy, and entertainment beyond the mundane demands of work and public life.[122] Oral histories too have shown that the experience of watching Western television was instrumental in teaching children the meaning of the private sphere itself—namely, which adults to trust or suspect in regard to this illegal yet widely practised 'anti-socialist' pastime.[123] And just as Western television-viewing marked the people's emotional withdrawal from state socialism, so too did it reflect the socialist state's retreat from socialism. The tacit acceptance of Western television was akin to the growing presence of Western goods and even currency in East German life from the 1970s on, as we shall see in Chapter 6. As one East European specialist has observed, by the 1970s socialist regimes across the East Bloc 'quietly abandoned their attempts to create a new, distinctively socialist material culture', replacing it 'with an engagement with patterns of Western consumer culture'.[124]

The private sphere thus became both a place and practice by the 1970s. In part this had to do with reduced work hours and more leisure time; however, it also was related to the lack of alternatives for identification and pleasure in public life, as the regime invested less and less resources in youth clubs, leisure centres, and other public venues. Sociologists were aware that GDR citizens were deriving less satisfaction from the public world of work, and directed their emotional investment instead into the private sphere of the family.[125] It became a form of personal protection, a refuge from the demands and pressures of the outside world. As East German novelist Claudia Rusch wrote:

In a land in which citizens were so regimented and controlled, life at home was a private space of retreat where one could be free from social pressures. Like a mask the prescribed correct GDR-citizendom was hung on a peg in the doorway whereafter people became who they really were: people with needs, desires, woes, irritations, humor, etc. The color palette was mixed in private. In my family we all saw the significance of the private sphere in the same way, as the only secure place of withdrawal.[126]

Another interviewee recalled: The 'private sphere was naturally all that what one discussed at home, or behind cupped hands...When it happened, all the windows and doors were first closed, and then you could talk...One especially prized the private sphere for this, since only within one's four walls were we able to be half-way secure, or at least so we thought'.[127]

To be sure, such attitudes were hardly unusual across Eastern Europe at the time.[128] Svetlana Boym, for instance, describes the significance of domestic culture in Moscow's high rises thus: 'In the 1960s an alternative "kitchen culture" emerged. The members of the Moscow intelligentsia who happened to live in their own separate flats started to have unofficial kitchen gatherings in their homes. . . . The kitchen provided a perfect informal setting for the subtle, casual but friendly intimacy that became a signature of that generation.'[129] This was scarcely the intention of the architects and designers. Rather than seeing the modern apartment as a site of socialist formation and ideological renewal, Boym's generation reworked these spaces as social sanctuaries against the regime. The same went for the GDR. The older the GDR got, the more important the private sphere—and especially the home—became for its citizens.[130]

But it is wrong to say that state abandoned the private sphere. The 1970s in no way spelt a de-escalation in measures used to monitor private lives. On the contrary, they were intensified considerably in scope and ambition. Hannah Arendt's comment that 'the four walls of one's private property offer the only reliable hiding place from the common public world, not only from everything that goes on in it but also from its very publicity, from being seen and begin heard' had little application east of the Berlin Wall.[131] This could be seen in various ways, such as the 'housing community' material discussed in Chapter 1. Admittedly, the more ham-fisted language of the housing communities as a vital means of 'raising national consciousness' and theoretically doing away with the private sphere in the name of national community had clearly fallen off under Honecker, as there was a discernible shift toward the defence of the nuclear family as the 'true cell' of socialist community and personality.[132] Nonetheless, the decade signalled a dilation of the state into family and private life all the same. The organization of competitions, festivals, and social events associated with the housing communities—to say nothing of the National Front-sponsored *Mach Mit!* (Join In!) programme to refurbish and beautify East German neighbour-hoods —actually intensified under Honecker. It was also during this time that the *Hausbuch* programme was significantly enlarged and more vigorously enforced.[133] Increasingly it was tied to security agencies, and in particular was considered 'an important part of the public work of the People's Police'.[134] Not least, the stepped-up activities of the Stasi in the 1970s and 1980s (much of which focused on activities within the home) further illustrates this abiding state obsession with the private sphere.

At first it may seem strange that these developments occurred in the 1970s. The potential threats from West Germany and the West more generally had been clearly mitigated by the construction of the Wall and the advent of Ostpolitik. National security, international recognition, and domestic stability had all been achieved, and a growing sense of normalization (including a more relaxed residential life and youth cultures) apparently pervaded the country. But as we have seen in Chapter 1, it was precisely this new distancing of state and citizen that incited renewed state apprehension about conduct in the home. For in the state's eyes, the home still remained an uncontrolled arena of individual freedom, private detachment, and potential political dissent. The 1950s campaign to construct new homes as symbols of domestic security and the good life eventually gave way to growing government fears that these same 'homes for heroes' had become dens of domestic misery and political menace. This seems to me a key, if neglected, effect of the famed Ostpolitik, in that the relaxation of East–West tensions—coupled with the widespread perception that the GDR would continue to fall further and further behind West German economic development—gave cause for state concern that the home warranted renewed political attention.

The 1977 publication of Maxie Wander's oral history of GDR women, *Guten Morgen, Du Schöne* (*Good Morning, Beautiful*) loudly spoke of this deep reservoir of dissatisfaction at the core of GDR domestic life. As noted in the last chapter, the book was extremely novel at the time, not least because it featured frank confessions by female citizens about 'real existing socialism'.[135] But if this became a kind of cult book in the GDR, it was hardly an isolated case. A sizeable number of 1970s and 1980s novels and artworks (see Chapter 7) made the same point, as alienation and domestic despair became new cultural themes.[136] Not that all the news was bad, however. One 1977 questionnaire, for instance, recorded that a majority of people polled were quite content with their home life, and went on to place 'good living conditions' next to 'good family life' and 'interesting work' as the most important indices of a 'satisfactory life'.[137] Even so, the SED could not fail to see what was happening. The increased contraction of social life to the home, or put differently, the appreciable value of the home as the cherished locus of relative freedom and pleasure, meant that private life now took on new political gravity, one that the state felt it needed to watch very carefully.

Such changes also marked a significant shift in the relationship between public and private. For all of its interest in the private sphere, the state in certain respects left families alone in the 1950s and 1960s. Indeed, no real SED family policy existed at the time. While it is certainly true that the Party tirelessly championed the nuclear family as the bedrock of social stability and political peace, and did much to socialize youth into the virtues of socialist ideology, the emergence of the family—and with it private life—as an object of state intervention was very much a product of the mid- to late 1960s, and grew dramatically in the 1970s. In part this was simply because the regime was preoccupied with the pressing issues of reconstruction, provisioning, and security in the 1950s. The 1961 construction of the Berlin Wall and *de facto* 'normalization' meant that the state was in a better position to look beyond crude productionism and infrastructure concerns towards more nagging social and domestic problems.

If nothing else, the state's growing concern with home life pointed up the dangerous interplay of privacy and politics at the heart of GDR domestic life. Just as in Stalin's Soviet Union, the notion of private life as closed sphere beyond state control continued to be rejected ideologically; yet the idea of 'personal life' as an individual realm open to public scrutiny was promoted by the state.[138] It was in this context that the home took on such political proportions in the GDR. The changing ideals of GDR domestic life—as noted in the two exhibitions under discussion—marked the shift in ideology towards a more industrially oriented 'socialist modern'. But looking at things from a purely aesthetic standpoint is limiting. For even if the decorative elements of the home may not have changed all that much from the mid-1960s, the sociological role of the home (both as desired outpost of surveillance and as a locus of resistance) did change dramatically. A 1977 editorial in the home decoration magazine *Kultur im Heim* captured the heightened significance of private life:

if the living space (*Wohnraum*) were only a repository of individual accents, subjective fantasies and 'tastemaking,' there would be no need to treat it as a social issue—it would be a purely private affair. But its primary significance in the education of the human being, in the richer formation of socialist conditions of reality, as well as in its chief function within social psychology makes its form a paramount public (*res publica*) affair.[139]

In the end, the home may not have been all that private or free, but it did serve as a kind of refuge and alternative world for many East Germans.

In the next two chapters we will look more closely at how these domestic ideals were contested at the local level, showing how they got entangled in changing expectations and demands of popular justice.

5

Property, Noise, and Honour

Neighbourhood Justice in East Berlin

Civil rights in the GDR may seem like an oxymoron to many. The stock supply of crude epithets used to describe East Germany's failed socialist state, ranging from SED-Tyranny, Red Totalitarianism, Stasi-State to *Unrechtsstaat,* imply that what most people understand as civil rights were non-starters under communist law. A well-known collection of essays comparing twentieth-century Germany and the United States as 'two cultures of rights' did not even mention the GDR.[1] Since the early 1990s dozens of best-selling histories, television programmes, and exhibitions have helped reinforce these perceptions by repeatedly trawling the GDR's lurid underworld of unfreedom, surveillance, and mass-produced misery. Even though most historians have refrained from such black-and-white renderings, a good deal of recent historiography continues to portray the GDR as twentieth-century Germany's 'second dictatorship', in effect framing its history in terms of its more famous forerunner's patent abuse of state power, civil law, and designated 'enemies of the state'. However overdrawn these comparisons have been, even the most diehard GDR sympathizers would struggle to deny the regime's low regard for civil rights and genuine democratic culture. The state's infamous flouting of the law and due process, together with the Orwellian chicanery of the state's security and police forces, make this plain enough.

And yet, it is worth recalling that citizen rights and 'socialist justice' were contentious topics in the GDR from the very beginning, and were perennial subjects of serious concern. Legal scholars unsurprisingly have been most interested in these issues, often going to great lengths to show that the whole GDR justice system was simply an arm of state power and flagrant political abuse.[2] While others like Inga Markovits and Klaus Westen have furnished much more nuanced portraits of GDR law and justice, few historians have followed their lead.[3] This is a great pity, since the field of civil law was quite complex in the GDR and was given unusual latitude over the decades.[4] Nowhere was this more apparent than with the informal 'dispute commissions', or *Schiedskommissionen,* which were set up in East German residential areas in 1963 to take pressure off the legal system and to initiate citizens into the workings of 'socialist legality'.[5] They were explicitly designed to complement the successful 'conflict commissions', or *Konfliktkommissionen,* which had been created ten years before as lay tribunals to deal with minor conflicts arising in the workplace. The brief of the dispute commissions, by contrast, was to settle quarrels between neighbours over sundry petty infractions and 'antisocial activities', with the express aim of re-educating offenders. By 1989 there were some 56,917 people serving as elected 'lay assessors' on over 5,700 dispute commissions nationwide.[6] So proud were GDR authorities of these dual 'social courts' that they were cited as late as 1989 as 'incontestable signs of the robustness of our people-oriented socialist justice system and the lawfulness of the socialist state'.[7] Since 1990 the GDR civil court system has remained one of most potent sources of nostalgia for many East German citizens.[8] While Western legal observers have long debated the political merits and meaning of these lay citizen courts,[9] they do illustrate East German citizens' extensive involvement in the state, what Mary Fulbrook has called the GDR's distinct form of 'participatory dictatorship'.[10]

What follows is an attempt to examine the role of these dispute commissions in socialist political life. Precisely because these hearings covered relatively minor infractions and thus did not invite the full machinery of the state justice system, they offer a unique glimpse into the inner workings of East German local justice. How notions of privacy were understood, presented, and adjudicated in residential communities by these neighbourhood dispute commissions is the main thrust of this chapter. To date these court records have not attracted much scholarly attention, in part because most work on GDR law tends to centre on criminal law and the machinations of the state's renowned security apparatus. Whereas other East German justice organs concentrated almost exclusively on the relationship between state and citizen, these informal citizen commissions dealt with something different, namely citizen–citizen conflict in residential communities. This chapter is based on an analysis of some 600 cases from the East Berlin districts of Friedrichshain, Treptow, Köpenick, and Lichtenberg, whose records, though far from complete, nonetheless detail the everyday tensions of East Berliners over the decades. While the first section addresses the historical background of these citizen courts, the second part will focus on three themes—personal property, noise, and slander—in order to show how socialist ideals and practices functioned at the neighbourhood level.

DISPUTE COMMISSIONS

From the very outset these citizen commissions were hailed as vital new organs of 'people's justice', precisely because they took up the small coin of socialist society. They addressed a range of citizen concerns that one might expect of small claims courts anywhere—petty theft, vandalism, truancy, minor assault, child support, failed rent payments, housing regulation violations, disturbances of the peace, insults, and sundry quarrels over personal property. While not grave enough to involve the more formal state justice system, these cases were still considered harmful 'offences against the very foundations of socialist morality'. Since they were not classified as criminal, the emphasis fell on re-educating the offender and re-establishing socialist standards of proper comportment. In cases of juvenile deliquency, for example, this often meant putting pressure on parents, teachers, and Free German Youth organizers to mind the child more carefully in the future, as well as informing the local police and the elected residential superintendent, or *Hausgemeinschaftsleiter*, about the outcome. According to official statistics, cases were almost always (reportedly up to 80 per cent) resolved 'harmoniously', foregrounding their effectiveness in repairing breaches of citizen conduct. Socialist citizen courts differed from liberal courts in that the point was not simply conflict adjudication, but also 'consciousness-raising', 'collective socialization', and the reconciliation of all parties. In this sense, socialist law was closely allied with the maintenance of social norms, whose cases often functioned as modern-day morality plays.

Procedurally, these 'quasi-courts' sought to break with traditional court proceedings in a number of ways. Formal courtrooms were avoided, and 'egalitarian' seating arrangements (gathering everyone around a large table) were recommended to foster an 'aura of informality'. Adopting a more casual approach was seen as the best means to bring about conciliation and rehabilitation. The vocabulary used to describe their actions was also telling: the tribunal was called a 'commission' rather than a court, the proceedings were referred to as 'deliberations' (*Beratungen*), and the punishment was labelled 'educational measures' (*Erziehungsmassnahmen*).[11] Given their informal nature, these courts were often termed 'not public', or *Nichtöffentlichkeit*, insofar as the court setting only included the parties involved, along with the presiding judge and lay assessors drawn from the community.[12] Still, there were clear links to the state, as commission jurists were often appointed by the National Front. While the compensation-based civil court system in the West was expressly rejected, the courts did levy small fines (up to 500 marks) and issue censures, resulting in public notices and formal apologies displayed in the buildings of residence. But this all depended on the people serving—a good many neighbourhood courts had seemingly little connection to state organs, and often enjoyed unusual freedom in their deliberations. The presence and casework of these commissions varied quite dramatically region to region, city to city, and even neighbourhood to neighbourhood. Nationally, two-thirds of them were located in rural or semi-rural communities (*Gemeinde*), and tended to be more numerous in newer cities (like Karl-Marx-Stadt) than in older ones, such as Dresden or Berlin.[13]

On average the Berlin neighbourhood commissions heard two to three cases a month, sometimes more. These numbers remained fairly steady from the early 1960s until the collapse of the regime in 1989, though there was a marked drop in the second half of the 1980s.[14] Protocols recorded the dispute and verdict, and often included letters from both parties. Overseeing the procedure was usually one presiding judge, along with ten to twelve lay assessors; but unlike Anglo-

American jurists, the assessors were closely involved in the case, often visiting and advising the parties as social workers. Announcements of commission meetings were displayed in public places, such as post offices or residency notice boards, though court appearance was not obligatory. If the accused failed to show, he was referred to ordinary civil courts. Dispute commissions met after work hours, usually convening Wednesday nights in National Front offices or other communal facilities. Many, however, actually met in the residences of the parties involved, literally taking state justice into the private homes of citizens.

Formally speaking, these social courts were brought to life with the passing of a 1953 ordinance (*Errichtung von Sühnestellen von 24 April 1953*) that created the conflict commissions as new judicial organs charged with hearing minor disputes arising in state-controlled enterprises. At the GDR's 2nd Party Congress the year before, First Secretary Walter Ulbricht had placed the 'building up of socialism' as the Socialist Unity Party's (SED) main priority, whereupon 'better developing a consciousness of justice' (*Rechtspflege*) was now identified as a 'matter for all citizens'. By the end of the decade the SED recognized the wider potential benefit of these citizen tribunals, passing a further ordinance (*Verordnung über die Sühnestellen-Schiedmannsordnung*) that extended the courts' competence of petty 'antisocial cases' to residential areas.[15] These new dispute commissions were formalized in 1963, and eventually embedded in Article 9 of the GDR Constitution as part of the campaign to give justice back to the Volk, making law 'the people's own'.[16]

The idea of these social courts was no East German invention, however. The German tradition of extra-juridical adjudication harks back to the beginning of the nineteenth century, when voluntary 'honorial societies' composed of various city elders heard minor citizen disputes in Prussia, Bavaria, and elsewhere. These informal nineteenth-century citizen courts were enlarged during the Weimar Republic mainly to relieve the overburdened legal system, and in 1938 were further expanded and integrated into the Third Reich's German Justice Front (*Deutsche Rechtsfront*) as a means of better binding citizen and state. From 1934 to 1940 there were some 15,000 social court jurists, or *Schiedsmänner*, serving annually in Prussia alone. By the autumn of 1945 a number of makeshift lay courts (*Schöffengerichte*) sprang up all over war-torn Germany as popular justice tribunals that adjudicated petty grievances. By 1948 there were already some 5,100 lay judges (*Orts- und Friedensrichter*) across the Soviet Zone, who heard some 15,000 civil disputes and 80,000 private complaints, the majority of which concerned housing issues.[17] What scattered files exist mainly dealt with cases of small property claims and landlord–tenant disagreements, in which renters often refused to pay full rent in light of the 'uninhabitability' of bomb-damaged residences.[18] Others concerned the itemized recovery of personal effects (mainly household goods) following the death or divorce of one partner; still others took up theft, violence, and even cases of ex-Wehrmacht soldiers in illegal possession of weapons after 1945.[19]

Nevertheless, the social courts' more direct antecedent was Lenin's revolutionary initiative to integrate newly communist citizens into the machinery of socialist justice. According to official GDR publications, their origins lay in 1918 when Lenin established these 'comrade courts' in the Petrograd military district as a means of shoring up military discipline in the Red Army;[20] the jurisdiction of these courts was widened a year later to cover violations of labour discipline in factories.[21] In the early 1930s such courts were established across the Soviet countryside and new urban residential areas; by 1938 there were over 45,000 of them in the Russian Republic alone. But they all but disappeared during the Second World War, as labour discipline cases were moved to higher tribunals, and the courts remained dormant until Khrushchev revived them in the late 1950s. The new premier's aim was to use them to help accelerate the transition to communism, in which the state functions of the courts would slowly be transferred to more public organizations.[22] Thanks in part to Khrushchev's lead, the GDR's social courts assumed a new tone and brief by the early 1960s. In 1961 GDR Minister of Justice Hilde Benjamin led an East German delegation of legal theorists on a study trip to Moscow, after which she was inspired to establish GDR versions of the Soviet comrade courts. Like in the Soviet Union, the emphasis was less on the repressive than on the restitutive, as these citizen courts were hailed as a fundamental step in the popularization of GDR civil culture. By early 1963 several pilot residential commissions were created in various East German cities, including Berlin.

By the end of 1967, there were already some 5,620 dispute commissions across the country.[23] While these numbers might seem surprisingly high, it is worth keeping in mind that participating in the state on this voluntary basis was not unusual in the GDR. Millions of East German citizens were involved in organizations such as parent governing boards, members of inspection teams (*Arbeiter- und Bauerinspektion*), and so-called 'confidence people' (*Vertrauensleute*) in factories and in residences. By the mid-1960s, the number of GDR citizens participating in such organizations was well above three million; over the course of a typical career, one in three workers was involved at one point in one of them. While no one would deny that these massive organizations were 'a natural dimension of state power',[24] they also functioned as a socialist form of civil society, in which citizens took seriously the task of self-government. This was particularly the case with these citizen courts, in that they were one of the few places in GDR life that was relatively free from state intervention, giving hundreds of thousands of citizens the experience of real decision-making power in solving neighbourhood conflicts each year.[25] Whereas the Soviet Union's hallowed comrade courts largely disappeared after Khrushchev's fall from grace, only to be revived again in the late 1970s, the GDR's dispute commissions enjoyed a continued presence in East German residential life.

Typically citizens aged between 40 and 60 years old sat on these volunteer-based juries. Younger members were occasionally included, especially if they were recommended by the Free German Youth organization. According to official figures, only around 35 per cent of jurists were SED members, and 45 per cent were National Trade Union (FDGB) members. Sometimes a member of the Auxiliary Police (ABV) sat on the commission as well. As for social composition, industrial workers accounted for 30–5 per cent of the lay assessors, whereas farm labourers made up around 25 per cent. Civil servant and bureaucrats accounted for around 15 per cent, while white-collar 'technical intelligence' rounded out another 10 per cent. Housewives made up around 5 per cent, and women in general comprised 30–5 per cent of the volunteers,[26] a figure which climbed to around 50 per cent by the late 1970s. The sociological profile of the jurists remained fairly unchanged over the decades.[27] Their voluntary service did not go unnoticed: jurists were rewarded with prizes, medals, and certificates.[28] Not surprisingly the press made much of the fact that everyday citizens were serving as lay judges and jurists, thus removing the elitist stigma of the judiciary in general.[29] Citizen satisfaction with the commissions was routinely reported for their ability to dispense socialist justice fairly and expeditiously.[30] At times these commissions actually competed with one another over the number of cases heard and harmoniously resolved, just as factories held competitions for filling production quotas.[31] Books, newspapers columns, and even television programmes were dedicated to broadcasting the activities of the citizen tribunals.[32] Several journals— including *Sozialistische Demokratie* and *Neue Justiz*—devoted considerable coverage to the social courts. And as early as 1954, the journal, *Der Schöffe*, was founded to broaden the appeal of the newly established conflict commissions and to help educate new jurists in the intricacies of socialist law. Its pages were filled with short articles and case studies about family law, rental agreements, and divorce settlements, and by 1956 it boasted 12,000 readers nationwide.

The perceived social benefits of this courts programme were what mattered most. In one 1961 Ministry of Justice report, it stated that the number of criminal cases across the GDR had decreased from 56,033 in 1958 to 55,866 in 1959 and then again to 45,847 in 1960. By contrast, the number of civil cases leapt from 2,869 cases in 1958 to 7,680 in 1959. The sudden jump in submitted civil cases in 1959 was explained as the positive effect of the establishment of the conflict commissions, in that citizens were supposedly internalizing the norms of socialist morality and developing confidence in the justice system to redress minor infractions. The report then concluded by singing the praises of the commissions' role in defusing potential conflict and integrating citizens into society more effectively, not least because it meant that ever more citizens now came in contact with the state's justice system.[33]

The potential usage of these courts for information-gathering was not lost on state authorities. One 1956 Ministry of Justice report, for example, stated that a principal element of the new courts was to gather information about social life that was otherwise hard to obtain, especially 'concerning the thousand small things that make life difficult for our people, the removal of which would significantly help ameliorate social relations'.[34] These courts might then be useful in helping confront 'the enemies of our state who try by all manner of sabotage, diversion and secret agency to undermine our goals'.[35] This was seen as all the more necessary, given that the people who usually filed private claims—housewives, self-employed workers, and the retired—were considered the very people who remained largely outside the state's network of mass organizations. In fact, the original November 1953 social court ordinance was passed in direct reaction to the major political upheavals of 16–17 June that year.[36] The problem for state officials was that residential areas—unlike the workplace—tended to resist state control. This was particularly so in the wake of the 1953 Uprising, as state officials found it difficult to penetrate housing communities. One July 1953 National Front report described the 'mood of the people' as wary and suspicious, and noted that the 'people are irritated by stepped-up neighbourhood surveillance'.[37] A National Front report ten years later stated that residents were still sceptical of state organizations in residential areas, and that many citizens—especially youth— were not very involved in communal life or activities.[38] To overcome this resistance, the courts were to maintain close contacts with the police, National Front, residential supervisors, and the formal justice system in identifying 'asocials' and 'rowdy behaviour' among residents, particular young people. In fact, the 1968 expansion of the dispute commissions across the GDR was a direct response to the threat posed by the Prague Spring that year, as the courts were seen to be able to help identify problem areas and citizens more quickly than the police could.[39]

Court records showed the extent to which the commissions were used to ferret out information about uncooperative citizens.[40] This was especially true for cases concerning young people who maintained distance from work and organized leisure activities. In many cases, there was extensive inquiry and discussion about the offender's work record, family background, and 'asocial lifestyle', with obligatory visits (and reports) from teachers, factory foremen, local youth directors, and lay assessors to ascertain the roots of nonconformity.[41] A 1971 case involving a boy caught stealing tennis clothes from his local tennis club generated a remarkable amount of paperwork and inquiry into family circumstances, in which the parents' divorce and the father's overly strict child-raising were held largely responsible for the boy's criminal behaviour.[42] These courts were partly involved in what might be called the 'deprivatization' of East German life, aiming in this case to overcome those remaining attitudes and habits that did not comply with the overarching ideals of East German socialist morality and communal living.

PERSONAL PROPERTY

What is so interesting about these inquisitorial cases was just how persistent these private, 'antisocialist' lifestyles remained over the years. This was most evident in the number of social court cases involving property disputes. By the mid-1960s property violations accounted for nearly 60 per cent of all crimes in the GDR, and remained about at that level during the 1970s and 1980s.[43] These crimes included infractions against what was called 'the collective property of the people', or *Volkseigentum*, as well as personal property.[44] Violations against the 'people's property' covered such things as shoplifting, stealing equipment from factories and embezzlement, and made up half of the property crimes in the GDR from the 1960s to the late 1980s.[45] Personal property by contrast included those objects designated in the GDR Constitution as embodying 'the satisfaction of material and cultural needs', such as consumer goods and property items bought, inherited, won, or given. Personal property cases covered the gamut of petty claims, ranging from stolen mopeds to damaged sports equipment to scratched automobiles. A large number of property cases—like those of the more formal civil courts—concerned conflicts between tenants and private landlords over unpaid rent and overdue house repairs. Others concerned battles between spouses and children over the inheritance of flats and personal items, with both sides drawing up elaborate lists of personal effects, producing makeshift wills, and summoning numerous witnesses to testify to the deceased's wishes about the object's rightful owner. No less frequent were fights between former married partners about how to divide up the household goods following a divorce. A good amount, too, dealt with conflicts between neighbours over property boundaries, usually regarding garden plots or overhanging trees. What is so remarkable about these property cases (and this was just as true of the formal civil courts) was that the ruling SED—ever-present in the rest of GDR life—was relatively absent from them, especially if they did not concern youth. Here the right to and protection of personal property was the only thing that mattered, giving the supposedly banished spectre of commodity fetishism a lively public forum. After all, these were by and large petit bourgeois conflicts over apartments, gardens, garages, furniture, and cars—the 'tiny enclaves of self-determination in an otherwise tight and regimented world'[46]—whose causes and concerns were not altogether different from what exercised petty claims courts west of the Berlin Wall.

Not surprisingly, the place and presence of personal property in socialist life was a source of great trepidation for communist authorities. As Inga Markovits ironically remarked, 'socialism was fascinated with property, just as Christianity was obsessed with sin'.[47] The concept of property was naturally central to Marxism, in that it was seen as the foundation of all political life and the driving force of global history. However, communism never wished to do away with property *tout court*, but only the bourgeois conception of it, as Marx and Engels explained in their 1848 *Communist Manifesto*. What they sought above all was to break free from the liberal logic and material injustice of private property, and for this reason Lenin's 1917 ordinance formally dissolving all private property served as Genesis 1 of modern economic revolution. But what about personal property? Despite his revolutionary beginnings, Lenin along with his economic planners, the so-called NEP-men, eventually introduced a mixed economy of private and socialist enterprise, providing legal protections for both. While Lenin had all but abolished testation in 1918 as a relic of the bourgeois past,[48] in no small measure because it was seen as a key element in maintaining the bourgeois conception of the family, inheritance rights were reintroduced into the civil codes of the other Soviet republics by 1922. For his part, Stalin busily campaigned to remove any last bastion of private enterprise from Soviet economic life, yet his 1936 Constitution did formally recognize and protect what was coyly called 'personal property' (*lichnaya sobstvennost*), as noted above all in Article 10: 'The personal right of citizens in their incomes and savings from work, in their dwellinghouses and subsidiary home enterprises, in articles of domestic economy and use and articles of personal use and comfort, as well as the right of citizens to inherit personal property, is protected by law.'[49] As Harold Berman argued, by the mid-1930s 'there was a new stress on personal ownership of one's house, of one's personal belongings, of one's savings account and government bonds', while inheritance too was 'freed from crushing taxation and a greater freedom of testation was introduced'.[50]

Rights to personal property were further expanded in the USSR after 1945. In part this was because communist leaders came to believe that the production, enjoyment and accumulation of consumer goods as personal property was an important spur to labour, as Aristotle posited long ago.[51] By 1948 'every citizen' enjoyed the right to buy or build one home (of one to two storeys and up to five rooms), and citizens were allowed to own livestock. Only six months after Stalin's death, Khrushchev set the tone by insisting that 'we must do away with the prejudice that it is a disgrace for workers to own cattle as personal property!' By 1957 taxes on inheritance were all but removed across the Soviet Union and Eastern bloc, leading one Western commentator to snigger that the USSR was actually 'a more inheritance-friendly environment than its western counterpart'.[52] Homes, cars, boats, dachas, books, jewellery, furniture, musical instruments, and household goods were all to be formally protected.[53] A 1961 USSR ordinance extended the personal property provisions laid out in the 1936 constitution to all Soviet satellite states.[54]

The GDR essentially followed the lead of the Soviet Union in terms of personal property protection. Inheritance, for example, remained a key feature of East Germany's Civil Code (even after its radical revision in 1975), and was firmly anchored in the GDR's 1968 Constitution (Art. 11, para. 1).[55] The right to a 'weekend-house' (like the Russian dacha) was expressly guaranteed in the 1975 Civil Code (ZGB), and even encouraged by the state in part as a sop to citizens who otherwise might consider emigration.[56] While Ulbricht's successor, Erich Honecker, may have dissolved virtually all privately owned enterprises in 1972, private homes and property remained expressly protected. His new 1975 code recognized the individual desire for goods as fundamental, and protected the right to—and ownership of—consumer objects as basic to all citizens.[57]

Precisely because GDR civil law legally preserved a veritable 'non-socialist' sphere, there was broad concern that it served as a kind of juridical Trojan Horse within the country's fortress of 'socialist law and justice'. Reformers consequently moved to close the gap between state and citizen by other means. Law was singled out as particularly decisive in this regard, as East German jurists busied themselves with using the citizen courts to help combat these new social dangers.[58]

In line with Marxist ideology, the roots of these social dangers were interpreted in terms of physical surrounding. Often this meant bad housing. Several dispute commission reports candidly argued that in newer buildings and residences, or *Volkseigene Neubauten*, there was apparently less civil conflict and casework. Older residential buildings, so they contended, were in very poor condition, and 'no longer correspond to the desires of today's residents'. This was interpreted as accounting for the escalation of conflict between tenants and landlords. That the intensity of the state's 'political-ideological work' was usually weaker in older residential areas was something noted as well. That said, the deeper cause was invariably attributed to the catch-all bugbear, 'capitalist behaviour'. According to the reports, the real reason why these old residences were prone to more 'anti-social activities' was that a good percentage of them (over half by the mid-1970s) tended to be privately owned properties, thus keeping alive the 'remnants of past worldviews' wherein citizens 'still believe that they can live egotistically only for themselves' and have no understanding of the 'foundations of socialist communal living'.[59] One 1971 Ministry of Justice guidebook for lay assessors summed up the logic by saying that crime in the DDR 'has it roots mainly in the influence of the imperialistic class enemy, in regressive thinking and lifestyles of a number of citizens, who have clung to the ideological holdovers of the [pre-socialist] past'.[60]

Ironically, what exacerbated the problem was the coming of socialist prosperity. At first this may seem puzzling, given the common image of East European socialism as one of mismanagement, privation, and mass-produced misery. But during the time that these dispute commissions took wing in the early 1960s, the Eastern bloc—and East Germany in particular—was in the beginning phases of its Great Leap Forward in 'consumer socialism'. By that time the so-called standard of living had become a key ideological battleground of cold war rivalry, as each system used economic success as a means of showcasing political legitimacy. At the USSR's 22nd Party Congress in 1961, for example, Khrushchev stressed the central importance of 'Everything for the People—Everything for the Welfare of the People!'[61] and each Eastern bloc leader followed suit in paying more heed to the 'citizen-consumer'. While its actual results may look meagre to us now, everyday socialist life was indeed undergoing major transformation. A new socialist 'mass culture' was beginning to materialize, complete with new shopping centres, mail-order catalogues, fashion, furniture, household goods, and shiny consumer durables of all varieties.[62] This may have been good news for

GDR economists and policy-makers, but it also meant that there were many more goods for the law—and the courts—to honour and protect. Where the rudimentary social courts in the early 1950s were primarily concerned with relatively scarce personal property items like family jewellery and sewing machines, the 1960s dispute commissions were faced with tens of thousands of claims about the new fruit of socialist consumer culture, such as televisions, motorcycles, sports equipment, camping gear, and automobiles. How important this was to GDR citizens was acknowledged by Ulbricht himself in 1960, who wrote that socialism can be attained only if the state plays its role in 'guaranteeing the protection of property and the rights of citizens'.[63] The genie of consumer desire was out of the bottle.

The ascendancy of Erich Honecker as First Secretary in 1971 changed little in this regard. The old Marxist notion that the coming of communism meant that the state—and with it the law—would wither away hardly came to pass; in fact, the social court system was significantly expanded in the 1970s in the name of educating citizens about socialist rights and justice. At the 9th Socialist Unity Party Congress in 1976, Honecker made clear that it was to help curb consumer desires, 'develop socialist society', and 'civilize' the masses about the norms of socialism one case at a time.[64] As one guidebook put it, these courts were to serve as a 'lever' in the 'historical transformation of I into We', one in which 'personal rights are not to cut people off from society, but rather will have a law-abiding and collectivizing effect in protecting us from egotistical, undisciplined and unrefined behavior'.[65] The language of intimidation was also on hand should these more anodyne pronouncements go unheeded. In one oft-cited 1959 Potsdam case, for example, the local civil court upheld the action of one citizen who smashed another's portable radio in the street on the grounds that the plaintiff was listening to illegal and hostile broadcasts on Radio in the American Sector (RIAS). The case was quoted to drive home the point that state ideology ultimately trumped personal property claims, and that the law would and should be used to assure that social life stayed socialist.[66]

But it was really morality itself that was deemed crucial in assuring that socialist society would not turn into its ideological enemy. The constitutional emphasis on 'the satisfaction of material and cultural needs' first articulated in Stalin's 1936 Constitution, and later included verbatim in the civil codes of all socialist republics after 1945, including the GDR, was intended to curb the demons of 'surplus value' and unrestrained consumerism. The heavy emphasis on morals at the time—what Dorothee Wierling calls the state's 'didactic dictatorship'—was scarcely limited to these courts, and could be seen throughout GDR society in the 1960s, as part of the desperate effort to hold together a society in the throes of febrile modernization and socialist transformation. The courts' crusade to rehabilitate petty offenders was part in the GDR's broader 1960s social engineering project to remake society after the erection of the Berlin Wall in 1961. That these infractions derived from a stubborn private property mentality thereby struck at the heart of the socialist project, and warranted serious attention. The notable absence of moralizing in GDR civil law cases from the late 1940s to the early 1960s—to say nothing of the infrequent mention of socialism itself—was now a thing of the past. By the mid-1960s the courts had stepped up their mission to restore socialist norms of good behaviour, often by hectoring offenders, shaming shirkers, and demanding public apologies. Hardly a verdict was passed without impassioned paternalistic admonitions such as 'you must understand that...', 'one must realize that in today's society...', or most frequently, 'the principles of socialism dictate that...'; for the assessors, the infractions were not just moral failings, but affronts against the very power and possibilities of socialism itself.

PEACE AND QUIET

But beneath the rhetoric and recriminations, these dispute commissions were also busy negotiating the social contract between citizens and the state. This was particularly so in cases concerning noise and 'disturbances of the peace' or *Hausfriedensbruch*, which accounted for some 20–30 per cent of the Berlin commissions' business by the 1970s and 1980s. Interestingly, the theme of peace and quiet was scarcely an issue in the 1950s and 1960s; few sounds were categorized as harmful, and thus actionable in court. On the contrary, it was widely accepted that the construction of socialism after the Second World War would be a noisy affair, and loud noise—especially industrial noise in cities—was viewed as a necessary and even welcome sign of progress. In the 1970s things changed, however, as noise became a growing source of residential conflict across the country, and even across the Eastern bloc.[67] At that time, there was growing concern among all socialist governments about the deleterious effects of excess noise in the workplace, insomuch as loud noise was seen as hindering workers' productive capacities. In the GDR, for example, there were a number of conferences in the 1970s on noise control both at work and at home.[68] Behind the state's new interest in the social effects of noise was the old Marxist notion of social reproduction, in which workers were seen as needing restful time at home to recoup their energies for the next working day. Controlling noise at work and at home was thus a key dimension of socialist welfare. Afterhours leisure was therefore 'not an alternative to work, but its extension; if its effectiveness was impeded by noise, this would undermine the central tenet of socialist society, productive work itself'.[69] Home life, too, was changing. Like everywhere else in Europe, GDR homes were being increasingly outfitted with modern appliances, such as dishwashers and televisions, whose noise penetrated the cramped quarters and thin walls of socialist housing units. People, moreover, were at home more often as a consequence of shortened work weeks and extended holidays, exposing them to more noise pollution from their neighbours. Carpets, curtains, and rugs were routinely used to dampen unwanted reverberation, and were standard features of socialist interiors across Eastern Europe. But it was also accompanied by a shift in sensibility. No longer was noise to be tolerated as simply an inevitable by-product of socialist life, at least not at home. Dispute commission records were filled with cases from the early 1970s on concerning disturbances of the peace, usually focusing on their neighbours' loud music, domestic squabbles, and raucous late night antics. Indeed, the noisy neighbour now emerged as a new 'enemy of the people', as peace and quiet became popular yardsticks with which to measure residential harmony and socialist civilization.

A few examples illuminate this point. In one 1969 case, a neighbour complained about what she felt was excessive piano practice by the neighbour's children. After a series of nasty rows in the hallway, the case was brought to the commission, which concluded: 'The commission is of the opinion that the fundamental principle of living together in a socialist community—mutual consideration—is not yet being respected, and the problem can be rectified with a little bit of good will.' To be sure, the tag phrase 'not yet' was quite conventional in these verdicts, implying that socialist society—while still under construction—was moving in the right direction.[70] More significant, though, was the sentiment that such behaviour was a violation of assumed and expected 'standards of socialist cohabitation'. Just as peace became the GDR's chief foreign policy issue in the Honecker era, so too did it become a central concern for residents in their everyday life. In another 1971 case, a female plaintiff claimed that her neighbour Frau G was making too much noise at night. To fortify her case, she submitted a detailed list of disturbing noises over a two-week period, including moving furniture around between 1 and 2 a.m. and watching television all hours of the night at high volume. In this instance the commission ended up scolding the tenant, threatening to kick her out if her 'asocial' behaviour continued. The judgment concluded with the standard admonition: 'Toward the members of our socialist community one must have a certain consideration that. . .' While this at first may not seem very noteworthy in itself, it did reveal the way in which citizens looked to the state as the guardian of a quiet domestic life and ordered residential community.[71]

A high percentage of these neighbourhood disturbance cases involved domestic animals. Typically this meant unruly, barking dogs, but not infrequently these cases concerned pets that attacked children, older neighbours, and/or other residents' domestic animals. Court records plainly show that dealing with animal disturbances played a considerable role in establishing and maintaining rules of courtesy in East German residential areas. One resident's case about the offensive odours in the common stairwell caused by his neighbour's four cats ended with his successful plea for 'including a new house ordinance in the rental contract'.[72] Elsewhere specific regulations were cited in the commissions' verdicts, and both parties often referred to the law to justify their positions. In one 1980 case, the plaintiff concluded her written complaint thus:

I would like to make the Auxiliary Police aware of Paragraph 38, Clause 10 of the City Statutes, in which it explicitly states that every pet owner is obliged to note in the name of *order, cleanliness and hygiene* that the socialist lifestyle of citizens is not to be disturbed. Moreover, I refer you to Paragraph 317 of the Socialist Civil Code, which states that all residents are obliged to fence in, either wholly or partially, his property if it obstructs the movement of others or violates the *interests of society*.[73]

These common cases about dogs effectively involved the whole machinery of local justice by invoking and reaffirming social rules of residential cooperation.

Complaints about noise in the GDR often moved into the area of rights as well. In one 1969 case, a couple filed a complaint that their neighbour played music very loud at night. The accusatory letter was unusually harsh in tone, and the signatures of three other building residents were appended in support. In the letter Fräulein H. was accused of having had many male visitors, and that her 'loud racket and screaming' during sexual intercourse often lasted until 2–3 a.m.; so loud was it that the complainant's young children were often woken up, giving the parents the awkward task of explaining to them what was happening. The letter added that 'we are of the opinion that house residents have the right to peace and quiet in their dwellings, without being bothered by such loud noises'. It concluded by saying ''as well as the undersigned, other building residents share the view that we cannot arrive at any workable residential arrangement with Fräulein H that corresponds with our socialist social order'.[74] Particularly revealing here was the manner in which citizens linked the moral norms of socialist society with their perceived right to peace and quiet. A 1974 case extended this logic. It concerned a collective petition lodged by several neighbours against another who was accused of complaining about everyone else. The usual procedure was thus reversed in this instance. Here the neighbours maintained that before Frau K arrived, they had 'a good housing community, as everyone understood one another and there were no arguments or disputes'. Everything apparently changed with the arrival of Frau K, who carped incessantly about the daily cacophony of noisy dogs, children, etc. But once again, the language was instructive: 'Many residents have been bothered by the behaviour of Frau K—it must be made clear that we don't live in a sanatorium, but rather in a housing community in which everyone has the right to lead their lives as is good and proper. Excessive noise is not a problem.'[75] While this particular case ended with both sides being asked to try to get along 'in a good neighbourly way', the rhetoric of rights was again invoked as a defence of privacy and the freedom to live as one wished so long as it did not unduly disturb others.

The importance of 'peace and quiet' has been fundamental to the development of the modern German state ever since the Napoleonic Wars, and its consolidation and expansion was in large measure based on its ability to keep revolutionary impulses under strict control. Indeed, it became central German state policy in the wake of political upheaval, stretching from the Karlsbad Decrees of 1819 to the Weimar Republic's Groener-Ebert Pact exactly one hundred years later, when peace and quiet was 'republicanized' as the mainstay of political order in the aftermath of the Great War.[76] Developments in the GDR did not fit this model so easily, though. After all, the GDR state—especially under Ulbricht—hardly saw itself as counter-revolutionary or conservative. The GDR was to carry the spirit of communist revolution to all corners of East German life, as the state's social reconstruction project to build a new 'antifascist order' atop the charred remnants of Nazism was the very antithesis of peace and quiet. Yet it was precisely under the 'Thermidorian' regime of Erich Honecker that peace and quiet returned as hallmark virtues of East German state and citizen alike, and it was during the 1970s that this theme emerged as a deeply held right in dispute commission proceedings.[77] For this reason, it is misleading to suggest, as some have, that this was somehow the expression of the 'most German' virtues of order and discipline, and that the SED simply 'instrumenta-lized' the 'Prussian-German' sensibility of law and order for its own ends. After all, communist comrade courts across the Soviet Union were faced with precisely the same complaints about the noisy and chaotic conditions of everyday social-ism. The wider implication is that this self-understood right to domestic tran-quillity was something that came from the citizens themselves, underscoring that the claim to peace and quiet was not somehow antithetical to the development of civil society. On the contrary, these court records amply reveal myriad efforts on the part of East Berliners to defend a distinct domestic space against which society—here, noisy neighbours—could not encroach.

INSULTS AND REPUTATION

Perhaps the most interesting cases among these courts were those concerning *Beleidigung* or *Verleumdung*, insults or defamation. Remarkably, no less than 50–60 per cent of all cases that I studied dealt with slander in some way or another. Such percentages were common across the country, and even increased over the decades.[78] Slander complaints were typically filed by older residents, and more often than not by women.[79] A good number of cases were filed by men however, sometimes on behalf of offended family members, against residents who breached their sense of honour in some manner. And according to reports, slander was especially rife in the capital. To be sure, the problem of insults was legion immediately after the war. One 1956 report admitted that the flood of refugees, expellees, and returning POWs often met a harsh reception from East German residents. There were indeed a good many cases of slurs of 'racial hatred' (*Völkerhass*) against Poles, Czechs, gypsies, as well as 'Russian bastards' (*Russen-kinder*) and 'Russian sluts' (*Russenhuren*). Likewise, the makeshift citizen courts heard dozens of cases of 'offended honour' filed by former Nazis subjected to frequent verbal abuse by their neighbours, who tarred them as 'old fascists', 'fascist sluts', and 'Nazi pigs'.[80] One protracted 1950 case involved a man who sought to reinstate his honour with the Soviet authorities after having been mistaken—and falsely jailed for four months—by a city resident for being a former *SA-Reichssturmführer* and 'Naziaktivist'. The frequency of slander cases after the war is not all that surprising, for it is precisely during periods of political upheaval and 'status revolutions' when cases of bruised personal honour and defamation have been at their most frequent historically. Take the dramatic leap in defamation cases in seventeenth-century England, for example, whose 'world turned upside down' witnessed rapid social mobility and a new 'cult of reputation'.[81] The same went for Germany after the First World War; but despite all of the upheaval attending the post-Nazi construction of state socialism, the number of slander cases brought before citizen courts was still relatively small until the early 1960s.

From the mid-1960s on, dispute commissions faced a steady stream of slander and defamation cases involving neighbours calling each other names in public. Among the most common terms of derision were 'lazy', 'stupid', 'stinky', 'slutty', 'fat cow', 'filthy whore', and 'dirty pig'. One 1968 file concerned a resident accusing his overbearing neighbour of 'behaving like a SA-Man', whereafter the accuser was made to retract his words and apologize publicly.[82] On occasion slander cases touched on racism against foreigners, though these were usually handled by the civil courts. One 1967 case, for example, involved three boys taunting and beating up a Guinean student in a Berlin pub, after which the student was granted compensation (to replace his teeth), while the leader of the gang was sentenced to three years in a work camp.[83] But such racially motivated slander cases were rare. More frequent were petty complaints of besmirched honour such as those filed by aggrieved housing community directors upset about being mocked by residents as overzealous or incompetent.[84] With time the courts' jurisdiction even extended beyond the residential areas. One 1969 case dealt with a dentist who was verbally abused in the waiting room by one of his patients, resulting in a notice hung in the clinic naming both offence and offender, with the demand for a public apology.[85] Another 1990 case concerned a drunken man in a café who subjected the waitress to a string of unseemly names, after which he was forced to demonstrate contrition and pay her 300 marks for his misbehaviour.[86] Typically, the hearings ended with the accused apologizing to both the plaintiff and the commission as a gesture of penitence and understanding; such an outcome was a source of great pride for the whole social court system, supposedly highlighting the reformability and reconciliation of socialist citizens. A note was then sent to the *Hausgemeinschaft* leader (and sometimes to the Auxiliary Police), indicating that the offender must be kept under close scrutiny in the future.

Needless to say, the concept of personal honour as a fundamental political issue has a long history.[87] It was central to Aristotle's *Nicomachean Ethics*, hailed by Luther as a 'treasure' which we 'cannot dispense with',[88] and considered by Kant as a 'gift of fortune' (*Glücksgaben*) in which "every person has a legal entitlement to due consideration from the people around him'.[89] While defamation as an actionable offence in court harked back to Roman law, in Germany it was not until the 1871 Constitution that it first found secure legal footing, building on the 'offence against honour' (*Ehrverletzung*) statute present in the Bavarian Civil Code of 1753 and in the Prussian Gesetzbuch of 1851. Slander and defamation were expanded in the Weimar Republic as civil offences, whereas the Third Reich published its own sizeable literature on defamation, recasting honour as the property of the racial community rather than the liberal individual citizen.[90] Nazi ideology and its racial laws touched defamation cases only to a limited extent at the local judicial level though, as personal honour cases were largely relegated to the Third Reich's own citizen courts from the mid-1930s onward.[91] After 1945 honour and individual dignity were embraced as part of the de-Nazification of German constitutional law and the postwar reinvention of human rights. It was enshrined in Article 12 of the 1948 UN Charter ('No one shall be subjected to arbitrary interference with his privacy, family, home or correspondence, nor to attacks upon his honour and reputation') and in Article 1 of the West German Basic Law.[92] Even if quite unwieldy in court, individual honour and reputation remained central planks of West German legal life.[93]

Things were different in the GDR, however. East German lawmakers were very keen to do away with the idea of the citizen versus the state, and in particular the liberal notion that individual rights and privileges were to be set against the encroachments of the collective. And yet, they wanted to ensure the dignity and honour of individual citizens as well. In the GDR the 1953 Social Courts Ordinance explicitly stated that lay judges were 'to be attentive to the honour of fellow citizens and to school them in responsible social behaviour'.[94] These cases were taken very seriously precisely because the citizenry supposedly stood at the centre of socialist society. GDR publicists never tired of making the point that, whereas capitalist society was based on exploitation, oppression, and degradation, socialist society was to be distinguished by 'comradely cooperation', mutual assistance, and the recognition of the dignity of the 'socialist personality'. Not that the East Germans were alone. Under Khrushchev honour, dignity, and defamation became legal topics in the USSR for the first time, making the 'right to the protection of one's honour and dignity' inalienable 'personal non-property rights' there.[95] Offences against the honour and dignity of the individual were thus construed as a transgression against the very spirit of socialism itself. What is more, insults were seen as having dangerous social effects. Like those cases dealing with noise, the peril lay in the fact that it 'disturbed the normal relations between people, undermining citizen self-awareness, the joy of life and work, as well as the desire to take part in social life'.[96] Slander (*üble Nachrede* and *Verleumdung*) was hence expressly covered (paras. 185–7) in the GDR's Socialist Civil Code, and the courts were to take the lead in remedying this social poison.

But why were the numbers of slander cases so high in the GDR from the 1960s on? Much of the explanation rests in the fact that the dispute commissions

were not fully set up until 1963, and it was only then that matters of neighbourhood agitation enjoyed a real forum. Conflict between neighbours was also an
unexpected consequence of 1960s social policy, whose combination of housing
density, residential surveillance, and forced neighbourhood mixing of social
classes in the name of 'socialist democracy' and political control often led to
deep mistrust and animosity among the locals.[97] Exacerbating the problem still
further was the poor state and supply of housing, not least because it was very
difficult to move away from unpleasant neighbours. This is not the way GDR
state authorities saw things, of course. For them, the roots of such antisocial
behaviour were almost always personal, not structural. Reports on commission
work placed the blame on long-time antagonism between old neighbours, the
pernicious activities of a few 'egotistic' bad apples and 'class enemies', and, more
typically, the ever-present 'capitalist residue' from the pre-socialist period.[98]
Insufficient residential organization and surveillance was also cited as a contributing factor,[99] sometimes resulting in the reprimanding of 'negligent' housing
community leaders.[100] Other more upbeat reports spun the evidence in a positive
light, claiming that the rising amount of civil casework concerning slander and
defamation simply reflected a growing sensitivity and awareness of 'socialist
justice' and personal honour more generally.[101]

Whatever the real or perceived causes, most of the slander complaints
concerned appeals to redress breaches of socialist standards of behaviour. In
one 1968 slander case, a mother, who was derided as an 'idiot' who had 'no
idea how to raise a child', wanted more than an apology. From her perspective,
the offender's actions gravely 'violated the very principles of our interpersonal
socialist relations', and thus the court 'should use the occasion to make this
known to the whole community'.[102] A 1973 letter from a plaintiff in another
slander case concluded in almost Victorian fashion: 'I beg the social court to
consider this case carefully, and to make clear to Frau H that hers is not a
dignified form of verbal intercourse between citizens in our [socialist] social
order.'[103] In these examples, norms of socialist decency were not just lofty ideals,
but were taken to heart as issues of social justice, and the commissions were
identified as the one place where basic etiquette could be reaffirmed publicly.
Sometimes the cases even concerned what was not said. Take a 1970 case, for
instance, in which a Berlin woman wrote in a handwritten letter that she had had
a long relationship with a man who lived nearby. Both were unmarried, but she
complained that her neighbours presumed that he was married, and thus that she
was engaged in an extramarital affair. According to her testimony, such rumours
were passed on to the local Auxiliary Police, 'who made two visits to my home to
inquire about my personal relationship, and to inspect my apartment'. All of this,
she continued, had brought her in 'disrepute', as residents 'keep their distance
from me, and harbour hostile attitudes toward me'. Her family doctor would not
even write 'Single' (*Alleinstehend*) on her illness certificate due to his apparent
knowledge of her relationship. As a result, she demanded a hearing before the

housing community in order 'to clear up any misunderstandings with her neighbours'.[104] In this particular case it is difficult to know whether it is really about the reach of the state security forces, the puritanical prejudices of this East Berlin housing block, or perhaps the paranoid fantasies of a troubled East Berlin resident. What it does show, though, is the degree to which citizens turned to the commissions as a receptive forum for addressing their social ills and moral injuries, often in the name of personal honour and socialist justice.

Moreover, insult cases often touched on issues of social inequality. To be sure, this issue was effectively taboo in the GDR, in that it flew in the face of the cherished myth of the classless society.[105] But everyone knew that this was not so, and often commission records reflected this social anger. Whereas the deeply resented injustices associated with unequal access to goods, housing, and Western currency were the subject of individual complaint letters to GDR state authorities, as we shall see in the next chapter, it was the preferential treatment toward Party officials, police, and government employees in the neighbourhood that resonated in honour violation cases.[106] In one 1974 case, for example, a retired woman sought to clear her name of being the source of undue noise in the building. She admitted that she often typed at 6 a.m., but that there was no reason why the People's Police had knocked on her door at 12.30 a.m.; in her accompanying statement she insisted that she had good relations with the local police, proudly admitting to have informed on other noisy residents in the past. She then accused another resident of being the real cause of the disturbing noise, and was offended that this resident, who worked for Ministry of State Security, was given the benefit of the doubt, while she by contrast was being treated as a 'second-class citizen'. An apology eventually was issued, but it was the slight on her honour by the authorities that was the real subject of discontent.[107] Moral outrage against privileged citizens found expression in other instances. In one 1989 file, a resident took umbrage that his neighbours constantly insulted the members of his family. According to his testimony, he found this especially galling given that the wife of the accused worked in the local law department, and was apparently abusing her position there to suppress any legal action against her and her partner. The offended plaintiff then finished on a note of moral threat, predicting the negative effects of such a miscarriage of justice on his own son: 'To me it is unclear how someone working in a law department is granted such unchecked freedom (*Narrenfreiheit*) in their private life to do as they please . . . Now I can no longer convincingly tell my son, who incidentally has been insulted by Frau N as well, why he should continue to have any confidence in state authorities.'[108] In these and other cases, the court records manifestly registered the hidden injuries of moral injustice that festered beneath the surface of socialist life.

Discernible, too, in these slander cases was an effort to defend one's private sphere. Even if the private sphere *per se* was not an actionable subject in GDR law, as it was in the West, citizens often used their cases to solicit the state to protect their citizen rights as private residents. A good illustration was a 1970 case in which a man filed that his neighbour's 'constant insults and abuse toward his [the plaintiff's] family' must be stopped. Herr H and his family were alleged to have repeatedly called the plaintiff's family lazy, stinky, and dirty, and Herr H himself apparently took great relish in shaking his rug full of dog hair from his balcony, knowing full well that it would drift into his neighbour's home through the open windows. The plaintiff ended his letter with the despairing words: 'Since my patience is now at an end, I am no longer willing to put up with this chicanery toward me and my family. I demand in light of the circumstances that deliberations with Family H be scheduled at once. Rules should be put in place so that my family can finally live undisturbed as citizens of this republic in our building.'[109] While this case remained unresolved and was eventually referred to a formal civil court hearing, the larger point is that citizens were looking more and more to the state as the guarantor of a peaceful private life.

By the 1980s the commissions were showing signs of decline. The issues that exercised the courts were still the same, though the number of cases tailed off after the mid-1980s.[110] There was markedly less reporting and paperwork in the court files; accompanying letters from complainants thinned out considerably, as the protocols simply recorded bare facts and outcomes. The trend was towards a speedy admonition, apology, and settlement, punctuated with a routine citation of the relevant civil code infraction. There was still some interest in reaffirming social norms, but the pronouncements were comparatively brief and dutiful. A 1981 case concerning a noisy neighbour concluded in this ritualized manner: 'Family P. must be made aware that they must remain true to the norms of collective life and the statutes pertaining to building regulations, municipal statutes and the Civil Code.'[111] Another case from the same year involving two neighbours fighting over the usage of a common water facility ended with the half-hearted verdict: 'The commission recommends to both parties that they forget the past and restore their former good neighbourly relations without demanding preconditions.'[112] The educational zeal that once fuelled these courts seemed all but spent, as the long-serving assessors appeared exhausted in the face of continuous petty disputes.[113] A 1988 case dealing with the constant quarrelling between two Berlin neighbours revealed even more frank resignation:

Such behavior has come to pass that the dignity and honour of both parties have been violated, which has not only affected the lives of the parties in their building, but has also exerted a negative influence on the other citizens in the building. The commission has already convened eight times to hear this case ... and has made clear in a concrete and comradely fashion that you are renters in this buildings and thus have no special rights ... These deliberations are still of no use (*wirkungslos*) to them nor the court.[114]

Not that fruitless outcomes were new; most 'useless' cases were simply referred to the higher civil courts. While this practice still continued for particularly complicated cases, more and more 'useless' cases were now simply adjourned and

abandoned. The reformatory mission had fallen off dramatically, giving way to
creeping pessimism about the possibility of either reforming offenders or eradicating petty crime from socialist soil.

What little high-minded language persisted was mostly directed towards
youth. In part this was due to the age of the lay assessors. While initially elected
to rotating four to five year posts, many citizens sat on these commissions for over
twenty years, not least because the courts were finding it more difficult to attract
younger jurists by the late 1970s and 1980s. According to one 1982 Berlin
report, the average age of social court assessors was 57, a marked difference from
the much younger average a generation before.[115] Some commentators have
viewed this trend as evidence of a broader 'retreat into the private sphere' in
the 1980s, as younger citizens opted out from serving on state-like organs,
especially those that peered into the private live of others.[116] At any rate, there
was little denying that 1980s cases often hinged on generational conflict. In one
1979 file, for example, a young man was accused of dumping excess snow into his
neighbours' gutter, damaging their walls and television antenna, as well as
insulting these elderly residents as 'dirty cows'; in its verdict the commission
averred in a paternalistic manner that 'it is a commandment of moral decency to
assist older citizens, above all in this case in repairing damages. It is also a
legal duty, as stated in Paragraph 323 and 325 of the Socialist Civil Code.'[117]
Likewise, a 1980 slander case reprimanded the young offender that 'it should be
expected that younger citizens show more consideration, politeness and respect
toward elderly people'.[118] The 1960s and early 1970s insistence that decency
and mutual cooperation were the bedrock of socialist society was not taking
root among younger citizens; and the commissions seemed ineffective in reforming the young.[119] Most troubling to the courts was that those young people who
were born, schooled, and socialized in the GDR possessed even less social grace,
respect, and solidarity towards their neighbours than their parents.

The changed tenor of the 1980s cases could be seen in other ways as well. For
one thing, one cannot help but detect a new-found aggressive tone in the
proceedings. Where complaints in the 1950s and 1960s were almost feudal in
their deference and delicacy towards authorities of any kind, the 1980s courts
witnessed remarkable insolence and cheek on the part of citizens toward their
peers. Some of this open hostility was there all along, especially concerning cases
of post-divorce disputes over personal property. What was new, however, was the
manifest impatience and impudence exhibited by citizens towards the judges, as
noted in the letters contained in case files. The once-standard decorum of citizen
pleas to the commission had dropped off markedly. A further indication of
changing neighbourly relations in the 1980s could be seen in the sharp increase
in cases involving fences and walls demarcating a citizen's territory from another's. Such disputes first emerged in the early 1970s (but they spiked in the
1980s) and were couched in a new tone.[120] In filing a 1986 complaint against a

neighbour on the grounds that his walnut tree was planted too close to the plaintiff's own fence and washing line, the latter wrote that

no man lives for himself alone; we all live in a society, a socialist society, and must be considerate of each another. If however someone for his own benefit infringes upon the justified rights and wishes of his neighbours . . . then it is hardly any wonder when his neighbours, who have long been patient and tolerant, will not put up with this kind of behavior anymore, and will resort to 'countermeasures'—in this case erecting a 2.5 meter high wall—in the name of law and justice![121]

Striking here is not only the ways in which this citizen had ably exploited the rhetoric of civil rights to his own advantage, but also the extent to which his language—despite the socialist patina—was indistinguishable from common bourgeois property law. As Markovits wrote, 'all bourgeois rights are modeled after property rights: they map our territory, set up fences against prospective intruders, or to quote Marx, they delineate the elbow room of the individual capitalist'.[122] Good fences may indeed make good neighbours, but in these property boundary disputes, East Berlin residential life did not look altogether different from its cold war rival. Fence-building cases were a sign of the times, reflecting the 1980s trend toward privacy, individualism, and social distance.[123]

* * *

From these court records as a whole, it is possible to conclude initially that East German socialist society—despite propaganda to the contrary—was really battling over distinctly 'bourgeois' notions of domestic order, propriety, and the good life. The commissions' growing sense of helplessness in combating 'capitalist egotism' may then be seen as an admission of the very limits of the socialist makeover of everyday citizens, as well as an implicit acknowledgement that these 'pre-socialist' bourgeois attitudes were here to stay. In a world defined by scarcity and material want, personal property became even more important, and unsurprisingly became the very stuff of local social friction. The same went for the high percentage of cases concerning violations of honour. After all, it is precisely in societies characterized by little flow of goods and money that honour—as a kind of non-transferrable private property—is held especially dear. That the state policed public debate as closely as it patrolled its national frontiers meant that these court confrontations between neighbours became one of the few places where citizens could vent their everyday grievances. But as always, this occurred within the strict limits of the GDR authoritarian state. That the social court system was developed and expanded in reaction to several 'system-critical' events—the 1953 Uprising, the 1961 erection of the Berlin Wall, and the 1968 Prague Spring—underlines the state's effort to use the commissions to multiply its power and paternalistic reach. From the authorities' perspective, the citizen commissions helped track residential strife and nonconformists in the name of 'socialist community'. Nonetheless, in these residential disputes about personal property and individual honour, collectivist ideals often lost out, as complainants effectively reworked the 'I–We' relationship to personal ends. Emphasis fell on preserving citizens' own property from the abuse of others— be it their homes, possessions, domestic tranquillity, and/or personal reputation, leading to a 'privatization' of social justice born of creeping political disillusionment. At the very least, these developments go some way to explaining why the world of personal property—everyday objects and memorabilia—figured so prominently in the infamous nostalgia wave (*Ostalgie*) among East Germans after Reunification.[124]

But consigning these developments to some sort of facile 'bourgeoisification' of GDR society overlooks other key issues. For instance, one could plausibly counter—and this is my second point—that these court records ultimately demonstrate a kind of citizen assertion of civil society. For some this may seem peculiar, not least because an influential strand of GDR historiography has worked to turn Marx on his head, arguing that it was society, and not the state, that eventually withered away under Soviet-style socialism. And yet, these files amply show that a certain expression of civil society—based on the protection of property, peace, privacy, and even courtesy—developed at the local level over the years, and that these dispute commissions played their part in making this possible. Admittedly, the classic liberal notion of an independent civil society flourishing in the social spaces between the family home and the state found no expression in the GDR, as state, society, and the private sphere were always blurred and overlapping. There was no critical public sphere, and Western-style civil rights, such as the freedom of speech, assembly, and emigration, were essentially off-limits, even after the signing of the Helsinki Accords in 1975. The cosy relationship between the justice system—including the social courts— and the National Front and local police makes this perfectly plain, as noted in several cases discussed above. The key point is that GDR civil society did not develop—as it did in the West—against the state, but rather very much within it. As a result, GDR citizen rights may never have added up to Western civil and political rights, but they were more in keeping with what T. H. Marshall long ago called modern 'social rights', defined as 'the right to a modicum of economic welfare and security . . . to live the life of a civilized being according to the standards prevailing in society'.[125] In this regard, perhaps the more important government document outlining the relationship between the GDR state and its citizenry was another one that appeared in 1975: the Socialist Civil Code. Like the Helsinki Accords, the GDR's new code covered questions of security and rights, but treated them from a decidedly socialist perspective. As we have seen, the code was an explicit effort to 'materialize' civil rights, safeguarding a host of property protections and 'subjective rights' for GDR citizens. An illustration from a 1978 book significantly called *Socialist Lifestyle and Personal Property* (Figure 15) perfectly captured this logic, as a family and its personal effects are literally sheltered by the regime's Socialist Civil Code, or ZGB.[126] This understanding was firmly in line with socialist governments' understanding of civil

Figure 15. Cartoon about the GDR's 1975 Civil Code's Protection of Family and Property, 1978.

rights at the time, to the extent that they saw the right to work, decent housing, health, higher education, and even 'rest and relaxation' as fundamental human rights, as opposed to the 'abstract' liberties celebrated by their cold war rivals.[127] A 1981 brochure entitled 'What Citizens Ask about Civil Law Rights' neatly reflected this official 'materialist' attitude. In it civil rights were confined to useful information on how to redress violations of public property; apply for house repairs; learn about your property rights concerning weekend houses and garages; report noise and other disturbances of the peace; and to find out who is responsible for building walls and fences between neighbours—complete with civil code citations.[128] From this perspective, the dispute commissions served at the front line of residential social rights conflicts for nearly three decades.

Thirdly, commission records underline just how seriously many residents took these broadcast norms of socialist behaviour. In this area, the state's ideological campaign succeeded far beyond expectations. Ulbricht's proud assertion before the Volkskammer in 1960 that 'our justice is the right to friendly cooperation, mutual assistance and respect for one another' became the very *raison d'être* for these citizen courts. In the end this idea of justice may not have given, as Ulbricht hoped, 'every citizen in our republic a fixed perspective in the fight for the victory of socialism';[129] it did however spur demands and expectations of popular justice. There are unfortunately no opinion polls or studies of how citizens viewed the commissions; no doubt many were mistrustful, regarding them as just another form of state snooping, while others embraced them as instruments to advance private interests.[130] But for those who did pursue personal grievances, the commissions provided ordinary citizens with a new rhetoric of redress against one another. What they arguably took most to heart were the original claims of Marxism itself—social justice and material compensation. In the GDR, civil rights always remained subordinate to economic rights; but once personal property became a protected fixture of GDR civil law, its citizens pressed for their social rights accordingly. That the GDR Civil Code of 1975 was a bestseller across the country, having sold some two million copies to a population of 16.7 million, attests to socialism's own burgeoning 'rights culture'.[131] However cynically citizens may have cited the code to advance their private claims, the point is that they embraced the law, the citizen court system, and ultimately the state itself as receptive organs of popular justice.[132]

Lastly, the social court records reveal something that flies in the face of conventional wisdom about the GDR, namely that the state played a key role in defending the private sphere of its citizens. This may appear incongruous to those committed to a Stasi-centric view of GDR history; while no one would deny the Stasi's remarkable reach into East German everyday life, its influence in the sphere of civil law, and in the social court system in particular, was relatively modest. In creating a quasi-public organ for hearing private disputes, the state provided an unusually frank forum for discussing infringements on citizen rights and socialist liberties. What united almost all of these complaints was the shared presumption that the state was there to provide for—and protect—a decent private life for all of its citizens. By the 1980s the SED was devoting increasing attention—and resources—to the security, cleanliness, and comfort of residential areas, above all in the name of political peace. But it was precisely this commonly noted distance between state and citizen that became a gnawing concern for the government; little wonder that it was during the apparent 'liberalization' of the 1970s when the East German state stepped up the surveillance of ordinary citizens as potential dissidents. Thus the commissions played a key role in gathering information about 'asocial' residents, as individuals were encouraged to criticize one another for their 'private' non-socialist misbehaviour. As a result, the state paradoxically served as both foe and guardian of the private sphere. The citizens' personal property claims—be they about goods, a quiet life, or honour—only intensified this paradox. In the end, the thousands of dispute commission cases afford a unique vista into the micropolitics of residential socialism from the early 1960s to the regime's demise, chronicling as they did the shifting values of socialist citizens toward the state and each another.

6

Socialism's Social Contract
Individual Citizen Petitions

Over the years, the GDR has gained a reputation as a cranky and unremitting 'complainer culture'. It is an image that West Germans have perpetuated with great frequency and relish since 1989, especially in the wake of the painful 'Solidarity Tax' imposed on them to share the financial burdens of Reunification. Yet the perception of the GDR as a veritable 'grumble *Gesellschaft*' was actually homegrown in East Germany, and one that went beyond the carpings of overwhelmed bureaucrats faced with an ever-dissatisfied population demanding basic goods and services.[1] In fact, the GDR's invention of the 'complainer-citizen' was hailed as a welcome and fundamental dimension of socialist life. Virtually from the outset the SED took great pains to build what one historian has ironically called an 'institutionalized culture of complaint'.[2]

This chapter sets out to recall the special place of the famed citizen petitions, or *Eingaben*, within East German life. What makes these citizen communications particularly interesting is the way that they straddled the line between public and private. By and large these complaints were sent to public addressees to deal with highly personal questions. Most were written by single authors, not groups, and were a main form of personal contact with the state under communism. By 1989 East Germans were writing over a million complaint letters a year, making this at once a mass-produced yet highly individualized mode of communication between citizen and state. As noted in the last chapter, individual civil rights and duties were taken very seriously in the GDR from the very beginning, reflecting shifting ideals about the relationship between socialist law and citizenship.

The use of citizen petitions as a source of historical research for modern Germany is hardly unique to GDR historiography. For at least two decades, citizen petitions have been well-integrated into the study of modern German legal history, and have been used by social historians since the 1970s to analyse everyday power relations—in particular worker culture—from the late nineteenth century onward.[3] Nonetheless, some of the most far-reaching analyses of citizen complaints of late have focused on East German history. While some historians have approached these sources primarily as instruments of authoritarian government, whose real value lay in their ability to 'reconcile critics with the regime through a combination of authoritarian practice and the rhetoric of

participatory democracy',[4] others have interpreted these letters as a rich repository of East German subjectivity and sociability—'ethnographic diaries' of GDR
citizens.[5] Underlying both views, however, is the assumption that these letters
essentially served as compensation for a very limited public sphere. No doubt this
complaint-system flew in the face of any normative conception of the liberal
public sphere as an arena of public, enlightened discourse. Yet the GDR's
Eingabe was probably the best-functioning and most used form of communication between citizens and state authorities, offering people without official
connections one of the few available avenues to redress wrongs or problems.
What Sheila Fitzpatrick has written about Stalinist culture is equally valid for the
GDR: the writing and reading of these letters 'is as close to a public sphere as one
is likely to get during the Stalin period'.[6] Moreover, they afford deep and unusual
vistas into the private lives and problems of average citizens. They show how
GDR citizens presented their anger, frustration and desires, and in so doing
revealed remarkable 'patterns of individualization' in an otherwise highly regulated society.[7] For this reason, they furnish some of the most revealing 'everyday
texts' of East German history,[8] casting a good deal of light on popular perceptions of the state and socialist justice.

THE RIGHT TO COMPLAIN

The right to petition was anchored in Article 3 of the GDR's 1949 Constitution.
East German Premier Walter Ulbricht himself championed its inclusion, arguing
that such a right functioned as a crucial means of better binding state and citizen.
During the 3rd Socialist Unity Party Congress the next year, GDR President
Wilhelm Pieck summarized the government's position, insisting that 'the intimate connection between the state apparatus and the people, the speedy resolution of all complaints, and the eradication of all bureaucratic obstacles
[obstructing the relationship between the people and the state] must be given
highest priority'.[9] Justification was traced back to Lenin, who saw such petitions
as part of the 'enlistment and education of the workers' into the 'daily administrative work of the state', thus a necessary step toward citizen self-government.[10]
By 1953 the citizen's right to petition was further expanded by a new law of the
State Council, which stated that such petitions were fundamental to the state's
'broader struggle for the further strengthening of the democratic order'. In SED
Party literature, the right to petition was now repeatedly hailed for its ability to
bring about 'great confidence in our state', 'the consolidation of socialist
democracy', as well as 'political-moral unity and growing socialist consciousness'.[11] So whereas complainants early on were often dismissed by government
authorities as querulous citizens with 'petit bourgeois backgrounds',[12] they
were now to be received with great respect and pride. Even the official term
used to describe the citizen communication shifted from *Beschwerde* to *Eingabe*,

since the former word was considered too coarse and negative. Former GDR Interior Minister Karl Steinhoff circulated a memorandum by the end of 1950 stating that 'every citizen of our GDR must feel personally spoken to from us'.[13] So vital was this connection between citizen complaints and socialist democracy in the eyes of the state that regional administrators were actually encouraged to compete for the highest quota of received citizen petitions.[14] In the country's revised 1968 and 1975 Constitutions, the formal right of complaint was enshrined as one of the most fundamental civil liberties of East German citizens (Article 103, para. 1), closely connected with the 'right of co-determination and participation' (*Mitbestimmung- und Mitgestaltungsrecht*) of all citizenry to engage in the affairs of state and society. The key passage read: 'Every citizen may turn to the representative bodies of the people, their individual members, or state and economic organizations, with *Eingaben* [suggestions, tips, requests or complaints]. This right is also available to social organizations and citizens' communities. Exercise of this right should not bring any disadvantages to them.' Further clauses guaranteeing the speedy 'processing of all citizen complaints' remained in force until 1990, since these petitions were considered integral to the GDR's larger socialist trinity: 'Work Together, Plan Together, Govern Together.'[15]

And complain they did. So much so that no state in history ever recorded as many citizen complaints as East Germany did. Already by 1952, three years after the country's founding, President Pieck personally received no fewer than 80,000 written citizen petitions. By 1962 the State Council received over 100,000 letters annually, and over 134,000 by 1988. But this was only the beginning. Thousands of complaints were sent to ministries as well as local and regional representatives on a monthly basis over four decades, adding up to hundreds of thousands of complaints filed every year, across every region. In 1989 alone, there were over one million formally filed citizen complaints nationwide. It is estimated that every household submitted at least one complaint letter over the course of the regime's forty-year reign.[16] And these were only the written complaints; by the mid-1970s, local Party representatives often held office hours in workplaces, during which local citizens could—and did—lodge their complaints orally if they preferred. Nowhere else has the world seen such an elaborate and institutionalized complaint culture. While some of this had to do with the country's sprawling and energetic bureaucracy, the extraordinary number of complaints was also due to the state's active encouragement of citizens to get involved in state affairs in this way.

But what did they complain about? Topics varied, but most every aspect of socialist life was ripe for complaint-letter writing. Of course certain themes— such as state repression, the Wall, the West, and the inability to travel freely— remained strictly off-limits for the first three decades of the regime;[17] but after the signing of the Helsinki Accords this too changed somewhat, as we shall see. In any case, most letters were explicitly written to address pressing personal problems and to resolve disputes. They concerned a whole range of consumer issues, such as inadequate housing, sanitary conditions, wage levels, working hours, holiday entitlement, public transportation, health facilities, air pollution, noise, childcare facilities, promised automobile parts, domestic repairs, food queues, consumer bottlenecks, insufficient cultural programmes, and other sundry problems. Some complained about 'asocials' in their midst, be they work-shy residents, alcoholics, or deadbeat fathers,[18] while others were angry that they could not arrange a party in the factory to celebrate a marriage announcement.[19] One featured a letter from the Ministry of People's Education that all teachers should be given flats with a work study area to carry out their work.[20]

Not surprisingly, these often spilled into political issues. In the 1950s a significant percentage of petitions concerned imprisoned family members and POWs, for example. Other East Berliners vented their spleen about using the Polish names of old German cities in former Prussia when being asked to fill out the residential Hausbuch about their place of birth.[21] After the construction of the Berlin Wall, authorities were inundated with a rash of petitions from people (especially East Berliners) to see family members.[22] Nonetheless, the most common topics were problems associated with the home, work, and welfare services; the quality and provisioning of badly undersupplied consumer goods; travel restrictions; transportation and pollution problems; and more general political dissatisfaction with local, regional, and national-level administration, to which I shall return later. This form of citizen action proved extremely popular, providing a rare chance to express genuine citizen concerns in a world not really of their making. As a result, the complaints variably served as barometers of common hopes and expectations, individual investment in the state, as well as a controlled and controllable outlet of everyday discontent.

The right to petition was not new to the twentieth century. It first originated in Roman law, and enjoyed numerous legal reincarnations over the centuries. It lay at the very heart of the Magna Charta, insofar as the document was essentially Parliament's petition of grievances against the English king. The right to petition was anchored in the Bill of Rights that concluded the 1688 Glorious Revolution, and was explicitly invoked by the American colonialists in 1776 and firmly rooted thereafter in the American Constitution of 1791. Across the Atlantic that same year, the French National Assembly made petition rights a key feature of its new revolutionary constitution. In several German lands, especially Prussia, such so-called *Bittschriften* were common across the eighteenth century.[23] Moreover, the 1848 Constitution drafted by the National Assembly in Frankfurt stated that 'every German has the right to submit in writing complaints and petitions to local authorities, national representatives and to the Reichstag itself'.[24] While the right to petition was formally diluted under Bismarck, it was fully reinstated in the Weimar Republic's 1919 Constitution as a signal commitment to democratic citizenship.

Less well-known is that such formal complaints were enshrined in West German civil society as well. The right to petition was made a key element of West German constitutional life, guaranteed in Article 17 of the Basic Law.[25] Its spirit was quite similar to the GDR's right to petition, with the same objective of overcoming bureaucratic blockages and resistance. Nonetheless, the West German constitutional provision of citizen complaints excluded the possibility of oral complaints and reduced such petitions to a merely consultative role. Unlike in the GDR, Article 17 makes plain that citizen petitions must be addressed to parliament, not state institutions or the executive. In practice the West German equivalent were much more public in character, in that complaints tended to function as 'mass petitions' used by various organizations to lobby influence and/or publicize a particular issue, such as environmental concerns.[26] While numbers of submitted petitions paled in comparison to East German standards, the Bundestag did receive nearly 50,000 annual complaints between 1972 and 1976 on topics ranging from social security, childcare, old age provisions, and the environment.[27]

But it is misleading to see the history of citizen petitions as simply part of the lineage of liberalism. After all, such complaint-writing was central to absolutism. It was common in France under Louis XVI in the form of the infamous *cahiers*, and was standard practice under the Russian tsars. Petitions to the tsar against abusive or corrupt officials played a key role in the tsarist system, reinforcing the popular myth of a 'just tsar' who protected the people from malicious administrators. In the Russian case, the right to petition was considered a private dialogue between aggrieved individuals and the sovereign, with which the monarch could defuse potential challenges to royal power. This special feature of Russian political life continued even after 1917, as new Soviet citizens were encouraged to write to the communist state with their concerns.[28] Lenin encouraged citizen engagement in this way, and in 1928 Stalin too called 'the masses, the millions of workers and peasants to the task of criticism from below'.[29] Such practices continued after 1945. In the period 1945–6, for example, the Russia's NKVD received over 500,000 letters from Soviet citizens complaining about their material situation and standard of living, as people were emboldened by the wartime experience to assert their rights.[30] Similar developments were manifest in the Third Reich: Hitler's Chancellery received more than 1,000 letters per working day, and Goering supposedly received about 2,000 letters daily from those seeking favours or wishing to make complaints. In Nazi Germany, petition letters to authorities became a favoured form of citizen activity.[31]

THE LANDLORD STATE

Even so, the centrality of the petitions as an instrument of benevolent paternalism was especially pronounced in the GDR, and assumed unusual political gravity there. While there were similar practices in the Soviet Union and in satellite states such as Bulgaria, nowhere was the citizen complaint system as elaborate as in the GDR. In part this had to do with the fact that the right to petition was fundamental to GDR notions of privacy and private rights. At first this may seem a little puzzling, given that privacy—to say nothing of private rights—was apparently one of the most severely rationed of East German commodities. But as we saw in the last chapter, private rights and private property persisted in various forms in the GDR. Not surprisingly, such issues vexed GDR lawyers and lawmakers. Various reform campaigns among GDR jurists from the late 1950s on to rewrite Germany's long-standing Civil Code according to evolving ideals of socialist citizenship sparked heated discussion about exactly what—and where—the private sphere was within state socialism. From 1945 to 1949, for example, East and West German jurists and lawyers alike aimed to rehabilitate the German Civil Code (Bürgerliches Gesetzbuch) of 1900 as the cornerstone of post-Nazi constitutional order. This civil code was based on a set of classic liberal 'negative freedoms' that assured the liberties of free, private citizens against the undue encroachments of the state. But with the intensification of the cold war and the stepped-up effort to accelerate the reach of 'socialist legality' to all aspects of East German life, the civil code was now targeted for 'modernization'. Ulbricht himself led the charge, citing Marx that a socialist civil code must aim 'to bring people out of social isolation and free them from the bourgeois mindset'.[32] For Ulbricht and the SED, the relationship of individuals to society needed to be brought in line with postwar socialist thought and practice.[33] Crucial here was the new ideological justification deriving from Stalin's idea of the 'active superstructure', which held that state actions (and not just economic transformation) were equally important in cultivating socialist consciousness and citizenship.

Law was singled out as particularly decisive in this regard. East German jurists busied themselves with remaking civil law for a new socialist world. This was neither easy nor obvious, however, not least because socialist civil law was riddled with holdovers from liberal jurisprudence, as noted in the last chapter. The failure to do away with private rights was no victory for individual rights in the GDR, however. If anything, this 'anomaly' within socialist political culture prompted renewed action to confront its potential harmful effects. Reformers then moved to close the gap between state and citizen by other means. Notably, the battlelines (and legal language) changed along the way. In the sphere of civil law, for instance, the distinction was no longer seen in terms of public versus private rights, as in liberal jurisprudence. Rather, it was slowly replaced with a new lexicon that treated conflicts as confrontations between civil rights and what was now known as the state's 'administrative right' or *Verwaltungsrecht*.

It was in this context that the written complaints became so important. For however much the right to petition was enshrined in the GDR constitution as a fundamental socialist right, instituted to help overcome the distance between state and citizen, there was widespread worry that the complaint system was inadvertently widening this gulf. Little wonder, then, that this development was greeted with apprehension by state officials, who thought that these written complaints actually undermined—not strengthened—'collective conscious-ness'.[34] While some officials were more upbeat, dismissing the tendency of citizens to use the petitions for expressly individual concerns as merely tempo-rary and transitional,[35] there was common state anxiety about the long-term effects of this institutionalized 'complaint culture'. In particular, it was seen as giving form to (and even championing) individual private concerns over those of the collective, especially since most complaints were written by private *Bürger* with specific private issues in mind.

The bureaucratic processing of these written complaints was a vital issue from the very beginning. The speedy turnaround was a source of pride for the regime, and the efficient processing of these complaints received wide press coverage.[36] But such expeditious reception was not often the case in reality. Complaints landed on the administrator's desk, and it was up to their discretion how to deal with them. Responsible institutions were commonly seen as lazy and even corrupt, and tended to reject applications on grounds that the petitioner was 'anti-socialist' in claim or attitude. Local administrators were encouraged to seek out personal conversations with the petitioners as a means of assuaging swelling discontent. For this reason, the petition-processing literature (handbooks, bro-chures, etc.) was as much about scolding incompetent administrators as it was addressing individual citizen dissatisfaction.[37]

The numerous handbooks for local, regional, and state-level party function-aries (which included housing community leaders and 'confidence men') drafted during the 1970s repeatedly reprimanded 'heartless' and 'unfeeling' bureaucrats for their poor service.[38] That state representatives were routinely chastened by the central government for not answering citizen complaints promptly enough was not only to guarantee the rights of socialist citizens; it was also to help overcome rampant 'bureaucratism' and the growing gap between state and citizen, a gap that the state knew very well existed and was in danger of opening up beyond repair. This was especially important since the law provided no possibility of independent legal appeal, nor did neglecting petitions carry any real conse-quences for the *Eingaben* processor. To be sure, communism's antipathy towards 'bureaucratism' was nothing new. In the early Soviet Union for example, the Soviet government constantly appealed to citizens to expose the misdeeds of state officials and unnecessary red tape. So intractable was the fight against 'bureau-cratism' that Lenin reportedly once said that 'this war is much more difficult than the civil war'.[39] The GDR's high-profile campaign in the mid-1970s to reduce the reply turnaround time for processing to such complaints to four weeks (down from four months) put even more pressure on these civil servants to keep the 'wheels of socialist democracy' turning.[40] As a consequence, the insensitive and indolent bureaucrat was as much a vilified figure as the individualist 'asocial' house resident.[41]

The 'confidence people' and especially the 'housing communities' were entreated to play more active roles in this regard. These housing administrators were urged to devote more attention to the private life of its citizens, as evidenced in the new 'housing community leader' handbooks. Calls for expanded communal control were largely driven by growing fears of violence and crime, particularly among youth, which spurred wide discussion in the 1960s and 1970s among GDR sociologists, educators, and social workers. For them, a great deal of the problem lay in identifying the roots of deviant behaviour within state socialism, especially since traditional Marxist sociology maintained that crime essentially sprang from capitalist sources (namely, economic inequality, material misery, and social alienation), all of which the GDR supposedly had overcome with its successful revolution. Residential life was increasingly singled out as largely responsible, giving rise to explosive new interest during the 1970s in studying 'socialist personality', 'socialist lifestyle', 'socialist living conditions', 'socialist childraising', 'socialist family life', and above all 'asocial behavior' as new targets of social reform.[42] The much-publicized development and nurturing of 'socialist justice' (*Rechtspflege*) among housing residents and in particular the creation of so-called 'social courts' in residential communities, as noted in the last chapter, were inspired by a similar concern.[43] State-level discussion about the significance of these complaints went hand in hand with the government's redoubled effort from the mid-1960s on to build up the fraying 'socialist community', especially in residential areas. In this context anti-socialist behaviour of all kinds was considered more dangerous than ever, and systematically targeted for 're-education'.[44] A good number of complaints written in the 1950s and 1960s focused on 'asocial' residents and 'unsocialist' behaviour.[45] Not that these complaints were always successful. Often the untoward efforts to tar neighbours' actions as criminal met with scepticism from authorities, and many wrote back to exonerate the accused. If nothing else, such action shows that the state authorities did take such denunciations seriously, typically checking them with *Volkspolizei* and other local organs of justice.

People sometimes looked elsewhere to plead their case. Frustration with a sprawling and overwhelmed state bureaucracy meant that they increasingly turned to other organizations with their troubles. Many Christians for example wrote to the Church with their material concerns, especially regarding housing, in the hope that the Church would play its historical role as key welfare institution in society. By the 1970s citizens also turned to the Stasi about poor work conditions, blocked job promotions, and administrative corruption, with the expectation that it would and could act on their behalf. Others complained about the Stasi. For example, citizens accused the Stasi of fixing matches for its football team, BFC Dynamo; the team dominated GDR football during the 1980s, and it was widely believed that the side received preferential treatment by referees. It was taken seriously enough that a Politburo member formally complained to Stasi Chef Erich Mielke, claiming that this was undermining the reputation of the FDGB Cup. Occasionally the national press, including *Neues Deutschland* and various football papers, also vented popular anger about the cosy relationship between referees and Mielke. Even the Stasi filed complaints to state authorities, usually about the poor quality of their flats.[46] Such examples demonstrate just how ubiquitous and normal this complaint culture was in all aspects of GDR life.

This complaint system was also a boon to the state. Administrators quickly realized that these complaint letters provided the regime with valuable intelligence about popular discontent. This was particularly prized in a world without real opinion polls or open votes. The SED was well aware that it was hardly a popular regime, not least because everyone knew that it owed its 'leading role' not to popular support, but rather to Soviet bayonets. German resistance to the Soviets was there from the beginning, due in large part to the rapes, thefts, and brutality perpetrated by the Soviet occupational forces during the endgame of the Second World War. Many East Germans also blamed the communists for their material hardships after the war, and saw the SED leaders as essentially Russian stooges. In the early 1960s the SED created an Institute for Opinion Research to gauge the morale of its Party faithful, and was surprised to learn that even its supporters harboured real reservations about SED policy and its running of the country.[47] Already in the 1950s the SED was making efforts to gather popular opinion as vital intelligence, having organized a number of so-called 'public discussions' on various issues of national concern—such as church–state relations, Civil Code reform, and rearmament—about which citizens did not hesitate to express their grievances. Party officials and state journalists were also routinely posted on public transport to take the temperature of popular opinion. Over the years they reported that most citizens were not all that convinced by the SED leadership's policy or competence, and tended to feel a sense of helplessness, apathy, and even apoliticism. Yet such dissatisfaction was tolerated by the SED, as long as it was expressed passively and privately, since most citizens—so the reports concluded—'preferred to concentrate on their local concerns and private lives rather than risk upsetting a rather precariously loaded applecart'.[48] In fact, largely due to the uncomfortable results, Honecker shut down the Institute in 1976, and the Stasi's own Central Evaluation and Information Group (ZAIG) stopped reporting on the populace at large that same year as well.[49] These developments made these complaint letters all the more vital as informal referenda on SED rule and good government.

They also registered changing images of the state–citizen relationship. As hard as it was for the state to answer—let alone attend to—all of these complaints, the system was very effective in channelling dissent into a manageable arena. Earlier (and potentially more explosive) notions of abstract civil rights were in practice being slowly replaced with more concrete demands for material betterment. Needless to say, the state always viewed privacy and private rights as potential fifth-column factors in GDR political life, best seen in the role played by one of its incarnations, religious devotion. But the right to petition was a form of private rights that the state was able to accept and handle. In this regard, East German sociologist Wolfgang Engler is off the mark when he asserted that the GDR state 'wanted modern life without modern citizens', deathly afraid as the regime supposedly was of citizens agitating for expanded political rights and constitutional privileges.[50] The complaint system showed this was not completely true, for the state did encourage individual citizen agitation, albeit in a very private and 'civilized' manner.

Such an ideal was elevated as state theory. In GDR parlance, the 'co-formation of the citizen's developmental possibilities' became the state's preferred image of the citizen's relationship to the state, and the *Eingabe* system became one of its hallmark manifestations. Here individual rights were increasingly expressed in terms of individualized material concerns addressed to the state as glorified landlord. Small wonder that the new metaphor of choice for describing the relationship between the state and citizen shifted to that of landlord and tenant, recasting the state's primary role as consumer service provider and guarantor of peace and order. This was the GDR version of the citizen as consumer.

Given that the state promised to provide for all, these seemingly banal problems of provisioning quickly shaded into quite trenchant political criticisms of the regime's ability to make good on its promises. This of course was the fruit of the regime's ideological campaign to subordinate civil rights to economic rights, which held the government accountable for all matters of daily welfare. That the complaint system built on and actively mobilized the language of direct democracy only made things more dangerous. It created a kind of vicious circle in which the initial idea of encouraging the complaints as a means of political control soon proved unwieldy and even counterproductive.[51] So even if the petitions did serve as instruments of surveillance to help track popular discontent and bureaucratic effectiveness, it was really a two-way surveillance in the end. Just as in Stalin's Russia, East German complaints also functioned as a form of popular surveillance over bureaucracy and the regime's intelligence-gathering on its citizens.[52]

NARRATING DISCONTENT

These complaints were by no means uniform or unchanging. Anyone researching on the topic cannot help but be struck not only with the volume of petitions, but also with the dizzying variety of style and appearance. They ranged from hastily scrawled notes to ten-page handwritten letters to meticulously typed accounts of personal injustice, complete with photographs as supporting evidence. With time the letters generally grew more formal and even formulaic in presentation, though black humour and irony remained in strong supply. Statistically, the peaks of complaint letter-writing were the 1960s and early 1980s, with significant drops in the 1970s. The addressees also changed. In the early 1950s many complaints were addressed to local 'confidence people' and housing community leaders. A surprising number of early 1950s letters were sent to President Wilhelm Pieck, an avuncular and much-loved figure in the early GDR. People across the country referred to him as a kindly 'father of the new nation' or the 'confidence man of the people' (*Vertrauensmann des Volkes*). In his period of office from 1950 to 1959 Pieck received some 1.65 million private missives.[53] Upon Pieck's death in 1960, the President's Office was closed, after which such citizen letters were then sent directly to Ulbricht's new State Council, which helped shore up the image of SED leaders as all-knowing and paternally responsible for everyone's welfare.

The complaint system marked a kind of materialization of civil rights. In the 1950s many *Eingaben* were written by firms to Ulbricht about economic issues, such as delivery problems and supply bottlenecks.[54] With time, however, most complaint letters were written by individuals, and concerned personal material circumstances. One 1954 report, for example, stated that 49 of 61 of Berlin-Friedrichain's January 1954 complaints concerned housing.[55] Another 1965 *Eingaben* report recorded that over 70 per cent of complaints concerned housing, often from young couples with small children in need of new accommodations.[56] To be sure, what exactly constituted 'home issues' was often quite elastic, since it could include demands for a new flat following a marriage, or grumbling about the unjust division of personal property after marital dissolution.[57] These letters reflected the broader trend toward more privatized notions of social justice over the decades. Such letter-writing also went hand in hand with a more general decline in various forms of the collective defence of worker interests across the country, such as strikes or unofficial work stoppages. While it would be exaggerated to attribute the flourishing complaint system as a direct cause, there was a manifest 'shift from collective interest representation to individual forms of intervention'.[58]

The focus on domestic problems was in large measure a result of the SED's family policy. The early Marxist dream of doing away with the family in the name of socialist collectivism was discarded across the communist world under Stalin, as the nuclear family made a strong comeback, and continued long after his death. In the GDR, it was clear that the aim was not to destroy the nuclear family, but to remould it as a haven of emotional affection and solidarity by removing its financial insecurities and gender inequalities. While it is certainly true that the SED tirelessly championed the nuclear family as the bedrock of social stability and political peace from the mid-1950s on, and expended considerable energy in socializing youth into the virtues of socialist ideology, the emergence of the family as an object of state intervention was very much a product of the mid to late 1960s, and intensified in the 1970s. In the late 1960s, the expanded scope of welfare policies into the home was largely introduced in the name of relieving overburdened mothers saddled with the lion's share of child-raising and housework. Notably, domestic reform initiatives (such as the campaign for new kitchens, heating systems, washing facilities, and modern appliances) were spearheaded by various women's groups, who successfully made the case to the government that family residential problems deserved urgent state assistance. A vast number of the *Eingaben*, for example, took the form of mothers complaining about the unheated and excessively damp conditions of their flats, which left the family and especially the children susceptible to sundry respiratory ailments. These developments thus need not be read as necessarily negative, since they were part and parcel of a more general 1970s idea of the 'therapeutic state' that strove to direct more attention to the care of at-risk families and vulnerable citizens, above all children and the elderly.

Like elsewhere in the Eastern bloc, the GDR featured its 'gray markets' and informal 'second economies' to compensate for the inadequacies of the state planned economies. People imaginatively organized their own networks of goods and services. With time the state turned a blind eye to this extralegal barter system, since everyone knew that getting adequate materials depended on participation in the semi-legal shadow economy outside the household or state sector.[59] House repairs for example were often done by hand with the aid of a barter economy, while tools and supplies were not infrequently pilfered from workplaces to make up for the lack of available material and state services. So prevalent was the need for skilled repair work that lonely hearts advertisements in the GDR commonly featured pleas for partners who were 'handy and skilled' (*handwerklich geschickt*) around the house.[60]

A good number of the complaints were animated by class injustice. The GDR's rudimentary citizen research agency, the Central Evaluation and Information Group (ZAIG), found that issues of class, gender, generation, and status still rankled among the people. The elderly complained that younger colleagues were unwilling to assume positions of responsibility, despite higher standards of living, and there was a good deal of resentment towards the privileges of SED functionaries.[61] Many citizens also voiced their anger about the presence and unequal availability of Western goods in GDR life. From the very beginning West Germany assumed a considerable 'shadow existence' in the material culture of the GDR, in the form of gifts, information, and cultural products. Gift packages from Western relatives in particular had long been a source of desire and envy, especially after the construction of the Berlin Wall.[62] But it was the regime's tacit approval of Western items, pop music, and even currency in the 1970s that many socialists found shocking and hypocritical. Dissident philosopher Wolfgang Harich spoke for many when he coyly remarked that economic life in the GDR was characterized less by the official slogan 'to each according to their labor' than 'to each according to where their [West German] aunt lives'.[63]

Not infrequently did letters conclude with a flurry of outrage that the state was not fulfilling its socialist promises of a decent material life for its citizens. Many would try to shame the local state representative by quoting Lenin on the importance of providing citizens with a decent standard of living, or reciting Article 4 of the GDR Constitution, which stated that 'all Power should serve the well-being of the Volk. It should secure the People's peaceful existence, protect its socialist society, guarantee a socialist lifestyle for its citizens, the free develop-ment of all persons and the preservation of their dignity.'[64] Typical is the following ending: 'You can believe me when I say that we are forced to live like animals [in this housing unit], and this in socialism!'[65] The nearly obligatory conclusion, 'In Socialist Greeting', was thus quite variable in meaning, ranging as it did from an expression of loyalty to irony to outright admonition.

Other strategies were deployed to shame local administrators into action. Complaint letters written in the 1950s and 1960s were on the whole much more modest and deferential, and often invoked key biographical issues to make an effective plea about resolving specific problems. Letter-writers would cite their pre-1949 communist activity and military service, social position, and SED loyalty (local party leader, residence director, etc.) to lend moral weight to their claim. Note the common preamble from a 1973 letter written directly to Honecker asking for a new apartment for the petitioner's ailing older daughter:

Dear Comrade Erich Honecker! After long consideration I have decided to turn to you with my very personal and bothersome problem, since I don't know what else to do, and hope that you can help me. My name is Lise P. I was a member of the Communist Party in 1944 and have been a member of our Party since 1949. My husband was Adolf P, who due to his antifascist activity was forced to emigrate. He fought as a brigadier in the Thälmann Unit in the Spanish Civil War and was severely wounded there, after which he was sent to Paris in 1937 for convalescence. This is where we met. Adolf and I were resistance fighters during the fascist occupation in France, and returned together to Germany after the war. Adolf worked as a member of the Central Committee from 1949 to 1961, and I have raised our children as conscious, Party-oriented fighters for our cause . . .[66]

The amount of detail and proof of Party loyalty was a standard mode of legitimizing the plea on moral grounds. The presumption was that state redress was part of the social contract with its citizens, and thus state inaction was a violation of this bargain. Yet the language got nastier with time. By the 1960s citizens used their citizen rights and activities to threaten the state. Many refused to vote or take part in elections should their complaints go unheeded. So frequent was this threat that the SED noted a strong correlation between national elections and the spike in the number of citizen petitions.[67] By the late 1970s some citizens even threatened suicide if their demands for travel or an adequate flat were not satisfied.[68] Others wrote that they would take their problem to higher authorities if left unaddressed. One 1966 handwritten letter complaining about the deplorable condition of his house and sanitary facilities concluded that the petitioner would 'take up the matter with the secretary of our esteemed State Council if nothing was done'.[69] Others insisted that they would go public with their problems to local newspapers, radio, and television stations, hoping that these media organs would champion their particular case and broadcast the injustices. One angry letter-writer finished his note about overdue house repairs with the sentence: 'If I receive yet another unsatisfying reply', then 'I will turn to the mayor and the press to take up the issue.'[70] By the 1970s still others threatened to file for emigration if their demands were not met.[71] One 1975 letter from a Halle resident combined these threats in a rush of vitriol: 'If we don't have a new flat by the 15th of August you can get our emigration ready or else we will send pictures abroad showing how GDR citizens live. We're living like animals, not human beings.'[72]

SPEAKING SOCIALIST

As a consequence, it would be misleading to paint citizens simply as victims. People were good at exploiting the system and using socialist civil rights language to extract concessions from state authorities.[73] While there are no statistics on the success of these complaints, it can be safely estimated that roughly a third were effective in having their concerns addressed, though this dropped in the 1980s in the face of growing material shortages. Like elsewhere in the socialist world, German citizens became adept at bluff, and learned the art of 'speaking Bolshevik' in their petitions.[74] In a 1981 letter from Ralf H. written to VEB Gaststätten HO Berlin as well as the SED District Leader, the Berlin Mayor's Office and the ABI, a young man voiced his outrage at the way that he and his punk friends had been treated by the restaurant's manager, who apparently shouted 'in a very impolite and aggressive tone "Get out of here, this is no club for scum; you all should be in jail and not sitting at a bar!"' What is interesting was how adeptly the petitioner cited the constitution and recent speech by Honecker to lodge his grievance:

According to Paragraph 103 of the GDR Constitution, the freedom and personality of all people is inalienable . . . This restaurant manager has breached the GDR Constitution and discriminated against citizens of the GDR. At the 10th Party Conference General Secretary Erich Honecker stated that 'in our state every person is equal and is to be treated equally' . . . In the interests of all citizens of our republic I thank you in advance and look forward to your response.[75]

In this case the complainant's plea was eventually overturned when it was revealed that the 'Punkers' themselves did not behave all that well that day, and had played their part in escalating the conflict. Still, the key issue is how adroitly people were now citing laws, constitutions, and Party speeches to buttress their claims.

Some readers may have detected the usage of human rights language here, which was invoked more and more by petitioners after the GDR signed the Final Act of the Helsinki Accords in 1975, and published the full text in the SED's mouthpiece newspaper, *Neues Deutschland.* The GDR's quest—along with the rest of the Eastern bloc—to use the Accords a means of gaining badly sought international legitimacy certainly succeeded, but at a certain price. For the GDR, the Accords effectively secured recognition of borders and its long-desired seat at the United Nations; but it also meant that the government was soon faced with new problems. To be sure, the GDR's entrance into the UN in 1973 implied that it agreed with its charter that freedom of movement was a basic international right; indeed, the GDR's 1974 constitution featured the clause: 'Everyone is free to leave every country, including his or her own.'[76] But the 1975 Accords intensified the issue. When the citizenry learnt that freedom of movement was included as an agreed human right, the number of individuals requesting exit visas skyrocketed, and many cited Helsinki in their applications to travel to West Germany. By the late 1970s there were on average 7,200 first-time applications and the granting of 4,600 exit visas. By the early 1980s these figured had jumped to 12,600 and 7,000 visas issued. In 1984—the high point—the numbers leapt again to 57,600 and 29,800, respectively.[77] A growing number of people now wrote directly to the UN (or even the Federal Republic's quasi-embassy in the GDR, the Permanent Mission) to plead their emigration cases.[78] The text of the Helsinki Accords may have been published only once in the newspapers, but the damage was done.

The story of how Eastern bloc activists—and especially the churches—capitalized on the Helsinki principles of human rights to challenge their home governments is quite well-known.[79] But what is so striking here is how this new lexicon was quickly exploited—albeit delicately—by ordinary GDR citizens to criticize the government. Claims that the state's subpar housing policy violated the 'norms of human cohabitation' (*Normen menschlichen Zusammenlebens*) were not uncommon.[80] A 1979 letter from a retired female train conductor recorded the deplorable state of her roof and toilet facilities, including pictures as supporting evidence. She cited her thirty-three-year work record and list of work awards, and then vented her spleen about her sense of gross injustice:

When I see stories in the press and on television about how young families receive new housing with the blessing of our state leaders, then I cannot help but ask myself what these people have done to deserve these 'dignified' dwellings (*menschenwürdiges Wohnen*)!! Is my long and genuine 'dignity of work' (*Arbeitswürdigung*) not good enough to receive the same? I ask you now my esteemed leaders with great urgency for a new apartment, in fulfilment of my constitutional right to a dignified dwelling, and I too want and deserve to live in a satisfactory and happy manner in our state.[81]

Still, citing such delicate human rights language was tricky. Not only was it dangerous to do so; it later came out that those petitions that directly invoked human rights laws were automatically discarded.[82] While this could not have been known at the time, most complainants used a slightly different tactic. Often the preferred mode of trying to shame the official into action was to quote recent Party speeches. A 1987 letter from East Berliner Gottfried F pleading for a new flat in his daughter's town was quite typical in this respect:

I have studied very carefully—as is my duty—the documents of the District Party Conference of the 11th SED Party Conference of 8 January 1987. In this respect I would like to refer to the speech by Comrade K, in which he said. 'For our state personal concerns and problems are never secondary issues . . . More energetically must we impress upon those responsible, who have often been indifferent or negligent in their unsatisfactory manner of handling the complaints of our citizens and fellow administrators.' Similar and even more pointed statements were also made by Comrade S. Since I am of the opinion that I am also a comrade and citizen to whom these sentences apply, I once again demand a quick resolution of my problem.[83]

In this case, his long-time SED affiliation and service were not judged effective enough in moving the official, so this complainant resorted to quoting official speeches with the hope of exposing the gap between word and deed. It was still a moral argument in the end, but it was more reflective of a burgeoning rights culture that was growing stronger by the year.

No less striking was the change in tone over the years. In the 1950s and 1960s complaint letters were relatively reserved and respectful. Just as with the social courts, citizens too showed great deference toward state authorities to advance their pleas. 'To the Very Honoured Minister' and 'Dear Esteemed Comrade' were standard modes of salutation, but there was also a discernible intimacy that blended comradeship and supplication. People for example wrote to Pieck as a benevolent patriarch who protects and pities his children, or as a trusted and understanding confidant. What characterized these letters as socialist was that, despite the formal openings, many citizens wrote in the comradely *Du* form of address to make their case. That letters to Erich Honecker for example were addressed with the informal *Du* form suggested this sense of intimate community.[84] In tone many letters were clearly drawing on conventions of writing to authorities that predated the socialist regime.[85] But at least through the mid-1960s, citizens generally accepted the material limitations and difficulties of the regime in these letters,[86] and couched their concerns by appealing to the state's claim to make good on socialism's ideals of social justice and material betterment. Callous bureaucrats were often blamed for these shortcomings, and comments such as 'we citizens of socialism cannot get along with crass rough administrative regulations and a "bureaucratic tone" (*Beamtenton*) against fellow citizens' were routinely cited as proof of mismanagement.[87] The larger point is that for the first two decades of the regime, these citizens generally wrote as polite supplicants, subjects, and victims in search of personal redress.

Things changed markedly in the 1970s and 1980s. Gone was the restrained and respectful in tone, as citizens grew more and more frustrated with administrators and their inability to solve the myriad everyday problems affecting the population. One elderly man writing in 1989 showed little moderation in tone in writing: 'What is this for a miserable economic policy? How furious do you think I am about these conditions? When you read in the soc[ialist] press [about the] "maximal satisfaction of the needs of the people and so on" and read on every page three times "everything for the benefit of the people," it makes me sick to my stomach.'[88] There was always an ample supply of humour in these letters, but nasty sarcasm was much more typical of the 1970s and 1980s, and the more traditional rhetoric of deference and expectation was becoming all but a thing of the past. Internal SED documents were quite frank in expressing their own anger that this changed tone was the symptom of an increasingly spoiled, disrespectful, and ungrateful society, and local and regional administrators made no bones about their frustration and impatience with an ever-demanding army of letter-writers. Yet the shift in tone can also be seen as a changed idea of citizenship, in that people addressed the state less as supplicants than as equal and deserving citizens. They were more demanding of their socialist rights, notably in the way that they cited the laws and SED speeches, and often brazenly pointed out misuse of resources in the public interest.[89] Where citizens once asked for mercy, they now demanded justice.

With time, though, the number of *Eingaben* was in danger of spiralling out of control. By the second half of the 1980s, this elaborate 'culture of complaint' was being overrun by over a million submitted petitions a year. Despairing as it was for local complaint processors, the state—at least in its official spin—continued to welcome these developments as a healthy sign of 'people's democracy'. Such sentiment departed dramatically from the early years of Honecker's rule, when the sharp decline in petitions in the early 1970s was hailed as evidence of the regime's new-found ability to satisfy the pressing concerns of its citizenry and to deliver higher standards of living for more and more East Germans.[90] By the late 1970s, however, the number of complaints shot back up, as rising standards bred rising expectations. This time around, the state greeted this rash of new complaints as good news for the republic, proof of the citizens' robust engagement with state affairs. As one administrator's handbook put it: 'The complaints make quite plain that citizens of our republic have become more mature, clever, experienced, independent and self-conscious, and with it the individual's responsibility toward the collective has grown as well.'[91]

The intensified politicization of these citizen complaints in the 1980s could be detected in a number of ways. For one thing, complaints about consumer goods now exceeded those about housing shortages.[92] Consumerism of course had long been a source of citizen unrest and complaints. The sharp rise in coffee prices in

1977 for example unleashed a torrent of *Eingaben* to state authorities, under-lining the extent to which consumer shortages had become crises of political legitimacy.[93] By the 1980s complaints about consumer goods and services were coming fast and furious. In 1988 the editors of the *Leipziger Volkszeitung* reported to their district leaders that fully half of all letters to the editors were complaints about subpar or unavailable goods and services in state shops.[94] The same went for the spike in travel requests to West Germany.[95] Travel became a topic of national discussion in the 1980s, as visa restrictions were somewhat eased under Honecker after his own visit to the West in 1987.[96] More dangerous to the regime, however, was that applicants were beginning to unite in their *Eingaben* requests, forming a new solidarity of the dissatisfied.[97] New self-styled 'Emigration Communities' emerged in cities like Jena, Dresden, and Berlin over the course of the 1980s, as would-be emigrationists boldly built associational networks across the country.[98]

By the early 1980s individual petitions were becoming collective again, reflecting a new self-confidence and emerging public sphere. A revealing marker of change was that signatories were less apprehensive about preserving their anonymity in more politically oriented, collectively written *Eingaben* to state authorities.[99] For the first two and a half decades of the regime, the shrivelling up of civil society meant that people were administered and monitored less as hostile social groups than as non-compliant private citizens. But now the ground was shifting. Much of this new petition-writing was inspired by Gorbachev's glasnost policies and his calls for a revived public sphere at the time. The once-taboo term of glasnost was now findings its way into citizen communications. In one hand-written letter dated 22 March 1989, Ulrich D assertively concluded that the GDR itself was in need of more glasnost and that the country would improve markedly with 'honest, critical and self-critical reportage'.[100] The East German media was also changing. In the spirit of glasnost, the *Berliner Zeitung* opened its pages to complaints about consumer goods shortages in late 1988, giving peti-tioners a new public forum for their complaints.[101] Citizen dissatisfaction, what one historian has suggestively called the 'inner consensus of GDR citizens', was beginning to take on broader political overtones.[102] With it the petition system went from being an instrument of control to the articulation of dissent, inadver-tently becoming 'the main source of uncoordinated resistance to SED rule in East Germany.'[103]

These changes also reflected a new attitude. Unlike in the 1950s and 1960s, there was little belief that these problems could be resolved. By the early 1980s there was a discernible impatience and rudeness on the part of citizens in addressing state authorities. Many wrote to Honecker directly as private citizens, and vented their criticism of state policy. In their eyes the social contract of exchanging political rights for prosperity had been broken. Trust in the state to make good on its claims to furnish a better future—let alone a decent present—deteriorated markedly. Disaffection spread, as did the need for more autonomy and distance from state affairs. Yet the complaints kept coming, even if they were written less in hope than in deepening anger, cynicism, and 'gallows humor'.[104] The people's affection for Honecker's policies had fostered 'a conditional loyalty that crumbled as the standard of living again declined'.[105]

In conclusion, this complaint system significantly shaped the relationship between citizen and state in the GDR over the decades. It revealed how the state very much treated its citizens as needy dependants addressing the all-powerful state as benevolent caretaker.[106] In doing so the state engendered a kind of 'infantile mentality', in which citizens were turned into children by the 'Father State'.[107] Such developments have prompted various scholars to argue that the GDR was fundamentally neo-absolutist in tone and outlook, and that its citizen complaint system drew on 'pre-democratic legal traditions' in constructing a 'private dialogue between individuals and the ruling elite'.[108] Citizen participation brought some unexpected results in its train, though. The conversation with the state was not only permitted but encouraged, as long as the system itself was not questioned. Because voices could be (and were) heard by the state, letter-writing gave citizens the feeling that they were not really living in a dictatorship, or at least in a qualified sense.[109] Constitutionally speaking, these relatively modest *Eingaben* became powerful 'weapons of weak' for those without power, privilege, or status, to the extent that people exploited the legal language, cultural codes, and narrative conventions to advance their claims.[110]

What this complaint system reveals is the extent to which East Germany's own version of the 'tyranny of intimacy' was equally casual and coercive, imposed and self-generating. While similar developments could be found in other Eastern bloc countries, the GDR was singular in both scope and intensity. After all, it was home to history's most perfected state security network and citizen petition system, both of which were explicitly designed to close the gap between state and individual. Put differently, it was precisely this strange fusion of privacy and politics in a world devoid of any real civil society that ultimately earmarked GDR social life. That the vast majority of these formal complaints were written by unaffiliated, disgruntled citizens disclosed a crucial dimension of GDR everyday culture, namely a privatization of politics on the one hand, and a politicization of the private on the other. Indeed, they could—and did—use their personal domestic concerns to criticize the state for not upholding expected standards of privacy, normality, and propriety. Odd as it may seem, the state's stepped-up monitoring of the private lives of its charges went hand in hand with the people's usage of these complaints to preserve and assure the existence of a decent private sphere free of undue state interference.

Similarly, the petition system effectively highlighted the centrality of the private sphere as a point of interaction between citizen and state. If nothing else, it underscored the point that the private sphere never really disappeared at all, or more precisely, was never allowed to disappear. In the end, the state had a great deal at stake in preserving its role as the paternal guardian of citizen privacy.

Evidence of this could be seen in the maintenance of proper hygiene and safety standards, noise levels, peaceful neighbourhoods, and domestic order more generally. The 1961 construction of the Berlin Wall, political stabilization, and economic improvement meant that the SED was in a better position to address long unattended social and domestic problems. What underlay many of these complaints was the presumption that the state was responsible for protecting and providing a decent private life. Here again, the state paradoxically served as both the foe and guardian of the private sphere. So however much the private sphere was in many ways a social fiction, it was one that was exploited and defended by state and citizenry alike. From this perspective, the complaint system was the perfect expression of both the imaginary and real status of the private realm in East German everyday life.

The political dimension of the complaint letters only intensified with time, as individual concerns with material shortcomings were transformed into fulsome critiques of the provider regime for not delivering promised goods, services, and socialist ideals. Its very success as a legitimate exchange point of state and citizen led to its eventual undoing, as the state found it harder and harder to honour its part of the socialist social contract.[111] In this sense, the *Eingaben* system both reflected and spurred the plebiscite character of the regime, driving home the key point to citizen letter-writers that material life (and even will of the authorities) was indeed transformable, even if the political system was not. Perhaps even more importantly, the letters challenged the received wisdom of GDR society withdrawing into isolated niches: the millions of complaint letters bespoke an engaged citizenry actively exercising their constitutional rights for personal ends.

By the 1970s, the private sphere was not only gaining more political recognition; it was beginning to enjoy new cultural representation too. In the next chapter we shall see how the private sphere emerged as a new dimension of socialist realism for East German photographers in the final two decades of the regime.

7

Picturing Privacy
Photography and Domesticity

Since the mid-1990s there has been growing interest in the study of East German visual culture, in part because the arts were apparently among the most vibrant and least effectively controlled cultural fields in the GDR. This was certainly the case for painting and film, and arguably even more so for photography.[1] The SED's efforts to transform artistic photography into crude regime-affirming propaganda enjoyed only limited success, and over the course of the 1970s and 1980s the realm of professional photography became ever more decentralized and diverse.[2] To some degree this had to do with the fact that the regime did not recognize photography as an art until very late—it was first included in the GDR's quadrennial National Art Exhibition in Dresden in 1982, and was less subject to the strictures imposed on painting or literature. This was particularly true after Honecker's assumption of power in 1971, as photographers were allowed—and even encouraged—to explore 'socialist realism' in new ways. It was precisely this relative benign neglect that seemingly accounted for the field's remarkable growth as what has been called the 'hidden paradise' of GDR culture.[3] One contributor to a 2008 English exhibition of East German photography went so far as to say that the 'development of autonomous photographic art in the German Democratic Republic is perhaps one of the most unlikely stories to have emerged from forty years of dictatorial rule in Eastern Germany'.[4]

Since 1989 a number of impressive retrospectives on East German *Fotokunst* have appeared,[5] but key aspects of this history have yet to be explored. One of the most interesting is the relationship between domesticity and photography. To date there is still very little work on the representation of private life in the GDR's visual arts, in large measure because the still reigning assumption is that communist visual arts supposedly focused on the world of work and public life to the exclusion of all else. What discussion there is about privacy has tended to dwell on the ways in which the personal lives of artists and writers were monitored and abused by the state.[6]

But what about photography? Whereas private life played little role in East German professional photography in the 1950s and early 1960s, the domestic sphere emerged as a new interest in the mid-1960s, and grew in intensity a decade later. By that time a new generation of East German *Fotokünstler* saw themselves as maverick chroniclers of 'real existing socialism' recording the private lives of ordinary East German citizens. This was a delicate undertaking, to be sure, especially in light of the regime's unflagging commitment to self-flattery and the prohibition of images that undermined the vaunted virtues and victories of the regime. But given the state's embracing of socialist realism as official ideology from the early 1950s on, as well as the much-touted relaxation of the Honecker era, photographers began to test the meaning of socialist realism from fresh perspectives. This chapter addresses how and why many of them chose to go indoors in the 1970s and 1980s, identifying the private domestic sphere as the authentic register and last outpost of GDR socialism.

POSTWAR SOCIALIST PHOTOGRAPHY

From the very beginning there were unique East German factors at play in determining what could or could not be photographed. Where socialist realism in the Soviet Union and China for example proudly featured mass rallies, marches, and shows of military power, GDR photography—given the Nazi past—studiously downplayed such martial imagery. The GDR's central place in cold war geography meant that other subject matters were also off-limits, such as photographing policemen, archaeological sites, or visiting relatives at train stations.[7] The two biggest events in GDR history—the 1953 Uprising and the 1961 construction of the Berlin Wall—found virtually no visual representation at all. Over the decades the Wall, the very symbol of the GDR, remained a forbidden subject of East German photography, lest its images aid would-be escapees.[8] This taboo was even enforced in cultural productions. In Konrad Wolf's film version of Christa Wolf's famous novel, *Divided Heaven*, the visual presence of the Berlin Wall was altogether absent.

Another special feature of the GDR's photographic culture was the Stasi. The mammoth secret police outfit was by far the largest photographic agent in the GDR, having compiled some 1.3 million photographs of suspicious persons and situations. Its interest in photography had its roots in specific theories and practices developed at the KGB, which by the 1950s was convinced that photography could play a decisive role in fighting crime. By 1952 the Stasi started to use photography for security operations, and its Observation Department (Section VIII) became one of the largest sectional units there. Secret agents were trained at the department's special observation and photography school, complete with instructions on how to use camera disguises effectively.[9] While early Stasi photography tended to concentrate on criminals and crime scenes,[10] with time the scope for surveillance photography expanded considerably. By the early 1960s the Wall became the secret subject of intense Stasi photographic activity, as agents used pictures to document measures taken to consolidate the border regime. A surprising amount of Stasi attention was also trained on empty

Figure 16. Stasi Photo of Dissident Folk Singer Wolf Biermann, early 1970s.

Autobahn junctions, bridges, and abandoned forest paths, on the assumption that they might serve as 'imaginary crimes scenes' of blackmarket exchanges and 'enemy contacts' of various kinds.[11] Prisoner photographs—especially their tattoos—featured prominently in the Stasi's visual archive as well.[12] Mostly, however, the Stasi's cameras were fixed on potential subversives, as noted in this typical surveillance snapshot of dissident folk singer Wolf Biermann (Figure 16). By the 1970s photography became the most important medium for espionage and secret intelligence. During secret house searches, Stasi agents routinely took documentary photographs of the domestic interiors of suspected citizens to peer into their private lives.[13] In the late 1970s and 1980s the Stasi hired operatives to befriend dissident groups so as to furnish intimate photographs of them at home. This was especially the case with punks, as the Stasi amassed an extensive photographic archive of its members and activities.[14] As a result oppositional groups in the late 1970s and 1980s were reluctant to photograph themselves, for fear that they would be seized by secret police as incriminating evidence. And they were not wrong. At the Potsdam protest against the 1968 Prague invasion, for example, Stasi officers used amateur film footage to record protesters.[15]

The power of images was understood in other ways as well. After the defeat of fascism, communists were convinced that a new revolutionized socio-economic order must be accompanied by a new post-fascist visual culture to enlighten and inspire those involved in building the New Jerusalem of state socialism. But this went far beyond doing away with the fallen regime's buildings, iconography, paintings, and propaganda imperium. For the SED, destroying Nazism's visual heritage was part and parcel of the broader campaign to combat the perils of

Western culture *tout court*, as the struggle against 'decadent-formalist bourgeois art' was fundamental to the new socialist regime's understanding of anti-fascism.[16] In the early postwar years there was concerted effort to rehabilitate the leading lights of Weimar modernism as antifascist cultural ballast, such as Max Beckmann, Otto Dix, and Willi Baumeister. The two leading East German visual arts journals, *Bildende Kunst* and *Fotografie*, were both founded in 1947 to lend support to the antifascist crusade. Early GDR photography looked to reconnect with the left-wing Weimar tradition of the *Arbeiter Illustrierte Zeitung*. Realistic imagery of war destruction was the main subject of photography after the ceasefire, as harrowing pictures of refugees, *Trümmer-frauen,* and shattered landscapes served as visual accusations of fascism's destructive patrimony.[17]

The official canonization of socialist realism in the early 1950s saw a radical shift in GDR photography. At this point there is no need to rehearse the infamous Realism Debate of 1951–2, but the point is that photography was quickly mobilized as an ideological weapon against the West. Ulbricht himself made clear that he wanted realism that would uplift and inspire.[18] Traditional subject matters such as landscapes, intimate portraits, and nudes were dismissed out of hand as 'bourgeois', decadent, or formalist.[19] Conventional family scenes were replaced by group images of workers, and the genre of artistic self-portraits— a key presence at the 1949 German National Art Exhibition in Dresden—all but disappeared in the 1950s.[20] As part of the new dispensation of socialist realism, workers were pictured as the new owners of the land and the means of production,[21] and there was a distinctive monumentalization of labour and labourers alike. To help things along, an ordinance was passed in 1951 to create stipends for artists to produce politically correct art work for the regime. In its train came an endless series of stylized pictures of joyous work brigades, agricultural activities, sweaty industrial labour, and sundry scenes of synchronized socialist life on the move.[22] Favourite socialist subjects in East Germany included the symbiosis between workers and machines, new scientific laboratories, cooperative sporting events, and enlightening classroom situations.[23] One East German ideologue summed up the idealism behind such realism: 'Realism is about laughing, happy life, our proud young people, our labourers and our beautiful German homeland. Abstract, formal compositions, which are illegible and elicit a false sentimentality, old style kitsch photography, all add up to isolation of art from the people and thus serve as objective support for imperialism.'[24]

In photography, things were slightly different. By the early 1950s photography, and especially press photography, was summoned as a new educational instrument to enlighten and ennoble the masses. Antipathy was levelled against the establishment of the MAGNUM agency by Henri Cartier-Bresson, Robert Capa, and others in 1947, as well as Edward Steichen's 1955 blockbuster international touring exhibition, 'The Family of Man'. The show's 'abstract universalism' of unity in diversity was seen as deviously masking the international class struggle, and thus was tarred as 'formalist, anti-democratic and decadent'.[25] Special ire was reserved for West Germany's most influential postwar photographer at the time, Otto Steinert, whose Bauhaus-inspired 'subjective photography' was vociferously condemned as 'personal petty bourgeois emotionality' fuelled by a 'worldview of emptiness' and 'existential fear'.[26] The West's attempted 'hijacking' of 'humanist culture' after the war prompted a new East German fusion of state and image-making, as the output and publication of photography in the GDR was targeted for central coordination. In 1958 the Central Commission for Photography was created within the Kulturbund under the direction of the polemicist Berthold Beiler, who threw down the gauntlet in terms of what passed as socialist photography. The state's heavy intervention in the photographic arts was given intellectual imprimatur in Beiler's 1959 essay, 'Parteilichkeit im Foto', and then in his 1967 *Die Gewalt des Augenblicks*. In them he not only vented his spleen against Steinert's subjective photography, but also attacked both the 'Family of Man' show and Karl Pawek's 'World Exposition of Photography' two years later as toxic Western subversion.[27]

In the cold war struggle for ideological supremacy, photographers were entreated to bear witness to the 'pulsating life' of socialism under construction. Socialist photography, wrote Beiler, 'would show the workers how they should see and how they should be, how to emerge from their protracted period of lethargy and become revolutionaries'. In the 1953 East Berlin show, 'Schöne deutsche Heimat', entrants were to show how 'all upright patriots' were 'to cultivate national, humanistic traditions, while ceaselessly fighting for unification of a democratic, independent and peace-loving Germany'.[28] To this end photography was to capture the 'pathos of reconstruction' for the emerging brave new world of East German socialism.[29] Herbert Hensky's iconic 1948 photo of coal miner Adolf Hennecke (Figure 17) set the tone for GDR socialist realist photography for the next two decades.[30] It was a picture of the heroic worker, whose indefatigable individual labour was inseparable from the will and destiny of the socialist project. No less important for the new genre of monumentalizing socialist heroes was Adolf Klimaschewsky's 1955 picture book of the GDR champion cyclist, Täve Schur, *Täve: Das Lebensbild eines Sportlers unserer Zeit*, which sold 59,000 copies.[31] The perceived power of photography to uplift the people took on heightened significance after the Uprising of June 1953, as Ulbricht insisted that photography should broadcast images of harmony, passion, and appreciation for socialist life. 1950s East German photography took its cue from Soviet traditions. The decade's worker portraits and stylized youthful faces, such as Wolf Spillner's *Worker Portrait* (Figure 18) or Carla Arnold's *Getting the Weeds* (Figure 19), were imbued with historical optimism and exalted socialist mission, repeatedly photographed in the context of muscular labour, marching youth brigades, busy factory workers, and energetic spectacles of urban reconstruction. The accent was placed on the idealized construction of a harmonious world free of 'social contradictions'.[32] Pictures were routinely retouched to

Figure 17. Herbert Hensky, *Adolf Hennecke* (1948).

maximize the desired effect. As Beiler himself wrote in 1959: by 'interfering with a gentle hand', one could 'turn possibility into reality. The only rule is that of all good directing: it must not be visible in the finished work.'[33] Historian Stefan Wolle acknowledged the numbing nature of these typical socialist realist photographs: 'it is precisely this mindless, blissful smile that is the single constant factor through the visual imagery of the GDR'.[34] The highly publicized 'Bitterfeld Way' of 1959 and 1964 to bring art and the masses closer together in the name of social unity only intensified this cultural crusade.[35] The slogan of 'Unity of Politics, Economics and Culture for the Entire People' was above all a call to fuse these separate spheres, not least because the country's revolutionary energy was seen as cooling off and in need of revitalization.[36] Photography was to help fortify 'socialist morality' by advancing a 'dogma of proximity to the People' as a means of bridging culture and the 'socialist community'.[37] This was a shotgun marriage of idealism and realism in which 1950s socialist realist photography did not really concern itself with 'what really was, but rather with what should be'.[38]

     This situation has led some to conclude that there were effectively two worlds of photographic representation in the GDR. On the one side was the idealized official arsenal of images, on the other the more gritty and unburnished 'documentary images of real life'.[39] Since the mid-1990s these more critically oriented

Figure 18. Wolf Spillner, *Arbeiterporträt* (1959).

Fotokünstler have been celebrated 'as a permanent visual assault (*Foto-Anschlag*) against the fake and retouched visual world of state propaganda'.[40] This dichotomy (at least until the early 1970s) was similarly articulated by the photographers themselves. As Ursula Arnold, one of the pioneering 1950s East German photographers, put it: 'The authorities wanted propaganda and enthusiasm—which no one except the Party functionaries believed in—so I kept my photography private and for myself, and made a commitment to telling the truth as I saw it.'[41] Gundula Schulze Eldowy shared the sentiment, remarking in 2007: 'I think that my ability to work and exhibit can partly be ascribed to my refusal to be cowed, but I was also careful: I hid my negatives because it was obvious to me that they [the Stasi] would eventually try to arrest me.'[42]

But assuming a neat separation of official and oppositional art is misleading, since there were many crossovers. The SED's ideological crusade of socialist realism

Figure 19. Carla Arnold, *Getting the Weeds* (*c*.1960).

was never able to seal off Western influences.[43] Despite the tireless condemnations from SED cultural authorities, the officially maligned 'Family of Man' exposition and subsequent Western photography books and shows exerted an enduring effect on GDR photography.[44] Even supposedly taboo Western themes—like the nude—found acceptance in venues like *Das Magazin* (founded in 1954) and other mainstream GDR media.[45] By the late 1950s a new generation of GDR photographers emerged whose influences included older Soviet figures like Rod-chenko, German photographers such as Heinrich Zille, August Sander, and Richard Peter Sr., as well as international pioneers like Robert Frank, Dorothea Lange, Walker Evans, Henri Cartier-Bresson, and later Diane Arbus.[46] In 1956 some of the leading East German photographers founded a new association, 'action fotografie', as well as a short-lived journal, *Fotografik—Zeitschrift für künstlerische Fotografie* to mark their arrival. As in painting, photography's 1950s concentration on the world of work gave way to a new concern with an expanded notion of the worker's life, including what he or she did between shifts and after work. In fact, the work break became a new subject of 1960s and 1970s photogra-phy, as did worker weddings and the world of leisure.[47] East German photogra-phers subtly took issue with the straitjacket of socialist realism, often by broaching themes of the disjunction of the individual from the collective, best seen in the

Figure 20. Arno Fischer, *Müritz* (1956).

work of Evelyn Richter, Ursula Arnold, and Arno Fischer. As noted in Figures 20 and 21, Arno Fischer's seemingly unrelated figures in *Müritz* and Ursula Arnold's *Zeitungsfrau*, both from 1956, challenged the conventional portraiture of socialist collective life by focusing on fleeting moments of isolation and solitude. Publishing such unusual images was not easy at the time, especially since there were no venues outside the state-controlled press, book market, museums, and cultural organs, like the Kulturbund.[48] But these maverick photojournalists managed to find work at the GDR's illustrated magazines, such as *Das Magazin, Für Dich, Sibylle, Sonntag,* or *Neue Berliner Illustrierte,* whose young readership and fashion orientation put a premium on innovation, fantasy, and arresting images of GDR life. The illustrated press's weekly circulation of ten million copies put these talented press photographers in demand for their ability to lend socialist modernity a fresh look.[49]

One thing that made GDR photography so distinctive was the predominance of women in the field. Whereas by contrast there were very few female GDR painters, the field of photography was strongly influenced by women, such as Evelyn Richter, Ursula Arnold, Helga Paris, Sibylle Bergemann, Gundula Schulze Eldowy, Ute Mahler, Renate Zeun, Eva Mahn, Tina Bara, and Christiane Eisler. Many of them, especially the younger generation, had studied at Leipzig's Hochschule für Grafik und Buchkunst, which offered the only postgraduate degree in photography in the country. In their own work they often

Figure 21. Ursula Arnold, *Zeitungsfrau* (1956).

looked to other female photographers, like Dorothea Lange, Gisela Freund, and above all Diane Arbus, for their inspiration as a kind of socialist version of 'magic realism'. This unique story was the subject of a 1991 catalog, *DDR Frauen fotografieren*. According to the show's curator, the explanation 'why women photograph differently' lay in women's social position in the GDR, particularly in the way that for them 'there is no separation between personal and public. This is the result of other life experiences, attitudes . . . Another reason for the different kind of photography lies in the growing self-consciousness of women and in their critical regard toward men—and themselves.'[50] Ursula Arnold sharpened the polemic when she remarked: 'If I ask myself what for me

Figure 22. Peter-Heinz Junge, *Unterwegs zur neuen Wohnung* (1974).

distinguishes women's reality from men's, the answer is: not to belong to the dominant group. My sympathy rests with the underdogs.'[51] Whatever one makes of this statement, there is no denying that women furnished many of the most trenchant emblems of the East German underside of 'real existing socialism'.

An important feature of this less conformist photography was the emptiness of urban life. This could be seen for example in Peter-Heinz Junge's 1974 *Unterwegs zur neuen Wohnung* (Figure 22). At first such a picture hardly seems all that novel, building as it did on the many press photos of smiling workers moving into Stalinallee from the mid-1950s on. But Junge's photograph darkly hints at the desolation and emptiness of these new flats, and as such coyly undermines the easy optimism of those earlier images. Evelyn Richter's series of fatigued banner-carriers marching before dilapidated buildings was plainly an ironic commentary on the regime as well. Most famous in this respect was Helga Paris's Halle series entitled *Houses and Faces*, 1983–5. Paris studied fashion and worked for *Neue Berliner Illustrierte*, but in this series she captured Halle's decomposing urban atmosphere, shrouded in wet grey, and shot in the unsparing sociological style of 1930s American Farm Security Administration photography.[52] Her series also indirectly draws on those German photographers who had taken pictures of ruins in the aftermath of the Second World War. These Halle residents may not have looked as devastated and the landscapes not as scarred and ruined, but these were very unflattering intimate pictures of a city—and by association—a nation in decay, what one critic called 'the wound-scapes (*Wundstellen*) of architecture and people'.[53] As seen in Figure 23, the coupling of melancholic children with these decrepit buildings dramatized the point even more so. Blighted surroundings, so goes the logic, had created blighted lives.[54] There was a sly Marxist subtext here, in that the colourless, crumbling cityscape

Figure 23. Helga Paris, *Untitled*, from the Series *Häuser und Gesichter*, Halle 1983–85.

seemed to rub off on the subjects themselves, though her figures do manage to retain a stubborn dignity despite the conditions. Little wonder, though, that Paris crossed swords with the censor for several years in trying to exhibit *Houses and Faces*, especially in Halle, since it was clearly interpreted as highly unsavoury images of Honecker's Germany.[55]

Another example of the intimacy of everyday urban life was Uwe Steinberg's 1971 series on *Elfriede Schilski Departs*. In it the photographer aimed to depict the very personal pain and suffering of an aged woman on her last day of work. As noted in Figure 24, Steinberg chronicled her retirement party with colleagues

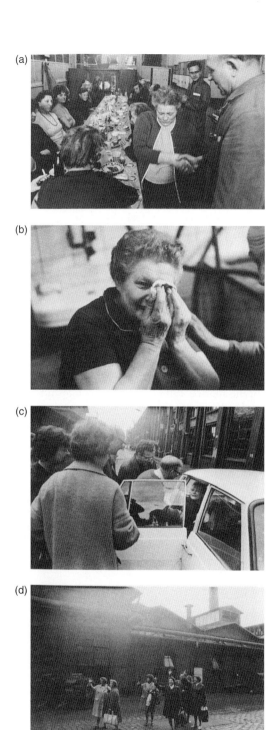

Figure 24a–d. Uwe Steinberg, *Elfriede Schilski Scheidet* (1971).

and friends, her teary emotional disconsolation, her departure in the car, and the almost funereal reaction from those left behind as the car sped away. These serial images punctuate social separation from work and collective life, a liminal moment in the relationship between individual and society.[56] As such Steinberg sought to go beyond what he dismissed as the 'political intention of persuasion' so prevalent among mainstream East German photography at the time, preferring instead a more 'honest' and emotional form of picture-making.[57] Here and elsewhere Steinberg's work captured what is usually reserved for private circles of friends and family, and reflected the decade's growing interest in penetrating the intimate world of unguarded personal feelings.

Under these circumstances, photographers were given more latitude to chronicle socialism as *Zeitdokumente*, serving as roaming sociologists with cameras. A milestone in documentary photography was the 'Porträtfotoschau' in Dresden and Berlin in 1971. Although there was a good deal of pious talk in the catalogue about 'socialist humanism' and 'the development of socialist personalities among the citizens of our republic', it was plain that these concepts were being radically remade.[58] The show featured a mix of styles, ranging from more casual, even intimate shots of Ulbricht to images of happy families playing together.[59] As noted in Figure 25, the accent was on individuality in ways that departed dramatically from the portrait-style photos of the 1950s and 1960s.[60] To paraphrase Dubcek, the deposed hero of the aborted 1968 Prague Spring reform movement, this was to be 'photography with a human face'.

In large measure this broadened sense of photographic realism can be attributed to the wind of change resulting from Honecker's assumption of power in

Figure 25. *Porträtfotoschau der DDR* (Berlin and Dresden, 1971), unpaginated.

1971. That year the SED's 8th Party Congress pledged to expand the idea of a 'developed socialist society', one that demanded artists 'use all of the means at their disposal to show how the socialist personality is formed in our time'.[61] This was interpreted as a call to take socialist realism in new directions. Much was made of Honecker's 'no taboos' claim to cultural pluralism, even if there were obvious limits to what was permissible at the time. Nevertheless, the visual arts directly benefited from the new policy.[62] Not only did the 1970s see the rehabilitation of older modernists, such as Paul Klee and Oskar Kokoschka, as new polestars in the GDR art journals; images of workers became more individualized, and the world of work itself was no longer the main focus. While this was not always greeted favourably,[63] socialist realism was opened up in new directions. The state was now keen to encourage artists to satisfy the subjective needs of the people, and to give them more freedom in their work.[64]

By the mid-1970s this issue had spilled into public debate. Exemplary in this respect was the year-long discussion in 1975 on the theme of whether art was or should be 'Societal and/or Private', which took place in the GDR's flagship art journal, *Bildende Kunst.* The debate was launched with the questions: 'Is the tendency toward intimate, private subject matter a departure from the so-called Great Themes? Is it not possible to consider all "small" themes as social? Is the devotion to "great" themes necessarily socially desirable?' Many different opinions were represented, and surprisingly critical views of both GDR culture—and indirectly the state—were quite bald. Notable too was the shared perception that private life had become a major theme of East German art over the last few years. No longer was it condemned as Western decadence. Rather, there was a tacit acceptance that the private sphere was a—if not perhaps the—key site for the development of the personality, and thus what happens there was of vital concern to socialist society in general. No less interesting was the way in which several contributors invoked the language of rights in making their cases. One artist for example argued that 'we have no right to exclude the whole subjective world of experience from reality, a world of experience to which belong feelings of fear and sadness, and perhaps even solitude or the need to be alone'. One East German art historian put the issue about the 'appreciation of the "private" subject' in terms of the United Nations Charter, arguing that if one 'denies in art the full range of human possibilities, then this violates our country's fruitful recognition of the UN Charter'.[65] The Helsinki Accords had been signed that summer, and citizens of the GDR—as noted in the previous chapter—were quick to exploit its potential promise for reform. But here was a case in which the private sphere—or at least the artistic representation of it—was brought to bear as a human right of the artist. The new thematic focus towards the private sphere was given official blessing in 1978 when Willi Sitte, President of the GDR Artists Union, stated in a speech that 'equally important for us is the private sphere of the workers, their relations to their families, to their environment, nature, sports and leisure . . . Increasingly art is turning to the personal destiny of the workers, his joys and concerns, the whole panoply of what makes up the everyday.'[66] By the National Art Exhibition in Dresden of 1977–8, private life had become a central theme. This was described—and justified—in terms of new official language of 'spiritual needs' and 'social psyche', wherein there was a new perceived connection between artists and the public through 'personal feelings'.[67]

Photography was now given more attention. The chances for GDR photographers to exhibit opened up considerably, culminating in the major 'Medium Fotografie' show in 1977 and the inclusion of photography in the National Art Exhibition in Dresden in 1982.[68] To support this trend, the Kulturbund backed photography as a vibrant field of socialist realism. It sponsored a number of photographic exhibitions of young photographers at new venues (the so-called 'kleine Galerien') through the 1970s. By 1975 the Kulturbund had created some 121 new galleries across the country, and the number rose to over 500 by 1989.[69] What is more, new semi-autonomous groups and showrooms were founded, such as Berlin's Gruppe Jugendfoto (1969–79) and Galerie Berlin (1978–80).[70] Several years before that, the GDR's Central Commission for Photography (ZKF) within the Kulturbund campaigned to promote amateur documentary photography. From the mid-1960s on workers were encouraged to take their own amateur photos at the workplace, and their work was proudly pinned up on factory announcement boards across the country.[71] Even the Stasi organized internal amateur photography exhibitions to inspire its employees.[72] So widespread was this campaign that one observer wrote that '[n]owhere was the popular interest in fellow workers and their immediate world greater than in the GDR and nowhere was it . . . so subjectively photographed with the Praktika or Praktisix [GDR cameras] as here'.[73]

TAKING THE CAMERA INDOORS

The defining trend of 1970s photography was the impulse to go indoors. In this photographers were by no means alone—such interest in home life was shared by East German writers, painters, and filmmakers, who all saw themselves as the new chroniclers of everyday domestic socialist life and private subjectivity.[74] Perhaps this was the logical result of the regime's own policies of building GDR society around the nuclear family. How the vaunted 'socialist community' actually functioned—and looked—at home was not limited to the arts though; it became an abiding concern across the social sciences in the 1970s, as East German sociologists now turned to the home to study the making of 'the socialist family', 'socialist lifestyle', and 'socialist personality'. Yet photographers took up the theme with particular relish. A certain curiosity about the non-work dimensions of people's lives was already present among 1960s photographers, such as Katja Worch, who started photographing families more intimately several years before most others did so.[75] But in general professional photographers rarely went inside the house, as if this private realm was not for the camera's scrutiny. Through the 1960s the public's visual representation of home life was the domain of advertising, the furniture industry, and home decoration literature. But things were changing. As one GDR curator put it in the mid-1970s: 'Apart from the workplace and family, life in this country takes place in large measure in private, since this is where people drink and celebrate—and photograph.'[76] Already a few years before, SED cultural authorities had conceded that 'the exact correlative of the brigade image is the family image in the personal–private sphere (*persönlich-privaten Sphäre*)'.[77] By the early 1970s, the factory, Party events, and the brigade had fallen off as sources of topical interest,[78] as photographers looked instead to what one East German critic at the time called 'personal intimacy and subjective authenticity' in the home.[79]

A good example can be found in Christian Borchert's images of families and domestic interiors taken in the 1970s and early 1980s. Like Steinberg, Borchert was interested in a new kind of realism, focusing on the everyday day so as to capture, as he put it, 'what was'.[80] He was a founding member of Gruppe Jugendfoto, and worked as a photographer for *Neue Berliner Illustrierte*. Borchert had an abiding fascination with the 'kleine Leute' of the country, subjecting them to what one critic described as a kind of 'photographic research through the serial structure'.[81] Using unusually wide-angle lenses, Borchert's pictures harked back to the interwar tradition of *Neue Sachlichkeit* and specifically to the work of August Sander, who was one of his main inspirations.[82] As seen in his *Family Portraits* in Figures 26 and 27, Borchert liked to photograph families and people at home. These were generally tidy working-class milieux, devoid of much decoration or vitality, exemplifying what one observer called 'ordinary good socialist life'.[83] His earlier work in shooting placards, gravestones, display windows, and monuments as historical artefacts enjoyed corresponding expression

Figure 26. Christian Borchert, from the series *Familienportraits I* (*c*.1980).

Figure 27. Christian Borchert, from the series *Familienportraits II* (1983).

here, to the extent that his snapshots of people at home have at once a *gemütlich* yet frozen quality about them.[84] For this reason his family pictures can be interpreted as a kind of post-revolutionary aesthetic reminiscent of the late Weimar Republic,[85] in which the millennial passions and frenzied social engineering projects of the GDR's first two decades had cooled off in a world now characterized by stasis, distance, and interiority.[86] Some have therefore read his work as a kind of testament of East German defeat and dullness, 'a whiff from the provinces, a world of top–down coordination (*Gleichgeschaltetsein*) in which people have given up'.[87] In any case, it is Borchert's muted and almost clinical sociological gaze at GDR domestic life that is so distinctive; his pictures are suffused with an unresolved interplay of individuality, sameness, and family collectivity. One critic perceptively wrote that Borchert was 'less a collector of object forms than a collector of feeling, moods and impressions'.[88]

But the notion that Borchert's was simply recycled Weimar portrait photography is misleading. Arguably the more accurate historical analogy is Biedermeier, as Borchert's family portraits of the 1970s have a good deal in common with early nineteenth-century Central European paintings. As noted in Figure 28, the Biedermeier family was foregrounded as the real social unit of society. In them the family was removed from the world of work and public life, portrayed indoors against the backdrop of their proud if simple material possessions. Biedermeier's patriarchal authority may be absent in Borchert's photographic work, but his is still a world in which social life has been largely confined to the family and domestic interiors. Recall too that Biedermeier celebrated a society of repose in the wake of revolution, which was characterized by two things: beefed-up state security (e.g. the Karlsbad Decrees) and a strong emphasis on the private virtues of peace, comfort, and domesticity.[89] Such attributes inform

Figure 28. J. Hartmann, *Familie des Forstmeisters Wilhelm Heinrich Seyd* (1845).

Borchert's family images as well, providing a visual framework for what has been called the GDR's own 'Biedermeier collectivism'.[90]

Not that this photographic turn towards chronicling the domestic interior as a new sociological space was unique to East Germany. Such trends found some echoes across the Eastern bloc and Soviet Union at the time.[91] No less interestingly, West German society was also experiencing a similar privatization of social life, and photographers there too were taking their cameras inside homes as social historians.[92] Herlinde Koelbl, for example, published similar work on West Germany, most notably in her 1980 book, *Das deutsche Wohnzimmer*. This popular picture book was motivated by the desire to capture the ways in which the 'dwelling is a reflection of the soul of the inhabitants', with a view to seeing how people have built 'intimate surroundings' beyond the prescriptive market-driven norms of the home decoration industry.[93] While some of the pictures (Figure 29) featured highly modernist interiors and inhabitants, others (Figure 30) depicted quite modest families flanked by their domestic things, not so

Figure 29. Herlinde Koelbl, *Dr. Christine L, 31, Zahnärztin* from her book, *Das deutsche Wohnzimmer* (1980).

Figure 30. Herlinde Koelbl, *Fritz B, 56, Bauingenieur, Gemeinderat, Gisela B, 46, Hausfrau,* from her book, *Das deutsche Wohnzimmer* (1980).

unlike their East German counterparts. West German apartments may have been more spacious (and their residents more smiley), but the similarities far outweighed the differences. The captions also gave the subjects the chance to summarize their attitude about family, home, and themselves.[94] Even the manner used to describe the subjects' identity was largely the same: in both cases the adults photographed were explicitly linked with their profession or principal activity (à la Sander). What seemed to mark Borchert's work as East German however was that—unlike Koelbl—he rarely included the subjects' first names and usually referred to the family as a unit, such as 'The N Family, Electrician and Clerical Worker'.

No doubt Borchert was also drawing on the informal and intimate style of the family snapshot to depict his figures. By the early 1960s, instant cameras were more and more common in the GDR, and Borchert was one of the GDR's best known photographers to bridge the gap in the world of *Fotokunst.* Enterprises tended to chronicle their achievements and events in this family album aesthetic, seemingly in an effort to promote the paternalist idea of the workplace as a second family.[95] Even the Stasi tended to chronicle The Firm's social events (balls, music evenings, hunting trips, etc.) in a manner strongly reminiscent of family albums.[96] Countercultures too, such as the famed Prenzlauer Berg literary scene in East Berlin, photographed themselves in a similar intimate style in chronicling their readings, happenings, and social gatherings, whose 'private counterworld as a space of retreat' has been described as a kind of 'biedermeierly' sensibility in its own right.[97] But where Borchert's work diverged from the genre of private family photography was that he did not use this familiar style to commemorate milestones and special events (such as weddings, birthdays, Jugendweihe celebrations, Christmas festivities, or other ritualized family occasions) as most families do.[98] Instead, Borchert sought the ordinary and everyday, the asymbolic and unadorned.

Other East German photographers followed Borchert's lead in identifying the home as the site of authentic social life in the GDR. Margit Emmrich did a series of *Wohnzimmer* in 1978. As noted in Figure 31, the atmosphere is again one of distance, featuring family members relaxing at home in spaces closed off from the outer world.[99] The resident's absent relationship to others beyond the home seems to find its substitute in the reserved community between people and things. Here the family seems hemmed in by the tightly arranged furniture ensemble, sitting rather stiffly behind their neatly presented *Kaffee und Kuchen* set. Much like Borchert, the family name and individual family member occupation (or age, if children) are listed in the caption, as if to catalogue these stern inhabitants in a kind of photographic zoology of domestic culture. But unlike Borchert, Emmrich undermined the formality of the staged family portrait by including their more familial first names in the caption. A markedly different mood is present in Ute Mahler's family portraits. As seen in Figure 32, her family images are not nearly so static. They are odd, Diane Arbus-inspired jumbles of

Figure 31. Margit Emmrich, *Wilfried D (42), Bäckermeister selbstständig, Elisabeth D (40), Verkauferin, Sohn, Jörg D (12), Schüler,* 1977, from her *Wohnzimmer* series, 1978.

unsettling figures and skewed lines. Unlike Borchert and Emmrich's more clinical sociological studies, Mahler's pictures of domestic life are more intimate and enigmatic, bestowing a stronger sense of individuality to the subjects.[100] The tighter camera angle and use of shadows lends the domestic setting a much more crowded and claustrophobic feel. Where all three photographers dramatically departed from Biedermeier, however, is with the relative absence of windows. While the use of domestic windows in painting dates back to seventeenth-century Holland, they became standard features of Biedermeier era portraits in the early nineteenth century.[101] As noted in the previous illustration, Biedermeier windows are typically depicted as open and beckoning, suggesting a clear and comfortable relationship to the world beyond the home. In Borchert, Emmrich, and Mahler's work, by contrast, the family seems boxed in by their interiors, untethered from the world altogether. Such imagery diverged from trends in East German painting at the time, which often foregrounded windows in domestic scenes or self-portraits.[102] Or put differently, one could argue that it was the television itself—which featured prominently in many of these photographs—that served as the window to the wider world for East Germans; the desire to travel and transport oneself to other places and times found its most popular expression in private

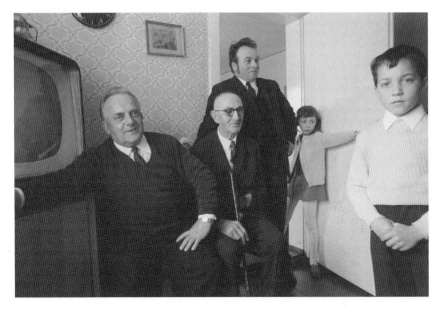

Figure 32. Ute Mahler, from the series *Zusammen Leben* (*Living Together*), 1981.

television-watching. In this, perhaps East German *Fotokünstler* were simply reflecting the wishes and habits of the inhabitants themselves.[103]

By the 1980s, things changed again. One of the residual socialist aspects of 1970s East German domestic photography was that people were still photographed in groups, even if this collectivity had been reduced to the family or just the couple.[104] In 1980s photography, the social aspect of domestic life largely dropped away. Noticeable too is that photographers were interested in tighter frames to close the distance between camera and subject.[105] This retreat into interiors was a trend of the 1980s, as the emphasis often fell on the individual alone in his or her dwelling. A good example was Bernd Lasdin's 1986–9 series, *So We Are*, or *So Sind Wir*, which took the portrait of the private sphere in new directions. As seen in Figure 33, the home is again used as a theatre of personal identity. In this case an older woman was featured in repose in her living room. Such a scene was a far cry from Paris or Steinberg's desire to strip away the staged artifice of mainstream socialist photography in the name of 'honest' realism; on the contrary, the accent here was on the self-styled theatricality of the enclosed interior.

To be sure, many of Lasdin's other photographs in this series were more in keeping with the realism found in Borchert and Ute Mahler, but this picture of theatrical individualism was not an isolated case. What was also novel in Lasdin's photography is that his subjects were encouraged to furnish their own settings and captions, echoing Koelbl's style of representation. Where Lasdin differed

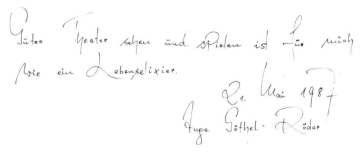

Figure 33. Bernd Lasdin, untitled from the series *So Sind Wir* (*So We Are*) (1986–1989).

from Koelbl however was that the subject's captions were handwritten, reminiscent of family albums.[106] In this almost bleached image of a 63-year-old actress
reclining in a chair in her frilly white living room, the subject writes that 'going to
the theater and acting are for me an elixir of life'. In a different way, Gundula
Schulze Eldowy's series of naked subjects at home also captured this interface of
1980s intimacy and domesticity. As noted in Figure 34, one of the photos from
her *Nudes* series, 1983–6, the domicile again emerged as a setting for identity,
though the postal worker Lothar (featured in a 1982 photo standing in the street
in his uniform) was here stripped of clothes as markers of status and station. But
this was less nakedness as naturalism than as a condition for private disclosure.

Figure 34. Gundula Schulze Eldowy, *Lothar*, 1983, from her series *Aktportraits* (1983–6).

Schulze Eldowy was one of the GDR's best known photographers of the nude. But in this instance there was little mass market eroticism; instead, this series sought to allow people to stage their nakedness at home for the camera, uncovering intimate worlds wherein supposedly there was 'nothing to hide'.[107] No less important is that this image was the first—and as far as I know the only—to represent an East German domestic interior in a state of dishevelled decay, effectively bringing indoors Helga Paris's sensibility of an urban cityscape in ruin.

Other photographers explored the theme of domestic intimacy. This could be seen in Tina Bara's work or in Eva Mahn's 1989 self-portraits. In each instance, the earlier interest in overexposed interiors and domestic furnishings gave away to more atmospheric portraits of unsmiling, unmade-up female subjects. Mirroring trends in 1970s and 1980s East German film, these photographers used female subjects to depict the collapse of the collectivist ethos that marked East German society and culture in earlier decades.[108] There were also new efforts to bring hidden aspects of private life into the camera's field of vision. Examples of representing private hardships could be seen in Karin Wieckhorst's 1985 series on disabled women, *Körperbehindert*, which depicted scenes of personal suffering and forgotten lives. The same goes for Renate Zeun's 1986 portraits of terminal cancer patients at hospitals, *Betroffen—Bilder einer Krebserkrankung*, in which she unflinchingly brought the lonely realm of illness and dying into the world of photography.[109] These photographers were pushing the limits of socialist realism by exposing the shadow lives of those who were marginalized or left behind in the grand socialist project of production, community, and mutual assistance. Occasionally this shift has been interpreted as marking a transition in the cultural self-representations of East German workers from the dominant social class to forlorn victims of industrial civilization.[110] But it is worth recalling that the sentiment that the old and disabled were being disowned by both Germanies in their effort to build rival social welfare states was expressed across the cold war divide in the early 1980s,[111] even if its visual representation was taken up more directly in East Germany.

Other novel elements could be found in 1980s photography of domestic life. Werner Mahler shot a series of residents in their dwellings over the course of several years, introducing an element of time into his portraits. In them residents were photographed against relatively unchanged interiors to draw attention to the effects of time on these people.[112] In them the 1950s love affair with the future had been replaced by wistful rumination about the past. In so doing, Mahler was returning to the very origins of photography itself, whose medium, as pioneering practitioner William Fox Talbot noted in 1839, was to chronicle 'the injuries of time'.[113] Lasdin also shot a similar series of 'before and after' photographs of East Germans in their residences over the period 1986–98, called *Zeitenwende* (1999). Interest in time's effects was even more prevalent in the work of Christiane Eisler, who showed young people—often punks—at home over the span of several years. Her work captured a discernible neo-Expressionist sensibility of the 1980s, replete with a deeply felt sense of anomie, isolation, and aggression. But unlike other photographers, Eisler often erased the domestic settings and personal context. Instead, people were photographed alone against blank canvasses (Figure 35). But if spatial markers were removed, temporal ones served as their replacements—in this case how a young woman's punk identity changed with age and motherhood. Such 'before and after' shots sometimes even involved death, including the suicide of a young man (Figure 36). In this case, the second image of the glowing wreath marked the spot in the war memorial near Halle where the troubled young man took his own life five years after the first photograph was taken. It is well-known that the GDR had one of the highest suicide rates in the world. For decades the regime denied the problem, blaming such 'private death' on the effects of capitalist misery.[114] But such denial began to fade in the 1980s, as the SED could not help but acknowledge the frequency of suicide and depression, grudgingly conceding that 'personal happiness and satisfaction are not automatic results of socialist society'.[115]

To be sure, suicide had long been a theme in literature, as manifest in Christa Wolf's *Nachdenken über Christa T* (1968), Ulrich Plenzdorf's *Die neuen Leiden des jungen W.* (1973), and Brigitte Reimann's *Franziska Linkerhand* (1974). In Maxie Wander's *Guten Morgen, Du Schöne* suicidal depression was mentioned on several occasions. Several films of the period also foregrounded suicidal

(a)   (b)

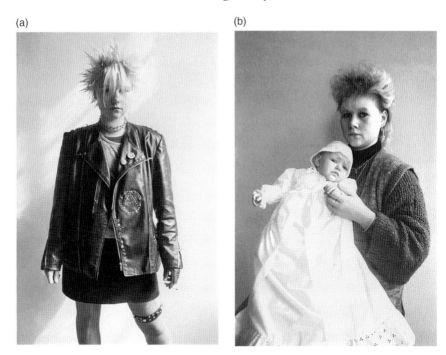

Figure 35a–b. Christiane Eisler, *Heike* (1983 and 1986).

tendencies, such as Konrad Wolf/Wolfgang Kohlhaase's 1979 *Solo Sunny* and
Siegfried Kühn's 1985 *Der Traum von Elch*, and the popular television programme
Polizeiruf 110 took up the issue of suicide in several episodes in the late 1970s.[116]
But it was the stark photographic representation of death that was new.

The theme of death was taken up directly in Rudolf Schäfer's work. The photo
shown in Figure 37 is from a series taken in Charité Hospital in Berlin in the
early 1980s with permission from the nurses and doctors, which chronicled
patients a few minutes after they had died. This series was part of Schäfer's
long-time interest in pushing photography into areas where little work had been
done. Death, as we have seen in Chapter 2, was a delicate theme for the GDR,
not least since Marxist-Leninism itself provided little solace for it. Indeed, the
historical optimism driving Marxist-Leninist philosophy was nursed by the
expectation that only under socialism—as one book put it in the early 1960s—
'the tragedy of human life would be overcome'.[117] For Marx, individual death
was always linked to the fate of humanity itself ('Gattung Mensch') and thus
death for socialist theorists appeared 'as a hard victory of the species over the
individual'.[118] It was also well-known that death in the state-run hospitals was a
forlorn and lonely experience, and the dying were given little beyond the most
basic care. Facilities did little to help relatives accompany the dying person

(a)   (b)

Figure 36a–b. Christiane Eisler, *Stefan* (1983 and 1988).

during their final days and hours, or to enable the bereaved to pay their last respects to the body after death.[119] Schäfer resented the way that modern societies—and not simply the GDR, or even socialist states—treated the dead. For him, the dead had sadly become the waste products of all consumer societies, and he deplored the way that death—like birth—had become confined to the antiseptic, isolating institution of the hospital, a world largely devoid of social ritual, friends, and family.[120] Perhaps for this reason his work found great resonance in West Germany at the time, since similar concerns were being raised there as well.[121] Schäfer's abiding concern was to capture the ultimate moment of individual withdrawal from the world, total self-absorption and finality, the literal and symbolic end of community itself. His was an effort to bestow greater dignity and peacefulness on the dead—'the dead deserve as much dignity and respect as the living'—and to accentuate a more traditional attitude of hope.[122] Schäfer's work thus embodied the secret sharing of photography and death that Roland Barthes neatly postulated: 'Contemporary with the withdrawal of rites, Photography may correspond to the intrusion, in our modern society, of an asymbolic death, outside of religion, outside of ritual, a kind of abrupt dive into literal Death.'[123] In the end, these images were less about death itself than about its stark privatization in modern society.

Figure 37. Rudolf Schäfer, *Visages de Mort/Totengesichter* (*Faces of Death*), early 1980s.

Several conclusions can be drawn from this. For one thing, this story of 1970s photo-realism makes clear that the ever-present Wall was not all that effective in shielding East German photography from Western influences. Despite the regime's best efforts, Western stylistic trends exerted a continual impact on GDR society and culture. In photography this could be seen in some of the modern-oriented images produced even at the height of 1950s socialist realism, and this only intensified through the 1970s and 1980s. The subterranean presence of Western modernism has been chronicled for painting, but this was even more pronounced with photography. Not that the influences were all one-way. East German photographers were occasionally exhibited in Viennese museums and West German photography journals, and Rudolf Schäfer in particular gained a good deal of publicity among West German photography galleries in the 1980s.[124] So while there were certainly formal differences between East and West, photographic modernism was in no way beholden to geopolitical confines. Subjectivity, abstraction, and alienation—all supposed Western themes deemed anathema to the SED—found surprisingly equal place in the GDR as well.[125] In this cultural field, just as with industrial design, home decoration, and advertising, the Wall ultimately proved very porous. No doubt most East German photographers were self-proclaimed realists until the end. In fact, no other branch of GDR culture—including painting and literature—clung to the precepts of socialist realism as long as photography, precisely because such realism retained its critical edge in documenting socialist experience. But if they were realists, they were also romantics in a certain sense. For the old romantic themes—from solitude to dignified individual death, from interior psychological states to the disconnection between self and society—were all rife in GDR photography, and resonated across 1970s and 1980s East German painting and film as well.[126]

Secondly, it is tempting to say that this 1970s and 1980s preoccupation with the private sphere confirmed the existence of Gaus's 'niche society.' But this model is quite limited, since it implies that East Germans had cut off their relations to public culture altogether in retreating to respites of family, friends, and weekend getaways. What these photographers amply show by contrast was not so much the unsullied world of private retreats, but rather how the domestic sphere was thoroughly shaped and affected by the world outside. How subjects arranged their lives in light of standardized living quarters or how the passage of time marked their being underlined their particular place in this particular society.[127] This was clear in Borchert's family images as well as in Eisler's portraits. Simply put, it was not so much that these photographers had somehow discovered the tender innocence of an unguarded private sphere. Rather, like those writing *Eingaben*, arguing their private property cases in court, suing for divorce, or defending religious rights, citizens were actively staging the place and importance of what was commonly called the *Privatsphäre* in GDR life. In this way, as we have seen elsewhere in this book, private life was less a fact or a place than a social claim and political assertion.

But this may be too simple, especially if we broaden the perspective. East German photography of domestic interiors and their inhabitants may not have looked all that different from their West German counterparts at the time, but that's where the similarity ended. Once photographers ventured outdoors into the city, for example, East–West German differences became crass. Not surprisingly, it was precisely urban documentary photographs that met the wrath of the SED censor. This could be seen in Arno Fischer's banned book on *Situation Berlin, 1954–1960*, whose pictures of pock-marked, divided Berlin (Figure 38) were considered too critical of the regime in the wake of the erection of the Berlin Wall a few months later. The same went for Helga Paris's melancholic portraits of Halle. By the late 1980s, Harald Hauswald's unflattering pictures of decrepid East Berlin street life (Figures 39 and 40) attracted special ire, and were forbidden to be published in the GDR. That they were published in West Germany in a 1987 book, *Ost-Berlin,* solidified Hauswald's reputation as a *persona non grata* in his own country.[128]

The larger point is that the SED had no qualms about allowing—and even encouraging—photographers to go inside private dwellings in order to chronicle

Figure 38. Arno Fischer, *Friedensfahrt* (*The Peace Race*), East Berlin, 1957.
The Peace Race, commonly known as the Course de la Paix, was a high-profile annual international amateur cycling competition that started in 1948. It connected the cities of Warsaw and Prague, and was generally dominated by riders from the communist countries. The East German team was the overall winner in 1957. Here Fischer captures several East Berliners watching the race from their homes in the Prenzlauer Berg section of East Berlin that year.

Figure 39. Harald Hauswald, *Oderbergerstrasse*, East Berlin (1987).

Figure 40. Harald Hauswald, *Dimitroffstrasse*, East Berlin (1987).

Figure 41. Walter Ulbricht with Workers from Forst District, February 1961.

Figure 42. Erich Honecker with Grosskopf family, Berlin-Marzahn, to mark the occasion of the construction of the GDR's one millionth apartment, 1978.

'real existing socialism' at home. After all, both Ulbricht and Honecker had long used images of themselves relaxing with socialist comrades at home as a means of lending the regime a populist touch, and to make good on the idea that decent housing was an emblem of political legitimacy and socialist promise (Figures 41 and 42). Of course this was part of a general trend of twentieth-century politics. As Barthes observed, the 'Age of Photography corresponds precisely to the explosion of the private into the public, or rather into the creation of a new social value, which is the publicity of the private.'[129] Such developments had particular resonance in Eastern bloc societies that aimed to do away with this public–private distinction altogether, at least early on. As we have seen over the course of this book, this public–private divide never disappeared in socialist life, however, and re-emerged with a vengeance in various forms across the GDR in the 1970s and 1980s. From this perspective, the advent of a kind of niche society, generally construed as a sign of Westernization and the end of socialism, was scarcely a dangerous development for the regime; on the contrary, it was accepted and even welcomed by the SED in the name of peace and stability. By the 1970s the tidy worker domicile was arguably the last best advertisement for state socialism, and government support for its chroniclers followed accordingly. Borchert's 'family pictures' for example received generous support from the Kulturbund, as did other photographers working on series of interiors and citizens at home. In part this is why Helga Paris (who shot a number of residents at home over her career) never turned her back on the cityscape as the true face of the regime, for she knew that what she called the 'sentimentality of niches' literally domesticated photography's critical realist edge and reformist mission.[130] The 'domestic turn' among GDR photographers in the 1970s and 1980s was therefore at once system-critical and system-sustaining, reflecting in the end the special symbolic significance that home interiors acquired in the socialist geography of Honecker's Germany.

Epilogue

The House of Spirits: 1989, Civil Rights
and the Reclamation of Private Life

Patiently endured so long as it seems beyond redress, a grievance comes to appear intolerable once the possibility of removing it crosses men's minds.[1]

Alexis De Tocqueville

In 1985 the American sociologist Richard L. Merritt conjectured about the possible effects of a future Reunification on the long-divided city of Berlin:

If the city is politically amalgamated on the basis of new international agreements, it will be fairly easy to rebuild a unified municipal government, and with it will be possible to construct the links to tie together divided water and sewage systems, streets and subway lines, and the like. More difficult to reconstruct will the sentimental ties of community. Reunification in the year, say, 2000 will come more than a half a century after the city's political division and almost 40 years after the appearance of the wall. By then there will be very few Berliners who will have a vivid memory of what it was like before 1945 and fewer still who will have any active contacts on the other side of the city . . . Rebuilding a common set of expectations, demands and identifications among Berliners will doubtless be a very slow process, quite possibly slower than that which had forced them apart in the first place.[2]

How prophetic Merritt was, and what he predicted would bedevil Berliners has been equally true for the nation as a whole. Twenty years on Germany is still suffering from the aftershocks of Reunification. While economic and political union has long been achieved, 'the sentimental ties of community' remain deeply troubled. 'Rebuilding a common set of expectations, demands and identifica-tions' has indeed been a 'very slow process', proving more illusory and intractable than expected. It was not long before the elated 1989 headlines that 'Germans were the happiest people in the world'[3] were replaced by raw recriminations and mutual misunderstandings, as 'Wessies' and 'Ossies' found little common ground in trying to get to grips with Germany's cold war past and post-cold war future. Across East Germany the euphoria of crumbling walls turned to feelings of *Anschluss* and melancholy, with a strong dose of victimization rhetoric to boot.[4]

One thing that has perplexed observers has been the stubborn persistence of a separatist East German cultural identity long after the heady days of 1989. The Wall may have been abruptly 'decommissioned' by popular demand two decades ago, yet it continues to exert a powerful presence in the hearts and minds of all Germans. The 1990s witnessed heated debate and quite nasty cultural wars about the East German past, especially regarding the designation of the defunct German Democratic Republic as Germany's 'second dictatorship' of the twentieth century. Topics ranged from trigger-happy border guards to the virtues of socialist painting, to what to do with East Berlin's delapidated government buildings. Official debates on the legacy of the GDR went to surprising lengths to ascertain whether the beloved children's nurseries or the Stasi best symbolized the fallen socialist republic.[5] What emerged were two divided and seemingly irreconcilable 'memory cultures' about the ex-GDR.[6]

In this context, many East Germans dug in their heels and defended their lost communist world with surprising passion and even longing. The 1990s phenomenon of *Ostalgie*, or East German nostalgia, for the socialist security of the past was in many ways a symptom of the disillusionment felt by many East Germans in the face of turbulent transition. By the mid-1990s polls revealed the remarkable fact that a large percentage of both West and East Germans preferred the old cold war order of a divided Germany. Such views still have some residual force. A poll conducted as late as 2007 showed that around 20 per cent of Germans 'would like to see the Wall rebuilt', and 'the desire to see the wall return is as high among former citizens of communist East Germany (the GDR) as it is among those from the west'. Only 3 per cent from the East said that they were 'very satisfied' with way that German democracy has worked out, whereas 73 per cent believe that socialism was a good idea in principle, but just poorly implemented.[7] Not that rosy reminiscence about the cold war past is a monopoly of East Germans. Similar trends were noted in Poland and Russia as well.[8] There was even a good deal of pining among West Germans ('Westalgie') for their secure and prosperous 'Bonn Republic'.[9] Many West Europeans too regretted the passing of the richer, more clubbish European Union of the 1980s.[10] Nevertheless, this look backward was particularly acute in East Germany, not least because it was the only former Eastern bloc country that did not enjoy national independence by 1990. Unlike the others, it was essentially absorbed by its cold war rival. East German disappointment also had to do with the way that Reunification occurred, to the extent that its historical drama passed from the noisy streets of Leipzig to closed-door Bundesbank negotiations, thus precluding East Germans from enjoying the fruits of having brought about the first successful revolution on German soil.

This disenchantment with the present has led to a kind of renewed privatization of life after 1989. The transition to democracy was really characterized by an elite-dominated period that oversaw the speedy institutionalization of new civil liberties and democratic structures. In the wake of Reunfication, citizens were demobilized, as the public tended to recede into private worlds of everyday activities, while policy-makers and scholars busied themselves with institutional design and political stability. As one scholar put it, the unification process 'left little or no room for citizen input. It was the hour of the policymaker and the bureaucrat', rendering people as the 'subjects, rather than agents, of change'.[11] Many became very defensive in the face of Reunification disaffection, and of West German ignorance and antipathy toward their former way of life.[12] Economic problems took centrestage, as most people were preoccupied with making ends meet in this new world, looking for jobs, paying bills, and tending families. What was heralded as Eastern Europe's 'rebirth of politics' in 1989 seemed no more than a passing episode.[13] Citizen withdrawal from public life was often interpreted as a bad sign for these Eastern bloc transitional democracies. East European intellectuals were not shy in expressing their horror toward the people's rapid retreat from the newly won public sphere after 1989 and their manifest desire afterwards to pursue purely personal concerns.[14]

For many East German citizens, their former semi-private lives became a shield of protection that took on various forms. Initially this was expressed in terms of defending the GDR's social accomplishments, such as childcare facilities, relative gender equality, and shared sense of intimate community. The oft-remembered warmth of East German social relations in neighbourhoods served as a key marker of memory for interviewees about the defunct republic.[15] Christians too lamented the break-up of old networks and the 'we-feeling' among congregations, as noted in numerous Christian memoirs written after 1989.[16] Eroticism even served as a site of *Ostalgie* too. The old idea that East Germans were more open and sexually liberated became a favourite refrain about the private pleasures and joys of life commonly experienced in an otherwise heavily regulated society, underlining the heightened importance that the private sphere had for East Germans.[17] A good deal of this *Ostalgie* also centered on the GDR's commonplace material artefacts, the remaindered hardware from a lost world. What appeared as a fleeting phenomenon has had a remarkable shelf-life, as these old everyday objects—clothes, housewares, foodstuffs—remain beloved (and commercially coveted) emblems of shared memory and identity. To be sure, the romance with material culture was in many ways a response to West German derision and condescension, which is still rife in contemporary Germany.[18]

The point is that East German memories tended to focus on domestic life in one form or another. Not that East Germans were alone in this regard. Home life has been the source of wistful reminiscences across the former Eastern bloc as well, as domestic spaces and things have served as favourite vehicles of national myths, cultural identity, and private history.[19] This echoed similar trends in Western Europe, Britain, and the United States during the 1980s, when the 1950s became the popular subject of misty memories about the can-do spirit, family cohesion, and moral order supposedly underlying the postwar's first decade of relative peace and plenty.[20] Objects also assumed unprecedented symbolic power for wartime survivors as reminders of lost stability and comfort. As Hannah Arendt put it in her 1958 book, *The Human Condition*, 'the things of the world have the function of stabilizing human life, and their objectivity lies in the fact that . . . men, their ever-changing nature notwithstanding, can retrieve their sameness, that is, their identity, by being related to the same chair and the same table'.[21] Such attitudes had resonances for East Germans after 1989 as well. Just as after 1945, durability and identity were no longer givens, and had to be reconstructed like everything else. It was precisely in this transitional context that the relationship between people and things—including the desire for durability— assumed heightened significance.[22] Underlying all of this post-1989 memory-making, however, was an assumed distinction between state and society, and it was the GDR's semi-private social world—informal networks, favourite pop culture artefacts, and tight subcultures—that attracted most attention and affection.

Others condemned the spirited defence of the niche society in the 1990s as simply an excuse for not getting involved or being held accountable for what happened before the demise of the SED regime.[23] It did not help that seemingly everyone claimed refuge in a niche after 1989. Honecker insisted that he knew little about the operations of the Stasi, since it was a separate department. Governmental officials (and their spouses) living in the government village of Wandlitz claimed that they simply retreated into the 'private sphere'.[24] Even Markus Wolf, the father and long-time chief of GDR's 'Department of Enlightenment', said that his foreign intelligence division (HVA) was his own unsullied 'niche'. As Timothy Garton Ash wrote:

> Those who worked for the state say 'it was not us, it was the Party.' Those who worked for the Party say 'it was not us, it was the Stasi.' Come to the Stasi, and those who worked for foreign intelligence say 'it was not us, it was the others.' Talk to them, and they say 'it was not our department, it was XX' . . . When the communists seized power in Central Europe, they talked of using 'salami tactics' to cut away the democratic opposition, slice by slice. Here, after communism, we have the salami tactics of denial.[25]

East German writer Jurek Becker scoffed at this myth-making, asserting that the SED government was lucky that it 'had to do with a population which readily subordinated itself, with citizens whose main act of opposition consisted of getting annoyed'.[26] In 1991 the famous East German folk singer Wolf Biermann dismissed this bout of *Ostalgie* in harsh terms: 'It stinks of self-pity in the East.'[27]

But as we have seen throughout this book, private life was not simply a defence. It could also be a social claim and political assertion. The events of 1989 provided good illustration in this respect. In these circumstances, notionally private concerns become real public issues. The desire to emigrate to the West, for instance, was generally considered a 'private affair', but took on new overtones in the autumn of 1989. A telling example was the dramatic occupation of the Dresden railroad station in November 1989, as would-be *Ausreiser* sought to board refugee-laden trains bound for the West, using the first-person plural in chanting 'Wir wollen raus!' As such these citizens were converting 'private exit into public exit,' and in so doing generating 'public voice and even organized delegation and negotiation with the authorities—all within a matter of days'.[28]

Most revealing in this respect was the citizens' symbolic storming of Berlin's Ministry of State Security fortress. The first assault on a Stasi building took place in Leipzig about a month after the breaching of the Wall in November 1989, and was repeated in various cities across the country. Across the GDR Stasi officers barricaded themselves in offices, frantically destroying incriminating files. Yet it was the televised seizure of East Berlin's massive Stasi headquarters in the Normannenstrasse on 15 January 1990 that attracted national attention. That day the New Forum dissident movement staged a demonstration in the parking lot of the Stasi complex. The other fourteen regional Stasi offices had already been taken over by local citizens, and their files were being transferred to the Berlin headquarters. Over 50,000 East Berliners assembled in front of the Stasi's forty-one-building Stasi compound, and things got increasingly unruly over the course of the bitterly cold winter day. Pleas for orderly conduct from Round Table leaders were of no avail, as people shouting 'We are the People' tore down the gates late that afternoon. Crowds surged inside, windows were smashed and offices ransacked. Portraits of Erich Honecker and Leonid Brezhnev were trampled, and files and furniture were thrown out of windows. Rooms were strewn with upturned files and dozens of burnt-out shredding machines. In the basement protesters discovered hidden stocks of fine French wine, cognac, champagne, and smoked eel, and used the Stasi's precious silver, Meissen china, and crystal glass collection to serve up a feast of savory delicacies and sweet revenge.[29] While the still SED-loyal press condemned these demonstrators as lawless 'rowdies' and 'vandals',[30] the significance of the event was plain to all. Journalists were quick to see the storming of the Bastille in 1789 as its historical analogy, as it too was an insurrectionary seizure of the hated old regime's most potent symbol of tyranny and arbitrary rule.[31]

Pulling back the curtain on the Stasi's surveillance empire became a subject of lurid fascination in the German press for the next few years, as the shocked public was fed a steady diet of harrowing revelations about the remarkable reach and monstrous machinations of history's most elaborate secret police outfit. A book of documents chronicling the Stasi's collapse became a bestseller.[32] While such corruption was actually quite modest, popular anger was deep and vociferous.[33] A phoneline was even set up for the purpose of reporting corruption. The outrage was less fuelled by the scandal of luxury than the hypocrisy that the SED leaders were supposedly the moral representatives of the working class.[34] This was followed by countless media exposés about the elitism and corruption of the ruling SED mandarins, as Party supremos and Stasi brass were reported to have been spoilt by lavish spending allowances, private automobiles, sports clubs, hunting lodges, travel privileges, and exclusive access to rare Western goods.

Honecker and his wife owned a fleet of fourteen cars, while Stasi Chief Erich Mielke enjoyed personal access to the Stasi's special hunting lodge and its 3,000-hectare stocked reserve near the Polish border. As dissident Jens Reich observed: 'The rage over the relative luxury and corruption of the nomenklatura was one of the strongest motives behind the uprising at the beginning of December which led to the overthrow of [Honecker's successor, Egon] Krenz. According to my observations, it was much broader, "closer to the people" and much more energetic and ready for action than were the peaceful demonstrations of September and October.'[35] The events of 15 January 1990 kicked off a wave of strikes across the country, as the SED's power was crumbling.[36] As another commentator put it: 'The hunting lodges and bungalows [of the government compound] of Wandlitz became like the diamond necklace of Marie Antoinette.'[37]

These tumultuous events sparked wide public discussion about what to do with the seized Stasi files. Although angry citizens spray-painted 'I Want My File!' on the walls of the occupied Stasi building, such demands found little initial support. In early March 1990, Round Table and New Forum leaders instead pleaded for the complete destruction of all data banks as a means of permanently disabling the old regime and starting afresh, and the still active East German Parliament—the Volkskammer—authorized this course of action later that month. The argument was that this information had been obtained illegally, and might be exploited again if the political climate changed for the worse. CDU Interior Minister Peter-Michael Diestel followed a similar line in asserting that these 'products of evil' could not be used to determine guilt and innocence, and that the misbegotten records of a 'police state' were hardly reliable instruments of social justice.[38] Files were thus ordered to be destroyed. Chancellor Kohl himself apparently advocated the destruction of files, insisting that they were cumbersome and a dangerous source of political poison. Other politicians feared that making the files public would lead to chaos and unrest. Minister President Lothar de Maizière went so far as to say that the revelations would lead to a situation in which 'there will no longer be neighbours, friends or colleagues, and may lead to violence and killings'.[39] While such fears were grossly exaggerated, Stasi agents and informants complained of rough treatment by the public. The word 'Stasi' was reportedly sprayed on cars and houses of the newly designated 'enemies of the people', and many former Stasi agents and collaborators were shunned, confronted, or assaulted by neighbours. One former Stasi agent wrote to Maizière about how he was being treated by family and neighbours: 'Our children have turned away from us; acquaintances do not know us any more; I had to give up my work and my sports club expelled me: I am scolded; there are threats to ignite my house; drunks create a pogrom atmosphere and it is to be foreseen that the gentle revolution probably will not end without a bloody confrontation.'[40] Ex-Stasi agents were frustrated, and many of them tended to withdraw into own private niches and alcoholic abuse.[41] In this topsy-turvy atmosphere, some committed suicide, while other agents got new jobs in consumer technology installation, security services, and private detective work.

Soon, however, new voices rose to champion the preservation of the files, and more importantly, the citizen's right to view his or her file. How much access was the crucial question. Differences of opinion tended to reflect party allegiances. Whereas the CDU favoured more restrictive access for citizens, the leftist or left-leaning parties (including the SPD, FDP, and Bündnis 90/Greens) favoured opening the captured files to citizens. By June 1990 the East German Parliament created a special commission to oversee the Stasi records, headed by dissident Rostock pastor and Volkskammer member, Joachim Gauck. The commission was thereafter known as the Gauck Authority. Giving citizens full access to their files was seen as 'compensation for the injuries of injustice' and a 'step toward the individual's self-determination and sovereign citizenship'.[42] But in the mean time, the Stasi files were to be turned over to the Federal Archives in the West German city of Koblenz, where they were to be stored away until the government could find a way of organizing the millions of seized dossiers. East German citizens reacted angrily to Bonn's administrative control of the files, fearing that information collected in the dossiers might be reused against them in the future and that this transfer still kept them in the dark about the Stasi's abuse of their civil rights. In September 1990 East German campaigners reoccupied the now derelict Stasi headquarters in protest, and even launched a high-profile hunger strike to draw public attention to the issue. Dissident Jens Reich summarized the dominant mood among East Germans at the time: 'This is our dirty laundry and our stink, and it is up to us alone to clean it up.'[43]

The protesters won their case, to the extent that it was agreed that the files would stay in East Germany 'in recognition of fact that they were an integral aspect of the East German past'.[44] To Gauck this was a great victory, since the files could serve as an effective means of democratizing East Germany: 'After all of the great words of revolution,' he argued, 'this is a matter of searching out those smaller, dirty words of betrayal that were the usual thing among our people,' and in so doing would inspire a new democratic attitude, 'awake, informed and driven by a will to achieve more justice and truth'.[45] The commission thus provided public and private bodies with access to information for criminal prosecution; screened individuals for jobs; and helped rehabilitate victims of Stasi persecution. In Gauck's eyes, 'the effort to make the Stasi files accessible is a continuation of efforts that began with the street demonstrations: to return power and knowledge to the people'.[46] A law, the Stasi-Unterlagen-Gesetz, was passed by the Bundestag on 20 December 1991, granting each individual the right to view the information stored in the GDR's secret police files. To legal theorists, the new law blended two opposing conceptions of privacy. On the one side stood the Federal Republic's constitutional right to 'informational self-determination' that the West German courts had enshrined in the early 1980s. On the other was the protection of privacy for the perpetrators and/or informants in the files, on the grounds that this information was obtained illegally and was not to be used to impugn the reputation or integrity of any party.[47] As such the Stasi law marked a successful fusion of West German liberal jurisprudence and East German civil rights activism, balancing the 'risks to privacy and the pursuit of social justice' that undergirded this new constitutional order.[48]

Gaining access to files was not all that joyous an occasion, however. Upon reading their files many citizens experienced the shock of revelation and pain of betrayal. Harrowing stories of husbands spying on wives and children informing on their parents drove home the extent to which the lines between state and society, public and private had been fully effaced in the GDR. Some dissidents confessed that learning the identity of those who had betrayed them was like a 'second savaging of Stasi victims',[49] not least because the press had a field day exposing the netherworld of complicity and cowardice. But the files were not only filled with woeful tales of betrayal and depravity; they also, as some found out to their pleasant surprise, featured great moments of moral defiance and civil courage. Newspaper editor Ulrich Schacter, for example, wrote an open thank you note to all of his friends after reading his file, extolling the fact that no one informed on him.[50] Such positive revelations were the exception that proved the rule. Interviewees generally admitted that their former existence looked different after reading their Stasi files, exposing the fact that their private lives were much less free or private than they had ever suspected.[51] Others argued that their post-Wall will to testimony was a deliberate effort to combat the false picture produced in the Stasi files. As dissident Vera Wollenberger put it: 'Our understanding, our feelings, our memories are the necessary corrective [to Stasi lies and legends].'[52] What is more, such file-reading occasionally led to some unexpected consequences. Reportedly, around 35 per cent of those who applied to see their Stasi files were told that they didn't actually have one. One psychologist ironically dubbed this syndrome 'file envy', or *Aktenneid*, as people were often jealous toward those with thick Stasi files as conspicuous proof of nonconformity and political resistance.[53]

Still, there is no denying that the whole process has been a great success. At the time of Reunification the Gauck Authority had merely 52 employees; by 1993 it had almost 3,500 on the books. Within one year of Reunification some 300,000 requests for screening public job candidates were filed. Between 1990 and 1993 over 2 million individuals applied to see their files. By 1997 Gauck had reported 3.7 million petitions for viewing files, 1.3 million of which were from private citizens alone.[54] Soon Gauck created a new investigative parliamentary committee, the so-called Enquete Commission, to address 'the history and consequences of the socialist dictatorship'. For this teams of academic experts and witnesses were called forth to testify and debate the effects of the regime on East German society. In the course of its tenure from 1992 to 1998, the commission oversaw numerous public hearings, culminating in two multi-volume published reports.

While for many this may have been truth without reconciliation, it did underline the earnestness with which the New Germany sought to work through the fallout of the deposed socialist republic by means of hard self-examination.

All of this was fundamental to the restoration of the *Rechtsstaat* and a liberal bourgeois order. Not surprisingly, much of the initial focus of what was called 'corrective justice' centred on property, whether in terms of selling off defunct East German factories or returning private property illegally acquired after 1945.[55] Apart from the legislation discussed above regarding the citizen's right to see his or her Stasi file, constitutional protections of private life came in other forms as well. Political safeguards against the invasion of privacy emerged at the international level in the 1990s. In 1993 the International Criminal Court, for instance, made denunciation a violation of human rights, following the language of the 1945 Control Act discussed in Chapter 1.[56] In any case, no other country put as much effort or resources into the investigations of the communist abuse of power. The Gauck Authority is again a ready example. By 1996 its budget was DM 234 million, more than the total defence budget of Lithuania.[57] In Romania and Hungary, secret police files were largely destroyed, and in Poland and Czechoslovakia most files remained under lock and key. As one East German SPD politician put it in the early 1990s, it was 'first time in German history, and perhaps in all of history that the opening of the files, the archives of a secret police and the victims' access to them has been accomplished'.[58] Though the *lustrace* laws in Czechoslovakia most closely resembled developments in East Germany, it was never as comprehensive in granting citizen access to personal files. More relevant to this study, the private repossession of Stasi files became East Germany's uniquely popular version of coming to terms with the communist past, serving as the symbolic new foundation of German democracy. For many citizens the constitutional right to see their files signalled the real end of the regime, marking the emergence of a civil society that never existed in the GDR. The popular reclamation of personal files was a kind of taking back of history, turning the old Marxist slogan of 'expropriating the expropriators' on its head. In this sense, seeing one's personal file was a 'reacquisition of biography' which offered at least a small measure of justice for those who suffered at the hands of the regime.[59] As noted in interviews, reading one's personal file was as important a milestone in their lives as the events of 1989 themselves, often even more so. It was the moment when the East German past was finally confronted head on and personally.

At first such personalized pursuits of justice may be taken as simply the typical reaction of people living under authoritarianism. As we have seen over the course of this book, in certain ways the regime inadvertently created a society of self-oriented materialists who increasingly looked after themselves at the expense of all else. In this regard one could invoke classic characterizations of eighteenth-century *Ancien Régime* tyranny as an historical precedent. After all, the division between a 'privileged domineering official realm' and a 'private realm character-ized by mutual suspicion' was a principal feature of Montesquieu's analysis of late eighteenth-century despotism.[60] Tocqueville, too, described *Ancien Régime* France in similar terms, writing that people under despotism were

far too much disposed to think exclusively of their own interests, to become self-seekers practicing a narrow individualism and caring nothing for the public good. Far from trying to counteract such tendencies, despotism encourages them, depriving the governed of any sense of solidarity and interdependence; of good-neighbourly feeling and a desire to further the welfare of the community at large. It immures them, so to speak, each in his or her private life and, taking advantage of the tendency they already have to keep apart, it estranges them still more.[61]

Such views about the atomization of society were retreaded by social scientists in the wake of Reunification in order to explain East Germans' supposed inability to cope with the transition to liberal democracy. The 'East German character'—a favourite theme of pop psychology after 1989—was widely described as a deficiency syndrome of 'congested feelings', dishonesty, and split personalities, most famously articulated in a 1990 bestseller by East German psychoanalyst Hans-Joachim Maaz, *Behind the Wall: The Inner Life of Communist Germany*.[62] In a follow-up book, Maaz diagnosed the 'crippled' East German psyche, portraying them as masters of self-deception, dissimulation, disavowal, and denial for having been socialized in a brutal world of communist tyranny and tutelage.[63] Others however countered that the socialist experience may have had some hidden positive effects on its citizens. Studies concluded that East Germans identified more strongly with personal and intimate relationships than West Germans, and that they drew real sustenance and satisfaction from their private lives and intimate circles of friends and family.[64] Still others contended that the communist version of the 'authoritarian personality' actually served as a good coping strategy developed for dealing with state socialism and its aftermath, to the extent that this fragmented world of self-initiative and self-reliance may have eased the adjustment to the liberalization of the ex-communist lands in the 1990s. As one Russian historian put it: 'This proliferation of secret, intimate spheres, created and controlled only by the individual, prepared the way to the easy public assertion of the value of privacy after 1991.'[65]

But this updated atomization model only goes so far. Recent oral history projects—along with interviews that I conducted—highlighted the role and importance of familiar (and familial) personal networks in surviving the confusion and chaos associated with the *Wende*.[66] For many the collapse of the state meant that the family stepped up to play a key role in weathering the rough transition from communism to capitalism, and helped people manage the fallout of Reunification on a personal level.[67] At times the strain was too much, however, as divorce rates among East Germans doubled from 1991 to 1996.[68] Marriages too were on the wane,[69] and East Germans had far fewer children in the 1990s.[70]

The churches were routinely cited as a key guardian of the private sphere—and not just for Christians, since their welfare network of hospitals, old people's homes, and youth groups touched many at-risk and needy people. It was also acknowledged that the churches played a decisive role in the events of 1989. As we saw in Chapter 2, the churches increasingly criticized the state and its ill effects on the populace over the decades. With time the great originator of the East German 'niche society' grew more and more dismayed with the way that people tended to 'retire into the private sphere', and helped create a new and dangerous 'counter-public sphere' in its own right in the late 1980s.[71] In this sense, the Church was effective in acting as an umbrella organization for many citizens (such as punks, gays, environmentalists, human rights activists) who by the 1980s had constructed 'counter-identities' against the prescribed model of the 'socialist personality'.[72] After 1989 a good many people returned to church. The baptism rate in Lutheran Churches doubled between 1989 and 1991, and the same went for participation in confirmation.[73] But claiming a 'rechristianiza-tion' of East Germany is off the mark, as many churches largely remained empty in the 1990s. Revealingly, death rituals changed too. After 1989 funeral services were largely privatized, and many new companies were established in the early 1990s to care for the dead. In its train came new funeral rites, as memorial plaques were introduced with the names of the deceased inscribed on them, in a clear break from long-standing socialist practice of de-individualizing death. What is more, many of these memorials appeared without family surnames, featuring only first names as a symbol of the deceased's shared intimacy with family and friends.[74]

Other traditions addressed in this book survived 1989. A good example is the 'youth dedication' ceremony discussed in Chapter 2. As late as 1990, 75 per cent of East German youth still underwent the Jugendweihe,[75] and around half of East German 14 year olds continued to do so during the 1990s.[76] Nowhere else in the Eastern bloc did such socialist youth rites of passage persist. But in East Germany this mainly was because the ceremony had changed in orientation. As noted, the ritual had been essentially hollowed out of any real socialist content over the course of the 1970s and 1980s, and celebrated more as a family tradition than anything else. By the early 1990s the trend was explicitly towards returning the Jugendweihe to its nineteenth-century 'free thinking' tradition. Today it serves as a reminder of these multiple pasts, a rite of humanist legacy, East German socialism, and family tradition.[77] In this way it has become another instance of tradition as *Eigensinn*, as people alter the meaning of these rituals to suit their personal interests and family customs.

Another example is the citizen complaint letters. Between 1989 and 1995 the number of *Eingaben*, for example, remained remarkably high, especially given that their old institutionalized 'culture of complaint' had died away. Years after Reunification ex-GDR citizens continued to solicit state authorities—in this case, the Bundestag—with their individual grievances. Old habits die hard—the collapse of the state thus did not deter the custom of regular letter-writing, though the addressee changed. At the very least, this provides some explanation of what West Germans disparagingly referred to as 'Jammerossis', or 'carping East Germans', were doing. To be fair, such post-*Wende* complaining wasn't limited to East Germans: West Germans did their share of public grumbling about the financial burdens of Reunification. Yet the continuation of these formally submitted complaint letters long after 1990 sheds some valuable light on why East Germans often saw the Federal Republic's justice system as cold and impersonal. As we saw in Chapter 6, such complaints were fundamental to socialist citizenship, and East German *Bürger* were very used to this direct interface with their state. For them personal rights—whether seen as a defence of peace, quiet, respect, and honour—were synonymous with social justice, and it was this impulse which arguably fuelled both the 1990s *Eingaben* and the 10,000 monthly requests to view one's personal files over the course of the 1990s.

Such instances of the remaking of private life after 1989 are usually construed as the cultural by-products of the 'de-communization' of East Germany. As one observer baldly put it: 'After decades of state aggression against the private sphere, these revolutions [of 1989] reinstituted the distinction between what belongs to the government and what is the territory of the individual. Emphasizing the importance of political and civil rights, they created a space for the exercise of liberal democratic values.'[78] But as this book has shown, it is wrong to say that the East German private sphere was somehow a retroactive invention after 1989 to compensate for post-Reunification despair. It was a real issue and cultural battleline, and was taken seriously by all sides long before 1989. In a world in which most social interaction was heavily monitored, the private sphere functioned for many citizens as a cherished locus of individuality, alternative identity-formation, and/or dissent and resistance. The private sphere—even if not always called as such—was defended, staged, and asserted as a semi-permeable haven from public life and prescribed collective identities, giving form to more private understandings of the self. Its practices ranged from individual retreat and prized isolation to shared intimacy and social bonding. Its protean quality and changing boundaries were what made it so resilient and intractable, and accounts for its irrepressible political place in a state that did its best to keep its potential power under control. In the end, private life was as much a claim and assertion as a fixed place or spatial barrier. The effort on the part of millions to take back stolen life stories after 1989 ('I Want My File!') serves as a rich reminder of how East German citizens saw their private life in relation to the state and to each other. This book goes some way in demonstrating how, why, and under what social conditions the private sphere under communism developed and flourished. In Eastern Europe politics were never coterminous with the public sphere, and often took place elsewhere, breeding in the honeycomb cells of state socialism. Unlike the Third Reich, the GDR ended not with a bang but a whimper. Recounting the centrality of the private sphere in the fallen socialist republic helps accounts for why the regime lasted so long, collapsed so easily, and died so unloved.

Notes

NOTES TO THE INTRODUCTION

1. www.ddr-museum.de, accessed 10 Sept. 2009. See too Richard Bernstein, 'Peek into This East German Museum, and it Peeks Back', *New York Times*, 20 July 2006.

2. Horst V., Eisenach, questionnaire, 15 May 2007; Karin and Konrad R, respectively, Berlin, interview, 17 July 2005.

3. Renate W., Weimar, interview, 16 July 2005.

4. Christiane M., Berlin, interview, 20 Apr. 2007.

5. Karl-Heinz B., Eisenach, questionnaire, 15 May 2007.

6. Irma G., Berlin, interview, 25 July 2005, and Norbert H., Berlin, questionnaire, 22 July 2005.

7. Werner L., Berlin, questionnaire, 28 June 2005.

8. Franziska T., Berlin, interview, 2005.

9. Hans M., Berlin, questionnaire, 29 June 2005.

10. Renate W., Berlin, interview, 16 July 2005.

11. Richard W. (name altered), Berlin, questionnaire, 5 July 2005, and Hans-Otto F., interview, Berlin, 30 Jan. 2007.

12. Nancy Travis Wolfe, *Policing a Socialist Society: The German Democratic Republic* (New York, 1992), 133. See too Barbara Miller, *Narratives of Guilt and Compliance in Unified Germany: Stasi Informers and their Impact on Society* (London, 1999).

13. Owen Evans, *Mapping the Contours of Oppression: Subjectivity, Truth and Fiction in Recent German Autobiographical Treatments of Totalitarianism* (New York and Amsterdam, 2006). Note as well the evocative memoir by Timothy Garton Ash, *The File: A Personal History* (London, 1997).

14. *Das Kollektiv bin ich: Utopie und Alltag in der DDR*, ed. Franziska Becker, Ina Merkel, and Simone Tippach-Schneider (Cologne, 2000).

15. *Fortschritt, Norm & Eigensinn: Erkundungen im Alltag der DDR*, ed. Dokumentationszentrum Alltagskultur der DDR, 1999 and more recently, *Erinnerungsorte der DDR*, ed. Martin Sabrow (Munich, 2009).

16. Frank Schumann, *Lotte und Walter: Die Ulbrichts in Selbstzeugnissen, Briefen und Dokumenten* (Berlin, 2003); Ed Stuhler, *Die Honeckers Privat: Liebespaar und Kampfgemeinschaft* (Berlin, 2005); Thomas Grimm, *Das Politbüro Privat: Ulbricht, Honecker, Mielke & Co aus der Sicht ihrer Angestellten* (Berlin, 2005); Peter Kirschey, *Wandlitz/Waldsiedlung: Die geschlossene Gesellschaft. Versuch einer Reportage, Gespräche, Dokumente* (Berlin, 1990); Susanne Hopf and Natalja Meier, *Plattenbau Privat: 60 Interieurs* (Berlin, 2004).

17. Jürgen Habermas, *The Structural Transformation of the Public Sphere*, tr. T. Berger (Cambridge, Mass., 1989 [1962]).

18. Craig Calhoun (ed.), *Habermas and the Public Sphere* (Cambridge, Mass., 1992). Classic is this regard is Karin Hausen, 'Family and Role-Division: The Polarisation of Sexual Stereotypes in the 19th Century,' in Richard Evans and W. R. Lee (eds.), *The German Family* (London, 1981).

19. Norbert Bobbio, 'The Grand Dichotomy: Public/Private', in his *Democracy and Dictatorship* (Minneapolis, 1989) and Beate Rössler, *Der Wert des Privaten* (Frankfurt, 2001).

20. Norbert Elias, *The Civilizing Process* (New York, 1978 [1939]), 190. Pioneering in this respect is Philippe Aries and Georges Duby (eds.), *The History of Private Life* (Cambidge, Mass., 1987–91), i–v.

21. Barrington Moore, *Privacy: Studies in Social and Cultural History* (Armonk, NY, London, 1984), 82.

22. Ibid. 267–77.

23. Arendt, *The Human Condition* (Chicago, 1958), 54.

24. Habermas, *Structural Transformation,* 11.

25. Raymond Williams, *Keywords: A Vocabulary of Culture and Society* (New York, 1976), 242–3. See too Richard Sennett, *The Fall of Public Man* (New York, 1974), 1–27 and 89–106.

26. Hannah Arendt, *The Origins of Totalitarianism* (New York, 1951), 176.

27. Carl J. Friedrich and Zbigniew Brzezinski, *Totalitarian Dictatorship and Autocracy,* 2nd rev. edn. (Cambridge, 1965 [1956]), 295–8. See too Moore, *Privacy,* 74–5, and Abbott Gleason, *Totalitarianism: The Inner History of the Cold War* (New York, 1995).

28. Article 8, Section 1, reads: 'Everyone has the right to respect for his private and family life, his home and his correspondence.'

29. Deborah Nelson, *Pursuing Privacy in Cold War America* (New York, 2002), 10–11, and 85–7.

30. Ibid., p. xiii, and Richard F. Hixson, *Privacy in a Public Society: Human Rights in Conflict* (New York, 1987), p. xv.

31. Serge L. Levitsky, *Copyright, Defamation and Privacy in Soviet Civil Law* (Alphen aan den Rijn, 1979), 447–59.

32. The provisions included the right to 'freedom of faith and of conscience' (Art. 4), 'privacy of post' (Art. 10), and the 'inviolability of the home' (Art. 13). Dietwalt Rohlf, *Der grundrechtliche Schutz der Privatsphäre* (Berlin, 1980).

33. Stefan Stolze, *Nachkriegsjahre: Erinnerungen 1945–1955* (Frankfurt, 1984), 118.

34. Marc Raeff, *The Well-Ordered Police State: Social and Institutional Change through Law in the Germanies and Russia, 1600–1800* (New Haven, Conn., 1983).

35. Gisa Austermühle, *Zur Entstehung und Entwicklung eines persönlichen Geheimsphärenschutzes von Spätabsolutismus bis zur Gesetzgebung des Deutschen Reiches* (Berlin, 2002) and Andreas Gestrich, *Absolutismus und Öffentlichkeit: Politische Kommunikation in Deutschland zu Beginn des. 18. Jahrhunderts* (Göttingen, 2004).

36. Marc Garcelon, 'The Shadow of the Leviathan: Public and Private in Communist and Post-Communist Society', in Jeff Weintraub and Krishan Kumar (eds.), *Public and Private in Thought and Practice: Perspectives on a Grand Dichotomy* (Chicago, 1997), 303–32.

37. Orlando Figes, *The Whisperers: Private Life in Stalin's Russia* (London, 2007), xxix–xxxvii.

38. Sheila Fitzpatrick, *Everyday Stalinism* (Oxford, 1999), as well as her *Tear Off the Masks! Identity and Imposture in Twentieth Century Russia* (Princeton, 2005). See too Sarah Davies, *Popular Opinion in Stalin's Russia: Terror, Propaganda and Dissent, 1934–1941* (Cambridge, 1997).

39. Svetlana Boym, *Common Places: Mythologies of Everyday Life in Russia* (Cambridge, 1994), esp. 93–5, and Oleg Kharkhordin, *The Collective and the Individual in Russia* (Berkeley, Calif., 1999). See too Deborah A. Field, *Private Life and Communist Morality in Khrushchev's Russia* (New York, 2007).

40. Vladimir Shlapentokh, *Public and Private Life of the Soviet People: Changing Values in Post-Stalinist Russia* (New York, 1989), as well as Lewis M. Siegelbaum (ed.), *Borders of Socialism: Private Spheres of Soviet Russia* (New York, 2006).

41. Tony Judt, *Postwar* (New York, 2005), 580; for China, see Yanxiang Yan, *Private Life under Socialism: Love, Intimacy and Family Change in a Chinese Village, 1949–1999* (Palo Alto, 2003).

42. Joseph Rothschild, *Return to Diversity: A Political History of East Central Europe since World War II* (New York, 1993), 208–9.

43. Vaclav Havel, 'The Power of the Powerless', in *Vaclav Havel: Living in Truth*, ed. Jan Vladislav (London, 1990), 36–122.

44. Karl Marx, 'Über die Pressefreiheit', 1842, quoted in Steven Pfaff, *Exit-Voice Dynamics and the Collapse of East Germany: The Crisis of Leninism and the Revolution of 1989* (Durham, 2006), 61.

45. Timothy Garton Ash, *'Und willst du nicht mein Bruder sein...': Die DDR Heute* (Hamburg, 1981). See too Rüdiger Henkel, *Rückzug ins Private: Individuelle Antworten auf den 'realen Sozialismus'* (Bonn, 1980).

46. Günter Gaus, *Wo Deutschland liegt: Eine Ortsbestimmung* (Hamburg, 1983), 117–19.

47. Ibid. 117.

48. Gabriel Almond and Sidney Verba, *The Civic Culture Revisited: Political Attitudes and Democracy in Five Nations* (New York, 1980). For a wartime celebration of England's 'niche society', see George Orwell, *The Lion and the Unicorn: Socialism and the English Genius* (London, 1941), 15. At times privacy has been elevated as a distinctive English national trait. Kate Fox, *Watching the English: The Hidden Rules of English Behaviour* (London, 2004), esp. 42–52.

49. Mark Mazower, *Dark Continent: Europe's Twentieth Century* (New York, 1998), xi.

50. Ralf Dahrendorf, *Society and Democracy in Germany* (New York, 1967), 285–96.

51. Jonathan Steele, *Socialism with a German Face: The State that Came in from the Cold* (London, 1977), 154.

52. Jens Hacker, *Deutsche Irrtümer: Schönfärber und Helfershelfer der SED-Diktatur im Westen* (Frankfurt, 1992).

53. Hendrik Bussiek, *Die real existierende DDR: Neue Notizen aus der unbekannten deutschen Republik* (Frankfurt/M, 1984) and Werner Filmer (ed.), *Alltag im anderen Deutschland* (Düsseldorf, 1985).

54. Theo Sommer, *Reise ins andere Deutschland* (Hamburg, 1986).

55. Alice Kahl, *Kollektivbeziehungen und Lebensweise* (Berlin, 1984), 139. Jutta Gysi, *Familienleben in der DDR* (Berlin, 1989), 161.

56. Garton Ash, *Und willst*, 13–14.

57. Freya Klier, *Abreisskalender* (1988), no page.

58. Joachim Staadt, *Eingaben: Die institutionalisierte Meckerkultur in der DDR* (Berlin, 1996), 1.

59. Dietrich Storbeck, 'Die Familienpolitik der SED und die Familienwirklichkeit in der DDR', in Peter Christian Ludz (ed.), *Studien und Materialien zur Soziologie der DDR* (Cologne, 1964), esp. 104–6.

60. R. C. van Caenegem, *An Historical Introduction to Western Constitutional Law* (Cambridge, 1995), 284. cited in Mazower, *Dark Continent*, 57.

61. Charlotte Beradt, *The Third Reich of Dreams: The Nightmares of a Nation, 1933–1939* (Wellingborough, 1985), 21.

62. Detlev Peukert, *Inside Nazi Germany: Conformity, Opposition and Racism in Everyday Life*, tr. R. Deveson (New Haven, Conn., 1987 [1992]), 236–42.

63. Marion A. Kaplan, *Between Dignity and Despair: Jewish Life in Nazi Germany* (Oxford, 1998).

64. Ian Kershaw, *Hitler, the Germans and the Final Solution* (New Haven, Conn., 2008), 198–9. One could argue that the 1987 Martin Broszat–Saul Friedländer exchange on the legacy of Nazism and history-writing in part pivoted on the issues of how racist ideology, action, and memory were internalized and privatized by ordinary Germans. The correspondence is tr. and repr. in English as 'A Controversy about the Historicization of National Socialism', *New German Critique*, 44 (Spring/Summer 1988), 85–126.

65. Konrad Jarausch, 'Care and Coercion: The GDR as Welfare Dictatorship', in his edited *Dictatorship as Experience: Towards a Socio-Cultural History of the GDR* (New York, 1999), 47–69.

66. Hans-Joachim Maaz, *Behind the Wall: The Inner Life of Communist Germany* (New York, 1995), 79. It originally appeared as *Der Gefühlsstau: Ein Psychogramm der DDR* (Berlin, 1990).

67. Greg Eghigian, 'Homo Munitus: The East German Observed', in Katherine Pence and Paul Betts (eds.), *Socialist Modern: East German Everyday Culture and Politics* (Ann Arbor, 2008), 41, 48.

68. Winfried Thaa *et al.*, *Gesellschaftliche Differenzierung und Legitimitätsverfall des DDR-Sozialismus* (Tübingen, 1992), 100, 177–8.

69. Alexis De Tocqueville, *The Old Regime and the French Revolution* (Garden City, NY, 1955 [1856]), 204–5.

70. Christoph Boyer and Peter Skyba (eds.), *Repression und Wohlstandsversprechen: Zur Stabilisierung von Parteiherrschaft in der DDR und CSSR* (Dresden, 1999).

71. Mary Fulbrook, *The People's State: East German Society from Hitler to Honecker* (New Haven, Conn., 2005), 236, 247.

72. Richard Bessel and Ralph Jessen (eds.), *Die Grenzen der Diktatur: Staat und Gesellschaft in der DDR* (Göttingen, 1996).

73. Dorothee Wierling, *Geboren im Jahr Eins: Der Jahrgang in der DDR: Versuch einer Kollektivbiographie* (Berlin, 2002), 170 and 387.

74. Charles Maier (ed.), *Changing Boundaries of the Political: Essays on the Evolving Balance between State and Society, Public and Private* (Cambridge, Mass, 1987).

75. Johannes Huinink *et al.*, *Kollektiv und Eigensinn: Lebensläufe in der DDR und danach* (Berlin, 1995) and Thomas Lindenberger (ed.), *Herrschaft und Eigen-Sinn in der Diktatur: Studien zur Gesellschaftsgeschichte der DDR* (Cologne, 1999).

76. Ehrhart Neubert, *Geschichte der Opposition in der DDR, 1949–1989* (Bonn, 1997), 23.

77. Sibylle Meyer and Eva Schulze, *Familien im Umbruch: Zur Lage der Familien in der ehemaligen DDR* (Stuttgart, 1992), 22, 77.

78. James C. Scott, *Weapons of the Weak: Everyday Forms of Peasant Resistance* (New Haven, 1985).

79. Pfaff, *Exit-Voice Dynamics*, 263.

80. Alf Lüdtke, 'Cash, Coffee-Breaks, Horseplay: Eigensinn and Politics among Factory Workers in Germany circa 1900', in Michael Hanagan and Charles Stephenson (eds.), *Confrontation, Class Consciousness and the Labor Process* (New York, 1982), 81–2. See too his *Eigensinn: Fabrikalltag, Arbeitererfahrungen und Politik vom Kaiserreich bis in den Faschismus* (Hamburg, 1993), as well as his edited *The History of Everyday Life* (Princeton, 1995).

81. Herzog, *Sex After Fascism,* 203.

82. Inga Markovits, 'Socialist vs. Bourgeois Rights: An East–West German Comparison', *University of Chicago Law Review,* 45 (1978), 612–36, 612.

83. Charles S. Maier, *Dissolution: The Crisis of Communism and the End of East Germany* (Princeton, 1997), 29.

84. Donna Harsch, *Revenge of the Domestic: Women, the Family and Communism in the German Democratic Republic* (Princeton, 2006), as well as Barbara Einhorn, *Cinderella Goes to Market: Citizenship, Gender and the Women's Movement in East Central Europe* (London, 1993).

85. Wierling, *Geboren,* 413.

86. Thaa *et al.*, *Gesellschaftliche Differenzierung,* 154–5, 167–9, and Roland Habich and Eckhard Priller, 'Soziale Lage und subjektives Wohlbefinden in der ehemaligen DDR', in Michael Thomas (ed.), *Abbruch und Aufbruch* (Berlin, 1992), 242.

87. Apart from those cited above, see e.g. Adelheid von Saldern, *Häuserleben* ((Bonn, 1997); Ina Merkel, *Utopie und Bedürfnis: Die Geschichte der Konsumkultur in der DDR* (Cologne, 1999); Katherine Pence, *Rations to Fashions: Gender and Consumer Politics in Cold War Germany* (Cambridge, 2010); Dagmar Herzog, *Sex After Fascism: Memory and Morality in Twentieth Century Germany* (Princeton, 2005); and Josie McLellan, 'State Socialist Bodies: East German Nudism from Ban to Boom', *Journal of Modern History,* 79 (Mar. 2007), 48–79, as well as her forthcoming, *Love in the Time of Communism* (Cambridge, 2011).

88. Corey Ross, *Constructing Socialism at the Grassroots: The Transformation of East Germany, 1945–1965* (London, 2000); Mark Allinson, *Politics and Popular Opinion in East Germany, 1945–1968* (Manchester, 2000); Inga Markovits, *Gerechtigkeit in Lüritz: Eine ostdeutsche Rechtsgeschichte* (Munich, 2006); Philipp Springer, *Verbaute Träume: Herrschaft, Stadtentwicklung und Lebensrealität in der sozialistischen Industriestadt Schwedt* (Berlin, 2006); Andrew I. Port, *Conflict and Stability in the German Democratic Republic* (Cambridge, 2007); and Jan Palmowski, *Inventing a Socialist Nation: Heimat and the Politics of Everyday Life in the GDR, 1945–1990* (Cambridge, 2009).

89. Patrick Major, *Behind the Berlin Wall: East Germany and the Frontiers of Power* (Oxford, 2010).

90. Sandrine Kott, 'Der Beitrag der französischen Sozialwissenschaften zur Erforschung der ostdeutschen Gesellschaft,' in Sandrine Kott and Emmanuel Droit (eds.), *Die ostdeutsche Gesellschaft: Eine transatlantische Perspective* (Berlin, 2006), 17.

91. Antoine Prost, 'Public and Private Spheres in France', in Antoine Prost and Gerald Vincent (ed.), *A History of Private Life,* v. *Riddles of Identity in Modern Times* (Cambridge, 1987), 7.

92. Katherine Pence and Paul Betts (eds.), *Socialist Modern: East German Everyday Culture and Politics* (Ann Arbor, 2008), esp. the introduction.

NOTES TO CHAPTER 1

1. Quoted in Alexandra Richie, *Faust's Metropolis: A History of Berlin* (London, 1998), 727.
2. Kristie Macrakis, *Seduced by Secrets: Inside the Stasi's Spy-Tech World* (Cambridge, 2008).
3. Annie Applebaum, *The Sunday Telegraph*, 21 Feb. 1999, book section, 13, and Tina Rosenberg, *The Haunted Land: Facing Europe's Ghosts After Communism* (London, 1995), 289.
4. Michel Foucault, *Discipline and Punish*, tr. A. Sheridan (New York, 1979), 214.
5. This language came from the verdict in a 1978 court case in Karl-Marx-Stadt, involving a theology student who has been given Orwell's novel by a West German acquaintance. He was sentenced to prison to twenty-eight months for 'incitement hostile to the state'. Mike Dennis, *The Stasi: Myth and Reality* (London, 2003), 62.
6. Anna Funder, *Stasiland* (London, 2003), 283.
7. Edward N. Peterson, *The Secret Police and the Revolution: The Fall of the German Democratic Republic* (Westport, Conn., 2002), 24.
8. Joachim Kallinach and Sylvia de Pasquale (eds.), *Ein offenes Geheimnis: Post- und Telefonkontrolle in der DDR* (Berlin, 2002).
9. John O. Koehler, *Stasi: The Untold Story of the East German Secret Police* (Boulder, Colo., 1999), 9.
10. Sonya Süss, 'Psychiater im Dienste des MfS', in Klaus Behnke and Jürgen Fuchs (eds.), *Zersetzung der Seele: Psychologie und Psychiatrie im Dienste der Stasi* (Hamburg, 1995), 255–293.
11. Rosenberg, *Haunted Land,* 290–1.
12. Hannah Arendt, *The Origins of Totalitarianism* (New York, 1973 [1951]), 431.
13. This phrase was first coined by American sociologist Richard Sennett in the conclusion to his well-known 1974 book, *The Fall of Public Man,* though he refers to 'intimacies of tyranny' in the plural. Richard Sennett, *The Fall of Public Man* (New York, 1974), 337.
14. Jens Gieseke, *Mielke-Konzern: Die Geschichte der Stasi, 1945–1990* (Stuttgart, 2001), 92.
15. David Childs, 'The Shadow of the Stasi', in Patricia J. Smith (ed.), *After the Wall: Eastern Germany After 1989* (Boulder, Colo., 1998), 93.
16. On this theme, see Jens Gieseke (ed.), *Staatssicherheit und Gesellschaft: Studien zum Herrschaftsalltag in der DDR* (Göttingen, 2007) and Jan Palmowski, *Inventing a Socialist Nation: Heimat and the Politics of Everyday Life in the GDR, 1945–1990* (Cambridge, 2009), esp. ch. 8.
17. Dennis, *Stasi*, 15.
18. Nancy Travis Wolfe, *Policing a Socialist Society: The German Democratic Republic* (New York, 1992), 74.
19. Charles Maier, *Dissolution* (Princeton, 1997), 47.
20. Mary Fulbrook, *Anatomy of a Dictatorship: Inside the GDR, 1949–1989* (Oxford, 1995), 48.
21. Gieseke, *Mielke-Konzern,* 70.
22. David Childs and Richard Popplewell, *The Stasi* (London, 1996), 86.
23. Mark Mazower, 'The Policing of Politics in Political Perspective', in his edited *The Policing of Politics in the Twentieth Century* (Oxford, 1997), 241–56.

24. Alf Lüdtke (ed.), *Sicherheit und Wohlfahrt: Polizei, Gesellschaft und Herrschaft im 19. und 20. Jahrhundert* (Frankfurt, 1992).

25. Peter Holquist, '"Information is the Alpha and Omega of our Work": Bolshevik Surveillance in its Pan-European Context', *Journal of Modern History*, 69/3 (Sept. 1997), 415–50.

26. Childs and Popplewell, *Stasi*, 33–46.

27. Norman M. Naimark, *The Russians in Germany: A History of the Soviet Zone of Occupation, 1945–1949* (Cambridge, Mass., 1995), 353–65.

28. Gieseke, *Mielke-Konzern*, 43.

29. Herbert Reinke, 'Policing Politics in Germany from Weimar to the Stasi' in Mazower, *Policing*, 91–101, and Childs and Popplewell, *Stasi*, 49.

30. Childs and Popplewell, *Stasi*, 77.

31. David E. Murphy, Sergei A. Kondrashev, and George Bailey, *Battleground Berlin: CIA vs. KGB in the Cold War* (New Haven, Conn., 1997), 286.

32. Gieseke, *Mielke-Konzern*, 75.

33. Childs and Popplewell, *Stasi*, 77.

34. Cited in Dennis, *Stasi*, 61.

35. Quoted in Fulbrook, *Anatomy*, 47.

36. Jürgen Lemke, *Ganz normal anders: Auskünfte schwuler Männer* (Berlin, 1989), 30–1.

37. Thomas Lindenberger, 'Creating State Socialist Governance: The Case of the Deutsche Volkspolizei', in Konrad Jarausch (ed.), *Dictatorship as Experience: Towards a Socio-Cultural History of the GDR* (New York and Oxford, 1999), 125–43.

38. Heinz Niemann, *Meinungsforschung in der DDR* (Cologne, 1993).

39. '"Geh'n Sie doch rüber, sträuben Sie sich nicht länger!" Sechs aus der DDR ausgebürgerte Sozialisten berichten', *Berliner Hefte: Zeitschrift für Kultur und Politik*, 6 (1978), 110–11.

40. The quotations derive from Orlando Figes, *Whisperers*, 2, 4.

41. See e.g. 'Spionage des "Sozialen Helferrings"', *Berliner Zeitung*, 26 Jan. 1950; 'Die Spionage- und Terrorzentralen in Westberlin', *Tägliche Rundschau*, 22 May 1952, and 'Amerikanisches Spionzentrum in der DDR zerschlagen', *Neues Deutschland*, 23 Sept. 1953.

42. 'Hausbuch für die Deutsche Demokratische Republik', *Der Tag*, 20 Dec. 1952.

43. Detlef Schmiechen-Ackermann, 'Der "Blockwart": Die unteren Parteifunktionäre im nationalsozialistischen Terror- und Überwachungsapparat', *Vierteljahreshefte für Zeitgeschichte*, 48/4 (2000), 575–602.

44. Michael Kater, *The Nazi Party: A Social Profile of Members and Leaders, 1919–1945* (Oxford, 1983), 192ff.

45. Murphy *et al.*, *Battleground Berlin*, 6.

46. Karl Bönninger, *Die Einrichtung der Haus- und Strassenvertrauensleute als Form der Teilnahme der Massen an der Leitung des Staates in der DDR* (Berlin, 1954), 15–86.

47. 'Büro des Präsidiums des Nationalrats der Nationalen Front des demokratischen Deutschland', Berlin, 15 May 1953, Bundesarchiv Berlin (BAB) DY6/0189.

48. According to one 1953 report, members of one Berlin Hausgemeinschaft helped 'motivate' the local residents by means of music and chanting the following refrain: 'Alles aus den Betten raus, wir kommen jetzt in Euer Haus! / Auf jeden von Euch

kommt es an, den Besten als Vertrauensmann!' 'Informationsbericht, Berlin, 30.3.53', DY 6/4626, BAB.

49. 'Vertrauliches Schreiben!', memo from the Ausschuss der Nationalen Front des demokratischen Deutschlands der Hauptstadt Berlin zur 1. Sekretäre der Stadtbezirke des demokratischen Sektors', 19 June 1953, DY6 /4626, BAB.

50. 'Protokoll der Tagung der Berliner Ausschusses der Nationalen Front am Montag, den 24. Juli 1961', 3–4, DY 6/2529, BAB.

51. 'Direktiv für die Tätigkeit einer Brigade des Nationalrats in Karl-Marx-Stadt Berlin', Büro des Präsidium, 2 Dec. 1961, DY 6/0189, BAB.

52. Untitled and unsigned typed letter, C Rep 104/476, Landesarchiv Berlin (LAB).

53. Karl-Heinz B, Eisenach, questionnaire, 15 May 2007.

54. Dorothee Wierling, 'Youth as Internal Enemy: Conflicts in the Education Dictatorship of the 1960s', in Katherine Pence and Paul Betts (eds.), *Socialist Modern: East German Everyday Culture and Politics* (Ann Arbor, 2008), 157–82.

55. 'Abschrift: Übersicht über die Meinung der einzelnen Kreise über die Tätigkeit der Kirchen unter der Jugend, 20.1.1948', MfS Allg. S 1030/ 67, Stasi-Archiv Berlin (SAB).

56. Abschlussbericht zum Operativ-Vorgang 'Burg', 14 Mar. 1978, MfS HA XX/4/ 2545, SAB.

57. MfS HA XX/4 2764, SAB.

58. MfS BV Berlin XX 3236, SAB.

59. 'Mein Name ist Günter C: Tonbandprotokoll eines politischen Häftlings aus der DDR', *Deutsche Zeitung* (West), 12 Feb. 1978, 21 and 'Carsten Lober: Schicksal eines Christen im "anderen Deutschland"', *Deutsche Evangelische Zeitung*, 15 Sept. 1979, 55.2/56, Landeskirchenarchiv Berlin (LKAB).

60. Childs and Popplewell, *Stasi*, 109.

61. Herbert Kietz and Manfred Mühlmann, *Konfliktursachen und Aufgaben der Zivil- und Familienrechtspflege* (East Berlin, 1969).

62. J. Ellinger, E. Lange, S. Petzold, and O. Schaefer, *Eingabenarbeit heute* (East Berlin, 1967), 81.

63. Thomas Lindenberger, 'Das Fremde im Eigenen des Staatssozialismus: Klassendiskurs und Exclusion am Beispiel der Konstruktion des "asozialen Verhaltens",' in Jan C. Behrends, Thomas Lindenberger, and Patrice Poutrus (eds.), *Fremde und Fremd-Sein in der DDR* (Berlin, 2003), 179–91.

64. Greg Eghigian, 'Homo Munitus', in Katherine Pence and Paul Betts (ed.), *Socialist Modern* (Ann Arbor, 2008), 37–70.

65. Ermittlungsbericht, BV für Staatssicherheit, Abt. VIII, Leipzig 31 Jan. 1988, MfS HA XX/4/3692, SAB.

66. Gieseke, *Mielke-Konzern,* 146.

67. Thomas Lindenberger, *Volkspolizei: Herrschaftspraxis und öffentliche Ordnung im SED-Staat, 1952–1968* (Cologne, 2003), 104–33, and Michel Christian, 'Ausschliessen und disziplinieren: Kontrollpraxis in den kommunistischen Partei der DDR und der Tschechoslowakei', in Sandrine Kott and Emmanuel Droit, *Die ostdeutsche Gesellschaft: Eine transatlantische Perspektive* (Berlin, 2006), 64–5.

68. Oleg Kharkhordin, *The Collective and the Individual in Russia* (Berkeley, Calif., 1999), 35–74.

69. Czeslaw Milosz, *The Captive Mind*, tr. Jane Zielonko (New York, 1981 [1951]), 75.

70. Fulbrook, *Anatomy*, 69.

71. Quoted in Travis Wolfe, *Policing*, 72.

72. Vera Wollenberger, 'Eine zweite Vergewaltigung', repr. in Hans-Joachim Schädlich (ed.), *Aktenkündig* (Berlin, 1992), 163.

73. Cited in Dennis, *Stasi*, 80.

74. Alison Lewis, 'En-Gendering Remembrance: Memory, Gender and Informers for the Stasi', *New German Critique*, 86 (Spring Summer 2002), 113–15. See too Belinda Cooper, 'Patriarchy within a Patriarchy: Women and the Stasi', *German Politics and Society*, 16/2 (1998), 1–31.

75. Barbara Miller, *Narratives of Guilt and Compliance in Unified Germany: Stasi Informers and their Impact on Society* (London, 1999), 20.

76. MfS HA XX/4/426, SAB.

77. Dennis, *Stasi*, 86–87.

78. Dagmar Herzog, 'East Germany' Sexual Evolution', in Pence and Betts, *Socialist Modern*, 79.

79. Andrew I. Port, 'Love, Lust and Lies under Communism: Family Values and Adulterous Liaisons in the German Democratic Republic', *Central European History*, forthcoming.

80. Felix Mühlberg, 'Die Partei ist eifersüchtig', in Katrin Rohnstock (ed.), *Erotik macht die Hässlichen schön* (Berlin, 1995), 122–43.

81. Timothy Garton Ash, *The File: A Personal History* (London, 1997), 174.

82. Barbara Bronnen and Franz Henny, *Liebe, Ehe, Sexualität: Interviews und Dokumente* (Munich, 1975), 36.

83. Sibylle Meyer and Eva Schulze, *Familien im Umbruch: Zur Lage der Familien in der ehemaligen DDR* (Stuttgart, 1992), 75.

84. Hans M., Berlin, questionnaire, 29 June 2005.

85. Jens Reich, 'Sicherheit oder Feigheit—der Kaefer im Brennglas', in Walter Süss and Siegfried Suckut (eds.), *Staatspartei und Staatssicherheit: Zum Verhältnis von SED und MfS* (Berlin, 1997), 25–37.

86. Jürgen Fuchs, 'Ich du er sie wir ihr sie: Eine "Kontaktierungs" Revue', *Kursbuch* (Mar. 1994), 41–58.

87. Freya Klier, *Abreiss-Kalender: Versuch eines Tagebuchs* (Munich, 1988), 262–72.

88. Robert Havemann Nachlass, RH 071, Matthias-Domaschk-Archiv in der Robert-Havemann-Gesellschaft e.V, Berlin (MDA).

89. Claudia Rusch, *Meine Freie Deutsche Jugend* (Frankfurt, 2003), 16–20.

90. Joachim Gauck, *Die Stasi-Akten: Das unheimliche Erbe der DDR* (Reinbek bei Hamburg, 1991), 26.

91. Dirk Verheyen, *United City, Divided Memories? Cold War Legacies in Contemporary Berlin* (Lanham, Md., 2008), 145.

92. Miller, *Narratives*, 101.

93. Robert Gellately, 'Denunciations in Twentieth Century Germany: Aspects of Self-Policing in the Third Reich and the German Democratic Republic', *Journal of Modern History*, 68/4 (Dec. 1996), 964.

94. Dietmar Riemann, 'Tagebuch einer Ausreise, 1986–1996', Nr 999, Deutsches Tagebuch-Archiv, Emmindingen (DTA).

95. Alison Owings, *Frauen: German Women Recall the Third Reich* (New Brunswick, NJ, 1993), 373–4.

96. Gertraud T., questionnaire, Berlin, 19 July 2005.

97. Paul Franzel, 'Mein Leben mit SED und Stasi im Nacken', 1995, 10/2, DTA.

98. Herbert Walter Rettig, 'Tagebücher, 1945–1960', Nr. 832/1–13, DTA; Anneliese Knappe, 'Jahre der Hoffnung, 1939–1955', Nr. 1194, DTA; as well as Riemann, unpaginated.

99. Marianne Wenzel, 'Aus dem Leben eines heimlichen Trinkers, Erfurt', Leipzig 1966, Nr. 718/1, and Wenzel, 'Gepeinigte Frauen, 1969', with additions by Marina Fiedler, Nr. 718/2, DTA.

100. Eva Schaefer, 'Tagebücher, 1958–1989', Nr. 93, DTA.

101. Gustav Rene Hocke, *Das europäische Tagebuch* (Wiesbaden, 1963).

102. See too Peter Fritzsche, *Life and Death in the Third Reich* (Cambridge, Mass., 2008).

103. Alexandra Garbarini, *Numbered Days: Diaries and the Holocaust* (New Haven, Conn., 2006) and Lawrence Langer, *Holocaust Testimonies: The Ruins of Memory* (New Haven, Conn., 1991).

104. Gustav Just, *Zeuge in Eigener Sache* (Berlin, 1990), 16–17.

105. Riemann, unpaginated.

106. Josie McLellan, *Antifascism and Memory in East Germany* (Oxford, 2004).

107. *Zwischenbericht: Eine Brigade, ihr Tagebuch und der Zirkel schreibender Arbeiter* (Leipzig, 1969), 5.

108. Dennis Tate, *Shifting Perspectives: East German Autobiographical Narratives Before and After the End of the GDR* (Rochester, NY, 2007).

109. Christiane M., Berlin, interview, 20 Apr. 2007; Ruth P., Berlin, interview, 30 Mar. 2007; and Renate S., Berlin, interview, 7 Mar. 2007.

110. Miller, *Narratives,* 95–6.

111. Childs and Popplewell, *Stasi,* 175.

112. Koehler, *Stasi,* 142.

113. 'Erste politisch-operative Auswertung der Schlussakte der Konferenz über Sicherheit und Zusammenarbeit in Europa', Berlin, 6 Aug. 1975, and 'Auswertung der Schlussakte der KSZE und erste politisch-operative Schlussfolgerungen', Berlin, 4 Sept. 1975, MfS HA XX/4/2343, SAB.

114. MfS HA XX/4/426, SAB.

115. 'Information: Veranstaltungen des Menschenrechtsprogramms der Kirchen zur Verwirklichung der Schlussakte von Helsinki vom 21. 11 bis 29.11.1984 in Eisenach, Bezirk Erfurt, 30.11.1984', MfS HA XX/4/1255, SAB.

116. Gieseke, *Mielke-Konzern,* 70.

117. Childs and Popplewell, *Stasi,* 176.

118. Gareth Dale, *Popular Protest in East Germany* (London, 2005), 122.

119. Uta Falck, *VEB Bordell* (Berlin, 1998).

120. Macrakis, *Seduced by Secrets,* 142–317.

121. Dennis, *Stasi,* 29.

122. Fulbrook, *Anatomy,* 27.

123. Sandra Pingel-Schliemann, *Zersetzen: Strategie einer Diktatur* (Berlin, 2003), 61–71.

124. Stichwort 'Zersetzung, operative', in Siegfried Suckut, *Das Wörterbuch der Staatssicherheit* (Berlin, 1996), 422.
125. Eghigian, 'Homo Munitus', 51–4.
126. Agnes Bensussan, 'Einige Characteristika der Repressionspolitik gegenüber politisch abweichendem Verhalten in der DDR in den 70er und 80er Jahren', in Kott and Droit, *Die ostdeutsche Gesellschaft*, 74.
127. Cited in Steven Pfaff, *Exit-Voice Dynamics and the Collapse of East Germany* (Durham, 2006), 71.
128. Gieseke, *Mielke-Konzern*, 186.
129. Renate Ellmenreich, 'Operative-Psychologische Strategien gegen Frauen', in Annette Maennel (ed.), *Frauen im Visier der Stasi* (Berlin, 1994), 8–18.
130. Instructions on how to conduct a thorough house search can be found in the internal People's Police booklet, *Die Durchsuchung und die Beschlagnahme* (Berlin, 1978). I thank Eli Rubin for this reference.
131. Dennis, *Stasi*, 113.
132. Pingel-Schliemann, *Zersetzen*, 196.
133. Reiner Kunze, *Deckname 'Lyrik'* (Frankfurt, 1990), 87–9. See too Erich Loest, *Die Stasi war mein Eckermann* (Göttingen, 1992).
134. Childs and Popplewell, *Stasi*, 110.
135. Pingel-Schliemann, *Zersetzen*, 362, 227.
136. Dennis, *Stasi*, 120, 137.
137. Childs and Popplewell, *Stasi*, 82.
138. Ibid. 62.
139. Dennis, *Stasi*, 218.
140. Milovan Djilas, 'The New Class', excerpted in Gale Stokes (ed.), *From Stalinism to Pluralism: A Documentary History of Eastern Europe since 1945* (Oxford, 1991), 103.
141. Martin Diewald, '"Kollektiv," "Vitamin B" und "Nische"? Persönliche Netzwerke in der DDR', in Johannes Huinink (ed.), *Kollektiv und Eigensinn* (Berlin, 1995), 223–60.
142. Jonathan Zatlin, *The Currency of Socialism* (Cambridge, 2007), 243–85.
143. Annette Kaminsky, 'Ungleichheit in der SBZ/DDR am Beispiel des Konsums: Versandhandel, Intershop and Delikat', in Lothar Mertens (ed.), *Soziale Ungleichheit in der DDR: Zu einem tabusierten Strukturmerkmal der SED-Diktatur* (Berlin, 2002), 57.
144. Dennis, *Stasi*, 217.
145. Maier, *Dissolution*, 40.
146. Travis Wolfe, *Policing*, 79.
147. Olaf Stieglitz, 'Sprachen der Wachsamkeit: Loyalitätskontrolle und Denunziation in der DDR und in den USA bis Mitte der 1950er Jahre', *Historical Social Research*, 26/2–3 (2001), 132.
148. Gellately, 'Denunciations', 959.
149. Excellent is the special issue on 'Practices of Denunciation in Modern European History, 1789–1989', ed. Sheila Fitzpatrick and Robert Gellately, in *Journal of Modern History* 68/4 (Dec. 1996) as well as Günter Jerouschek, Inge Marssolek, and Hedwig Röcklein (eds.), *Denunziation: Historische, juristische und psychologische Aspekte* (Tübingen, 1997).

150. Horst Luther, 'Denunziation als soziales und strafrechtliches Problem in Deutschland in den Jahren 1945–1990', in Jerouschek *et al.*, *Denunziation*, 259.

151. Irina Scherbakowa, 'Die Denunziation im Gedächtnis und in den Archiv-dokumenten', in Jerouschek *et al.*, *Denunziation*, 168–72.

152. Figes, *Whisperers*, 38.

153. Fitzpatrick, 'Signals from Below: Soviet Letters of Denunciation in the 1930s', *Journal of Modern History*, 68/4 (1996), 117.

154. Fred Hahn, *Lieber Stürmer: Lesebriefe an das NS-Kampfblatt 1924 bis 1945* (Stuttgart, 1978).

155. Klaus-Michael Mallmann and Gerhard Paul, 'Omniscient, Omnipotent, Omnipresent? Gestapo, Society and Resistance', in David Crew (ed.), *Nazism and German Society* (New York, 1994), 166–96.

156. Sace Elder, 'Murder, Denunciation and Criminal Policing in Weimar Berlin', *Journal of Contemporary History*, 41/3 (2006), 406–7.

157. Gellately, 'Denunciations', 934–44. See also Pamela E. Swett, *Neighbors and Enemies: The Culture of Radicalism in Berlin, 1929–1933* (New York, 2004), 214–31.

158. Katrin Dördelmann, 'Denunziation im Nationalsozialismus: Geschlechtsspezifische Aspekte', in Jerouschek *et al.*, *Denunziation*, 161.

159. Gisela Diewald-Kerkmann, *Politische Denunziation im NS-Regime, oder die kleine Macht der 'Volksgenossen'* (Bonn, 1995).

160. John Connelly, 'The Uses of the the Volksgemeinschaft: Letters to the NSDAP Kreisleitung Eisenach, 1939–1940', *Journal of Modern History*, 68/4 (Dec. 1996), 899–930.

161. Elder, 'Murder', 413.

162. Klaus Behnke and Jürgen Wolf, 'Die Auserwählten,' in Behnke and Fuchs, *Zersetzung der Seele*, 329.

163. Cited in Gellately, 'Denunciations', 961.

164. Diewald-Kerkmann, *Politische Denunziation*, 131.

165. Helmut Müller-Enbergs (ed.), *Inoffiziele Mitarbeiter des Ministeriums für Staatssicherheit: Richtlinien und Durchführungsbestimmungen* (Berlin, 1996), 23–4.

166. Gieseke, *Mielke-Konzern*, 56.

167. Brigitte Reimann, *Ich bedauere nichts: Tagebücher, 1955–1963* (Berlin, 2001), 85–6, 103.

168. Helmut Müller-Enbergs, 'Warum wird einer IM? Zur Motivation bei der inoffiziellen Zusammenarbeit mit dem Staatssicherheitsdienst', in Behnke and Fuchs, *Zersetzung der Seele,* 111–12.

169. Miller, *Narratives*, 55–64.

170. Klaus Behnke and Jürgen Wolf (eds.), *Stasi auf dem Schulhof: Der Missbrauch von Kindern und Jugendlichen durch das Minsterium für Staatssicherheit* (Berlin, 1998), 13.

171. Niemann, *Meinungsforschung*, 56.

172. Dennis, *Stasi*, 97–101.

173. Müller-Enbergs, 'Warum', 104–5.

174. Cited in Gieseke, *Mielke-Konzern*, 125–6.

175. Scherbakowa, 'Die Denunziation', 180, and Müller-Enbergs, 'Warum', 105.

176. Miller, *Narratives*, 45.

177. Childs and Popplewell, *Stasi*, 109.

178. Miller, *Narratives,* 68–9.

179. Annette Maennel, *Auf sie was Verlass: Frauen und Stasi* (Berlin, 1995), 67 and 114.

180. Reiner Kunze, *Deckname 'Lyrik'* (Frankfurt, 1990), 39–40, 73–4.

181. Childs and Popplewell, *Stasi*, 111.

182. Vera Wollenberger, 'Eine zweite Vergewaltigung', and Günther Kunert, 'Meine Nachbarn', both reprinted in Hans-Joachim Schädlich (ed.), *Aktenkündig* (Berlin, 1992), 162 and 48–9, respectively.

183. Klaus Hartung, 'Infamie und Vergangenheit: Schnur, Rühe und die Selbstbestimmung', *Die Tagezeitung,* 15 Mar. 1990.

184. Stephen Kotkin, *Magnetic Mountain: Stalinism as a Civilization* (Berkeley, Calif., 1995), esp. ch. 5.

185. James C. Scott, *Seeing like a State: How Certain Schemes to Improve the Human Condition have Failed* (New Haven, Conn., 1998), 32.

186. Jürgen Habermas, 'Bemerkungen zu einer verworren Diskussion', *Die Zeit,* 10 Apr. 1992, 17–19.

187. Lindenberger, 'Creating', 126.

188. Gieseke, *Mielke-Konzern,* 122, 157.

189. Klaus Behnke, 'Die Ohnmacht der Kinder', in Behnke and Wolf, *Stasi auf dem Schulhof,* 177.

190. Hans Fuchs, 'Erlebtes, Erinnerungen, Gedanken', 1996, p. 18, Nr. 64, DTA.

191. Alexander von Plato, 'Denunziation im Systemwechsel: Verhaftete, Deportierte, Lagerhäflinge in der SBZ um 1945', *Historical Social Research,* 26/2–3 (2001), 201.

192. Kharkhordin, *Collective,* 270.

193. Scott, *Seeing like a State,* 101.

NOTES TO CHAPTER 2

1. U. Jeremias, *Die Jugendweihe in der Sowjetzone* (Bonn, 1958) and Hans Köhler, *Christentum und Jugendweihe* (Bonn, 1958). For English versions, Robert Tobias, *Communist–Christian Encounter in East Europe* (Indianapolis, 1956), 524–50 and Richard W. Solberg, *God and Caesar in East Germany* (New York, 1961).

2. The Federal Republic's 1990s Enquete Commission dedicated two volumes to the role of the Church in the GDR. *Materielien der Enquete-Kommission 'Aufarbeitung von Geschichte und Folgen der SED-Diktatur in Deutschland',* vi. *Kirchen in der SED-Dikatur,* 1–2 (Baden-Baden, 1995).

3. Friedrich Wilhelm Graf, 'Eine Ordnungsmacht eigener Art: Theologie und Kirchenpolitik im DDR-Protestantismus', in Hartmut Kaelble, Jürgen Kocka, and Hartmut Zwahr (eds.), *Sozialgeschichte der DDR* (Stuttgart, 1994), 305.

4. Most important are Gerhard Besier, *Der SED-Staat und die Kirche: Der Weg in die Anpassung* (Munich, 1993); Robert F. Goeckel, *The Lutheran Church and the East German State: Political Conflict and Change under Ulbricht and Honecker* (Ithaca, NY, 1990); Horst Dähn, *Konfrontation oder Kooperation? Das Verhältnis von Staat und Kirche in der SBZ/DDR 1945–1980* (Opladen, 1982); Reinhard Henkys (ed.), *Die evangelischen Kirchen in der DDR* (Munich, 1982) and Frederic Spotts, *The Churches and Politics in Germany* (Middletown, Conn., 1973).

5. Albrecht Döhnert, 'Die Jugendweihe', in *Deutsche Erinnerungsorte III*, ed. Etienne Francois and Hagen Schulze (Munich, 2001), 347–60.

6. Christiane Griese, '*Bin ich ein guter Staatsbürger, wenn ich mein Kind nicht zur Jugendweihe schicke*': *Die Deutung von Phänomenen der Erziehungsrealität in Berichten an die Volksbildungsadministration der DDR-Analyse. Analyse von Wahrnehmungsmustern und Handlungsstrategien im Umgang mit kirchlicher Jugendarbeit* (Baltmannsweiler, 2001); Georg Diederich, Bernd Schäfer, and Jörg Ohlemacher, *Jugendweihe in der DDR: Geschichte und politische Bedeutung aus christlicher Sicht* (Schwerin, 1998); Christian Fischer, *Wir haben Eurer Verlöbnis vernommen: Konfirmation und Jugendweihe im Spannungsfeld* (Leipzig, 1998); Detlef Urban and Hans Willi Weinzen, *Jugend ohne Bekenntnis? 30 Jahre Konfirmation und Jugendweihe im anderen Deutschland 1954–1984* (Berlin, 1984); and Bo Hallberg, *Die Jugendweihe: Zur deutschen Jugendweihetradition* (Göttingen, 1979).

7. Johannes Hamel, *A Christian in East Germany* (London, 1960), 18–20.

8. Ibid. 125–6. See too Karl Barth and Johannes Hamel, *How to Serve God in a Marxist Land* (New York, 1959).

9. Czeslaw Milosz, *The Captive Mind*, tr. Jane Zielonko (New York, 1981 [1951]), 60, 80.

10. Spotts, *Churches and Politics*, x.

11. Quoted ibid. 99.

12. Diederich *et al.*, *Jugendweihe*, 6.

13. Detlef Pollack, 'The Situation of Religion in Eastern Germany After 1989', in Patricia J. Smith (ed.), *After the Wall: Eastern Germany After 1989* (Boulder, Colo., 1998), 162.

14. 'Abschrift: Übersicht über die Meinung der einzelnen Kreise über die Tätigkeit der Kirchen unter der Jugend, 20. 1. 1948', MfS Allg. S 1030/67, MfS, Stasi-Archiv, Berlin (SAB).

15. Propst Heinrich Grüber, *Erinnerungen aus sieben Jahrzehnten* (Berlin, 1968), 327–8.

16. Anselm and Gundula Tietsch, *Die 40 Jahre: Erinnerungen an 40 Jahren als Pfarrer in der DDR* (1996), 9, Landeskirchenarchiv, Berlin (LKAB).

17. 'Betr: Sachgebiet Kirche—Bericht über die jungsten aktuellsten negativen Ereignisse, Verwaltung Sachsen, Dresden, 12. 10. 1950', MfS/AS 180/66, SAB.

18. MfS HA XX/4/426, SAB.

19. Spotts, *Churches and Politics*, 208–12.

20. Solberg, *God and Caesar*, 39.

21. Mary Fulbrook, *Anatomy of a Dictatorship* (Oxford, 1995), 92.

22. Spotts, *Churches and Politics*, 184–6.

23. Harsch, *Revenge*, 205.

24. Ibid. 206–7.

25. Ibid. 210.

26. *Kleines Politisches Wörterbuch* (Berlin, 1978), 416, quoted in Fulbrook, *Anatomy*, 95.

27. Richard Stites, *Revolutionary Dreams: Utopian Vision and Experimental Life in the Russian Revolution* (Berkeley, Calif., 1989), 109–14.

28. Klemens Richter, 'Toten-Liturgie: Der Umgang mit Tod und Trauer in der Bestattungsriten der DDR', in Hansjakob Becker, Bernhard Einig, and Peter-Otto Ullrich (eds.), *Im Angesicht des Todes: Ein interdisziplinares Kompendium* (St. Ottilien, 1987), 242–55.

29. Hallberg, *Die Jugendweihe,* 75.

30. Joachim Chowanski and Rolf Dreier, *Die Jugendweihe: Eine Kulturgeschichte seit 1852* (Berlin, n.d.), 45–60.

31. Marina Chauliac, 'Die Jugendweihe zwischen familiarem und politischem Erbe der DDR: Zur Erfindung einer neuen Tradition', in Sandrine Kott and Emmanuel Droit (eds.), *Die ostdeutsche Gesellschaft: Eine transatlantische Perspective* (Berlin, 2006), 203.

32. Walter Ulbricht, 'Geleitwort', *Weltall* (1954), 2.

33. Fischer, *Eurer Verlöbnis,* 48–57.

34. Quoted ibid. 92.

35. Chauliac, 'Jugendweihe', 204.

36. *Wie gestalten wir unser persönliches Leben,* Material für die 8. Jugendstunde (Berlin, 1956), 4.

37. Ibid., as well as Jeremias, *Jugendweihe,* 60.

38. *Wir sehen und erleben, wie die Arbeiter und Bauern unseren Staat regieren, oder Wir lieben unsere Deutsche Demokratische Republik,* Material für die 9. Jugendweihe (Berlin, 1957), 18.

39. 'Programm der Jugendstunden', *Jugendweihe,* 10/6–7 (1964/5), 4–7.

40. Arvan Gordon, 'Recent Trends in the GDR Jugendweihe: State and Church Attitudes', *Religion in Communist Lands,* 13/2 (1985), 157–65.

41. Dorothee Wierling, *Geboren im Jahr Eins* (Berlin, 2002), 245.

42. Döhnert, *Jugendweihe,* 140.

43. *Jugendstunde: Der Sozialismus siegt!* (Berlin, 1962) and *Hinweise, Anregungen, Materielien zur Gestaltung sozialistischen Feierstunden* (Berlin, 1963).

44. Informationskontrolle an Magistrat von Gross-Berlin, Amt für Information, 12.10.1951, C Rep 104/576, LAB.

45. ''Jugendweihe—Eintritt ins Leben', *Berliner Zeitung,* 9 Dec. 1954.

46. Letter from Jugendweihe-Aussschuss an Liebe Eltern!, Finsterwalde, Feb. 1955, 35/532. LKABB.

47. Döhnert, *Jugendweihe,* 129.

48. Hans Mickinn, 'Wir dulden keine Verletzung der Verfassung', *Märkische Volkstimme,* 16 Dec. 1955.

49. Abschrift aus 'Ostsee-Zeitung', Greifswald, 10 Jan. 1955, 35/532, LKAB.

50. Jeremias, *Jugendweihe,* 72.

51. Urban and Weinzen, *Jugend ohne Bekenntnis?,* 119.

52. 'Abschrift Jugendweihe von Ev. Konsistorium Berlin-Brandenburg', 18 Oct. 1955, typescript, 35/532. LKAB.

53. Letter from Pfarrer Dr. Schmidt an den Kreisaussschuss für Jugendweihe im Kreis Spremberg, 12 Feb. 1955, 35/532. LKAB.

54. Döhnert, *Jugendweihe,* 127.

55. 'Kirchenleitung der Evangelischen Kirche in Berlin-Brandenburg an die Gemeinden der Evangelischen Kirche in Berlin-Brandenburg', 30 Nov. 1954, 35/532. LKAB.

56. Döhnert, *Jugendweihe,* 127.

57. 'Abschrift der Ev. Kirche in Deutschland', Kirchenkanzlei, Berlin Stelle, Betr. Elternversammlung, 29 Aug. 1955, 35/532. LKAB.

58. Döhnert, *Jugendweihe,* 142.

59. 'Bischofliches Ordinariat Berlin an Magistrat von Gross-Berlin z. Hd des Stellvertreters des Herrn Oberbürgermeisters Herrn Fechmer', 5 Mar. 1956, as well as 'Abschrift der Bischof von Berlin', 25 Aug. 1958, C Rep 104/576. LAB.

60. 'Werbung für die Jugendweihe: Beeinflussung in Ferienlagern—Sollzahlen wurden nicht erreicht', *Die Welt*, 4 July 1956.

61. See in particular C Rep 104/282, LAB.

62. Most influential was A. S. Makarenko, *Ein Buch für Eltern* (Berlin, 1966 [1958]). For his influence, see Sheila Fitzpatrick, *The Cultural Front: Power and Culture in Revolutionary Russia* (Ithaca, NY, 1992), 250–6.

63. *Schule und Elternhaus in der Sowjetunion: Methodische Anleitungen des Deutschen Pädagogischen Zentralinstituts zur Weiterbildung aller Lehrer und Erzieher* (Berlin, 1952), 9–11.

64. Ibid. 25.

65. 'Telegram des Ministers Wandel', *Elternhaus und Schule,* 1/1 (Mar. 1952), 11.

66. See *Elternhaus und Schule: Erfahrungsaustausch über die Zusammenarbeit zwischen Lehrern und Eltern* (Berlin, 1961).

67. Hans Kleffe, 'Lohn und Strafe', *Elternhaus und Schule,* 1/2 (Apr. 1952), 4–5.

68. 'Kinder brauchen Taktgefühl', *Elternhaus und Schule,* 20/1 (Jan. 1971), 23, and 'Wenn Eltern Schimpfen', *Elternhaus und Schule,* 12/83 (Dec. 1983), 10–11.

69. In 1966 the journal introduced a set of short publications on child-raising under the title, *Kleine pädagogische Bibliothek für Eltern.* See too Margot Besse, *Die Zusammenarbeit zwischen Krippe und Elternhaus* (Berlin, 1978).

70. 'Der Evangelische Bischof von Berlin: Kammer für Erziehung und Unterricht an "'Sehr verehrter Herr Amtbrüder!"', Oct. 1945, Anlage 4, 1.02.04/104 Gnaden-Kirchengemeinde, LKAB.

71. 'Handreichung für die Kirchliche Erziehungswoche vom 20. bis 26. April 1947', 1.02.04/104 Gnaden-Kirchengemeinde, LKAB.

72. Alfred Jagielski, 'Bericht von einer Versammlung der christlichen Kirche in Bohnsdorf aus Anlass der Elternausssschusswahlen', 14 Oct. 1951, C Rep 104/576, LAB.

73. 'Die Evangelische Kirchenleitung Berlin-Brandenburg an die Gemeindekirchenräte in unserem Kirchengebiet', 16 Jan. 1964, C Rep 104/576, LAB.

74. Cited in Jeremias, *Jugendweihe,* 99.

75. Jens Reich, 'Das Schneckenhaus Freiheit nach innen: Anpassung nach aussen', *Berliner Zeitung,* 15/16 (June 2002), 4–5.

76. Interviews with Christiane M., 20 Apr. 2007, Berlin; Ruth P., 30 Mar. 2007, Berlin; and Renate S., 7 Mar. 2007, Hans-Otto F., 30 Jan. 2007, Bernd A., 29 Jan. 2007, Berlin. I also made use of information provided in eight questionnaires on Christian private life distributed to a Protestant congregation in Eisenach, courtesy of Angela Brock.

77. 'Volkspolizei-Inspection Lichtenberg—Abteilung Erlaubniswesen—an das PdVP Berlin, Abt. Erlaubniswesen, Lichtenberg', 22 Dec. 1958, C Rep 104/576, LAB.

78. Christoph Klessmann, 'Relikte des Bildungsbürgertums in der DDR', in Kaelble *et al., Sozialgeschichte der DDR,* 265–6.

79. 'Kampf gegen die Spionage- und Agentenorganisation "Junge Gemeinde"', 1954, p. 6, no other publishing info. File 55.2/217, LKAB.

80. Sabine Gries, '"Negative" Jugendliche: Jugenddeliquenz in der DDR aus der Sicht des Ministeriums für Staatssicherheit', in Lothar Mertens and Sabine Gries (eds.), *Arbeit, Sport und DDR-Gesellschaft* (Berlin, 1996), 147–72.

81. 'Bericht über die Arbeitstagung der Kirchenteilung am 27.2.1958 über das Thema Konfirmation—Jugendweihe', Abteilung für Innere Angelegenheiten/Referat Gesellschaftsfragen, Berlin, C Rep 104/93, LAB.

82. Jeremias, *Jugendweihe*, 9.

83. *Pseudosakrale Staatsakte in der Sowjetzone* (Bonn, 1959), 14.

84. *Der Liebe Gott und der Sputnik* (Berlin, 1958).

85. Quoted in Jeremias, *Jugendweihe*, 95.

86. 'Zur Jahreswende', *Jugendweihe*, 4/12 (1958), 8.

87. Günter Vogel, *Als Pfarrer in der DDR: Erlebnisse zwischen 1948–1990* (Berlin, 1992), 34, and Hans-Martin Krusche, *Pfarrer in der DDR: Gespräche über Kirche und Politik* (Berlin, 2002), 362.

88. Klaus Hugler, *Missbrauchtes Vertrauen: Christliche Jugendarbeit unter den Augen der Stasi* (Neukirchen-Vluyn, 1994), 35–6.

89. Quoted in Krusche, *Pfarrer*, 82–3.

90. Solberg, *God and Caesar*, 233.

91. Jeremias, *Jugendweihe*, 32.

92. Solberg, *God and Caesar*, 233–8.

93. Erwin Heretsch, *Gegen den Strom: Notizen eines DDR-Christen* (Leipzig, 1998), 39–40.

94. Jeremias, *Jugendweihe*, 10.

95. Circular from Evangelisches Konsistorium, Berlin-Brandenburg an alle Pfarrerämter der Evangelischer Kirche, Berlin-Brandenburg, 27 Sept./Jan. 1956, Gnaden-Kirchengemeinde, 1 02 04, 106, LKAB.

96. D. Mitzenheim, 'Wort des Landesbischofs an die Gemeinden', Sammelrundschreiben 9/55, May 1955, 55.2/217, LKAB.

97. Beglaubigte Abschrift an den Kirchenrat von Buckow/Mark. Schweiz, 25 Jan. 1955, 35/532. LKAB.

98. 'Einschreiben an das Evang. Konsistorium, Berlin', 19 Nov. 1956, 35/532. LKAB.

99. 'Not-Konfirmation wird abgelehnt: Zwang zur Jugendweihe bedrängt vielen Familien', *Welt*, 31 Dec. 1960.

100. 'Kirchliche Erziehungskammer für Berlin an den Magistrat von Gross-Berlin, Amt für Gesellschaftsfragen', 21 April 1959, LAB C Rep 104/576, and 'Erfüllungsbericht zum Arbeitsplan des Referates Gesellschaftsfragen III. Quartal 1955', Berlin, 19 Oct. 1955, C Rep 104/93. LAB.

101. 'Der Kirchenkampf in der Sowjetzone: Evangelische Kirche unter wachsendem Druck, Misserfolg der "Jugendweihen"', *Süddeutsche Zeitung*, 4 May 1955, and 'Kinder in der Entscheidung: Jugendweihe und Konfirmation in der Zone', *Frankfurter Allgemeine Zeitung*, 16 May 1955, unpaginated.

102. *Pseudosakrale Staatsakte in der Sowjetzone* (Bonn, 1959), as well as Köhler, *Christentum und Jugendweihe* (Bonn, 1958).

103. 'Auch Pfarrer müssen sich entscheiden: Bürger des Ostseebezirkes sagen ihre Meinung', *Ostsee-Zeitung*, 9 Dec. 1957.

104. 'Offener Brief an Frau Huschenhoefer und andere Muetter in Marnitz und Umgebung', 6 July 1958, from Direktor Walter Awe, Stellv. Direktor Kurt Fischer and Frau Eva Buenger, 55.2/217, LKAB.

105. Christoph Klessmann, 'Evangelische Pfarrer im Sozialismus—Soziale Stellung und politische Bedeutung in der DDR', in L. Schorn-Schuette and W. Sparn (eds.), *Evangelische Pfarrer: Zur sozialen und politischen Rolle einer bürgerlichen Gruppe in der deutschen Gesellschaft des 18. bis 20. Jahrhunderts* (Stuttgart, 1997), 192. See too his edited *Kinder der Opposition: Berichte aus Pfarrhäusern in der DDR* (Gütersloh, 1993).

106. Krusche, *Pfarrer*, 35.

107. Interview with Christiane M., 20 Apr. 2007, Berlin.

108. Vogel, *Als Pfarrer,* 100–1.

109. Quoted in Krusche, *Pfarrer*, 53.

110. Karl-Heinz Eber, 'Begegnungen mit "daruben" (DDR)', West German Minister from Nurnberg, unpublished MS 1991–2, CX 16, LKAB, and Fischer, *Eurer Verlöbnis,* 100–1.

111. Norbert Schneider, *Familie und private Lebensführung in West- und Ostdeutchland* (Stuttgart, 1994), 61.

112. Gerd Doss, *Jugendweihe* 8 (1970), 7, quoted in Fischer, *Eurer Verlöbnis,* 198.

113. Fischer, *Eurer Verlöbnis,* 74–7, 128; Döhnert, 'Jugendweihe', 354.

114. Pollack, 'Situation', 165.

115. Cited in Döhnert, *Jugendweihe*, 135.

116. Walter Leo, 'Ja, das geloben wir: Jugendweihe in Ost-Berlin', *Zeit-Magazin,* 17 May 1974, 4–5.

117. Fulbrook, *Anatomy,* 104.

118. 'Vor einem neuen Lebensabschnitt', *Neues Deutschland,* 25 Mar. 1975.

119. H. Hafta, 'Niederschrift über die Besprechung von Fragen der Jugendweihe am 23. September 1957', 4, 35/532. LKAB.

120. Detlef Pollack, 'Von der Volkskirche zur Minderheitskirche: Zur Entwicklung von Religiosität und Kchlichkeit in der DDR', in Hartmut Kaelble, Jürgen Kocka, and Hartmut Zwahr (eds.), *Sozialgeschichte der DDR* (Stuttgart, 1994), 282.

121. Wolfgang Heinrich Hebeler, 'Die Möglichkeit einer kirchlichen Jugendarbeit in Mitteldeutschland', Universität Erlangen-Nürnberg, 1968, 55.2/206, LKAB.

122. Blaue Briefe, Berliner Information, 16 Dec. 1958, 1-2, 35/531. LKAB.

123. Fritz Hermann, 'Die Ohnmacht der Gespaltenen: Kirchlicher Alltag in Mittel-deutschland', *Christ und Welt,* 3 Jan 1969, 24, and Harald Steffahn, '. . . das nimmt ein gutes End: Eine sterbende Kirche?', *Die Zeit,* 12 Oct. 1973.

124. 'Pfarrer predigen in Wohnstuben: Ein Bericht über das Gemeindeleben in der DDR', *Sonntagblatt Bayern,* 38/70 (1970).

125. Felix Robin Schulz, 'Death in East Germany, 1945–1990', D.Phil., University of York, 2005, 283. See too the excellent discussion in Monica Black, *Death in Berlin: From Weimar to Divided Germany* (New York, 2010), 216–228.

126. Quoted in Fulbrook, *Anatomy,* 102.

127. Klemens Richter, 'Bestattungsriten in der DDR', *Deutschland-Archiv,* 7/1987, 733–9, and 'Weil die Religion den Menschen laehmt', *Neuer Tag,* 10 Apr. 1958.

128. Katherine Verdery, *The Political Lives of Dead Bodies: Reburial and Postsocialist Change* (New York, 1999) and Paul Betts, 'When Cold Warriors Die: The State Funerals of Konrad Adenauer and Walter Ulbricht', in Alon Confino, Paul Betts, and Dirk Schumann (eds.), *Between Mass Death and Individual Loss: The Place of the Dead in Twentieth Century Germany* (Oxford and New York, 2008), 151–78.

129. Felix Schulz, 'Disposing the Dead in East Germany, 1945–1990', ibid. 117.

130. Solberg, *God and Caesar*, 248–9; Black, *Death in Berlin*, 223.

131. Goeckel, *Lutheran Church*, 20.

132. Freidank, *Alles Hat Am Ende Sich Gelohnt: Material für weltliche Trauerfeiern* (Leipzig, 1972), 5–6. It was republished in 1982 as *Der Tag hat sich geneigt: Zur Gestaltung weltlicher Trauerfeiern*.

133. Stites, *Revolutionary Dreams*, 114.

134. Simone Ameskamp, 'Fanning the Flames: Cremation in Late Imperial and Weimar Germany,' in Confino *et al.*, *Mass Death*, 93–112.

135. Schulz, 'Death', 230.

136. Freidank, *Alles Hat*, 5–13.

137. Schulz, 'Death', 119, 130, 139–51.

138. 'Aktenvermerk: Gespräch mit Herrn Michael Knofel am 29.1.1980 bezüglich einer Eingabe beim Staatsrat wegen Todesanzeige', Rat des Stadtbezirks Friedrichshain, LAB C Rep 104/476.

139. Cornelia Geissler, 'Unter der Erde der DDR', *Kursbuch,* 114 (Berlin, 1993), 87.

140. Goeckel, *Lutheran Church*, 21–2.

141. Jonathan Steele, *Socialism with a German Face* (London, 1977), 158.

142. Fulbrook, *Anatomy*, 105.

143. Urban and Weinzen, *Jugend ohne Bekenntnis?* 85.

144. Cora Granata, 'The Cold War Politics of Cultural Minorities: Jews and Sorbs in the German Democratic Republic, 1976–1989', *German History,* 27/1 (January, 2009), 60–83.

145. Quoted in Goeckel, *Lutheran Church*, 173.

146. Graf, 'Ordnungsmacht', 305. See too Manfred Stolpe, 'Zehn Jahre Bund der Evangelischen Kirchen in der DDR: Anmerkungen zur kirchlichen Entwicklung nach 1968', *Die Zeichen der Zeit,* 11 (1979), 416, quoted in Fischer, *Eurer Verlöbnis,* 186.

147. Goeckel, *Lutheran Church*, 242–3.

148. Detlef Urban, 'Kirchen treten an die Öffentlichkeit', in Henkys, *Evangelische Kirchen*, 328–54.

149. Rotraut Simons, *'Der Pfarrer bleibt vom Bild her problematisch': Ausgewahlte Dokumente der Auseinandersetzung mit der Darstellung von Christen in Kinofilmen in der DDR 1956–1989/90* (Berlin, 2003), 7.

150. Horst Dähn and Joachim Heise, *Luther und die DDR: Der Reformator und das DDR-Fernsehen 1983* (Berlin, 1996).

151. Katharina Kunter, *Die Kirchen im KSZE-Prozess 1968–1978* (Stuttgart, 2000), 132–4.

152. 'Ausarbeitung negativer kirchlicher Kräfte aus den Landeskirchen Berlin-Brandenburg und Sachsen zum Thema: "Jugendweihe" und "Menschenrechte"', 28 June 1976, MfS HA XX/4/2341, SAB.

153. Bernd Eisenfeld, *Kriegsdienstverweigerung in der DDR—ein Friedensdienst?* (Frankfurt, 1978), 90–139.
154. 'Erste politisch-operative Auswertung der Schlussakte der Konferenz über Sicherheit und Zusammenarbeit in Europa', Berlin, 6 Aug. 1975, and 'Auswertung der Schlussakte der KSZE und erste politisch-operative Schlussfolgerungen', Berlin, 4 Sept. 1975. MfS HA XX/4/2343, SAB.
155. 'Dienstberatung in der Dienststelle des Staatssekretärs für Kirchenfragen', 22 Jan. 1976, Berlin, p. 2, original emphasis. C Rep 104/326, LAB.
156. 'Information: Veranstaltungen des Menschenrechtsprogramms der Kirchen zur Verwirklung der Schlussakte von Helsinki vom 21. 11 bis 29.11.1984 in Eisenach, Bezirk Erfurt', 30 Nov. 1984. MfS HA XX/4/1255, SAB, and Albrecht Schönherr, *Gratwanderung* (Berlin, 1992), 28.
157. MfS HA XX/4 1991 and 'Bericht zum Gespräch mit dem Bausoldatenkreis am 31.05.1983', Weimar, 21 June 1983, MfS HA XX/9 1895, SAB.
158. Goeckel, *Lutheran Church*, 124.
159. Interview, Henryk G., 31 Jan. 2007, Berlin. See too Paul Kaiser and Claudia Petzold (eds.), *Boheme und Diktatur in der DDR: Gruppen, Konflikte, Quartiere, 1970–1989* (Berlin, 1997), 94–9.
160. 'Abschlussbericht zum Operativ-Vorgang "Burg"', 14 Mar. 1978, MfS HA XX/4/2545, SAB.
161. 'Beratung des ZK der SED, Gen. Bellmann, mit den Mitarbeitern f. Kirchenfragen der Bezirke Potsdam, Frankfurt/Oder, Cottbus und der Hauptstadt am 15.7.1971 in Cottbus', 20 July 1971, p. 4. C Rep 104/326, LAB.
162. Quoted in Fischer, *Eurer Verlöbnis*, 200.
163. Rulo Melchert, 'Und wenn er religiös ist?' *Junge Welt*, 5 Jan. 1972.
164. 'Post an uns zu "Unter vier Augen"', *Junge Welt*, 12 and 19 Jan. 1972.
165. ''Keine Freundschaft zwischen Marxisten und Christen', *Frankfurter Rundschau*, 6 Jan. 1972, and 'FDJ: Weltanschauung geht vor Liebe', *Morgenpost*, 6 Jan. 1972.
166. Fischer, *Eurer Verlöbnis*, 209–10.
167. Tietsch, *Die 40 Jahre*, 33.
168. Kurt Marti, *Erinnerungen an die DDR und einige ihrer Christen* (Zurich, 1994).
169. Wolf Dieter Zimmermann, 'Die Rüststätte wurde zur Raststätte', *Deutsches Allgemeines Sonntagsblatt*, 5, 1 Feb. 1973.
170. Dietmar Linke, *Niemand kann zwei Herren dienen: Als Pfarrer in der DDR* (Hamburg, 1988), 197.
171. 'Information über die Kontrolle von Gottesdienst am 7. Mai 1989 in der Hauptstadt', no more biblio., p. 4, C Rep 104/576, LAB.
172. 'Dem Sozialismus "geweiht"', *Kölnische Rundschau*, 17 Apr. 1982.
173. Chauliac, 'Jugendweihe', 206.
174. 'Festliches zur Jugendweihe: Geschmacksvolle Sonderkollektion des Instituts für Bekleidungskultur', *Neues Deutschland*, 25 Nov. 1956, as well as 'Moderne gekleidet zur Jugendweihe', *Junge Welt*, 23 Jan. 1965; 'Schöner Tag im schönen Kleid', *Junge Welt*, 16 Jan. 1970; 'Chic zur Jugendweihe', *Berliner Zeitung*, 13 Jan. 1975; 'Wieder Jugenweihe und Mode', *Berliner Zeitung*, 19 Jan. 1978.
175. 'Jugendweihe und Mode', *Berliner Zeitung*, 10 Jan. 1966, and '"Jugendweihe und Mode" am Alex', *Der Morgen*, 16 Jan. 1974.

176. 'Marx auf der Zunge, Moped im Sinn: Eva Windmöller berichtet über 20 Jahre Jugendweihe in der DDR', *Stern*, 5 June 1975.

177. 'Aus dem Tagebuch des Schüler Adelbert', *Deutsche Lehrerzeitung*, 22 Apr. 1977.

178. 'Eltern und Jugendweihe', *Jugendweihe*, 8/1982, 1–7.

179. 'Jugendweihe—Sozialistische Volkssitte im 30. Jahr', *Aktuelle Kamera*, 25 Mar. 1984, 55.2/217, LKAB.

180. 'So sind wir! Sonderheft Jugendweihe', *Für Dich*, 8/1974.

181. Geissler, 'Unter der Erde', 88.

182. Pollack, 'Von Volkskirche', 277.

183. Detlef Pollack, *Kirche in der Organisationsgesellschaft* (Stuttgart, 1994), 387–8.

184. Schulz, 'Death', 213 and 13.

185. Horst Albrecht, 'Hin und wieder noch ein Engel: Die Sitten auf deutschen Friedhoefen haben sich radikal gewandelt', *Die Zeit*, 46, 11 Nov. 1988, 86. By the mid-1980s one quarter of West German funerals were presided over by professional speechmakers (*Rede-Profis*). Rüdiger Scheidges, 'Grabrede ohne Pfarrer: Das letzte Wort spricht heute oft nicht mehr der Geistliche, sondern ein Rede-Profi', *Frankfurter Rundschau*, 27 Nov. 1989.

186. Meier, 13.

187. Ronald Inglehart (ed.), *The Silent Revolution: Changing Values and Political Styles among Western Publics* (Princeton, 1977).

188. Dagmar Herzog, *Sex After Fascism: Memory and Morality in 20th Century Germany* (Princeton, 2005), 186.

189. Harald Schultze and Waltraut Zachhuber, *Spionage gegen eine Kirchenleitung* (Magdeburg, 1994).

190. Steven Pfaff, *Exit-Voice Dynamics and the Collapse of East Germany* (Durham, 2006).

191. Stefan-Ludwig Hoffmann, *The Politics of Sociability: Freemasonry and German Civil Society, 1840–1918*, tr. Tom Lampert (Ann Arbor, 2007).

192. Reinhart Koselleck, *Critique and Crisis: Enlightenment and the Pathogenesis of Modern Society* (Cambridge, 1988 [1959]), 75.

193. Friedrich Engels, 'Anti-Dühring', quoted in Goeckel, *Lutheran Church*, 24.

NOTES TO CHAPTER 3

1. Udo Grashoff, *'In einem Anfall von Depression . . .': Selbsttötung in der DDR* (Berlin, 2006) and Giselher Spitzer, *Wunden und Verwundungen: Sportler als Opfer des DDR-Dopingsystems* (Cologne, 2007).

2. Lothar Mertens, *Wider die sozialistische Familiennorm: Ehescheidungen in der DDR, 1950–1989* (Opladen and Wiesbaden, 1998), 34.

3. Johannes Huinink and Michael Wagner, 'Partnerschaft, Ehe und Familie in der DDR', in Johannes Huinink *et al.* (eds.), *Kollektiv und Eigensinn* (Berlin, 1995), 145–88.

4. Mertens, *Wider*, 13.

5. Michael Wagner, *Scheidung in Ost- und Westdeutschland* (Frankfurt, 1997), 303.

6. Ibid. 307.

7. Roderick Phillips, *Putting Asunder: A History of Divorce in Western Society* (Cambridge, 1988).

8. Besides Mertens and Wagner, see Dirk Blasius, *Ehescheidung in Deutschland* (Göttingen, 1987) and Inga Markovits, 'Marriage and the State: A Comparative Look at East and West German Family Law', *Stanford Law Review*, 115 (Nov. 1971), 116–99.

9. Irene Böhme, *Die da drüben: Sieben Kapitel DDR* (Berlin, 1982), 106–7.

10. Robert G. Moeller, 'The Elephant in the Living Room: Or Why the History of Twentieth Century Germany Should be a Family Affair', in Karen Hagemann and Jean H. Quataert (eds.), *Gendering Modern German History: Rewriting Historiography* (New York, 2007), 237.

11. Robert G. Moeller, *Protecting Motherhood: Women and the Family in the Politics of Postwar West Germany* (Berkeley, Calif., 1993).

12. Lutz Niethammer, 'Privat-Wirtschaft: Erinnerungsfragmente einer anderen Umerziehung', in Lutz Niethammer (ed.), *Hinterher merkt man dass es richtig war, dass es schiefgegangen ist: Nachkriegs-Erfahrungen im Ruhrgebiet* (Bonn, 1983), esp. 46–54.

13. Atina Grossmann, 'Trauma, Memory and Motherhood: Germans and Jewish Displaced Persons in Post-Nazi Germany, 1945–1949', in Richard Bessel and Dirk Schumann (eds.), *Life after Death: Approaches to a Cultural and Social History of Europe During the 1940s and 1950s* (Cambridge, 2003), 93–128.

14. 'Entwicklungsstand der sozialistischen Feiern anlässlich der Eheschliessung', Rat des Stadtbezirks Berlin-Mitte, 1962, C Rep 131-012/5155, LAB.

15. Notiz: Sozialistische Eheschliessung, Monika H und Hans T', Berlin, 5 Apr. 1962, C Rep 131-012/5155, LAB.

16. Cited in Gesine Obertreis, *Familienpolitik in der DDR 1945–1980* (Opladen, 1986), 115.

17. Moeller, *Protecting Motherhood*, 5, 102.

18. Jutta Gysi, 'Die Zukunft von Familie und Ehe: Familienpolitik und Familienforschung in der DDR', in Günter Burkart (ed.), *Sozialisation und Sozialismus* (Pfaffenhofen, 1990), 33–41.

19. Bernhard Klose, *Ehescheidung und Ehescheidungsrecht in der DDR: Ein ostdeutscher Sonderweg?* (Baden-Baden, 1996), 21–34.

20. Gabriele Czarnowski, *Das kontrollierte Paar: Ehe- und Sexualpolitik im Nationalsozialismus* (Weinheim, 1991), 80.

21. Michelle Mouton, *From Nurturing the Nation to Purifying the Volk: Weimar and Nazi Family Policy, 1918–1945* (Cambridge, 2007), 36.

22. Richard Bessel, *Germany after the First World War* (Oxford, 1993), 232.

23. Blasius, *Ehescheidung*, 164–87, and Helmuth Peuckmann, *Härteklausel zur Begrenzung des objektiven Zerrüttungsprinzips?*, Ph.D. diss., Albert-Ludwigs-Universität zu Freiburg, 1975, 16–17.

24. Adelheid von Saldern, 'Victims or Perpetrators? Controversies about the Role of Women in the Nazi State', in David Crew (ed.), *Nazism and German Society 1933–1945* (London, 1994), 146.

25. Stefan Chr. Saar, 'Familienrecht im NS-Staat: Ein Überblick', in Peter Salje (ed.), *Recht und Unrecht im Nationalsozialismus* (Münster, 1985), 82.

26. Blasius, *Ehescheidung*, 190.

27. Elizabeth D. Heineman, *What Difference does a Husband Make? Women and Marital Status in Nazi and Postwar Germany* (Berkeley, Calif., 1999), 23.

28. Wagner, *Scheidung*, 157. Nazi divorce law also recognized four additional grounds for 'no-fault' divorces: mental disorder, mental illness, contagious disease, and infertility, which were cited liberally to justify marital dissolution. Mouton, *Nurturing*, 92.

29. Kathrin Nahmmacher, *Die Rechtspechung des Reichsgerichts und der Hamburger Gerichte zum Scheidungsgrund des Para 55 EheG 1938 in den Jahren 1938 bis 1945* (Frankfurt, 1999) and Patricia Szobar, 'Telling Sexual Stories in the Nazi Courts of Law', *Journal of the History of Sexuality*, 11/1–2 (2002), 131–62.

30. Blasius, *Ehescheidung*, 196, Czarnowski, *Das kontrollierte Paar*, 79–97.

31. Adolf Hitler, *Mein Kampf*, 252, cited in Mouton, *Nurturing*, 35.

32. Dr H. Michaelis, *Das Neue Gesetzbuch, Kontrollrat-Gesetz Nr. 16 vom 20.2.1946* (Berlin, 1947), 9.

33. Heineman, *Difference*, 46.

34. Mouton, *Nurturing*, 64–5.

35. Atina Grossmann, *Reforming Sex: The German Movement for Birth Control and Abortion Reform, 1920–1950* (Oxford, 1995), 193 and Norman Naimark, *The Russians in Germany* (Cambridge, Mass., 1995), 69–140.

36. Donna Harsch, *Revenge of the Domestic* (Princeton, 2006), 23.

37. Ibid. 27, and Heinemann, *Difference*, 119.

38. Quoted in Dagmar Herzog, *Sex After Fascism* (Princeton, 2005), 189.

39. Case R19.45, Karton 1066 Nr. 1 R 45, 6 June 1945, C Rep 341 StM, LAB, as well as Case 2R.2.45, 9 Aug. 1945, Karton 2 R 45/5 R45, 1945, C Rep 333, StM LAB.

40. Case 2R.317.45, 23 Aug. 1945, Karton 2 R 45/5 R45, C Rep 333, StM, LAB.

41. Case 2R.2.45, 9 Aug. 1945, Karton 2 R 45/5 R45, C Rep 333, StM, LAB.

42. Case 985/50, 14 Sept. 1948, Karton 1191 Nr. 16 Ra 50, 1950, C Rep 341 StM, LAB.

43. Maria Hoehn, *GIs and Fräuleins: The German-American Encounter in 1950s West Germany* (Chapel Hill, NC, 2002).

44. Case 1R280.45, 20 Aug. 1945, Karton 1067 Nr. 1 R 45, C Rep 341 StM, LAB.

45. Case 1R 163/45, 29 June 1945, Karton 1068 Nr. 1 R 45, C Rep 341 StM, LAB.

46. Irmgard Weyrather, *Muttertag und Mutterkreuz: Der Kult um die 'deutsche Mutter' im Nationalsozialismus* (Frankfurt, 1993), 85–124.

47. Frank Biess, *Homecomings: Returning POWs and the Legacies of Defeat in Postwar Germany* (Princeton, 2006).

48. Heineman, *Difference*, 116.

49. Case Ra 989.50, 3 Sept. 1948, Karton 1195 Nr. 16/R/50, C Rep 341 StM, LAB.

50. Lutz Niethammer, Alexander von Plato, and Dorothee Wierling, *Die volkseigene Erfahrung: Eine Archäologie des Lebens in der Industrieprovinz der DDR* (Berlin, 1991), 356–62.

51. Case 392/50, 23 Feb. 1949, Karton 1191 Nr. 16 Ra 50, 1950, C Rep 341 StM, LAB.

52. Case R639/49, Karton 1191 Nr. 16 Ra 50, C Rep 341 StM, LAB.

53. Mouton, *Nurturing*, 71.

54. Young-Sun Hong, ' "The Benefits of Health must Spread among All": International Solidarity, Health and Race in the East German Encounter with the Third World', in K. Pence and P. Betts (eds.), *Socialist Modern* (Ann Arbor, 2008), 183–210.

55. Annette F. Timm, 'Guarding the Health of Worker Families in the GDR: Socialist Health Care, Bevölkerungspolitik, and Marriage Counselling, 1945–1970', in Peter Hübner and Klaus Tenfelde (eds.), *Arbeiter in der SBZ-DDR* (Essen, 1999), 464, 472.

56. Case Ra 81/57, 9 Apr. 1957, Karton 1659 Nr. 346B/57, C Rep 341 StM, LAB.

57. Case Ra16/57, 18 Jan. 1957, Karton 1656 Nr. 346B/56, C Rep 341 StM, LAB.

58. 'Protokoll über die Sitzung der Schöffen und Geschworenen', 31 May 1950, Treptow, Berlin, C Rep 145-01/94, LAB.

59. Helmut Ostmann, 'Welche prozessrechtlichen Aufgaben stellt das neue Familienrecht?', *Neue Justiz,* 8/9 (Apr. 1955), 227–34.

60. Mouton, *Nurturing,* 71.

61. Peuckmann, *Härteklausel* 33.

62. Case Ra20/57, 22 Jan 1957, Karton 1656, Nr. 346B/56, C Rep 341 StM, LAB.

63. Mertens, *Wider,* 22.

64. Harsch, *Revenge,* 221.

65. Case Ra 85/57, 29 Mar. 1957, Karton 1657 Nr. 346B/56, C Rep 341 StM, LAB.

66. Case Ra 214/57, 8 Nov. 1957, Karton 1659 Nr. 346B/57, C Rep 341 StM, LAB.

67. Case Ra22/57, 24 Jan. 1957, Karton 1656 Nr. 346B/56, C Rep 341 StM, LAB.

68. Sabine Gries, *Kindermisshandlung in der DDR: Kinder unter dem Einfluss traditionell-autoritärer und totalitärer Erziehungsleitbilder* (Münster, 2002).

69. *Gewalt- und Sexualkriminalität: Erscheinungsformen Ursachen Bekämpfung* (Berlin, 1970), esp. 155 ff.

70. An exception is Linda Gordon, *Heroes of their own Lives: The Politics and History of Family Violence, Boston, 1880–1960* (Urbana, Ill., 2002).

71. Case Ra 14/57, 15 Dec. 1956, Karton 1656 Nr. 346B/56, C Rep 341 StM, LAB.

72. Case 85/57, 15 Apr. 1957, Karton 1659 Nr. 346B/57, C Rep 341 StM, LAB.

73. Case Ra 100/57, 15 May 1957, Karton 1660 Nr. 346B/57, C Rep 341 StM, LAB.

74. Quoted in Heineman, *Difference,* 193.

75. Case F199/66, 19 July 1966, Karton 1651 Nr. 342 F/66, C Rep 341 StM, LAB.

76. Mertens, *Wider,* 36.

77. Harsch, *Revenge,* 294.

78. 'Erfahrungen und Probleme aus der Tätigkeit von Schieds-Kommissionen', Berlin, 27 Nov. 1963, 15, DP1/1243, BAB. For comparison, see Brian LaPierre, 'Private Matters or Public Crimes: The Emergence of Domestic Hooliganism in the Soviet Union, 1939–1966,' in Siegelbaum, *Borders of Socialism,* 191–207.

79. Klose, *Ehescheidung,* 295.

80. Case F22/60, 6 May 1960, Karton 1619 Nr. 241 F/60, C Rep 341 StM, LAB.

81. Inga Markovits, *Gerechtigkeit in Lüritz: Eine ostdeutsche Rechtsgeschichte* (Munich, 2006), 99.

82. Dorothee Wierling, *Geboren im Jahr Eins* (Berlin, 2002), *passim.*

83. Markowits, *Gerechtigkeit,* 100.

84. Uta C. Schmidt, 'Die "Schlüsselkinderzählung" als geschlechterpolitische Inszenierung im Kalten Krieg : Einführende Überlegungen zu "Geschlecht" und "Kalter Krieg"', in Thomas Lindenberger (ed.), *Massenmedien im Kalten Krieg: Akteure, Bilder, Resonanzen* (Cologne, 2006), 181.

85. Gerhard Poller, 'Ein Kreisgericht zieht Schlussfolgerungen aus der Rechtsspechung in Ehesachen', *Neue Justiz,* 12/23 (1958), 810.

86. Case F191/66, 26 Aug. 1966, Karton 1651 Nr. 342 F/66, C Rep 341 StM, LAB.

87. Mouton, *Nurturing*, 39–45.

88. Timm, 'Guarding the Health', 487.

89. Klose, *Ehescheidung*, 146–7.

90. Markowits, *Gerechtigkeit*, 118. In 1968, these Berlin centres logged 1,673 visits; by 1972 the figure leapt to 5,238. Timm, 'Guarding the Health', 491.

91. Obertreis, *Familienpolitik*, 6.

92. Harsch, *Revenge*, 296.

93. Siegfried Schnabl, *Mann und Frau Intim* (12th edn. Berlin, 1979), 26.

94. Quoted in Herzog, *Sex After Fascism*, 195.

95. Ibid. 211.

96. Wolfgang Polte, *Unsere Ehe* (8th rev. edn. Leipzig, 1980), 131, 137–8, cited in Herzog, *Sex After Fascism*, 214, and see too Karl Marx and Friedrich Engels, *Vom Glück der Gemeinsamkeit: Über Liebe, Freundschaft, Solidarität* (Berlin, 1985).

97. Deborah A. Field, 'Irreconcilable Differences: Divorce and Conceptions of Private Life in the Khrushchev Era', *Russian Review*, 57 (Oct. 1998), 599–613.

98. Markovits, 'Marriage', 141.

99. Case F115/66, 24 May 1966, Karton 1655 Nr. 344 F/66, C Rep 341 StM, LAB.

100. Walter Ulbricht, *Programmatische Erklärung des Vorsitzenden des Staatrates der DDR Walter Ulbricht, vor der Volkskammer am 4. Oktober 1960* (Berlin, 1960), 59.

101. Gunilla-Frederike Budde, *Frauen der Intelligenz: Akademinkerinnen in der DDR 1945–1975* (Göttingen, 2003), 202–7, 219–20.

102. Brigitte Hering and Harald Wessel, 'Liebe, Ehe und Familie im Geiste des sozialistischen Humanismus', in Richard Halgasch (ed.), *Wir bleiben zusammen* (Leipzig, 1971), 176.

103. Case F109/66, 13 May 1966, Karton 1655 Nr. 344 F/66, C Rep 341 StM, LAB.

104. Case F438/60, Karton 1642 Nr. 250 F/60, C Rep 341 StM, LAB.

105. Case F438/60, 12 Sept. 1960, Karton 1642 Nr. 250 F/60, C Rep 341 StM, LAB.

106. Case F440/60, 13 Sept. 1960, Karton 1642 Nr. 250 F/60, C Rep 341 StM, LAB.

107. Case F199/66, 6 Sept. 1966, Karton 1651 Nr. 342 F/66, C Rep 341 StM, LAB.

108. Case F191/66, 25 Aug. 1966, Karton 1651 Nr. 342 F/66, C Rep 341 StM, LAB.

109. Case 169/60, 2 Apr. 1960, Karton 1643 Nr. 250 F/60, C Rep 341 StM, LAB, original emphasis.

110. Case F111/66, 16 May 1966, Karton 1655 Nr. 344 F/66, C Rep 341 StM, LAB.

111. Case F170/66, 2 Aug. 1966, Karton 1650 Nr. 342 F/66, C Rep 341 StM, LAB.

112. Harsch, *Revenge*, 296.

113. Mertens, *Wider*, 51–2.

114. Bettina Jakob, *Liebe und Ehe am Scheideweg ins neue Jahrtausend: Ein sozialhistorischer Blick auf Liebe, Ehe, Trennung und Scheidung vom Hochmittelalter bis heute* (Berlin, 2005), 94–5.

115. Wagner, *Scheidung*, 157.

116. Klose, *Ehescheidung*, 203.

117. Harri Harrland and Rudolf Hiller, 'Familienrechtliche Konflikte im Spiegel der Gerichtsstatistik', *Neue Justiz*, 16/20 (1962), 622.

118. Anita Grandke and Klaus-Peter Orth, 'Rechtssoziologische Untersuchungen zur Stabilität von Ehen in der DDR', *Staat und Recht*, 21/1 (1972), 50.

119. Mertens, *Wider*, 28.
120. Ibid. 49.
121. 'Analyse von 36 Urteilen aus dem Jahre 1975 und 1976', Stadtbezirksgericht, Berlin-Mitte, C Rep 301, Karton 404/Kiste 82/83, LAB.
122. Case 346F 947.73, 11 Feb. 1974, F-Senat 109 Urteile 1974, 1–98, Stadtgericht-Berlin, LAB.
123. Case 3BF 28.71, 3 May 1971, Familie-Urteile 1971, 1–100, Stadtgericht-Berlin, LAB.
124. Herbert Kietz and Manfred Mühlmann, *Konfliktursachen und Aufgaben der Zivil- und Familienrechtspflege* (Berlin, 1969).
125. Kurt Wünsche, 'Die Aufgabe des Ministers der Justiz auf dem Gebiet der soz. Rechtspflege', *Neue Justiz* (1969), 67–8.
126. Markovits, *Gerechtigkeit*, 103.
127. Ibid., and Monika Wiedemeyer, 'Psychologische Aspekte in der Tätigkeit der Ehe- und Familienberatungsstellen', *Neue Justiz*, 28/12 (June 1974), 363–5.
128. *Sozialistische Beziehungen in Familien und Hausgemeinschaften bewusster gestalten* (Berlin, 1971) and Richard Halgasch, 'Ehe und Ehescheidung in unserer Gesellschaft', in Halgasch, *Wir bleiben zusammen*, 9–52.
129. Schneider, 255.
130. A. Grandke and K-P Orth, 'Rechtssoziologische Untersuchungen zur Stabilität von Ehen in der DDR,' *Staat und Recht* (1972), 49.
131. Jutta Gysi, ed., *Familienleben in der DDR* (East Berlin, 1989), 50.
132. Schneider, 25.
133. John R. Gillis, *For Better, For Worse: British Marriages 1600 to the Present* (New York, 1985), 318.
134. Josie McLellan, 'State Socialist Bodies: East German Nudism from Ban to Boom', *Journal of Modern History*, 79 (Mar. 2007), 48–79.
135. Maxie Wander, *Guten Morgen, Du Schöne: Protokolle nach Tonband* (Berlin, 1977), 9, 13.
136. Mertens, *Wider*, 60.
137. Barbara Bronnen and Franz Henny, *Liebe, Ehe, Sexualität in der DDR: Interviews und Dokumente* (Munich, 1975).
138. Rita Wenzel, '1975: Internationales Jahr der Frau: Zur Verwirklichung der Gleichberechtigung von Mann und Frau in Ehe und Familie', *Staat und Recht* (1975), 946–56.
139. Rudolf Neubert, 'Was nicht in der Statistik steht', in Halgasch, *Wir bleiben zusammen*, 55, and Schnabl, *Mann und Frau Intim*, 27–8.
140. Klose, *Ehescheidung*, 125.
141. Case 3BF 25.71, 5.4.71, Familie-Urteile, 1971, 1–100, Stadtgericht-Berlin, LAB.
142. Case F196/66, 2 Sept. 1966, Karton 1651 Nr. 342 F/66, C Rep 341 StM, LAB.
143. Der Vorstand, Kollegium der Rechtsanwälte in Berlin, 'Studien zu den Ursachen der Ehescheidung', 13 June 1978, 3, C Rep 368/311, Stadtbezirksgericht, LAB.
144. Ibid. 5.
145. Halgasch, *Wir bleiben zusammen*, 23.
146. 'Im Sozialismus ist Liebe keine Privatsache', *Berliner Zeitung* (West), 27 Feb. 1974.
147. 'Jede vierte Ehe scheitert in der DDR: Die SED ist ratlos und verwirrt', *Rheinische Post*, 10–11 Aug. 1974.

148. Jonathan Steele, *Socialism with a German Face* (London, 1977), 157.
149. Case 3BF 42.71, 6.9.1971, Familie-Urteile 1971, 1–100, Stadtgericht-Berlin, LAB.
150. Case 3BF 11.71, 19.4.71, Familie-Urteile 1971, 1–100, Stadtgericht-Berlin, LAB.
151. Case 109 BFB 81.74, 24 June 1974, F-Senat 109 Urteile 1974, 1–98, Stadtgericht-Berlin, LAB.
152. Mouton, *Nurturing*, 51.
153. Hartmut Berghoff, 'Zur Einflussnahme auf Ehekonflikte als Leitungsaufgabe im Betrieb', *Arbeit und Arbeitsrecht*, 27/4 (1972), 107, cited in Mertens, *Wider*, 31, and Markovits, "Marriage', 181.
154. Case 65, 28 Jan. 1970, C Rep 334/ 23, Stadtbezirkgericht Treptow, 1977–1989, LAB.
155. Klose, *Ehescheidung*, 147.
156. GDR sex manuals thus began to target younger audiences in the 1980s, as seen with Kurt Starke's *Junge Partner* (Leipzig, 1980) and Walter Friedrich's *Liebe und Ehe bis 30* (Leipzig, 1984).
157. Bronnen and Henny, *Liebe*, 86.
158. Case 17 FE 469.88, 5 May 1989, Familie-Urteile 1989, 1–150, Stadtgericht-Berlin, LAB.
159. Case 16F 101/85, 7 Nov. 1985, Familie-Urteile 1985, 151-, Stadtgericht-Berlin, LAB.
160. Case 10F 293/86, 2 Mar. 1987, Familie-Urteile 1986, 201-, Stadtgericht-Berlin, LAB.
161. Mertens, *Wider*, 64.
162. Klose, *Ehescheidung*, 226; Markovits, *Gerechigkeit*, 121.
163. Herzog, *Sex After Fascism*, 200.
164. Harsch, *Revenge*, 234.
165. Timm, 'Guarding the Health', 486.
166. Karl-Heinz Mehlan, *Wunschkinder? Familienplanung, Antikonzeption und Abortbe-kämpfung in unserer Zeit* (Greifenwald zu Rudolstadt, 1969), 133–69.
167. Lynn Abrams, 'The Personification of Inequality: Challenges to Gendered Power Relations in Nineteenth Century Divorce Courts', *Archiv für Sozialgeschichte*, 38 (1998), 48.
168. Herzog, *Sex After Fascism*, 188.
169. Lynne Carol Halem, *Divorce Reform: Changing Legal and Social Perspectives* (New York, 1980).
170. Heineman, *Difference*, 73.
171. Detlev Peukert, *Inside Nazi Germany* (New Haven, Conn., 1987), 236–42.

NOTES TO CHAPTER 4

1. Gavriel Rosenfeld, *Munich and Memory: Architecture, Monuments and the Legacy of the Third Reich* (Berkeley, Calif., 2000); Brian Ladd, *The Ghosts of Berlin: Confronting German History in the Urban Landscape* (Chicago, 1997); H. Glenn Penny, *Objects of Culture: Enthnology and Ethnographic Museums in Imperial Germany* (Chapel Hill, NC, 2002); Elizabeth Ten Dyke, *Dresden: A Paradox of Memory and History* (London, 2002); Janet Ward, *Weimar Surfaces: Urban Visual Culture in the 1920s* (Berkeley, Calif., 2001); and Eli Rubin, *Synthetic Socialism: Plastics and Dictatorship in the German Democratic Republic* (Chapel Hill, NC, 2008).

2. See e.g. *Geschichte des Wohnens*, iv. *Reform Reaktion Zerstörung*, ed. Gert Kähler (Stuttgart, 1996) and *Geschichte des Wohnens*, v. *Von 1945 bis Heute*, ed. Ingeborg Flagge (Stuttgart, 1999). See also Joachim Petsch, *Eigenheim und Gute Stube: Zur Geschichte des bürgerlichen Wohnens* (Cologne, 1989).

3. Lutz Niethammer and Alexander von Plato (eds.), *'Wir kriegen jetzt andere Zeiten': Auf der Suche nach der Erfahrung des Volkes in nachfaschistischen Ländern* (Berlin, 1985) and *When the War was Over: Women, War and Peace in Europe, 1940–1956*, ed. Claire Duchen and Irene Bandhauer-Schoffmann (London, 2000).

4. Maiken Umbach, *German Cities and Bourgeois Modernism, 1890–1924* (Oxford, 2009).

5. Barbara Miller Lane, *Architecture and Politics in Germany, 1918–1945* (Cambridge, 1968).

6. Ralf Dahrendorf, *Society and Democracy in Germany* (New York, 1967), 285–96. See too Robert Moeller, *Protecting Motherhood: Women and the Family in the Politics of Postwar West Germany* (Berkeley, Calif., 1993) and Erica Carter, *How German is She? Postwar West German Reconstruction and the Consuming Woman* (Ann Arbor, 1997).

7. Hannah Arendt, *The Human Condition* (Chicago, 1958), esp. 22–78, and Jürgen Habermas, *The Structural Transformation of the Public Sphere* (Cambridge, 1989 [1962]).

8. Joy Parr, *Domestic Goods: The Material, the Moral and the Economic in the Postwar Years* (Toronto, 1999), 21–39; D. Albrecht, *World War II and the American Dream: How Wartime Building Changed a Nation* (Washington, DC, 1995); and Detlev Peukert, *Inside Nazi Germany* (New Haven, Conn., 1987), 247.

9. Paul Betts, *The Authority of Everyday Objects* (Berkeley, Calif., 2004), esp. 23–72.

10. *Parteiauftrag: Ein neues Deutschland*, ed. Dieter Vorsteher (Berlin, 1997) and Paul Betts, 'The Politics of Post-Fascist Aesthetics: 1950s West and East German Industrial Design', in Richard Bessel and Dirk Schumann (eds.), *Life After Death* (Cambridge, 2003), 290–321.

11. Outstanding in this respect is Greg Castillo, *Cold War on the Home Front: The Soft Power of Midcentury Design* (Minneapolis, 2010). The famed Nixon–Khrushchev 'kitchen debate', in which the then-US Vice President and the Soviet Premier sparred over the meaning of modern kitchen appliances at the American Pavilion of the 1959 Moscow Fair, is perhaps the most dramatic instance of the more general politicization of material culture. Elaine Tyler May, *Homeward Bound: American Families in the Cold War Era* (New York, 1988), 17–18, and Mary Nolan, 'Consuming America, Producing Gender,' in R. Laurence Moore and Maurizio Vaudagna (eds.), *The American Century in Europe* (Ithaca, NY, 2003), 243–61.

12. W. L. Guttmann, *Workers' Culture in Weimar Germany* (New York, 1990), 54–106, 287–313.

13. Quoted in Werner Kirchoff, 'Schlusswort auf der gemeinsamen Tagung des Sekretariats des Nationalrats und des Ministerium für Bauwesen am 24. Oktober 1973', DY 6/2349, Bundesarchiv Berlin (BAB). Engels's *Zur Wohnungsfrage* was republished as a pamphlet in 1948, and was widely quoted in reports and Party journalism.

14. Richard Stites, *Revolutionary Dreams* (Berkeley, Calif., 1989), esp. 190–222; Milka Bliznakov, 'Soviet Housing During the Experimental Years, 1918 to 1933', in William Craft Brumfield and Blair A. Ruble (eds.), *Russian Housing in the Modern Age* (Cambridge, 1993), 85–149.

15. Herbert Riecke, *Mietskasernen im Kapitalismus, Wohnpaläste im Sozialismus: Die Entwicklung der Städte im modernen Kapitalismus und die Grundsätze des sozialistischen Städtebaus* (Berlin, 1954), 7.

16. Ibid. 36–7. See too *Wie komme ich zur einer Wohnung?* (Berlin, 1954) and Gisela Karau, *Sozialistischer Alltag in der DDR* (East Berlin, 1970), esp. 24–6.

17. Susan Reid and David Crowley (eds.), *Style and Socialism: Modernity and Material Culture in Post-War Eastern Europe* (Oxford, 2000), esp. the introduction.

18. Betts, *Authority*, 241–3, and Castillo, *Cold War*, 59–84.

19. Christoph Klessmann, *Zwei Staaten, Eine Nation: Deutsche Geschichte, 1955–1970* (Bonn, 1997), 406–7.

20. Thomas Hoscislawski, *Bauen zwischen Macht und Ohnmacht: Architektur und Städtebau in der DDR* (Berlin, 1991), esp. 38–43, 101–11, and 297–310; and Castillo, *Cold War*, 31–57.

21. Peter Marcuse and Fred Staufenbiel (eds.), *Wohnen und Stadtpolitik im Umbruch: Perspektiven der Stadterneuerung nach 40 Jahre DDR* (Berlin, 1991) and Klaus von Beyme, *Der Wiederaufbau: Architektur und Städtebau in beiden deutschen Staaten* (Munich, 1987).

22. Herbert Nicolaus and Alexander Obeth, *Die Stalinallee* (Berlin, 1997), 233–50, and Tilo Köhler, *Unser die Strasse—Unser der Sieg: Die Stalinallee* (Berlin, 1993).

23. 'Sixteen Principles for the Restructuring of Cities in the German Democratic Republic,' in Joan Ockman (ed.), *Architecture Culture, 1943–1968: A Documentary Anthology* (New York, 1993), 127–8.

24. 'Der Kampf gegen den Formalismus und Literatur, für eine fortschrittliche deutsche Kultur', *Tägliche Rundschau*, 18 Apr. 1951, quoted in Castillo, 'Marshall Plan Modernism', 15.

25. Walter Ulbricht, 'Sozialistischer Wohnungsbau in Siebenjahrplan', *Deutsche Architektur*, 8/12 (1959), 645.

26. Walter Ulbricht, 'Die grosse Aufgaben der Innenarchitektur beim Kampf um eine neue deutsche Kultur', 1952, quoted in Castillo, *Cold War*, 54.

27. Quoted in Kurt Liebknecht, 'Die Architektur der Wohnung für die Werktätigen unter besonderer Berücksichtigung des Möbels', in *Besser Leben—Schöner Wohnen: Raum und Möbel* (East Berlin, 1954), 8.

28. Jakob Jordan, 'Vorwort', ibid. 3.

29. Jakob Jordan, 'Über einige Aufgaben des Instituts für Innenarchitektur der Deutschen Bauakademie', *Deutsche Architektur*, 3 (1954), 9.

30. Quoted in Castillo, *Cold War*, 95.

31. Ibid. 10.

32. Ibid. 14.

33. *Besser Leben*, 3.

34. Liebknecht, 'Die Architektur', 74.

35. This was still the case by the late 1950s. See 'Eine Antwort an Frau Edith S.', *Kultur im Heim*, 2 (1959), 3, and Castillo, *Cold War*, 103.

36. Claudia Freytag, 'Neue Städte—Neues Wohnen: "Vorbildliche Wohnkultur" in Wolfsburg und Stalinstadt', in Rosemarie Beier (ed.), *Aufbau West Aufbau Ost: Die Planstädte Wolfsburg und Eisenhüttenstadt in der Nachkriegszeit* (Berlin, 1997), 318.

37. As a result the periphery—the GDR, Poland, and Czechoslavakia—was at the forefront of Eastern bloc design.

38. Nikita Khrushchev, *Besser, billiger und schneller bauen* (East Berlin, 1955), 28ff., in Thomas Topstedt, 'Wohnen und Städtebau in der DDR', in Ingeborg Flagge (ed.), *Geschichte des Wohnens* (Stuttgart, 1999), v. 486.

39. Topstedt, 'Wohnen und Städtebau', 485.

40. Hein Köster, 'Schmerzliche Ankunft in der Moderne', in NGBK (ed.), *Wunderwirtschaft: DDR-Konsumkultur in den 60er Jahren* (Cologne, 1996), 99.

41. Castillo, *Cold War*, 174.

42. Adelheld von Saldern, *Häuserleben* (Berlin, 1995), 315.

43. 'P2 macht das Rennen: Wohnungsbau als sozio-kulturelles Programm', in *P2 und Tempolinsen* (Berlin, 1996), 98.

44. In the early 1960s the architect emerged as a new cultural hero in the GDR, as perhaps best seen in the novels Karl-Heinz Jacobs, *Beschreibung eines Sommers* (1963); Erik Neutsch, *Spur der Steine* (1964); Brigitte Reimann, *Franziska Linkerhand* (1974); as well as Stefan Heym's posthumously published *Die Architekten* (2000).

45. Dolores L. Augustine, *Red Prometheus: Engineering and Dictatorship in East Germany, 1945–1990* (Cambridge, Mass., 2007).

46. The original passage comes from Marx and Engels, 'Deutsche Ideologie', in *Werke*, iii (Berlin, 1959), 28.

47. Petra Gruner, '"Neues Leben, neues Wohnen"', in NGBK, *Wunderwirtschaft*, 95.

48. Betts, *Authority*, esp. 212–48.

49. Nicolaus and Obeth, *Stalinallee*, 233–50.

50. Winifried Stallknecht, Herbert Kuschy, and Achim Fetz, 'Architekten Wohnen im Versuchsbau P2', *Kultur im Heim,* 1/1964, 3–7.

51. Karin Zachmann, 'A Socialist Consumption Junction: Debating the Mechanization of Housework in East Germany, 1956–1957', *Technology and Culture,* 43/1 (Jan. 2002), 73–99, as well as Susan E. Reid, 'The Khrushchev Kitchen: Domesticating the Scientific–Technological Revolution,' *Journal of Contemporary History* 40/2 (April 2005), 289–316.

52. Donna Harsch, 'Squaring the Circle: The Dilemmas and Evolution of Women's Policy', in Patrick Major and Jonathan Osmond (eds.), *The Workers' and Peasants' State: Communism and Society in East Germany under Ulbricht* (Manchester, 2002), 151–70.

53. Topstedt, 'Wohnen und Städtebau', 523.

54. Ina Merkel, 'Der aufhaltsame Aufbruch', and Jochen Fetzer, 'Gut verpackt . . .', in NGBK, *Wunderwirtschaft*, 11–15 and 104–11, respectively.

55. Martin Kelm, *Produktgestaltung im Sozialismus* (Berlin, 1971), 81. See too Eli Rubin, 'The Form of Socialism without Ornament: Consumption, Ideology and the Rise and Fall of Modernist Design in the German Democratic Republic', *Journal of Design History,* 19/2 (2006), 155–67.

56. Merkel, 'Consumer Culture in the GDR; or How the Struggle for Antimodernity was Lost on the Battlefield of Consumer Culture', in Susan Strasser, Charles McGovern, and Matthias Judt (eds.), *Getting and Spending: European and American Consumption in the Twentieth Century* (Cambridge, 1998), 290.

57. Quoted in Horst Redeker, *Chemie gibt Schönheit* (Berlin, 1959), 14. For discussion, see Rubin, *Synthetic Socialism*, 81–119.

58. Jennifer A. Loehlin, *From Rugs to Riches: Housework, Consumption and Modernity in Germany* (Oxford, 1999).

59. Merkel, . . . *Und Du, Frau auf der Werkbank* (Berlin, 1990), esp. 43–105.

60. Dr Moedel, 'Marktforschung: Eine Führungsaufgabe in der Industrie', *Die Wirtschaft*, 3/1966, Beilage.

61. See e.g. Harald Lorenz, 'Grundlagen für die Gestaltung des Möbelsortiments', Institut für Marktforschung, 1969, DL102/393, BA Dahlwitz/Hoppegarten (BADH).

62. Werner Bischoff and Waltraud Niecke, 'Grundlagen für die Gestaltung des Möbelsortiments im Perspectiv—und Prognosezeitraum', 1971, Institut für Marktforschung, DL 102/554, BADH.

63. Annette Kaminsky, *Wohlstand, Schönheit, Glück: Kleine Konsumgeschichte der DDR* (Munich, 2001), 71–115, and Ina Merkel, *Utopie und Bedürfnis: Die Geschichte der Konsumkultur in der DDR* (Cologne, 1999), 144–50.

64. Erhard Krause, 'Die Angebots- und Nachfragesituation bei Pölstermöbeln bis 1965', Leipzig, 1963, DL 102/243, BADH.

65. Waltraud Nieke und Werner Bischoff, 'Tendenzen der Entwicklung des Wohnbedürfnisse und der Nachfrage nach Wohnraummöbeln', Institut für Marktforschung, 1971, 4, DL 102/591, BADH.

66. Hanns Hopp, 'Ansprüche zur Eröffnung der Arbeitstagung für Innenarchitektur am 14.3.1952', 19, SAMPO DH2/DBA/A41, BAB.

67. Anna-Sabine Ernst, 'The Politics of Culture and the Culture of Everyday Life in the DDR in the 1950s', in David E. Barclay and Eric Weitz (eds.), *Between Reform and Revolution: German Socialism and Communism from 1840 to 1990* (New York, 1998), 489–506.

68. Ibid. 503 n. 7.

69. For fuller discussion, Paul Betts, 'Manners, Morality and Civilization: Reflections on Post-1945 German Etiquette Books', in Frank Biess and Robert Moeller (eds.), *Histories of the Aftermath: The Legacies of World War II in Comparative European Perspective* (Oxford and New York, 2010).

70. Karl Smolka, *Gutes Benehmen von A bis Z* (Berlin, 1957), 7–8.

71. Karl Kleinschmidt, *Keine Angst vor guten Sitten: Ein Buch über die Art miteinander umzugehen* (Berlin, 1961), 18–19.

72. Ibid. 39, 20; Schweikert and Hold, *Guten Tag, Herr von Knigge! Ein heiteres Lesebuch für alle Jahrgänge über alles, was 'anständig' ist* (Leipzig, 1959), 62, 251.

73. Schweikert and Hold, *Guten Tag*, 8.

74. Jörg Roesler, 'Die Produktsbrigaden in der Industrie der DDR', in Hartmut Kaelble, Jürgen Kocka, and Hartmut Zwahr (eds.), *Sozialgeschichte der DDR* (Stuttgart, 1994), 158.

75. See too Kanzei des Staatrates der DDR (ed.), *Ein glückliches Familienleben—Anliegen des Familiengesetzbuches der DDR* (Berlin, 1965).

76. Quoted in *Kahlschlag: Das 11. Plenum des ZK der SED 1965: Studien und Dokumente* (Berlin, 1991), 241.

77. Angela Brock, 'The Making of the Socialist Personality: Education and Socialisation in the German Democratic Republic, 1958–1978', Ph.D thesis, University College London, 2005, and Maria Elisabeth Müller, *Zwischen Ritual und Alltag: Der Traum von einer sozialistischen Persönlichkeit* (Frankfurt, 1997).

78. Vera Dunham, *In Stalin's Time: Middle-Class Values in Soviet Fiction* (Cambridge, 1979), 13.

79. Schweickert and Hold, *Guten Tag,* 210–11.

80. Gutachten von Hirte über Smolkas *Benehmen ist nicht nur Glückssache,* 23 June 1958, DR1/5078, BAB.

81. Gutachten von R. Dänhardt über Smolkas, *Benehmen ist nicht nur Glückssache,* 23 May 1958, DR1/5078, BAB.

82. Eric Weitz, *Creating German Communism, 1890–1990: From Popular Protests to Socialist State* (Princeton, 1997), 372. See too Nicholas Timasheff, *The Great Retreat* (New York, 1946), 317.

83. Cited in Gareth Dale, *Popular Protest in East Germany* (London, 2005), 91.

84. Barbara Einhorn, *Cinderella Goes to Market: Citizenship, Gender and Women's Movements in East Central Europe* (London, 1993).

85. Merkel, *Und Du, passim,* and Harsch, *Revenge of the Domestic* (Princeton, 2006).

86. Ernst, 'Politics of Culture', 494.

87. Karl Smolka, *Junger Mann von heute* (Berlin, 1964), 8.

88. See e.g. Rudolf Neubert, *Die Geschlechtsfrage: Ein Buch für junge Menschen* (Rudolfstadt, 1956) as well as *Das neue Ehebuch: Die Ehe als Aufgabe der Gegenwart und Zukunft* (Rudolfstadt, 1957).

89. Dagmar Herzog, *Sex After Fascism* (Princeton, 2005), 184–219.

90. 'Gutachen von Günter K. Thews über Kleinschmidt's *Keine Angst vor guten Sitten* (1961)', 31 May 1961, BAB DR1/5014a. See too the 'Gutachten von Hirte über Smolkas *Benehmen ist nicht nur Glückssache*', 23 June 1958, DR1/5078, BAB.

91. Smolka, *Junger Mann,* 47.

92. Kleinschmidt, *Keine Angst,* 56.

93. Ibid., preface unpaginated.

94. Ibid. 27.

95. Walter Schmidt, Georg Iggers, and Hendrik Bussiek, *Die real existierende DDR: Neue Notizen aus der unbekannten deutschen Republik* (Frankfurt am Main, 1985), 57–8.

96. Einhorn, *Cinderella,* 57–9.

97. Jonathan Steele, *Socialism with a German Face* (London, 1977), 153.

98. Norbert F. Schneider, *Familie und private Lebensführung in West- und Ostdeutschland* (Stuttgart, 1994), 25.

99. Jutta Gysi (ed.), *Familienleben in der DDR* (East Berlin, 1989), 50.

100. Topstedt, 'Wohnen und Städtebau', 523. See too Susanne Hopf and Natalja Meier, *Plattenbau Privat: 60 Interieurs* (Berlin, 2004).

101. Waltraud Niecke, 'Die Entwicklung des Bevölkerungsbedarf nach Wohnraummöbeln in Zeitraum bis 1985', Institut für Marktforschung, 1979, DL 102/1339, BADH.

102. Stefan Wolle, *Die heile Welt der Diktatur: Alltag und Herrschaft in der DDR, 1971–1989* (Munich, 2001), 362–6.

103. Ina Merkel, 'Leitbilder und Lebensweise von Frauen', in Kaelble *et al.,* 366.

104. Mark Pittaway, *Eastern Europe, 1939–2000* (London, 2004), 110.

105. Monika Grams, 'Vorwort', *Kultur im Heim,* 1 (1988), 1.

106. Thomas Gensicke, 'Sind die Ostdeutschen konservativer als die Westdeutschen?', in Rolf Reissig and Gert-Joachim Glaessner (eds.), *Das Ende eines Experiments: Umbruch in der DDR und deutsche Einheit* (Berlin, 1991), 285.

107. Werner L., Berlin, questionnaire, 28 June 2005. See too Carsten Keller, *Leben im Plattenbau: Zur Dynamik sozialer Ausgrenzung* (Frankfurt, 2005), 22–6.

108. Isolde Deutsch, *Hammer, Zirkel, Gartenzaun: Die Politik der SED gegenüber den Kleingärten* (Berlin, 2003).

109. Steele, *Socialism,* 13, 151.

110. Stephen Lovell, *Summerfolk: A History of the Dacha, 1710–2000* (Ithaca, NY, 2003) and Bernard Wheaton and Zhedek Kavan, *The Velvet Revolution: Czechoslovakia, 1988–1991* (Boulder, Colo., 1992), 9.

111. Nicole Andries and Majken Rehder, *Zaunwelten: Zäune und Zeitzeugen: Geschichten zur Alltagsgeschichte der DDR* (Marburg, 2005).

112. Benno Weiss, untitled typescript, p. 103, Nr. 7194, Walter Kempowski-Archiv, Akademie der Künste, Berlin (WKA).

113. Norbert H., Berlin, questionnaire, 22 July 2005.

114. Karin and Konrad R., respectively, Berlin, interview, 17 July 2005.

115. Dirk Philipsen, *We were the People: Voices from East Germany's Revolutionary Autumn of 1989* (Durham, 1993), 117.

116. Steven Pfaff, *Exit-Voice Dynamics and the Collapse of East Germany* (Durham, 2006), 73.

117. Brigitte Deja-Löhlhöffel, *Freizeit in der DDR* (West Berlin, 1986), 98–104.

118. Mary Fulbrook, *Anatomy of a Dictatorship* (Oxford, 1995), 5.

119. Pfaff, *Exit-Voice,* 74.

120. Tony Judt, *Postwar* (New York, 2005), 499.

121. Hans-Hermann Hertle and Stefan Wolle, *Damals in der DDR: Der Alltag im Arbeiter- und Bauernstaat* (Munich, 2006), 331.

122. Michael Meyen, 'Ein Stück Privatleben: Die Anfänge des Fernsehens in der DDR', *Deutschland-Archiv,* 33 (2000), 207–16.

123. Dorothee Wierling, *Geboren im Jahr Eins* (Berlin, 2002), 468.

124. Mark Pittaway, *Eastern Europe, 1939–2000* (London, 2004), 123.

125. Gislinde Schwarz and Christine Zenner, *Wir wollen mehr als ein Vaterland* (Reinbek, 1990), 93. See too Autorenkollektiv under the direction of Georg Assmann and Gunnar Winkler, *Zwischen Alex und Marzahn: Studie zur Lebensweise in Berlin* (East Berlin, 1987) and Alice Kahl, Steffen H. Wilsdorf, and Herbert F. Wolf, *Kollektivbeziehungen und Lebensweise* (East Berlin, 1984).

126. Claudia Rusch, Berlin, questionnaire, 26 July 2005.

127. Andreas F., Berlin, interview, 18 July 2005.

128. Slavenka Drakulic, *How We Survived Communism and Even Laughed* (London, 1992), esp. 91–2.

129. Svetlana Boym, *Common Places* (Cambridge, 1994), 148.

130. Saldern, *Häuserleben,* 313, 329, and Alfons Silbermann, *Das Wohn-Erlebnis in Ostdeutschland* (Cologne, 1993), esp. 84–133.

131. Arendt, 'The Public Realm and the Private Realm', in *The Hannah Arendt Reader,* ed. Peter Baehr (New York, 2000), 212.

132. *Sozialistische Beziehungen in Familien und Hausgemeinschaften bewusster gestalten* (Berlin, 1971).

133. 'Vermerk: Information des Leiter der Abt. PM/BDVP Neubrandenburg', 12 Dec. 1972, DO1/46357, BAB.

134. Werner Symmangk and Edwin Plenikowski, 'Formen, Methoden und Organisation der Arbeit mit den Hausbuchbeauftragten in einem Meldestellenbereich', 1971, DO1/46632, BAB.

135. Maxie Wander, *Guten Morgen, Du Schöne* (Berlin, 1977).

136. Katharina Belwe, 'Zwischenmenschliche Entfremdung in der DDR: Wachsender materieller Wohlstand versus Verlust an sozialen Kontakten', in *Die DDR in der Ära Honecker* (Opladen, 1988), 499–513.

137. Alice Kahl, 'Zum Verhältnis von Wohnzufriedenheit und Wohnortverbundenheit an neuen Wohnungsbaustandorten in der DDR', *Wissenschaftliche Zeitschrift der Humboldt-Universität zu Berlin: Gesellschafts- und sprachwissenschaftliche Reihe,* 28/4 (1979), 532.

138. Orlando Figes, *The Whisperers* (London, 2007), 160–1.

139. Friedrich Moebius, 'Der Wohnraum als "Abbild" und "Aktion"', *Kultur im Heim,* 4/1977, 34.

NOTES TO CHAPTER 5

1. Manfred Berg and Martin Geyer (eds.), *Two Cultures of Rights: The Quest for Inclusion and Participation in Modern America and Germany* (Cambridge, 2002).

2. See e.g. Roger Engelmann and Clemens Vollnhals (eds.), *Justiz im Dienste der Parteiherrschaft: Rechtspraxis und Staatssicherheit in der DDR* (Berlin, 2000) and Jürgen Weber and Michael Piazolo (eds.), *Justiz im Zwielicht: Ihre Rolle in Diktaturen und die Antwort des Rechtsstaates* (Munich, 1998).

3. Inga Markovits, *Gerechtigkeit in Lüritz: Eine ostdeutsche Rechtsgeschichte* (Munich, 2006), 'Pursuing One's Rights under Socialism', *Stanford Law Review,* 38 (1986), 689–761; 'Socialist vs. Bourgeois Rights: An East-West German Comparison', *University of Chicago Law Review,* 45 (1978), 612–36, and *Sozialistisches und bürgerliches Zivilrechtsdenken in der DDR* (Cologne, 1969); Klaus Westen and Joachim Schleider, *Zivilrecht im Systemvergleich: Das Zivilrecht der Deutschen Demokratischen Republik und der Bundesrepublik Deutschland* (Baden-Baden, 1984) and Klaus Westen (ed.), *Das neue Zivilrecht der DDR nach dem Zivilgesetzbuch von 1975* (Baden-Baden, 1977); see too Joachim Göhring, 'Ohne pauschale Verdammnis und Nostalgie: Überlegungen zur aktuellen Beschäftigung mit dem ZGB der DDR', in Jörn Eckert and Hans Hattenhauer (eds.), *Das Zivilgesetzbuch der DDR vom 19. Juni 1975* (Goldbach, 1995), 9.

4. Klaus Westen, 'Das Menschenbild des ZGB der DDR', in Eckert and Hattenhauer, *Zivilgesetzbuch,* 105.

5. Peter W. Sperlich, *The East German Social Courts: Law and Popular Justice in a Marxist-Leninist Society* (Westport, Conn., 2007); Hans-Andreas Schönfeldt, *Vom Schiedsmann zur Schiedskommission: Normendurchsetzung durch territoriale gesellschaftliche Gerichte in der DDR* (Frankfurt, 2002); Felix Herzog, *Rechtspflege: Sache des ganzen Volkes?* (Baden-Baden, 1999); Lothar Habermann, 'Schiedskommissionen in der DDR: Eine Dokumentation', in Christoph Rennig and Dieter Strempel (eds.), *Justiz im Umbruch: Rechtstatsächliche Studien zum Aufbau der Rechtspflege in den neuen Bundesländern* (Cologne, 1996), 191–283; and Nancy Travis Wolfe, 'Social Courts in the GDR and Comrades' Courts in the Soviet Union: A Comparison', in David Childs, Thomas A. Baylis, and Marilyn Rueschemeyer (eds.), *East Germany in Comparative Perspective* (London, 1989), 60–80.

6. Habermann, 'Schiedskommissionen', 191.

7. ''Die DDR—ein sozialistischer Rechtsstaat', 1989, C Rep 334/23, Landesarchiv Berlin (LAB). For background, K. Sieveking, *Die Entwicklung des sozialistischen Rechtsstaatsbegriffs in der DDR* (West Berlin, 1975), 67ff.

8. Joachim Göhring and Axel Dost, 'Zivilrecht', in Uwe-Jens Heuer (ed.), *Die Rechtordnung der DDR: Anspruch und Wirklichkeit* (Baden-Baden, 1995), 475.

9. Friedrich Christian Schroeder, *Das Strafrecht des realen Sozialismus: Eine Einführung am Beispiel der DDR* (Opladen, 1983), 137–63.

10. Mary Fulbrook, The *People's State* (New Haven, Conn., 2005), esp. 1–22.

11. Travis Wolfe, 'Social Courts', 65, 69.

12. 'Bericht über die Entwicklung der Tätigkeit der Schiedsmänner und Vorschläge für eine Neuregelung', Berlin, 8 July 1961, 7–8, DP 1/1241, BAB.

13. Habermann, 'Schiedskommissionen', 263, 228–9. Berlin was quite unique in this respect, with far fewer dispute commissions than other cities. In 1966 Berlin had only 96 commissions (with 1,305 jurists), compared to 388 commissions (3,912 jurists) in Dresden and 625 commissions (5,498 jurists) in Karl-Marx-Stadt. Herzog, *Rechtspflege*, 33. Perhaps because there were fewer of them, Berlin commissions tended to have roughly twice the casework as the national average in the neighbourhoods that I studied.

14. Again, statistics varied. In 1982–3 e.g. Berlin-Süd reportedly heard only 12 cases for that year, while Berlin-Köpenick registered 88 deliberations. Sperlich, *East German Social Courts*, 227.

15. Herzog, *Rechtspflege*, 11–22.

16. 'Presseinformationen des Ministeriums der Justiz', 1965, quoted in Herzog, *Rechtspflege*, 138.

17. Schönfeldt, *Schiedsmann*, 1–3, 9, 59.

18. e.g. Case 2C 144/45, 31 Oct. 1945, C Rep 343/28, LAB.

19. Cases 2 Ms 22.50-2.55.50 and 7 Ms. 59.50, 18 Aug. 1950, C Rep 343/28, LAB.

20. Hilde Benjamin, *Zur Geschichte der Rechtspflege der DDR, 1949–1961* (Berlin, 1981), 255ff.

21. Travis Wolfe, 'Social Courts', 60–1.

22. In practice they mostly issued reprimands and warnings, imposed 10 ruble fines and occasional evictions.

23. 'Bericht über die Wahl der Schiedskommissionen im I. Quartal 1968', Ministerrat der DDR, 5 June 1968, DP1/VA/ 2042, BAB.

24. Renate Hürtgen, *Zwischen Disziplinierung und Partizipation: Vertrauensleute des FDGB im DDR-Betrieb* (Cologne, 2005), 9.

25. Schönfeldt, *Schiedsmann*, 323.

26. Habermann, 'Schiedskommissionen', 263.

27. 'Bericht über den Stand der Bildung und Tätigkeit von Schieds-Kommissionen', Berlin, 9 Sept. 1965, DP1/VA/2042, BAB.

28. Sperlich, *East German Social Courts*, 172.

29. 'Neue Respektpersonen', *Neues Deutschland*, 22 Oct. 1964, 1.

30. ''Zement aufgewirbelt', *Nationalzeitung*, 14 Nov. 1964.

31. One 1964 newspaper article praised the Berlin district of Friedrichshain for its unusually high number of citizens sitting on residential commissions (79) and

number of cases heard in a year (110), concluding that it was the 'first district in the republic that has social courts in each one of its residential units'. '125mal Rechtsprechung im Wohngebiet: Friedrichshain bei Schiedskommissionen an erster Stelle', *Der Morgen*, 27 Nov. 1964.

32. Sperlich, *East German Social Courts*, 39. See too Kurt Görner, *Zwischen Tat und Urteil: Über Strafverfahren, Ehescheidungen und Zivilprozesse* (Berlin, 1963).

33. 'Bericht über die Entwicklung der Tätigkeit der Schiedsmänner', DP1/1241, BAB.

34. Schönfeldt, *Schiedsmann*, 37.

35. 'Arbeitsplan der Abteilung Innere Angelegenheiten für das 2. Halbjahr 1961', Magistrat von Gross-Berlin, 20 July 1961, C Rep 104/20, LAB.

36. Schönfeldt, *Schiedsmann*, 30, 37.

37. 'Besprechungen mit den Instrukteuren des Nationalrats, den Sekretaren des demo. Sektors und den Instrukteuren und politischen Mitarbeitern des Berliner Sekretariats', 1 July 1953, DY 6/4627, BAB.

38. 'Argumente und Meinungen aus den verschiedensten Kreisen der Bevölkerung', 14 June 1963, DY6/4633, BAB.

39. Herzog, *Rechtspflege*, 36.

40. 'Schiedskommissionen haben sich bewährt', *Berliner Zeitung am Abend*, 20 Nov. 1964.

41. Sperlich, *East German Social Courts*, 194–204.

42. Case 104/71, C Rep 334/31, LAB.

43. Michael Benjamin and Harry Creuzberg, *Die Übergabe von Strafsachen an die Konflikt- und Schiedskommissionen* (Berlin, 1966), 73.

44. On the USSR expropriation of German property after the war, Tilman Bezzenberger, 'Wie das Volkseigentum geschaffen wurde: Die Unternehmens-Enteignungen in der Sowjetischen Besatzungszone 1945–1948', *Zeitschrift für neuere Rechtsgeschichte*, 19 (1997), 210–48.

45. Arnold Freiburg, *Kriminalität in der DDR: Zur Phänomenologie des abweichenden Verhaltens im sozialistischen deutschen Staat* (Opladen, 1981), 82–102.

46. Markovits, *Gerechtigkeit*, 8.

47. Ibid. 41.

48. Z. Szirmai (ed.), *The Law of Inheritance in Eastern Europe and the People's Republic of China* (Leyden, 1961), 19.

49. Quoted in E. L. Johnson, *An Introduction to the Soviet Legal System* (London, 1969), 109.

50. Harold J. Berman, *Justice in the USSR: An Interpretation of Soviet Law* (Cambridge, Mass., 1963), 51.

51. Murad Ferid, 'Zur Problematik des Eigentumsrecht als Rechtsinstitut', in Ferid *et al.*, eds., *Das Eigentum im Ostblock* (West Berlin, 1958), 6.

52. Quoted in Rüdiger Thomson, 'Das persönliche Eigentum im Recht der UdSSR', ibid. 55–7.

53. Hans Wiedemann, *Das sozialistische Eigentum in Mitteldeutschland* (Cologne, 1965), 108.

54. Dieter Pfaff, *Das sozialistische Eigentum in der Sowjetunion* (Cologne, 1965), 28.

55. Gerhard Lingelbach, 'Zum Erbrecht im ZGB', in Eckert and Hattenhauer, *Zivilgesetzbuch*, 160–73.

56. Hans Hattenhauer, "Datschenrecht', ibid. 140–59. By 1989 a third of GDR urban dwellers owned small gardens or weekend houses.

57. Walther Hadding, "Der Vertrag zu Rechten Dritter im ZGB der DDR', ibid. 132.

58. Markovits, *Sozialistisches und bürgerliches Zivilrechtsdenken in der DDR* (Cologne, 1969), 28.

59. "Erfahrungen und Probleme aus der Tätigkeit von Schieds-Kommissionen', 27 Nov. 1963, 12, DP1/1243, BAB.

60. Ministerium der Justiz, *Leitfaden für Schiedskommissionen* (Berlin, 1971), 20.

61. Cited in Gerhard Springer, 'Zum persönlichen Eigentum der Bürger', in *Probleme des sozialistischen Zivilrechts* (Berlin, 1962), 83.

62. NGBK (ed), *Wunderwirtschaft* (Cologne, 1996) and more generally, Susan Reid and David Crowley (eds.), *Style and Socialism* (Oxford, 2000).

63. Springer, 'Zum persönlichen Eigentum', 87.

64. Herzog, *Rechtspflege*, 47.

65. Herbert Kietz and Manfred Mühlmann, *Die Erziehungsaufgaben im Zivilprozess und die Rolle der gerichtlichen Entscheidungen* (Berlin, 1962), 10–11, 34–5.

66. Ulrich Drobnig, 'Dingliche Rechte im Zivilgesetzbuch der DDR', *Recht in Ost und West*, 20 (1976), 14.

67. Rossitza Guentcheva, 'Sounds and Noises in Socialist Bulgaria', in John Lampe and Mark Mazower (eds.), *Ideologies and National Identities: The Case of Twentieth Century Southeastern Europe* (Budapest, 2004), 211–34.

68. Ernst Ehwald, Klaus Dörter Klaus, and Rudolf Junghaus, *Probleme der Landeskultur und der Lärmbekämpfung* (Berlin, 1982). See too Abt. Gesundheits- und Sozialwesen Sekretariat Amtsarzt Kollegin Kern, Betr: Eingabenentwicklung in der Kreishygiene-Inspektion', 17 Nov. 1976, p. 3, C Rep 134–16/150, LAB.

69. Guentcheva, 'Sounds', 217. See too Steven E. Harris, '"I know all the Secrets of My Neighbours:" The Quest for Privacy in the Era of the Separate Apartment,' in Siegelbaum, *Borders of Socialism*, 171–189.

70. Case 56, 13 Nov. 1969, C Rep 334/43, LAB.

71. Case 100, 6 Aug 1971, C Rep 334/43, LAB.

72. Case 40, 10 July 1968, C Rep 334/27, LAB.

73. Familien Kurt S. gegen Frau Alice V, 11 June 1980, original emphasis, C Rep 343/11, LAB.

74. Case 59, 12 Nov. 1969, C Rep 334/27, LAB.

75. Case 4/74, 9 Oct. 1974, C Rep 334/25, LAB.

76. Thomas Lindenberger, 'Ruhe und Ordnung', in Etienne Francois and Hagen Schulze (eds.), *Deutsche Erinnerungsorte II* (Munich, 2001), 469–84.

77. Ibid. 481–2.

78. Habermann, 'Schiedskommissionen', 199.

79. In 1966 e.g. 60% of the slander offenders were between 40 and 60 years old. Habermann, 'Schiedskommissionen', 241.

80. Schönfeldt, *Schiedsmann*, 18–19.

81. M. Lindsay Kaplan, *The Culture of Slander in Early Modern England* (Cambridge, 1997), esp. 12–33.

82. Case 36, 7 Nov.1968, C Rep 334/25, LAB.

83. Case 96/67, undated, C Rep 344/65, LAB.

84. Case 57, 3 July 1969, C Rep 334/23, LAB.

85. Case 47, 12 June 1969, C Rep 334/43, LAB.
86. Unnumbered case, 10 Jan. 1990, C Rep 343/21, LAB.
87. Friedrich Zunkel, 'Ehre, Reputation', in Otto Brunner, Werner Conze, and Reinhart Koselleck (eds.), *Geschichtliche Grundbegriffe* (Stuttgart, 1975), 1–63.
88. Martin Luther, 'Der Grosse Katechismus (1529): Das achte Gebot', in Kurt Aland (ed.), *Luther Deutsch: Die Werke Martin Luthers in neuer Auswahl für die Gegenwart*, iii. *Der neue Glaube* (Göttingen, 1983), 11, 84, cited in Rudolf Mackeprang, *Ehrenschutz im Verfassungsstaat* (Berlin, 1990), 15.
89. Immanuel Kant, *Metaphysik der Sitten, Tugendlehre*, paras. 38 and 40, cited in Hans Joachim Hirsch, *Ehre und Beleidigung: Grundfragen des strafrechtlichen Ehrenschutzes* (Karlsruhe, 1967), 7.
90. Markus Brezina, *Ehre und Ehrenschutz im nationalsozialistischen Recht* (Augsburg, 1987) and Jörg Ernst August Waldow, *Der strafrechtliche Ehrenschutz in der NS-Zeit* (Baden-Baden, 2000).
91. Schönfeldt, *Schiedsmann*, 3.
92. In the 1946 Land Hessen Constitution, Article 3 stated that 'Leben und Gesundheit, Ehre und Würde des Menschen sind unantastbar.' The UN article was reproduced as Article 17 of the 1966 International Covenant on Civil and Political Rights.
93. Alexander Ignor, *Der Straftatbestand der Beleidigung* (Baden-Baden, 1995). By the 1980s the GDR's dispute commissions were handling two and a half times more insult and defamation cases than West German criminal courts. Markovits, 'Pursuing One's Rights under Socialism', *Stanford Law Review*, 38 (1986), 689–744.
94. Quoted in Schönfeldt, *Schiedsmann*, 31.
95. Khrushchev's defense of citizen honour was seen as a key step in his de-Stalinization policies. Serge L. Levitsky, 'Preface', *Copyright, Defamation and Privacy in Soviet Civil Law* (Alphen aan den Rijn, 1979), pp. xi–xvii and 3–6.
96. Lucie Frenzel and Hans Weber, *Der strafrechtliche Schutz der Persönlichkeit in der DDR* (Berlin, 1957), 80, and Karl-Heinz Beyer, 'Bemerkungen zur weiteren Tätigkeit des Schiedsmanns wegen Beleidigungen', *Der Schöffe*, 10 (1963), 243–5.
97. Beate Völker and Henk Flap, 'The Comrades' Belief: Intended and Unintended Consequences of Communism for Neighborhood Relations in the Former GDR', *European Sociological Review*, 13 (1997), 241–65.
98. 'Probleme aus der Tätigkeit der Schiedskommissionen bei der Beratung von Beleidigungsachen', 18 Nov. 1966, C Rep 135-12/12, LAB.
99. 'Rathausgespräch über die Schiedskommissionen', *Sozialistische Demokratie*, 16 Oct. 1964.
100. Case 60/1979, 12 Sept. 1979, C Rep 343/11, LAB.
101. Frenzel and Weber, *Der strafrechtliche Schutz*, 78.
102. Case 40, 10 July 1968, C Rep 334/27, LAB.
103. Unnumbered 1970 case, C Rep 334/27, LAB.
104. Case 123/73, 11 Jan. 1973, C Rep 334/31, LAB.
105. Lothar Mertens (ed.), *Soziale Ungleichheit in der DDR* (Berlin, 2002) and Winfried Thaa *et al.*, *Gesellschaftliche Differenzierung und Legitimätsverfall des DDR-Sozialismus* (Tübingen, 1992).
106. Heike Solga, *Auf dem Weg in eine klassenlose Gesellschaft? Klassenlagen und Mobilität zwischen Generationen in der DDR* (Berlin, 1995), esp. 19–92.
107. Case 6/74, 6 May 1974, C Rep 334/25, LAB.

108. Eingaben, Stadtgericht Berlin, 12 Apr. 1989, C Rep 343/21, LAB.
109. Case 71, 8 July 1970, C Rep 334/27, LAB.
110. Herzog, *Rechtspflege*, 70, though other Berlin commissions did not record much change.
111. Case 19/1981, undated, C Rep 343/11, LAB.
112. Case 9/1981, undated: C Rep 343/8, LAB.
113. Uwe-Jens Heuer, 'Rechtsverständnis in der DDR', in his edited *Rechtsordnung*, 72.
114. Case 9/88, undated, C Rep 343/13, LAB.
115. 'Bericht über die Tätigkeit der SK Wendenschloss/Kietzer Feld', 18 Mar. 1982, C Rep 343/11, LAB and Habermann, 'Schiedskommissionen', 264.
116. Herzog, *Rechtspflege*, 65.
117. Unnumbered case, 12 June 1979, C Rep 343/10, LAB.
118. Unnumbered case, 3 Dec. 1980, C Rep 343/10, LAB.
119. Sven Korzilius, *'Asoziale' und 'Parasiten' im Recht der SBZ/DDR: Randgruppen im Sozialismus zwischen Repression und Ausgrenzung* (Cologne, 2005), 660–4.
120. Unnumbered case, 16 May 1972, C Rep 343/14, LAB.
121. Case 13/86, 13 Aug. 1986, C Rep 343/11, LAB.
122. Markovits, 'Socialist vs. Bourgeois Rights', *University of Chicago Law Review*, 45 (1978), 614.
123. Nicole Andries and Majken Rehder, *Zaunwelten: Zäune und Zeitzeugen—Geschichten zur Alltagskultur der DDR* (Marburg, 2005).
124. Paul Betts, 'The Twilight of the Idols', *Journal of Modern History*, 72 (2000), 731–65.
125. T. H. Marshall, *Citizenship and Social Class* (Cambridge, 1992 [1949]), 26.
126. Manfred Mühlmann, *Sozialistische Lebensweise und persönliches Eigentum* (East Berlin, 1978), 10.
127. Georg Brunner (ed.), *Menschenrechte in der DDR* (Baden-Baden, 1989).
128. Gustav-Adolf Lübchen, *Was Bürger zum Zivilrecht fragen* (Berlin, 1981). See too Klaus Gläss and Manfred Mühlmann, *Bürger-Hausgemeinschaft-Wohngebiet* (Berlin, 1981), 77–87.
129. Quoted in Heuer, 'Rechtsverständnis', 59.
130. Pre-1989 interviews with GDR citizens who had some commission involvement were generally supportive of the social court system. Sperlich, *East German Social Courts*, 249.
131. Daniel John Meador, *Impressions of Law in East Germany* (Charlottesville, Va., 1986), 180, and Markovits, 'Pursuing', 745.
132. Schönfeldt, *Schiedsmann*, 323. On post-1989 scepticism from ex-GDR citizens towards the Federal Republic's justice system, Elisabeth Noelle-Neumann, 'Rechtsbewusstsein im wiedervereinigten Deutschland', *Zeitschrift für Rechtssoziologie*, 16 (1995), 121–55.

NOTES TO CHAPTER 6

1. Andrew I. Port, *Conflict and Stability in the German Democratic Republic* (Cambridge, 2007), esp. 112–39.
2. Joachim Staadt, *Eingaben: Die institutionalisierte Meckerkultur in der DDR* (Berlin, 1996).

3. Klaus Tenfelde and Helmut Trischler (ed.), *Bis vor die Stufen: Bittschriften und Beschwerden von Bergarbeitern im Zeitalter der Industrialisierung* (Bonn, 1986) and Alf Lüdtke, *Eigen-Sinn* (Hamburg, 1993).

4. Jonathan Zatlin, *The Currency of Socialism: Money and Political Culture in East Germany* (Cambridge, 2007), 287, and Staadt, *Eingaben,* esp. the introduction.

5. Felix Mühlberg, *Bürger, Bitten und Behörden: Geschichte der Eingabe in der DDR* (Berlin, 2004), 7, and Ina Merkel (ed.), '*Wir sind doch nicht die Meckerecke der Nation!' Briefe an das Fernsehen der DDR* (Berlin, 2000), 18.

6. Sheila Fitzpatrick, 'Supplicants and Citizens: Public Letter-Writing in Soviet Russia in the 1930s', *Slavic Review,* 55/1 (Spring 1996), 78.

7. Mary Fulbrook, The *People's State* (New Haven, Conn., 2005), 270–1.

8. Ruth Reiher (ed.), *Mit sozialistischen und anderen Grüssen: Porträt einer untergangenen Republik in Alltagstexten* (Berlin, 1995).

9. Protokoll der Ersten Parteikonferenz der SED, Berlin, 1949, 242, quoted in Annett Kästner, 'Die Verfolgung zivilrechtlicher Ansprüche im Eingabenweg auf dem Gebiet des Mietrechts', in Rainer Schröder (ed.), *Zivilrechtskultur der DDR,* ii (Berlin, 1999), 133.

10. Traudel Ritter, *Eingabenarbeit* (Berlin, 1971), esp. 14–29.

11. J. Ellinger, E. Lange, S. Petzold, and O. Schaefer, *Eingabenarbeit heute* (East Berlin, 1967), 8, 15.

12. Wolfgang Menzel, *Das Vorschlags- und Beschwerderecht der Werktätigen der Deutschen Demokratischen Republik* (East Berlin, 1956), 82–3.

13. Cited in Mühlberg, *Bürger,* 71.

14. Wolfgang Bernet, 'Verwaltungsrecht: Entwicklung und Zustand der Verwaltungsrechtswissenschaft der DDR', in Uwe-Jens Heuer, *Die Rechtsordnung der DDR* (Baden-Baden, 1995), 421.

15. Bettina Theben, 'Eingabenarbeit: Zur Rolle der volkeigenen Betriebe bei der Schlichtung zivilrechtlicher Streitigkeiten mit Bürgern', in Schröder, *Zivilrechtskultur,* ii. 97.

16. Mühlberg, *Bürger,* 7.

17. Fulbrook, *People's State,* 270.

18. See the letters contained in Eingaben, 1962–3, C Rep 131/12/6, Landesarchiv Berlin (LAB).

19. Letter, 10 Jan. 1964, C Rep 131/12/6 LAB.

20. Letter from M. Honecker of the Ministry of People's Education to Ministry of Building Construction, DH 1/39252, Bundesarchiv Berlin (BAB).

21. Eingabenanalyse, Gross-Berlin: Rat des Stadtbezirks Mitte, 10 Oct. 1963, C Rep 131/12/6, LAB.

22. Eingabenanalyse, 1962–3, C Rep 131/12/6, LAB.

23. Mühlberg, *Bürger,* 32.

24. Johann Heinrich Kumpf, *Petitionsrecht und öffentliche Meinung im Entstehungsprozess der Paulskirchenverfassung 1848/1849* (Frankfurt am Main, 1983), 23–144.

25. Article 17: 'Everyone has the right, whether individually or in league with others, to lodge complaints and petitions in writing to local authorities and national representatives.' This right was expanded in a *Bundesverfassungsgericht Beschluss* from April 1953, and was further strengthened in 1975 with an expanded Article 45c of the Basic Law.

26. Zatlin, *Currency of Socialism,* 291–2.

27. Brigitte Grunert, *Der Bürger und sein Petitionsrecht* (Berlin, 1978), 45.

28. Orlando Figes, *The Whisperers* (London, 2007), 36.

29. Golfo Alexopoulos, 'Exposing Illegality and Oneself: Complaint and Risk in Stalin's Russia', in Peter H. Solomon, Jr (ed.), *Reforming Justice in Russia, 1864–1996* (Armonk, NY, 1997), 169.

30. Figes, *The Whisperers,* 459.

31. Robert Gellately, 'Denunciations in Twentieth Century Germany', *Journal of Modern History,* 68/4 (Dec. 1996), 950.

32. Ulbricht auf der Babelsberger Konferenz vom 2. und 3.4. 1958, Protokoll, 38, cited in Inga Markowits, *Sozialistisches und bürgerliches Zivilrechtsdenken in der DDR* (Cologne, 1969), 9.

33. *Marxistisch-leninistische allgemeine Theorie des Staates und des Rechts,* iii. *Der sozialistische Staat* (Berlin, 1975), 255, 260.

34. Ulrich Löffler, 'Eingaben im Bereich des Zivilrechts', in Rainer Schröder (ed.), *Zivilrechtskultur der DDR,* i (Berlin, 1999), 217.

35. Karl Hönl, 'Die Eingaben der Werktätigen als Mittel der Demokratisierung der Arbeitsweise des Staatsapparates', *Staat und Recht* (1953), 700.

36. 'Vermerk: Noch zu erledigen', *Neues Deutschland,* 5 Dec. 1969.

37. 'Taube Ohren für Eingaben', *Neues Deutschland,* 18 Nov. 1970.

38. Ellinger *et al., Eingabenarbeit heute,* 43 and *Eingaben: Bürger gestalten Kommunalpolitik mit* (East Berlin, 1989).

39. Alexopoulos, 'Exposing Illegality', 169.

40. Theben, 'Eingabenarbeit', 99.

41. Ibid. 103.

42. Thomas Lindenberger, 'Das Fremde im Eigenen des Staatssozialismus: Klassendiskurs und Exclusion am Beispiel der Konstruktion des "asozialen Verhaltens"', in Jan C. Behrends, Thomas Lindenberger, and Patrice Poutrus (eds.), *Fremde und Fremd-Sein in der DDR* (Berlin, 2003), 179–91.

43. Mühlberg, *Bürger,* 134.

44. Herbert Kietz and Manfred Mühlmann, *Konfliktursachen und Aufgaben der Zivil- und Familienrechtspflege* (East Berlin, 1969).

45. Mühlberg, *Bürger,* 196, 224–6.

46. Mike Dennis, The *Stasi* (London, 2003), 217–18, 136.

47. Heinz Niemann, *Die geheimen Berichte des Instituts für Meinungsforschung an das Politbüro der SED* (Cologne, 1993), esp. 56–8.

48. Mark Allinson, 'Popular Opinion', in Patrick Major and Jonathan Osmond (eds.), *The Workers' and Peasants' State* (Manchester, 2002), 110.

49. Patrick Major, *Behind the Berlin Wall* (Oxford, 2010), 17.

50. Wolfgang Engler, *Die Ostdeutschen: Kunde von einem verlorenen Land* (Berlin, 2000), 61.

51. Zatlin, *Currency of Socialism,* 301.

52. Fitzpatrick, *Everyday Stalinism,* 177.

53. Mühlberg, *Bürger,* 77–80, 275.

54. See the petitions gathered DC 20/3528 and 3609, BAB.

55. 'Berichterstattung für den Monat Januar 1954, Gross-Berlin Rat des Stadtbezirks Friedrichshain', 5 Feb. 1954, C Rep 135-01/149, LAB.

56. 'Eingabenanalyse für das I. Quartal 1965', C Rep 148-01/210, LAB.

57. Löffler, 'Eingaben', 224.

58. Fulbrook, *People's State*, 286.

59. Mark Pittaway, *Eastern Europe, 1939–2000* (London, 2004), 128.

60. Lothar Mertens, *Wider die sozialistische Familiennorm* (Opladen and Wiesbaden, 1998), 47.

61. Dennis, *Stasi*, 219–20.

62. Christian Härtel and Petra Kabus (eds.), *Das Westpaket* (Berlin, 2000).

63. Cited in Ross, *East German Dictatorship*, 68.

64. Merkel, *Meckerecke*, 104.

65. Repr. ibid. 107.

66. 'Letter to Erich Honecker', Rat des Stadtbez. Friedrichshain, 27 Feb. 1973, C Rep 135-01/414, LAB.

67. Zatlin, *Currency of Socialism*, 305 n. 60.

68. Staadt, *Eingaben*, 30, 34.

69. 'W. S. an Herrn Bürgermeister H, Rat des Stadtbezirks Friedrichshain', 17 Mar. 1966, C Rep 135-01/401, LAB.

70. 'Eingabe von Manfred K.', 28 Feb. 1972, Berlin, C Rep 135-09/95, LAB, and Merkel, *Meckerecke*, 47–375.

71. Mühlberg, *Bürger*, 232–45; Port, *Conflict*, 268.

72. Quoted in Major, *Behind*, 211.

73. Various stories are recounted in Sieglinde Peters, *Mein Hand für mein Produkt* (Berlin, 1996).

74. Stephen Kotkin, *Magnetic Mountain* (Berkeley, Calif., 1995), 198–237.

75. Ralf H. an VEB Gaststätten HO Berlin, 2 Dec. 1981, C Rep 135-12, 1001, LAB.

76. Major, *Behind*, 202.

77. Gareth Dale, *Popular Protest in East Germany* (London, 2005), 87.

78. Major, *Behind*, 217.

79. Daniel C. Thomas, *The Helsinki Effect: International Norms, Human Rights and the Demise of Communism* (Princeton, 2001).

80. 'Eingabe: Fortgesetzte Rühestörung durch Familie L', 13 Sept. 1981, C Rep 134-12/1457, LAB.

81. 'Eingabe an Stadtrat im Bez. Lichtenberg', 13 Mar. 1979, C Rep 147-01/154, LAB.

82. Major, *Behind*, 203.

83. 'Betr: Schriftliche Bitte einer Wohnraumlenkung', 7 Ju;y 1986, Berlin, 5.3.1987, C Rep 151-02/43, LAB.

84. Monika Deutz-Schroeder and Joachim Staadt (eds.), *Teuer Genosse: Briefe an Erich Honecker* (Berlin, 1994).

85. A similar tone can be found in the Nazi era complaint letters discussed in John Connelly, 'The Uses of the Volksgemeinschaft', *Journal of Modern History*, 68/4 (Dec. 1996), 899–930.

86. Zatlin, *Currency of Socialism*, 302.

87. 'Letter to Frau Bürgermeister Kurzia, Weissensee, Berlin', 15 Sept. 1965, C Rep 148-01/210, LAB.

88. Quoted in Zatlin, *Currency of Socialism*, 303.

89. Staadt, *Eingaben*, 5–6.

90. Merkel, *Meckerecke,* 24.

91. Ellinger *et al., Eingabenarbeit heute,* 26.

92. Zatlin, *Currency of Socialism,* 299.

93. Dale, *Popular Protest,* 73, and Staadt, *Eingaben,* 41–8.

94. Cited in Steven Pfaff, *Exit-Voice Dynamics and the Collapse of East Germany* (Durham, 2006), 45.

95. Merkel, *Meckerecke,* 18.

96. Fulbrook, *People's State,* 278.

97. Stefan Wolle, *Die heile Welt der Diktatur* (Berlin, 1998), 286.

98. Major, *Behind,* 218.

99. Dale, *Popular Protest,* 123.

100. 'Ulrich Drawe an Generalsekr. des ZK d. SED Erich Honecker', 22 Mar. 1989, Nachlass Bärbel Bohley, BBo 040, Matthias-Domaschk-Archiv in der Robert-Havemann-Gesellschaft e.V, Berlin.

101. Zatlin, *Currency of Socialism,* 316.

102. Merkel, *Meckerecke,* 40.

103. Zatlin, *Currency of Socialism,* 315.

104. Merkel, *Meckerecke,* 12.

105. Donna Harsch, *Revenge of the Domestic* (Princeton, 2006), 316.

106. Inga Markovits, 'Rechtsstaat oder Beschwerdestaat? Verwaltungsrechtschutz in der DDR', *Recht in Ost und West,* 5 (1987), 265–81.

107. Irene Böhme, *Die da drüben: Sieben Kapitel DDR* (West Berlin, 1982), 41–3.

108. Zatlin, *Currency of Socialism,* 288.

109. Fulbrook, *People's State,* 270.

110. James C. Scott, *Weapons of the Weak* (New Haven, Conn., 1985).

111. Zatlin, *Currency of Socialism,* 320.

NOTES TO CHAPTER 7

1. Eugen Blume and Roland März (eds.), *Kunst in der DDR: Eine Retrospektive der Nationalgalerie* (Berlin, 2003); Daniela Berghahn, *Hollywood behind the Wall: The Cinema of East Germany* (Manchester, 2005); and Joshua Feinstein, *The Triumph of the Ordinary: Depictions of Daily Life in East German Cinema, 1945–1989* (Chapel Hill, NC, 2002).

2. Heinz Hoffmann and Rainer Knapp (eds.), *Fotografie in der DDR: Ein Beitrag zur Bildergeschichte* (Leipzig, 1987), 14.

3. Thomas Honickel, 'Wir sind das Volk: Ostdeutsche Fotografie 1956 bis 1989', in Norbert Moos (ed.), *Utopie und Wirklichkeit: Ostdeutsche Fotografie, 1956–1989* (Bönen, 2005), 7.

4. Chris McIntyre, 'Foreword', in Nicola Freeman and Matthew Shaul (eds.), *Do Not Refreeze: Photography behind the Berlin Wall* (London, 2008), 7.

5. Besides Moos, *Utopie,* see too *Foto-Anschlag: Vier Generationen ostdeutscher Fotographen* (Leipzig, 2001) and Karl Gernot Kuehn, *Caught: The Art of Photography in the German Democratic Republic* (Berkeley, Calif., 1997).

6. See e.g. Peter Boethig (ed.), *MachtSpiele: Literatur und Staatssicherheit* (Leipzig, 1993). A notable exception is Birgit Poppe, *Freizeit und Privatleben in der Malerei der DDR: Formen und Funktionen neuer Motive der Leipziger Schule nach 1970* (Frankfurt am Main, 2000).

7. Rudolf Vedler, 'Fotografierverbote', *Fotografie* (March 1962), 82–3, 96, quoted in Kuehn, *Caught*, 65.

8. Elena Demke, 'Mauerfotos in der DDR: Inszenierung, Tabus, Kontexte', in Karin Hartewig and Alf Lüdtke (eds.), *Die DDR im Bild: Zur Gebrauch der Fotografie im anderen deutschen Staat* (Göttingen, 2004), 90–106.

9. Karin Hartewig, *Das Auge der Partei: Fotografie und Staatssicherheit* (Berlin, 2004).

10. Kristie Macrakis, *Seduced by Secrets: Inside the Stasi's Spy-Tech World* (Cambridge, 2008), 226–9.

11. Axel Dossmann, 'Transit: Die Autobahn im Blick von Polizei und Staatssicherheit', in Hartewig and Lüdtke, *DDR*, 107–21.

12. Karin Hartewig, 'Botschaften auf der Haut der Geächten: Die Tätowierung von Strafgefangenen in Fotographien der Staatssicherheit', ibid. 125–44.

13. Hartewig, *Auge*, 10, 29.

14. Macrakis, *Seduced by Secrets*, 243–4; Hartewig, *Auge*, 128–9.

15. Rainer Eckhart, 'Fotographie in der DDR zwischen Opposition und Repression', in *Foto-Anschlag*, 136–9.

16. See for Alexander Dymschitz, 'Über die formalistische Richtung in der deutschen Malerei', *Tägliche Rundschau*, 19 and 24 Nov. 1948, and Herbert Sandberg, 'Der Formalismus und die neue Kunst', *Tägliche Rundschau*, 17 Dec. 1948. Ludger Derenthal, *Bilder der Trümmer- und Aufbaujahre: Fotographie im sich teilenden Deutschland* (Marburg, 1999), 228.

17. Peter Pachnicke, 'Anmerkungen zur einer Geschichte der DDR-Fotografie 1945 bis 1960', in *Frühe Bilder: Eine Ausstellung zur Geschichte der Fotographie in der DDR* (Leipzig, 1985), 1–2.

18. Corinna Halbrehder, *Die Malerei der Allgemeinen Deutschen Kunstausstellung: Kunstausstellung der DDR*, i–vii (Frankfurt, 1995), 186.

19. Kuehn, *Caught*, 17.

20. Halbrehder, *Die Malerei*, 50–1.

21. Hubertus Gassner and Eckhart Gillen (eds.), *Kultur und Kunst in der DDR seit 1970* (Lahn-Giessen, 1977), 149.

22. Pachnicke, 'Anmerkungen', in *Frühe Bilder*, 1–2.

23. Kuehn, *Caught*, 40.

24. Ernst Nitsche, 'Realismus und Formalismus in der Fotografie', *Die Fotografie*, 7/4 (1953), 113.

25. Ulrich Domröse, 'Nichts ist so einfach wie es scheint', in Ulrich Domröse (ed.), *Nichts ist so einfach wie es scheint: Ostdeutsche Photographie, 1945–1989* (Berlin, 1992), 10.

26. Berthold Beiler, *Probleme über Fotografie: Parteilichkeit im Foto* (Halle, 1959), 34.

27. Jörn Glasenapp, *Die deutsche Nachkriegsfotografie: Eine Mentalitätsgeschichte in Bildern* (Paderborn, 2008), 161–88 and 211–57, and most recently, Astrid Ihle, 'Photography as Contemporary Document: Comments on the Conceptions of the Documentary in Germany after 1945', in Stephanie Barron and Sabine Eckmann (eds.), *Art of Two Germanys: Cold War Cultures* (New York, 2009), 186–205.

28. Kuehn, *Caught*, 10, 29.

29. Wolfgang Kil, 'Bilder vom Sein und vom Bewusstsein: Denkanstösse zu einer Fotogeschichtsschreibung DDR 1945–1965', *Bildende Kunst*, 2 (1987), 59–61.

30. Heinz Hoffmann and Rainer Knapp (eds.), *Fotografie in der DDR: Ein Beitrag zur Bildergeschichte* (Leipzig, 1987), 20–30. See too Silke Satjukov, '"Früher war das eben den Adolf . . .": Der Arbeitsheld Adolf Hennecke', in Silke Satjukow and Rainer Gries (eds.), *Sozialistische Helden: Eine Kulturgeschichte von Propangandafiguren in Osteuropa und der DDR* (Berlin, 2002), 115–32.

31. Stefan Schweizer, 'Täve Schur und das Bild der 'Diplomaten im Traininganzug: Zur bildlichen Inszenierung von Spitzensportlern in der DDR', in Hartewig und Lüdtke, *DDR*, 69–86. See too Norbert Rossbach, 'Der Radsportler Gustav-Adolf Schur', in Satjukow and Gries, *Sozialistische Helden*, 133–46.

32. Martin Damus, *Malerei der DDR: Funktionen der bildenden Kunst im Realen Sozialismus* (Hamburg, 1991), 102.

33. Beiler, *Probleme*, 58, quoted in Kuehn, *Caught*, 50.

34. Stefan Wolle, 'The Smiling Face of Dictatorship: On the Political Iconography of the GDR', in *German Photography, 1870–1970: Power of a Medium* (Cologne, 1997), 127.

35. See Hans Pischner's untitled opening remarks in *Fünfte Deutsche Kunstausstellung Dresden 1962* (Dresden, 1962), x–xi.

36. Hubertus Gassner and Eckhart Gillen, 'Kultur und "subjektiver Factor" in der DDR: Zur Debatte und das Konzept der "Arbeitskultur" in den 70er Jahren', in Hubertus Gassner and Eckhart Gillen (eds.), *Kultur und Kunst in der DDR seit 1970* (Giessen, 1977), 9–39.

37. Gerhard Henninger, 'Probleme einer sozialistischen Fotokunst', *Fotokunst* (Jan. 1961), 418.

38. Karin Thomas, *Kunst in Deutschland seit 1945* (Cologne, 2002), 120.

39. Bernd Lindner, 'Abbild und Einmischung: Sozialdemokratische Fotografie in der DDR', in *Foto-Anschlag*, 18.

40. Hermann Schäfer, 'Vorwort', *Foto-Anschlag*, 7.

41. Quoted in Matthew Shaul, 'Once Thawed—Do Not Refreeze', in Freeman and Shaul (eds.), *Do Not Refreeze*, 13.

42. Ibid. 16.

43. Ulrike Goeschen, *Vom sozialistischen Realismus zur Kunst im Sozialismus* (Berlin, 2001).

44. Peter Pachnicke, 'Suche nach Individualität', *Bildende Kunst*, 2 (1987), 69; Moos, *Utopie*, 15.

45. Josie McLellan, 'Visual Dangers and Delights: Nude Photography in East Germany', *Past and Present* (Aug. 2009), 143–74.

46. 'Über Ausbildung, Vorbilder, Kontakte', in Moos, *Utopie*, 16; Lindner, 'Abbild', 19.

47. Halbrehder, *Die Malerei*, 110.

48. Domröse, 'Nichts', 13–14.

49. Moos, *Utopie*, 9–10.

50. Gabriele Muschter (ed.), *DDR Frauen fotografieren: Lexicon und Anthologie* (Berlin, 1991), 7.

51. Ibid. 28.

52. Inka Schube, 'Und alles riecht nach Nachkrieg: Zu den Fotographien von Helga Paris', in Inka Schube (ed.), *Helga Paris: Fotographien* (Hanover, 2004), 6.

53. Muschter, 'Sehen', 242. See too Albrecht Wiesener, 'Halle an der Saale—Chemiemetropole oder "Diva im Grau"?', in Hartewig and Lüdtke, *DDR*, 51–68.

54. Ulrich Domröse, 'Rede zur Verleihung des Hannah-Hoch-Preises, 2004', in *Helga Paris, Fotographien, 1968–1996* (Berlin, 2004), 7. See too Matthias Flagge, 'Helga Paris, Christian Borchert', in *Foto-Anschlag, 56–7*.

55. The series was first published in 1986 with some modifications ('grey' changed to 'occasionally grey', etc.) and then reissued as *Diva in Grau* in 1990, with more texts. Helmut Brade, 'Häuser und Gesichter: Halle, 1983–1985', in *Helga Paris*, 286.

56. *Uwe Steinberg: Fotographien, 1957–1983* (Berlin, 1983), unpaginated.

57. Ibid.

58. *1. Porträtfotoschau der DDR* (Dresden and Berlin, 1971), unpaginated.

59. Ibid.

60. *Fotografie in der DDR*, 119.

61. Ibid. 117.

62. In painting some of these changes were afoot a few years before. At the 1967 Deutsche Kunstausstellung, for example, there was a discernibly new emphasis on still-lives, and even the return of the private lives of artists in artistic representations of the period, so much so that critics worried about the emergence of isolation and loneliness in these new works. Halbrehder, *Die Malerei,* 165. In fact, Diether Schmidt's *Ich War, Ich Werde Sein* (1968) was an explicit effort to counter this trend, arguing that self-portraiture was born of alienation with Dürer and Raphael and Rembrandt, and reached its high point during the period of 1890 to 1920. In his estimation, the flourishing of self-portraiture was a mark of class conflict, homelessness and alienation, and socialist countries had thankfully overcome the need for the genre.

63. Gassner and Gillen, *Kultur und Kunst,* 189.

64. Ulrike Niederhofer, *Die Auseinandersetzung mit dem Expressionismus in den bildenden Kunst im Wandel der politischen Realität der SBZ und der DDR, 1945–1989* (Frankfurt am Main, 1996), 250.

65. 'Gesellschaftliches und (oder ?) Privates', *Bildende Kunst,* 23/6 (1975), 306, and 23/8 (1975), 466, respectively.

66. Willi Sitte, 'Rechenschaftsbericht des VIII. Kongress des Verbandes Bildender Künstler der DDR' (Berlin, 1978), 23, quoted in Poppe, *Freizeit,* 133.

67. Halbrehder, *Die Malerei,* 219.

68. Photography did play a small part in the 1949 Dresden Deutsche Kunstausstellung. Derenthal, *Bilder,* 154.

69. *Foto-Anschlag,* 145.

70. 'Gruppe JUGENDFOTO BERLIN 1969–1979', *Bildende Kunst,* 4 (1984), 162–77.

71. Petra Clemens, '"Betriebsgeschehen" im VEB Forster Tuchfabriken—im Fotos und beim Fotographien', in Hartewig and Lüdtke, *DDR*, 169–85. See too Berthold Beiler, 'Vom Arbeiterfotografen zum fotografierenden Arbeiter', *Fotografie,* 4 (1971), 24–5.

72. Hartewig, *Auge,* 192.

73. Honickel, 'Wir sind das Volk', 7.

74. Kuehn, *Caught,* 109.

75. *Frauenbilder: Leben vor '89: Fotographien Katja Worch, Porträt Holde-Barbara Ulrich* (Berlin, 1995), 33, and *Frühe Bilder,* 80.

76. Honickel, 'Wir sind das Volk', 7.
77. Friedrich Möbius, 'Erkenntnis und Gestaltung: Zu Problemen des Mehrfigurenbildes auf der VI. Deutschen Kunstausstellung', *Bildende Kunst,* 6 (1968), 330, quoted in Poppe, *Freizeit,* 75.
78. *Fotographie in der DDR,* 65.
79. Pachnicke, 'Anmerkungen', 6.
80. 'Gegen das Verschwinden: Matthias Flagge im Gespräch mit Christian Borchert am 13. Januar 1996', in *Christian Borchert: Zeitreise, Dresden, 1954–1995* (Dresden, 1986), 203.
81. Peter Pachnicke, 'Suche nach Individualität: Porträtfotografie der 80er Jahre', *Bildende Kunst,* 2 (1987), 64.
82. T. O. Immisch, 'Familien: Ein sozialdokumentarisches Projekt', in *Familien in der DDR: 36 Fotographien von Christian Borchert,* no date, Nachlass Borchert, Berliner Galerie, Berlin.
83. Kuehn, *Caught,* 112.
84. Elke Erb, 'Das Eigene Bild', in *Christian Borchert: Gruppenbilder und Künstlerporträts* (Cottbus, 1980), 6.
85. See Helmut Lethen, *Cool Conduct: The Culture of Distance in Weimar Germany,* tr. Don Reneau (Berkeley, Calif., 2002).
86. Similar trends could be seen in 1970s film as well. Feinstein, *Triumph,* 6–7.
87. Gabriele Muschter, 'Sehen mit anderen Augen', in Gabriele Muschter and Rüdiger Thomas, *Jenseits der Staatskultur: Traditionen autonomer Kunst in der DDR* (Munich, 1992), 239.
88. Flagge, 'Helga Paris, Christian Borchert', in *Foto-Anschlag,* 57.
89. Angelike Lorenz, *Das deutsche Familienbild in der Malerei des 19. Jahrhunderts* (Darmstadt, 1985).
90. Charles Maier, *Dissolution* (Princeton, 1997), 29. See Stefan Wolle, *Die heile Welt der Diktatur* (Munich, 2001), 381–2.
91. Svetlana Boym, *Common Places* (Cambridge, 1994), 121–64.
92. Heino R. Möller, *Innenräume/Aussenwelten: Studien zur Darstellung bürgerlichen Privatheit in Kunst und Warenwerbung* (Giessen, 1981).
93. Herlinde Koelbl, *Das deutsche Wohnzimmer* (Lucerne and Frankfurt, 1980), 132.
94. In the first picture, the female resident writes that 'I am a modern woman and love modern living. I have succeeded in combining career, marriage and children.' In the second, the husband writes that 'I have shaped the face of my community during my time as mayor, and it has maintained its own standing thanks to my personal engagement', while his partner writes that 'when the children go to bed, I can finally enjoy being myself'.
95. Clemens, 'Betriebsgeschehen', 169–70.
96. Hartewig, *Auge,* 183, 206.
97. Paul Kaiser and Claudia Petzold (eds.), *Boheme und Diktatur in der DDR: Gruppen, Konflikte, Quartiere, 1970-1989* (Berlin, 1997), 42.
98. On family photographs, see Pierre Bourdieu, *Photography: A Middle-Brow Art,* tr. Shaun Whiteside (London, 1990 [1965]), esp. 19–31. For background on German private photography, Timm Starl, *Knipser: Die Bildgeschichte der privaten Fotografie in Deutschland und Österreich von 1880 bis 1980* (Munich, 1985).

99. Peter Guth, 'Margit Emmrich, Gerhard Gäbler,' in *Foto-Anschlag*, 84.
100. Kuehn, *Caught*, 184.
101. Helga Mobius, 'Ausblicke: Fenster als Bildgegenstand', *Bildende Kunst*, 9 (1979), 434–8.
102. Poppe, *Freizeit*, 69–75.
103. Rolf Sachsse, 'Ostkreuz versus Bilderberg: Ost- und Westdeutscher Bildjournalismus im Vergleich', in Hartewig and Lüdtke, *DDR*, 214.
104. See e.g. Hermann Peters, 'Zur Problematik des Gruppenbildes', *Bildende Kunst*, 3 (1970), 115–19, and Erika Klingenburg, 'Engagement in der Sache Famlienbild', *Bildende Kunst*, 9 (1973), 438–42. Parallel developments occurred in painting. Damus, *Malerei der DDR*, 247.
105. Andreas Krase, 'Das Authentische des Wirklichen: Künstlerische Fotografie in der DDR', in Blume and März, *Kunst*, 79.
106. Karin Hartewig, 'The Sentimental Eye: Family Photographs in the 19th and 20th Century', in Klaus Tenfelde (ed.), *Pictures of Krupp: Photography and History in the Industrial Age* (Munich, 1994), 215–40.
107. Gabriele Muschter, 'Frauen fotografieren anders', in *Bildende Kunst*, 2 (1988), 51.
108. Daniela Berghahn, *Hollywood behind the Wall*, 175–211.
109. Muschter, *DDR Frauen fotografieren*, 12.
110. Damus, *Malerei der DDR*, 306–9.
111. Gisela Helwig, *Am Rande der Gesellschaft: Alte und Behinderte in beiden deutschen Staaten* (Cologne, 1980). One historian has gone so far as to say that the old and retired in the GDR were seen by the SED as the 'Abfallprodukte der Leistungsgesellschaft'. Wolle, *Die heile Welt*, 300.
112. Werner Mahler, 'Harald Z', in OSTKREUZ (ed.), *Östlich von Eden: Von der DDR nach Deutschland, 1974–1999* (Vienna and Munich, 2000), 56.
113. Quoted in Kuehn, *Caught*, 1.
114. Friedrich Engels, 'Die Lage der arbeitenden Klasse in England', in *Marx-Engels-Werke*, ii (Berlin, 1976), 344, cited in Udo Grashoff, *'In einem Anfall von Depression...'* (Berlin, 2006), 274.
115. Antonia Grunenberg, *Aufbruch der inneren Mauer: Politik und Kultur in der DDR, 1971–1990* (Bremen, 1990), 193.
116. Grashoff, *In einem Anfall*, esp. 450–66.
117. T. I. Oiserman, *Die Entfremdung als historische Kategorie* (Berlin, 1965), 120.
118. Karl Marx, *Ökonomisch-philosophische Manuskripte* (Leipzig, 1974), 188, cited in Grashoff, *In einem Anfall*, 272.
119. Mary Fulbrook, *The People's State* (New Haven, Conn., 2005), 99.
120. Rudolf Schäfer, 'Rudi Schäfer und Gosbert Adler am 4 Juni 1985', in Gosbert Adler and Wilmar Koenig, *DDR Foto* (East Berlin, 1985), 54–7.
121. Sachsse, 'Ostkreuz', 224.
122. Schäfer, 'Rudi Schäfer und Gosbert Adler', 54–7.
123. Roland Barthes, *Camera Lucida: Reflections on Photography*, tr. Richard Howard (New York, 1981), 92.
124. See e.g. *Rudolf Schäfer: Der ewige Schlaf/Visages de morts* (Hamburg, 1989), unpaginated.

125. Katherina Belwe, 'Zwischenmenschliche Entfremdung in der DDR: Wachsender materieller Wohlstand versus Verlust an sozialen Kontakt', in Gert-Joachim Glaessner (ed.), *Die DDR in der Ära Honecker: Politik Kultur Gesellschaft* (Opladen, 1988), 499–513.

126. Feinstein, *Triumph*, 117–19, 131, and Damus, *Malerei der DDR,* 291–315.

127. Schäfer, 'Rudi Schäfer und Gosbert Adler', 10.

128. Harald Hauswald, *Ost-Berlin* (Munich, 1987). For discussion, Hartewig, *Auge*, 153–66.

129. Barthes, *Camera Lucida*, 98. For architecture, see Beatriz Colomina, *Privacy and Publicity: Modern Architecture as Mass Media* (Cambridge, Mass., 1994).

130. Flagge, 'Helga Paris, Christian Borchert', in *Foto-Anschlag*, 57.

NOTES TO EPILOGUE

1. Quoted in Mark Mazower, *Dark Continent: Europe's 20th Century* (New York, 1998), 361.

2. Richard L. Merritt, 'Interpersonal Transactions across the Wall', in Richard Merritt and Anna J. Merritt (eds.), *Living with the Wall: West Berlin, 1961–1985* (Durham, 1985), 182–3.

3. *Berliner Morgenpost* headline, 10 Nov. 1989, quoted in Kuehn, 267.

4. Charles Maier, *Dissolution* (Princeton, 1997), 285–329. The 'Germans as Victims' theme became a key dimension of German identity politics in the late 1990s. See Bill Niven, *Germans as Victims? Remembering the Past in Contemporary Germany* (Basingstoke, 2006).

5. Martin Sabrow *et al.* (ed.), *Wohin treibt die DDR-Erinnerung? Dokumentation einer Debatte* (Göttingen, 2007), esp. 56, 257, 321.

6. Armin Mitter and Stefan Wolle, *Untergang auf Raten* (Munich, 1993), 7.

7. Kate Connolly, 'Wall Remembered: Germans Hanker after Barrier', *Guardian*, 8 Nov. 2007, 20.

8. According to 1994 polls, 36% of Poles said that would gladly have their old system back. Tina Rosenberg, *The Haunted Land* (London, 1995), p. xviii.

9. Tobias Dürr, 'On "Westalgia": Why West German Mentalities and Habits Persist in the Berlin Republic', in Dieter Dettke (ed.), *The Spirit of the Berlin Republic* (New York, 2003), 38. For an early version of West German nostalgia, see Otthein Rammstedt and Gert Schmidt (eds.), *BRD Ade! Vierzig Jahre in Rück-Ansichten* (Frankfurt, 1992), esp. 13–28.

10. On Western European 'Westalgie', see Timothy Garton Ash, 'Europa unterschätzt seine Macht masslos', *Die Presse*, 12 Nov. 2007.

11. Jennifer Yoder, *From East Germans to Germans? The New Postcommunist Elites* (Durham, 1999), 18.

12. Wolf Lepenies, *Folgen einer unerhorten Begebenheit: Die Deutschen nach der Vereinigung* (Berlin, 1992), 27.

13. Winfried Thaa, *Die Wiedergeburt des Politischen: Zivilgesellschaft und Legitimitätskonflikt in den Revolutionen von 1989* (Opladen, 1996).

14. Eva Kolinsky, 'Exodus to the Private Realm', *Times Higher Education Supplement*, 29 Jan. 1993, 15–18.

15. Harald Woldemar Meyer, 'Mein Lebenslauf', 1995, Nr. 534, DTA and Sabine Mitschke, 'Geschichte des Hauses Albert-Schweitzer-Str 1 in Bautzen seit 1945', 1999, Nr 790/II, 2, DTA.

16. Klaus Hugler, *Missbrauchtes Vertrauen: Christliche Jugendarbeit unter den Augen der Stasi* (Neukirchen-Vluyn, 1994), 88–9.

17. Uta Kolano, *Nackter Osten* (Frankfurt am Oder, 1995), 44–5.

18. Thomas Roehe's tirade, *Arbeiten wie bei Honecker, leben wie bei Kohl: Ein Plädoyer für das Ende der Schonfrist* (Frankfurt, 1999) mocked the East Germans as lazy and shiftless, supposedly preferring to work like in the old days under Honecker, but wanting to live (and be paid) as West Germans under Kohl. Even more extreme was Louise Endlich's *Neuland: Ganz einfache Geschichte* (Berlin, 1999), in which the West German could barely hide her middle-class snobbery in ridiculing the East Germans as uncouth and uncivilized, shockingly unaware how to eat or behave properly.

19. Andras Gero and Ivan Petö, *Unfinished Socialism: Pictures from the Kadar Era* (Budapest, 1997); Daphne Berdahl, '(N)ostalgie for the Present: Memory, Longing and East German Things', *Ethnos,* 64/2 (1999), 192–211.

20. Paul Betts, 'Remembrance of Things Past: Nostalgia in West and East Germany, 1980–2000', in Paul Betts and Greg Eghigian (eds.), *Pain and Prosperity: Reconsidering Twentieth Century German History* (Stanford, Calif., 2003), 178–208.

21. Arendt, *The Human Condition* (Chicago, 1958), 137.

22. Paul Betts, 'Twilight of the Idols: East German Memory and Material Culture', *Journal of Modern History,* 72 (Sept. 2000), 731–65.

23. Barbara Miller, *Narratives of Guilt and compliance in Unified Germany* (London, 1999), 103.

24. Peter Kirschey, *Wandlitz/Waldsieldung—Die geschlossene Gesellschaft: Versuch einer Reportage, Gespräche, Dokumente* (Berlin, 1990), 41.

25. Timothy Garton Ash, *The File* (London, 1997), 150, 175.

26. *Jurek Becker,* ed. I. Heidelberger-Leonard (Frankfurt/M., 1992), 76.

27. Quoted in Miller, *Narratives,* 134.

28. Albert O. Hirschman, 'Exit, Voice and the Fate of the German Democratic Republic: An Essay in Conceptual History', *World Politics,* 45 (Jan. 1993), 198–9.

29. John O. Koehler, *The Untold Story of the East German Secret Police* (Boulder, Colo., 1999), 407–9.

30. Anne Worst, *Das Ende eines Geheimdienstes: Oder, wie lebendig ist die Stasi?* (Berlin, 1991), 32–8.

31. Robert Darnton, *Berlin Journal, 1989–1990* (New York, 1991), esp. 120–6.

32. Armin Mitter and Stefan Wolle (eds.), *Ich liebe Euch doch alle! Befehle und Lagebericht des MfS Januar–November 1989* (Berlin, 1990).

33. Volker Klemm, *Korruption und Amtsmissbrauch in der DDR* (Stuttgart, 1991), 71–4.

34. Mary Fulbrook, *Anatomy of a Dictatorship* (Oxford, 1995), 39 n. 22.

35. Quoted in Gareth Dale, *The East German Revolution of 1989* (Manchester, 2006), 150.

36. Ibid. 200.

37. Edward N. Peterson, *The Secret Police and the Revolution* (Westport, Conn., 2002), 241.

38. A. James McAdams, *Judging the Past in Unified Germany* (Cambridge, 2001), 61.

39. Lothar de Maizière, 'Rede von der Volkskammer am 15.9.1990', cited in Silke Schumann, *Vernichten oder Offenlegen? Zur Entstehung des Stasi-Unterlagen-Gesetzes: Eine Dokumentation der offentlichen Debatte 1990/1991*, ed. BstU (Berlin, 1995), Dok. 143.
40. Cited in Nancy Travis Wolfe, *Policing a Socialist Society* (New York, 1992), 134.
41. Jens Gieseke, *Mielke-Konzern: Die Geschichte der Stasi, 1945–1990* (Stuttgart, 2001), 232. See too *Stasi-Intern: Macht und Banalität* (1990).
42. Gieseke, *Mielke-Konzern*, 247.
43. Schumann, *Vernichten oder Offenlegen?*, 111–12.
44. Mike Dennis, *The Stasi* (London, 2003), 238.
45. Quoted in McAdams, *Judging*, 62–3.
46. Rosenberg, *Haunted Land*, 296.
47. McAdams, *Judging*, 59–60.
48. Dennis, *Stasi*, 238–9.
49. Vera Wollenberger, 'Eine zweite Vergewaltigung', repr. in Hans-Joachim Schädlich (ed.), *Aktenkündig* (Berlin, 1992), 164.
50. Rosenberg, *Haunted Land*, 298.
51. Ruth P, Berlin, interview, 30 Mar. 2007.
52. Vera Wollenberger, *Virus der Heuchler* (Berlin, 1992), 8.
53. Lutz Rathenow, 'Teile zu keinem Bild oder das Puzzle von der geheimen Macht,' in Hans-Joachim Schädlich (ed.), *Aktenkündig* (Berlin, 1992), 64.
54. *Zweiter Tätigkeitsbericht des Bundesbeauftragten für die Unterlagen des Staatssicher-heitsdienstes der ehemaligen Deutschen Demokratischen Republik 1995* (Berlin, 1995), 4–7.
55. McAdams, *Judging*, 124–56.
56. Cited in Hinrich Rüping, 'Denunziation im 20. Jahrhundert als Phänomen der Rechtsgeschichte', *Historical Social Research/Historische Sozialforschung*, 26/2–3 (2001), 42.
57. Garton Ash, *The File*, 195.
58. Cited in Dirk Verheyen, *United City, Divided Memories* (Lanham, Md., 2008), 151.
59. Miller, *Narratives*, 125–32.
60. Montesquieu, *The Spirit of the Laws* (New York, 1949), 20–115.
61. Alexis De Tocqueville, *The Old Regime and the French Revolution* (New York, 1955), p. xiii, quoted in Jowitt, 'The Leninist Legacy', in Vladimir Tismaneanu (ed.), *The Revolutions of 1989* (London, 1999), 218.
62. Hans-Joachim Maaz, *Behind the Wall: The Inner Life of Communist Germany* (New York, 1995); it originally appeared as *Der Gefühlsstau: Ein Psychogramm der DDR* (Berlin, 1990).
63. Hans-Joachim Maaz, *Die Entrüstung: Deutschland, Stasi, Schuld und Sündenbock* (Berlin, 1992), 41ff.
64. Cited in Greg Eghigian, 'Homo Munitus', in Katherine Pence and Paul Betts (eds.), *Socialist Modern* (Ann Arbor, 2008), 39.
65. Oleg Kharkhordin, *The Collective and the Individual in Russia* (Berkeley, Calif., 1999), 357. For an East German version, see Wolfgang Engler, *Die Ostdeutschen als Avantgarde* (Berlin, 2004).
66. Sibylle Meyer and Eva Schulze, *Familien im Umbruch* (Stuttgart, 1992), 110.

67. Peter Franz and Ulfert Herlyn, 'Familie als Bollwerk oder als Hindernis? Die Rolle der Familienbeziehungen bei der Bewältigung der Vereinigungsfolgen', in Norbert F. Schneider and Angelika Tölke (eds.), *Familie und Lebenslauf im gesellschaftlichen Umbruch* (Stuttgart, 1995), 90–102.

68. Lothar Mertens, *Wider die sozialistische Familiennorm* (Opladen and Wiesbaden, 1998), 91.

69. Kurt Starke, *Nichts als die reine Liebe: Beziehungsbiographien und Sexualität im sozialen und psychologischen Wandel: Ost-West-Unterschiede* (Lengerich, 2005).

70. Dirk Konietzka and Michaela Kreyenfeld (eds.), *Ein Leben ohne Kinder: Kinderlosigkeit in Deutschland* (Wiesbaden, 2007).

71. Sigrid Meuschel, 'Revolution in a Classless Society', in Gert-Joachim Glaessner and Ian Wallace (eds.), *The German Revolution of 1989* (Oxford, 1992), 152–3.

72. Iris Häuser, *Gegenidentitäten: Zur Vorbereitung des politischen Umbruchs in der DDR: Lebensstile und politische Soziokultur in der DDR-Gesellschaft der achtziger Jahre* (Münster, 1996).

73. Detlef Pollack, 'The Situation of Religion in Eastern Germany after 1989', in Patricia J. Smith (ed.), *After the Wall: Eastern Germany After 1989* (Boulder, Colo., 1998), 171.

74. Felix Robin Schulz, 'Death in East Germany, 1945–1990', D.Phil., University of York, 2005, 127, 219, 305.

75. Andreas Meier, *Jugendweihe—JugendFEIER: Ein deutsches nostalgisches Fest vor und nach 1990* (Munich, 1998), 14.

76. Marina Chauliac, 'Die Jugendweihe zwischen familiarem und politischem Erbe der DDR: Zur Erfindung einer neuen Tradition', in Sandrine Kott and Emmanuel Droit (eds.), *Die ostdeutsche Gesellschaft: Eine transatlantische Perspective* (Berlin, 2006), 198.

77. Ibid. 209, 213.

78. Vladimir Tismaneanu, 'Introduction', *Revolutions,* 14.

Bibliography

ARCHIVES

Bundesarchiv Berlin-Lichterfelde (BAB)
Bundesarchiv, Dahlwitz-Hoppegarten (BADH)
Landesarchiv Berlin (LAB)
Landeskirchenarchiv, Berlin (LAKB)
Deutsches Tagebuch-Archiv, Emmindingen (DTA)
Walter Kempowski-Archiv, Akademie der Künste, Berlin (WKA)
Matthias-Domaschk-Archiv in der Robert-Havemann-Gesellschaft e.V, Berlin (MDAB)
Ministerium für Staatssicherheit (Stasi) Archiv, Berlin (SAB)

INTERVIEWS

In addition, I held long interviews with 10 people during my research year in Berlin 2006–2007, and distributed a questionnaire about private life that same year, of which I received thirty detailed responses. In 2005 Dr Angela Brock conducted (and transcribed) twenty additional interviews as part of a British Academy grant to support the research of this project. These sources have been integrated into the body of the text at various points, and I have anonymized their names as requested.

References to archival sources, individual book chapters and journal articles will be found in the endnotes above, and only some of them are included again here.

PUBLISHED SOURCES

Allinson, Mark, *Politics and Popular Opinion in East Germany, 1945–1968* (Manchester, 2000).

Andries, Nicole, and Majken Rehder, *Zaunwelten: Zäune und Zeitzeugen—Geschichten zur Alltagsgeschichte der DDR* (Marburg, 2005).

Arendt, Hannah, *The Human Condition* (Chicago, 1958).

—— *The Origins of Totalitarianism* (New York, 1973 [1951]).

Aries, Philippe, and Georges Duby, eds., *The History of Private Life* (Cambidge, Mass., 1987–91), i–v.

Augustine, Dolores L., *Red Prometheus: Engineering and Dictatorship in East Germany, 1945–1990* (Cambridge, Mass., 2007).

Austermühle, Gisa, *Zur Entstehung und Entwicklung eines persönlichen Geheimsphärenschutzes von Spätabsolutismus bis zur Gesetzgebung des Deutschen Reiches* (Berlin, 2002).

Autorenkollektiv under the direction of Georg Assmann and Gunnar Winkler, *Zwischen Alex und Marzahn: Studie zur Lebensweise in Berlin* (East Berlin, 1987).

Badstübner, Evemarie, ed., *Befremdlich Anders: Leben in der DDR* (Berlin, 2000).

Barthes, Roland, *Camera Lucida: Reflections on Photography*, tr. Richard Howard (New York, 1981).

Behnke, Klaus, and Jürgen Fuchs, eds., *Zersetzung der Seele: Psychologie und Psychiatrie im Dienste der Stasi* (Hamburg, 1995).

—— and —— eds., *Stasi auf dem Schulhof: Der Missbrauch von Kindern und Jugendlichen durch das Minsterium für Staatssicherheit* (Berlin, 1998).

Behrends, Jan C., Thomas Lindenberger, and Patrice Poutrus, eds., *Fremde und Fremd-Sein in der DDR* (Berlin, 2003).

Berdahl, Daphne. '(N)ostalgie for the Present: Memory, Longing and East German Things', *Ethnos*, 64/2 (1999), 192–211.

Berghahn, Daniela, *Hollywood behind the Wall: The Cinema of East Germany* (Manchester, 2005).

Besier, Gerhard, *Der SED-Staat und die Kirche: Der Weg in die Anpassung* (Munich, 1993).

Bessel, Richard, and Ralph Jessen, eds., *Die Grenzen der Diktatur: Staat und Gesellschaft in der DDR* (Göttingen, 1996).

Besser Leben—Schöner Wohnen: Raum und Möbel, exh. cat. (East Berlin, 1953).

Betts, Paul, 'The Twilight of the Idols: East German Memory and Material Culture', *Journal of Modern History*, 72 (2000), 731–65.

—— 'Remembrance of Things Past: Nostalgie in West and East Germany, 1980–2000', in Paul Betts and Greg Eghigian (eds.), *Pain and Prosperity: Reconsidering Twentieth Century German History* (Stanford, Calif., 2003), 178–208.

—— 'The Politics of Post-Fascist Aesthetics: 1950s West and East German Industrial Design', in Richard Bessel and Dirk Schumann (eds.), *Life After Death: Violence, Normality and the Reconstruction of Postwar Europe* (Cambridge, 2003), 290–321.

—— *The Authority of Everyday Objects: A Cultural History of West German Industrial Design* (Berkeley, Calif., 2004).

—— 'When Cold Warriors Die: The State Funerals of Konrad Adenauer and Walter Ulbricht', in Alon Confino, Paul Betts, and Dirk Schumann (eds.), *Between Mass Death and Individual Loss: The Place of the Dead in Twentieth Century Germany* (Oxford and New York, 2008), 151–78.

—— 'Manners, Morality and Civilization: Reflections on Post–1945 German Etiquette Books', in Frank Biess and Robert Moeller (eds.), *Histories of the Aftermath: The Legacies of World War II in Comparative European Perspective* (New York, 2010).

Biess, Frank, *Homecoming: Returning POWs and the Legacies of Defeat in Postwar Germany* (Princeton, 2006).

Black, Monica, *Death in Berlin: From Weimar to Divided Germany* (New York, 2010).

Blasius, Dirk, *Ehescheidung in Deutschland* (Göttingen, 1987).

Böhme, Irene, *Die da drüben: Sieben Kapitel DDR* (Berlin, 1982).

Bönninger, Karl, *Die Einrichtung der Haus- und Strassenvertrauensleute als Form der Teilnahme der Massen an der Leitung des Staates in der DDR* (Berlin, 1954).

Bourdieu, Pierre, *Photography: A Middle-Brow Art*, tr. Shaun Whiteside (London, 1990 [1965]).

Boyer, Christoph, and Peter Skyba, *Repression und Wohlstandsversprechen: Zur Stabilisierung von Parteiherrschaft in der DDR und CSSR* (Dresden, 1999).

Boym, Svetlana, *Common Places: Mythologies of Everyday Life in Russia* (Cambridge, 1994).

Brock, Angela, 'The Making of the Socialist Personality: Education and Socialisation in the German Democratic Republic, 1958–1978', Ph.D. thesis, University College London, 2005.

Bronnen, Barbara, and Franz Henny, *Liebe, Ehe, Sexualität: Interviews und Dokumente* (Munich, 1975).

Budde, Gunilla-Frederike, *Frauen der Intelligenz: Akademikerinnen in der DDR 1945–1975* (Göttingen, 2003).

Carter, Erica, *How German is She? Postwar West German Reconstruction and the Consuming Woman* (Ann Arbor, 1997).

Castillo, Greg, 'Marshall Plan Modernism in Divided Germany', in David Crowley and Jane Pavitt (eds.), *Cold War Modern: Design 1945–1970* (London, 2009).

—— *Cold War on the Home Front: The Soft Power of Midcentury Design* (Minneapolis, 2010).

Childs, David, and Richard Popplewell, *The Stasi: The East German Intelligence and Security Service* (London, 1996).

Connelly, John, 'The Uses of the the Volksgemeinschaft: Letters to the NSDAP Kreisleitung Eisenach, 1939–1940', *Journal of Modern History*, 68/4 (Dec. 1996), 899–930.

Cooper, Belinda, 'Patriarchy within a Patriarchy: Women and the Stasi', *German Politics and Society*, 16/2 (1998), 1–31.

Czarnowski, Gabriele, *Das kontrollierte Paar: Ehe- und Sexualpolitik im Nationalsozialismus* (Weinheim, 1991).

Dähn, Horst, *Konfrontation oder Kooperation? Das Verhältnis von Staat und Kirche in der SBZ/DDR 1945–1980* (Opladen, 1982).

Dahrendorf, Ralf, *Society and Democracy in Germany* (New York, 1967).

Dale, Gareth, *Popular Protest in East Germany, 1945–1989* (London, 2005).

—— *The East German Revolution of 1989* (Manchester, 2006).

Damus, Martin. *Malerei der DDR: Funktionen der bildenden Kunst im Realen Sozialismus* (Hamburg, 1991).

Darnton, Robert, *Berlin Journal, 1989–1990* (New York, 1991).

Davies, Sarah, *Popular Opinion in Stalin's Russia: Terror, Propaganda and Dissent, 1934–1941* (Cambridge, 1997).

Deja-Löhlhöffel, Brigitte, *Freizeit in der DDR* (West Berlin, 1986).

Dennis, Mike, *The Stasi: Myth and Reality* (London, 2003).

Der Liebe Gott und der Sputnik (Berlin, 1958).

De Tocqueville, Alexis, *The Old Regime and the French Revolution* (New York, 1955).

Deutsch, Isolde, *Hammer, Zirkel, Gartenzaun: Die Politik der SED gegenüber den Kleingärten* (Berlin, 2003).

Deutz-Schroeder, Monika, and Joachim Staadt, eds., *Teuer Genosse: Briefe an Erich Honecker* (Berlin, 1994).

Diederich, Georg, Bernd Schäfer, and Jörg Ohlemacher, *Jugendweihe in der DDR: Geschichte und politische Bedeutung aus christlicher Sicht* (Schwerin, 1998).

Diewald-Kerkmann, Gisela, *Politische Denunziation im NS-Regime, oder die kleine Macht der 'Volksgenossen'* (Bonn, 1995).

Döhnert, Albrecht, 'Die Jugendweihe', in *Deutsche Erinnerungsorte III*, ed. Etienne Francois and Hagen Schulze (Munich, 2001), 347–60.

Dokumentationszentrum Alltagskultur der DDR Fortschritt, ed., *Norm und Eigensinn: Erkundungen im Alltag der DDR* (Berlin, 1999).

Drakulic, Slavenka, *How We Survived Communism and Even Laughed* (London, 1992).

Eghigian, Greg, 'Homo Munitus: The East German Observed', in Katherine Pence and Paul Betts (eds.), *Socialist Modern: East German Everyday Culture and Politics* (Ann Arbor, 2008), 37–70.

Einhorn, Barbara, *Cinderella Goes to Market: Citizenship, Gender and Women's Movements in East Central Europe* (London, 1993).

Elder, Sace, 'Murder, Denunciation and Criminal Policing in Weimar Berlin', *Journal of Contemporary History*, 41/3 (2006), 406–7.

Elias, Norbert, *The Civilizing Process* (New York, 1978 [1939]).

Elternhaus und Schule: Es muss ein Herzschlag sein: Erfahrungsaustausch über die Zusammenarbeit zwischen Lehrern und Eltern (Berlin, 1961).

Engelmann, Roger, and Clemens Vollnhals, eds., *Justiz im Dienste der Parteiherrschaft: Rechtspraxis und Staatssicherheit in der DDR* (Berlin, 2000).

Engler, Wolfgang, *Die Ostdeutschen: Kunde von einem verlorenen Land* (Berlin, 2000).

Ernst, Anna-Sabine, 'The Politics of Culture and the Culture of Everyday Life in the DDR in the 1950s', in David E. Barclay and Eric Weitz (eds.), *Between Reform und Revolution: German Socialism and Communism from 1840 to 1990* (New York, 1998), 489–506.

Feinstein, Joshua, *The Triumph of the Ordinary: Depictions of Daily Life in East German Cinema, 1945–1989* (Chapel Hill, NC, 2002).

Ferid, Murad, Eberhardt Pfuhl, and Rüdiger Thomsen, eds., *Das Eigentum im Ostblock* (West Berlin, 1958).

Field, Deborah A., 'Irreconcilable Differences: Divorce and Conceptions of Private Life in the Khrushchev Era', *Russian Review*, 57 (Oct. 1998), 599–613.

Figes, Orlando, *The Whisperers: Private Life in Stalin's Russia* (London, 2007).

Fischer, Christian, *Wir haben Eurer Verlöbnis vernommen: Konfirmation und Jugendweihe im Spannungsfeld* (Leipzig, 1998).

Fitzpatrick, Sheila, 'Supplicants and Citizens: Public Letter-Writing in Soviet Russia in the 1930s', *Slavic Review*, 55/1 (Spring, 1996).

—— *Everyday Stalinism: Ordinary Life in Extraordinary Times: Soviet Russia in the 1930s* (Oxford, 1999).

—— *Tear Off the Masks! Identity and Imposture in Twentieth Century Russia* (Princeton, 2005).

Flagge, Ingeborg, ed., *Geschichte des Wohnens, v. Von 1945 bis Heute* (Stuttgart, 1999).

Freidank, G. E., *Alles Hat Am Ende Sich Gelohnt: Material für weltliche Trauerfeiern* (Leipzig, 1972).

Freeman, Nicola, and Matthew Shaul, eds., *Do Not Refreeze: Photography behind the Berlin Wall* (London, 2008).

Friedrich, Carl J. and Zbigniew Brzezinski, *Totalitarian Dictatorship and Autocracy*, 2nd rev. edn. (Cambridge, 1965 [1956]).

Fulbrook, Mary, *The People's State: East German Society from Hitler to Honecker* (New Haven, 2005).

—— *Anatomy of a Dictatorship: Inside the GDR, 1949–1989* (Oxford, 1995).

Funder, Anna, *Stasiland* (London, 2003).

Garcelon, Marc, 'The Shadow of the Leviathan: Public and Private in Communist and Post-Communist Society', in Jeff Weintraub and Krishan Kumar (eds.), *Public and Private in Thought and Practice: Perspectives on a Grand Dichotomy* (Chicago, 1997), 303–32.

Garton Ash, Timothy, *The File: A Personal History* (London, 1997).

—— *'Und willst du nicht mein Bruder sein...': Die DDR Heute* (Hamburg, 1981).

Gauck, Joachim, *Die Stasi-Akten: Das unheimliche Erbe der DDR* (Reinbek bei Hamburg, 1991).

Gaus, Günter, *Wo Deutschland liegt: Eine Ortsbestimmung* (Hamburg, 1983).

Gellately, Robert, 'Denunciations in Twentieth Century Germany: Aspects of Self-Policing in the Third Reich and the German Democratic Republic', *Journal of Modern History*, 68/4 (Dec. 1996), 931–67.

Gieseke, Jens, *Mielke-Konzern: Die Geschichte der Stasi, 1945–1990* (Stuttgart, 2001).

—— ed., *Staatssicherheit und Gesellschaft: Studien zum Herrschaftsalltag in der DDR* (Göttingen, 2007).

Goeckel, Robert F., *The Lutheran Church and the East German State: Political Conflict and Change Under Ulbricht and Honecker* (Ithaca, NY, 1990).

Glasenapp, Jörn, *Die deutsche Nachkriegsfotografie: Eine Mentalitätsgeschichte in Bildern* (Paderborn, 2008).

Gläss, Klaus, and Manfred Mühlmann, *Bürger-Hausgemeinschaft-Wohngebiet* (Berlin, 1981).

Grashoff, Udo, *'In einem Anfall von Depression...': Selbsttötung in der DDR* (Berlin, 2006).

Gries, Sabine, *Kindermisshandlung in der DDR: Kinder unter dem Einfluss traditionell-autoritärer und totalitärer Erziehungsleitbilder* (Münster, 2002).

Griese, Christiane, *'Bin ich ein guter Staatsbürger, wenn ich mein Kind nicht zur Jugendweihe schicke'* (Baltmannsweiler, 2001).

Grimm, Thomas, *Das Politbüro Privat: Ulbricht, Honecker, Mielke & Co aus der Sicht ihrer Angestellten* (Berlin, 2005).

Grossmann, Atina, *Reforming Sex: The German Movement for Birth Control and Abortion Reform, 1920–1950* (Oxford, 1995).

Grunenberg, Antonia, *Aufbruch der inneren Mauer: Politik und Kultur in der DDR, 1971–1990* (Bremen, 1990).

Guttmann, W. L., *Workers' Culture in Weimar Germany: Between Tradition and Commitment* (New York, 1990).

Gysi, Jutta, ed., *Familienleben in der DDR* (East Berlin, 1989).

Habermann, Lothar, 'Schiedskommissionen in der DDR: Eine Dokumentation', in Christoph Rennig and Dieter Strempel (eds.), *Justiz im Umbruch: Rechtstatsächliche Studien zum Aufbau der Rechtspflege in den neuen Bundesländern* (Cologne, 1996), 191–283.

Habermas, Jürgen, *The Structural Transformation of the Public Sphere* (Cambridge, 1989 [1962]).

Hacker, Jens, *Deutsche Irrtümer: Schönfärber und Helfershelfer der SED-Diktatur im Westen* (Frankfurt, 1992).

Halgasch, Richard, ed., *Wir bleiben zusammen* (Leipzig, 1971).

Hallberg, Bo, *Die Jugendweihe: Zur deutschen Jugendweihetradition* (Göttingen, 1979).

Hamel, Johannes, *A Christian in East Germany* (London, 1960).

Harsch, Donna, *Revenge of the Domestic: Women, the Family and Communism in the German Democratic Republic* (Princeton, 2006).

—— 'Squaring the Circle: The Dilemmas and Evolution of Women's Policy', in Patrick Major and Jonathan Osmond (eds.), *The Workers' and Peasants' State: Communism and Society in East Germany under Ulbricht* (Manchester, 2002), 151–70.

Härtel, Christian, and Petra Kabus, eds., *Das Westpaket* (Berlin, 2000).

Hartewig, Karin, *Das Auge der Partei: Fotografie und Staatssicherheit* (Berlin, 2004).

—— and Alf Lüdtke, eds., *Die DDR im Bild: Zur Gebrauch der Fotografie im anderen deutschen Staat* (Göttingen, 2004).

Hausen, Karin, 'Family and Role-Division: The Polarisation of Sexual Stereotypes in the 19th Century', in Richard Evans and W. R. Lee (eds.), *The German Family* (London, 1981).

Häuser, Iris, *Gegenidentitäten: Zur Vorbereitung des politischen Umbruchs in der DDR: Lebensstile und politische Soziokultur in der DDR-Gesellschaft der achtziger Jahre* (Münster, 1996).

Havel, Vaclav, 'The Power of the Powerless', in Vaclav Havel, *Living in Truth*, ed. Jan Vladislav (London, 1990), 36–122.

Heineman, Elizabeth D., *What Difference does a Husband Make? Women and Marital Status in Nazi and Postwar Germany* (Berkeley, Calif., 1999).

Helwig, Gisela, *Jugend und Familie in der DDR* (Berlin, 1984).

Henkel, Rüdiger, *Rückzug ins Private: Individuelle Antworten auf den 'realen Sozialismus'* (Bonn, 1980).

Henkys, Reinhard, ed., *Die evangelischen Kirchen in der DDR* (Munich, 1982).

Heretsch, Erwin, *Gegen den Strom: Notizen eines DDR-Christen* (Leipzig, 1998).

Herzog, Dagmar, *Sex After Fascism: Memory and Morality in 20th Century Germany* (Princeton, 2005).

Herzog, Felix, *Rechtspflege—Sache des ganzen Volkes? Studien zur Ideologie und Praxis der Gesellschaftsgerichte in der DDR mit dem Schwerpunkt der nachbarschaftlichen Sozialkontrolle durch die Schiedskommissionen in den Wohngebieten* (Baden-Baden, 1999).

Hinweise, Anregungen, *Materialien zur Gestaltung sozialistischer Feierstunden* (Berlin, 1963).

Hirschman, Albert O., 'Exit, Voice and the Fate of the German Democratic Republic: An Essay in Conceptual History', *World Politics*, 45 (Jan. 1993), 173–202.

Hocke, Gustav Rene, *Das europäische Tagebuch* (Wiesbaden, 1963).

Hoehn, Maria, *GIs and Fräuleins: The German-American Encounter in 1950s West Germany* (Chapel Hill, NC, 2002).

Hoffmann, Heinz, and Rainer Knapp, eds., *Fotografie in der DDR: Ein Beitrag zur Bildergeschichte* (Leipzig, 1987).

Hoffmann, Stefan-Ludwig, *The Politics of Sociability: Freemasonry and German Civil Society, 1840–1918*, tr. Tom Lampert (Ann Arbor, 2007).

Holquist, Peter, '"Information is the Alpha and Omega of our Work": Bolshevik Surveillance in its Pan-European Context', *Journal of Modern History*, 69/3 (Sept. 1997), 415–50.

Hopf, Susanne, and Natalja Meier, *Plattenbau Privat: 60 Interieurs* (Berlin, 2004).

Hoscislawski, Thomas, *Bauen zwischen Macht und Ohnmacht: Architektur und Städtebau in der DDR* (Berlin, 1991).

Huinink, Johannes, Karl-Ulrich Mayer, and Martin Diewald, eds., *Kollektiv und Eigensinn: Lebensverläufe in der DDR und danach* (Berlin, 1995).

Inglehart, Ronald, ed., *The Silent Revolution: Changing Values and Political Styles among Western Publics* (Princeton, 1977).

Jarausch, Konrad, ed., *Dictatorship as Experience: Towards a Socio-Cultural History of the GDR* (Oxford, 1999).

Jeremias, U., *Die Jugendweihe in der Sowjetzone* (Bonn, 1958).

Jerouschek, Günter, Inge Marssolek, and Hedwig Röcklein, eds., *Denunziation: Historische, juristische und psychologische Aspekte* (Tübingen, 1997).

Judt, Tony, *Postwar* (New York, 2005).

Jugendstunde: Der Sozialismus siegt! (Berlin, 1962).

Kaelble, Hartmut, Jürgen Kocka, and Hartmut Zwahr (eds.), *Sozialgeschichte der DDR* (Stuttgart, 1994).

Kahl, Alice, Steffen H. Wilsdorf, and Herbert F. Wolf, *Kollektivbeziehungen und Lebensweise* (East Berlin, 1984).

Kaiser, Paul, and Claudia Petzold, eds., *Boheme und Diktatur in der DDR: Gruppen, Konflikte, Quartiere, 1970–1989* (Berlin, 1997).

Kallinach, Joachim, and Sylvia de Pasquale, eds., *Ein offenes Geheimnis: Post- und Telefonkontrolle in der DDR* (Berlin, 2002).

Kaminsky, Annette, *Wohlstand, Schönheit, Glück: Kleine Konsumgeschichte der DDR* (Munich, 2001).

Karau, Gisela, *Sozialistischer Alltag in der DDR* (East Berlin, 1970).

Kelm, Martin, *Produktgestaltung im Sozialismus* (Berlin, 1971).

Kharkhordin, Oleg, *The Collective and the Individual in Russia* (Berkeley, Calif., 1999).

Kietz, Herbert, and Manfred Mühlmann, *Konfliktursachen und Aufgaben der Zivil- und Familienrechtspflege* (East Berlin, 1969).

Kinder der Opposition: Berichte aus Pfarrhäusern in der DDR (Gütersloh, 1993).

Kleinschmidt, Karl, *Keine Angst vor guten Sitten: Ein Buch über die Art miteinander umzugehen* (Berlin, 1961).

Klemm, Volker, *Korruption und Amtsmissbrauch in der DDR* (Munich, 1991).

Klessmann, Christoph, *Zwei Staaten, Eine Nation: Deutsche Geschichte, 1955–1970* (Bonn, 1997).

Klier, Freya, *Abreiss-Kalender: Versuch eines Tagebuchs* (Munich, 1988).

Klose, Bernhard, *Ehescheidung und Ehescheidungsrecht in der DDR: Ein ostdeutscher Sonderweg?* (Baden-Baden, 1996).

Koelbl, Herlinde, *Das deutsche Wohnzimmer* (Lucerne and Frankfurt, 1980).

Koehler, John O., *Stasi: The Untold Story of the East German Secret Police* (Boulder, Colo., 1999).

Köhler, Hans, *Christentum und Jugendweihe* (Bonn, 1958).

Köhler, Tilo, *Unser die Strasse—Unser der Sieg: Die Stalinallee* (Berlin, 1993).

Kolano, Uta, *Nackter Osten* (Frankfurt am Oder, 1995).

Kolinsky, Eva, 'Exodus to the Private Realm', *Times Higher Education Supplement*, 29 Jan. 1993.

Korzilius, Sven, *'Asoziale' und 'Parasiten' im Recht der SBZ/DDR: Randgruppen im Sozialismus zwischen Repression und Ausgrenzung* (Cologne, 2005).

Koselleck, Reinhart, *Critique and Crisis: Enlightenment and the Pathogenesis of Modern Society* (Cambridge, 1988 [1959]).

Kotkin, Stephen, *Magnetic Mountain: Stalinism as a Civilization* (Berkeley, Calif., 1995)

Kott, Sandrine, and Emmanuel Droit, *Die ostdeutsche Gesellschaft: Eine transatlantische Perspektive* (Berlin, 2006).

Krusche, Hans-Martin, *Pfarrer in der DDR: Gespräche über Kirche und Politik* (Berlin, 2002).

Kuehn, Karl Gernot, *Caught: The Art of Photography in the German Democratic Republic* (Berkeley, Calif., 1997).

Kunze, Reiner, *Deckname 'Lyrik'* (Frankfurt, 1990).

Ladd, Brian, *The Ghosts of Berlin: Confronting German History in the Urban Landscape* (Chicago, 1997).

Lewis, Alison, 'En-Gendering Remembrance: Memory, Gender and Informers for the Stasi', *New German Critique*, 86 (Spring/Summer 2002), 103–34.

Lemke, Jürgen, *Ganz normal anders: Auskünfte schwuler Männer* (Berlin, 1989).

Lepenies, Wolf, *Folgen einer unerhorten Begebenheit: Die Deutschen nach der Vereinigung* (Berlin, 1992).

Levitsky, Serge L., *Copyright, Defamation and Privacy in Soviet Civil Law* (Alphen aan den Rijn, 1979).

Lindenberger, Thomas, 'Creating State Socialist Governance: The Case of the Deutsche Volkspolizei', in Konrad Jarausch (ed.), *Dictatorship as Experience: Towards a Socio-Cultural History of the GDR* (New York and Oxford, 1999), 125–43.

—— ed., *Herrschaft und Eigen-Sinn in der Diktatur: Studien zur Gesellschaftsgeschichte der DDR* (Cologne, 1999).

—— 'Das Fremde im Eigenen des Staatssozialismus: Klassendiskurs und Exclusion am Beispiel der Konstruktion des "asozialen Verhaltens"', in Jan C. Behrends, Thomas Lindenberger, and Patrice Poutrus (eds.), *Fremde und Fremd-Sein in der DDR* (Berlin, 2003), 179–91.

—— *Volkspolizei: Herrschaftspraxis und öffentliche Ordnung im SED-Staat, 1952–1968* (Cologne, 2003).

Loest, Erich, *Die Stasi war mein Eckermann* (Göttingen, 1992).

Lorenz, Angelike, *Das deutsche Familienbild in der Malerei des 19. Jahrhunderts* (Darmstadt, 1985).

Lovell, Stephen, *Summerfolk: A History of the Dacha, 1710–2000* (Ithaca, NY, 2003).

Lüdtke, Alf, *Eigen-Sinn: Fabrikalltag, Arbeitererfahrungen und Politik vom Kaiserreich bis in den Faschismus* (Hamburg, 1993).

—— ed., *The History of Everyday Life* (Princeton, 1995).

Maaz, Hans-Joachim, *Der Gefühlsstau: Ein Psychogramm der DDR* (Berlin, 1990).

—— *Die Entrüstung: Deutschland, Stasi, Schuld und Sündenbock* (Berlin, 1992).

McAdams, A. James, *Judging the Past in Unified Germany* (Cambridge, 2001).

McLellan, Josie, *Antifascism and Memory in East Germany: Remembering the International Brigades, 1945–1989* (Oxford, 2004).

—— 'State Socialist Bodies: East German Nudism from Ban to Boom', *Journal of Modern History*, 79 (March 2007), 48–79.

—— 'Visual Dangers and Delights: Nude Photography in East Germany', *Past and Present* (Aug. 2009).

Macrakis, Kristie, *Seduced by Secrets: Inside the Stasi's Spy-Tech World* (Cambridge, 2008).

Maennel, Annette, *Frauen im Visier der Stasi* (Berlin, 1994).

Maier, Charles, ed., *Changing Boundaries of the Political: Essays on the Evolving Balance between State and Society, Public and Private* (Cambridge, Mass., 1987).

—— *Dissolution: The Crisis of Communism and the End of East Germany* (Princeton, 1997).

Major, Patrick, *Behind the Berlin Wall: East Germany and the Frontiers of Power* (Oxford, 2010).

—— and Jonathan Osmond, eds., *The Workers' and Peasants' State: Communism and Society in East Germany under Ulbricht, 1945–1971* (Manchester, 2002).

Materielien der Enquete-Kommission 'Aufarbeitung von Geschichte und Folgen der SED-Diktatur in Deutschland', vi. *Kirchen in der SED-Dikatur*, 1–2 (Baden-Baden, 1995).

Markovits, Inga, *Sozialistisches und bürgerliches Zivilrechtsdenken in der DDR* (Cologne, 1969).

—— 'Marriage and the State: A Comparative Look at East and West German Family Law', *Stanford Law Review*, 115 (Nov. 1971), 116–99.

—— 'Socialist vs. Bourgeois Rights: An East–West German Comparison', *University of Chicago Law Review*, 45 (1978), 612–36.

—— 'Rechtsstaat oder Beschwerdestaat? Verwaltungsrechtschutz in der DDR', *Recht in Ost und West*, 5 (1987), 265–81.

—— 'Pursuing One's Rights under Socialism', *Stanford Law Review*, 38 (1986), 689–761.

—— *Gerechtigkeit in Lüritz: Eine ostdeutsche Rechtsgeschichte* (Munich, 2006).

Marti, Kurt, *Erinnerungen an die DDR und einige ihrer Christen* (Zurich, 1994).

Marshall, T. H., *Citizenship and Social Class* (Cambridge, 1992 [1949]).

May, Elain Tyler, *Homeward Bound: American Families in the Cold War Era* (New York, 1988).

Mazower, Mark, ed., *The Policing of Politics in the Twentieth Century* (Oxford, 1997).

—— *Dark Continent: Europe's Twentieth Century* (New York, 1998).

Merkel, Ina, *. . . Und Du, Frau auf der Werkbank: Die DDR in den 50er Jahren* (Berlin, 1990).

—— *Utopie und Bedürfnis: Die Geschichte der Konsumkultur in der DDR* (Cologne, 1999).

—— ed., *'Wir sind doch nicht die Meckerecke der Nation!' Briefe an das Fernsehen der DDR* (Berlin, 2000).

Merritt, Richard, and Anna J. Merritt, eds., *Living with the Wall: West Berlin, 1961–1985* (Durham, 1985).

Mertens, Lothar, *Wider die sozialistische Familiennorm: Ehescheidungen in der DDR, 1950–1989* (Opladen and Wiesbaden, 1998).

—— ed., *Soziale Ungleichheit in der DDR: Zu einem tabusierten Strukturmerkmal der SED-Diktatur* (Berlin, 2002).

Meyen, Michael, 'Ein Stück Privatleben: Die Anfänge des Fernsehens in der DDR', *Deutschland-Archiv*, 33 (2000), 207–16.

Meyer, Sibylle, and Eva Schulze, *Familien im Umbruch: Zur Lage der Familien in der ehemaligen DDR* (Stuttgart, 1992).

Miller, Barbara, *Narratives of Guilt and Compliance in Unified Germany: Stasi Informers and their Impact on Society* (London, 1999).

Milosz, Czeslaw, *The Captive Mind*, tr. Jane Zielonko (New York, 1981 [1951]).

Mitter, Armin and Stefan Wolle, eds., *Ich liebe Euch doch alle! Befehle und Lageberichte des MfS Januar-November 1989* (Berlin, 1990).

—— and —— *Untergang auf Raten* (Munich, 1993).

Moeller, Robert G., *Protecting Motherhood: Women and the Family in the Politics of Postwar West Germany* (Berkeley, Calif., 1993).

—— 'The Elephant in the Living Room: Or Why the History of Twentieth Century Germany should be a Family Affair', in Karen Hagemann and Jean H. Quataert (eds.), *Gendering Modern German History: Rewriting Historiography* (New York, 2007), 228–50.

Möller, Heino R., *Innenräume/Aussenwelten: Studien zur Darstellung bürgerlichen Privatheit in Kunst und Warenwerbung* (Giessen, 1981).

Montesquieu, *The Spirit of the Laws* (New York, 1949).

Moore, Barrington, *Privacy: Studies in Social and Cultural History* (Armonk, NY, and London, 1984).

Moos, Norbert, ed., *Utopie und Wirklichkeit: Ostdeutsche Fotografie, 1956–1989* (Bönen, 2005).

Mouton, Michelle, *From Nurturing the Nation to Purifying the Volk: Weimar and Nazi Family Policy, 1918–1945* (Cambridge, 2007).

Mühlberg, Felix, 'Die Partei ist eifersüchtig', in Katrin Rohnstock (ed.), *Erotik macht die Hässlichen schön* (Berlin, 1995), 122–43.

—— *Bürger, Bitten und Behörden: Geschichte der Eingabe in der DDR* (Berlin, 2004).

Mühlmann, Manfred, *Sozialistische Lebensweise und persönliches Eigentum* (East Berlin, 1978).

Müller-Enbergs, Helmut, ed., *Inoffiziele Mitarbeiter des Ministeriums für Staatssicherheit: Richtlinien und Durchführungsbestimmungen* (Berlin, 1996).

Murphy, David E., Sergei A. Kondrashev, and George Bailey, *Battleground Berlin: CIA vs. KGB in the Cold War* (New Haven, Conn., 1997).

Muschter, Gabriele, ed., *DDR Frauen fotografieren: Lexicon und Anthologie* (Berlin, 1991).

Naimark, Norman M., *The Russians in Germany: A History of the Soviet Zone of Occupation, 1945–1949* (Cambridge, Mass., 1995).

Nelson, Deborah, *Pursuing Privacy in Cold War America* (New York, 2002).

Neubert, Rudolf, *Das neue Ehebuch: Die Ehe als Aufgabe der Gegenwart und Zukunft* (Rudolfstadt, 1957).

Nicolaus, Herbert, and Alexander Obeth, *Die Stalinallee: Geschichte einer deutschen Strasse* (Berlin, 1997).

Niethammer, Lutz, ed., *'Hinterher merkt man dass es richtig war, dass es schiefgegangen ist:' Nachkriegs-Erfahrungen im Ruhrgebiet* (Bonn, 1983).

—— Alexander von Plato, and Dorothee Wierling, *Die volkseigene Erfahrung: Eine Archäologie des Lebens in der Industrieprovinz der DDR* (Berlin, 1991).

Niemann, Heinz, *Meinungsforschung in der DDR: Die geheimen Berichte des Instituts für Meinungsforschung an das Politbüro der SED* (Cologne, 1993).

P2 und Tempolinsen: Alltagskultur der DDR (Berlin, 1996).

Obertreis, Gesine, *Familienpolitik in der DDR 1945–1980* (Opladen, 1986).

Palmowski, Jan, *Inventing a Socialist Nation: Heimat and the Politics of Everyday Life in the GDR, 1945–1990* (Cambridge, 2009).

Pence, Katherine, *Rations to Fashions: Gender and Consumer Politics in Cold War Germany* (Cambridge, 2010).

—— and Paul Betts, eds., *Socialist Modern: East German Everyday Culture and Politics* (Ann Arbor, 2008).

Peterson, Edward N., *The Secret Police and the Revolution: The Fall of the German Democratic Republic* (Westport, Conn., 2002).

Peukert, Detlev, *Inside Nazi Germany* (New Haven, Conn., 1987).

Pfaff, Steven, *Exit-Voice Dynamics and the Collapse of East Germany: The Crisis of Leninism and the Revolution of 1989* (Durham, 2006).

Phillips, Roderick, *Putting Asunder: A History of Divorce in Western Society* (Cambridge, 1988).

Pingel-Schliemann, Sandra, *Zersetzen: Strategie einer Diktatur* (Berlin, 2003).

Pittaway, Mark, *Eastern Europe, 1939–2000* (London, 2004).

Pollack, Detlef, *Kirche in der Organisationsgesellschaft* (Stuttgart, 1995).

Poppe, Birgit, *Freizeit und Privatleben in der Malerei der DDR: Formen und Funktionen neuer Motive der Leipziger Schule nach 1970* (Frankfurt am Main, 2000).

Port, Andrew I., *Conflict and Stability in the German Democratic Republic* (Cambridge, 2007).

Prost, Antoine, and Gerald Vincent, eds., *A History of Private Life, v. Riddles of Identity in Modern Times* (Cambridge, 1987).

Pseudosakrale Staatsakte in der Sowjetzone (Bonn, 1959).

Reid, Susan, E., 'The Khrushchev Kitchen: Domesticating the Scientific–Technological Revolution,' *Journal of Contemporary History* 40/2 (April 2005), 289–316.

Reid, Susan, and David Crowley, eds., *Style and Socialism: Modernity and Material Culture in Post-War Eastern Europe* (Oxford, 2000).

Reimann, Brigitte, *Ich bedauere nichts: Tagebücher, 1955–1963* (Berlin, 2001).

Richie, Alexandra, *Faust's Metropolis: A History of Berlin* (London, 1998).

Richter, Klemens, 'Bestattungsriten in der DDR', *Deutschland-Archiv*, 7 (1987), 733–9.

Riecke, Herbert, *Mietskasernen im Kapitalismus, Wohnpaläste im Sozialismus* (Berlin, 1954).

Rohlf, Dietwalt, *Der grundrechtliche Schutz der Privatsphäre* (Berlin, 1980).

Rosenberg, Tina, *The Haunted Land: Facing Europe's Ghosts after Communism* (London, 1995).

Ross, Corey, *The East German Dictatorship* (London, 2002).

—— *Constructing Socialism at the Grassroots: The Transformation of East Germany, 1945–1965* (London, 2000).

Rössler, Beate, *Der Wert des Privaten* (Frankfurt, 2001).

Rubin, Eli, 'The Form of Socialism without Ornament: Consumption, Ideology and the Rise and Fall of Modernist Design in the German Democratic Republic', *Journal of Design History*, 19/2 (2006), 155–67.

—— *Synthetic Socialism: Plastics and Dictatorship in the German Democratic Republic* (Chapel Hill, NC, 2008).

Rusch, Claudia, *Meine Freie Deutsche Jugend* (Frankfurt, 2003).

Sabrow, Martin, ed., *Erinnerungsorte der DDR* (Munich, 2009).

Sabrow, Martin, Rainer Eckert, Monika Fincke, and Klaus-Dietmar Henke, eds., *Wohin treibt die DDR-Erinnerung? Dokumentation einer Debatte* (Göttingen, 2007).

Schädlich, Hans-Joachim, ed., *Aktenkündig* (Berlin, 1992).

Schnabl, Siegfried, *Mann und Frau Intim* (Berlin, 1979, 12th edn.).

Schneider, Norbert F., *Familie und private Lebensführung in West- und Ostdeutschland: Eine vergleichende Analyse des Familienlebens 1970–1992* (Stuttgart, 1994).

Schönfeldt, Hans-Andreas, *Vom Schiedsmann zur Schiedskommission: Normendurchsetzung durch territoriale gesellschaftliche Gerichte in der DDR* (Frankfurt, 2002).

Schule und Elternhaus in der Sowjetunion: Methodische Anleitungen des Deutschen Pädagogischen Zentralinstituts zur Weiterbildung aller Lehrer und Erzieher (Berlin, 1952).

Schulz, Felix Robin, 'Death in East Germany, 1945–1990', D.Phil., University of York, 2005.

Schumann, Silke, *Vernichten oder Offenlegen? Zur Entstehung des Stasi-Unterlagen-Gesetzes: Eine Dokumentation der öffentlichen Debatte 1990/1991* (Berlin, 1995).

Scott, James C., *Weapons of the Weak: Everyday Forms of Peasant Resistance* (New Haven, Conn., 1985).

—— *Seeing Like a State: How Certain Schemes to Improve the Human Condition Have Failed* (New Haven, Conn., 1998).

Siegelbaum, Lewis H. (ed.), *Borders of Socialism: Private Spheres of Soviet Russia* (New York, 2006).

Sennett, Richard, *The Fall of Public Man* (New York, 1974).

Shlapentokh, Vladimir, *Public and Private Life of the Soviet People: Changing Values in Post-Stalinist Russia* (New York, 1989).

Silbermann, Alfons, *Das Wohn-Erlebnis in Ostdeutschland* (Cologne, 1993).

Smolka, Karl, *Junger Mann von heute* (Berlin, 1964).

—— *Gutes Benehmen von A bis Z* (Berlin, 1957).

Solberg, Richard W., *God and Caesar in East Germany* (New York, 1961).

Solga, Heike, *Auf dem Weg in eine klassenlose Gesellschaft? Klassenlagen und Mobilität zwischen Generationen in der DDR* (Berlin, 1995).

Sommer, Theo, *Reise ins andere Deutschland* (Hamburg, 1986).

Sozialistische Beziehungen in Familien und Hausgemeinschaften bewusster gestalten (Berlin, 1971).

Sperlich, Peter W., *The East German Social Courts: Law and Popular Justice in a Marxist-Leninist Society* (Westport, Conn., 2007).

Spotts, Frederic, *The Churches and Politics in Germany* (Middletown, Conn., 1973).

Staadt, Joachim, *Eingaben: Die institutionalisierte Meckerkultur in der DDR* (Berlin, 1996).

Starl, Timm, *Knipser: Die Bildgeschichte der privaten Fotografie in Deutschland und Österreich von 1880 bis 1980* (Munich, 1985).

Steele, Jonathan, *Socialism with a German Face: The State that Came in from the Cold* (London, 1977).

Stites, Richard, *Revolutionary Dreams: Utopian Vision and Experimental Life in the Russian Revolution* (Berkeley, Calif., 1989).

Stuhler, Ed, *Die Honeckers Privat: Liebespaar und Kampfgemeinschaft* (Berlin, 2005).

Swett, Pamela E., *Neighbors and Enemies: The Culture of Radicalism in Berlin, 1929–1933* (New York, 2004).

Szirmai, Z., ed., *The Law of Inheritance in Eastern Europe and the People's Republic of China* (Leyden, 1961).

Tate, Dennis, *Shifting Perspectives: East German Autobiographical Narratives before and after the End of the GDR* (Rochester, NY, 2007).

Ten Dyke, Elizabeth, *Dresden: A Paradox of Memory and History* (London, 2002).

Thaa, Winfried, *Die Wiedergeburt des Politischen: Zivilgesellschaft und Legitimitätskonflikt in den Revolutionen von 1989* (Opladen, 1996).

—— Iris Häuser, Michael Schenkel, and Gerd Meyer, *Gesellschaftliche Differenzierung und Legitimätsverfall des DDR-Sozialismus: Das Ende des anderen Wegs in der Moderne* (Tübingen, 1992).

Thomas, Daniel C., *The Helsinki Effect: International Norms, Human Rights and the Demise of Communism* (Princeton, 2001).

Tismaneanu, Vladimir, ed., *The Revolutions of 1989* (London, 1999).

Tobias, Robin, *Communist–Christian Encounter in East Europe* (Indianapolis, 1956).

Travis Wolfe, Nancy, 'Social Courts in the GDR and Comrades' Courts in the Soviet Union: A Comparison', in David Childs, Thomas A. Baylis, and Marilyn Rueschemeyer (eds.), *East Germany in Comparative Perspective* (London, 1989), 60–80.

—— *Policing a Socialist Society: The German Democratic Republic* (New York, 1992).

Urban, Detlef, and Hans Willi Weinzen, *Jugend ohne Bekenntnis? 30 Jahre Konfirmation und Jugendweihe im anderen Deutschland 1954–1984* (Berlin, 1984).

Verdery, Katherine, *The Political Lives of Dead Bodies: Reburial and Postsocialist Change* (New York, 1999).

Verheyen, Dirk, *United City, Divided Memories? Cold War Legacies in Contemporary Berlin* (Lanham, Md., 2008).

Völker, Beate, and Henk Flap, 'The Comrades' Belief: Intended and Unintended Consequences of Communism for Neighborhood Relations in the Former GDR', *European Sociological Review*, 13 (1997), 241–65.

Von Saldern, Adelheid, *Häuserleben: Zur Geschichte städtischen Arbeiterswohnens vom Kaiserreich bis heute* (Berlin, 1995).

Vorsteher, Dieter, ed., *Parteiauftrag: Ein neues Deutschland* (Berlin, 1997).

Wagner, Michael, *Scheidung in Ost- und Westdeutschland: Zum Verhältnis von Ehestabilität und Sozialstruktur seit den 30er Jahren* (Frankfurt and New York, 1997).

Wander, Maxie, *Guten Morgen, Du Schöne: Protokolle nach Tonband* (Berlin, 1977).

Weitz, Eric, *Creating German Communism, 1890–1990: From Popular Protests to Socialist State* (Princeton, 1997).

Westen, Klaus, and Joachim Schleider, *Zivilrecht im Systemvergleich: Das Zivilrecht der Deutschen Demokratischen Republik und der Bundesrepublik Deutschland* (Baden-Baden, 1984).

Wiedemann, Hans, *Das sozialistische Eigentum in Mitteldeutschland* (Cologne, 1965).

Wie gestalten wir unser persönliches Leben, Material für die 8. Jugendstunde (Berlin, 1956).

Wierling, Dorothee, *Geboren im Jahr Eins: Der Jahrgang in der DDR: Versuch einer Kollektivbiographie* (Berlin, 2002).

Wir sehen und erleben, wie die Arbeiter und Bauern unseren Staat regieren, oder Wir lieben unsere Deutsche Demokratische Republik, Material für die 9. Jugendweihe (Berlin, 1957).

Wolle, Stefan, *Die heile Welt der Diktatur: Alltag und Herrschaft in der DDR, 1971–1989* (Munich, 2001).

Wollenberger, Vera, *Virus der Heuchler: Innenansicht aus Stasi-Akten* (Berlin, 1992).

Worst, Anne, *Das Ende eines Geheimdienstes: Oder, wie lebendig ist die Stasi?* (Berlin, 1991).

Wunderwirtschaft: DDR-Konsumkultur in den 60er Jahren, ed. NGBK (Cologne, 1996).

Yan, Yanxiang, *Private Life Under Socialism: Love, Intimacy and Family Change in a Chinese Village, 1949–1999* (Palo Alto, 2003).

Yoder, Jennifer, *From East Germans to Germans? The New Postcommunist Elites* (Durham, 1999).

Zachmann, Karin, 'A Socialist Consumption Junction: Debating the Mechanization of Housework in East Germany, 1956–1957', *Technology and Culture*, 43/1 (Jan. 2002), 73–99.

Zatlin, Jonathan, *The Currency of Socialism: Money and Political Culture in East Germany* (Cambridge, 2007).

Index